1,000,000 Books

are available to read at

---

www.ForgottenBooks.com

Read online
Download PDF
Purchase in print

ISBN 978-1-333-54297-9
PIBN 10517594

This book is a reproduction of an important historical work. Forgotten Books uses
state-of-the-art technology to digitally reconstruct the work, preserving the original format
whilst repairing imperfections present in the aged copy. In rare cases, an imperfection in
the original, such as a blemish or missing page, may be replicated in our edition. We do,
however, repair the vast majority of imperfections successfully; any imperfections that
remain are intentionally left to preserve the state of such historical works.

Forgotten Books is a registered trademark of FB &c Ltd.
Copyright © 2018 FB &c Ltd.
FB &c Ltd, Dalton House, 60 Windsor Avenue, London, SW19 2RR.
Company number 08720141. Registered in England and Wales.

For support please visit www.forgottenbooks.com

1 MONTH OF
FREE
READING

at
www.ForgottenBooks.com

By purchasing this book you are eligible for one month membership to ForgottenBooks.com, giving you unlimited access to our entire collection of over 1,000,000 titles via our web site and mobile apps.

To claim your free month visit:
www.forgottenbooks.com/free517594

* Offer is valid for 45 days from date of purchase. Terms and conditions apply.

English
Français
Deutsche
Italiano
Español
Português

www.forgottenbooks.com

Mythology Photography **Fiction**
Fishing Christianity **Art** Cooking
Essays Buddhism Freemasonry
Medicine **Biology** Music **Ancient
Egypt** Evolution Carpentry Physics
Dance Geology **Mathematics** Fitness
Shakespeare **Folklore** Yoga Marketing
Confidence Immortality Biographies
Poetry **Psychology** Witchcraft
Electronics Chemistry History **Law**
Accounting **Philosophy** Anthropology
Alchemy Drama Quantum Mechanics
Atheism Sexual Health **Ancient History**
Entrepreneurship Languages Sport
Paleontology Needlework Islam
Metaphysics Investment Archaeology
Parenting Statistics Criminology
Motivational

MOTHER MABEL DIGB

A BIOGRAPHY OF THE SUPERIOR GENERAL OF THE SOCIETY OF THE SACRED HEART
1835–1911

By ANNE POLLEN

WITH A PREFACE BY CARDINAL BOURNE

AND ILLUSTRATIONS

LONDON
JOHN MURRAY, ALBEMARLE STREET, W.
1914

[All rights reserved.]

PREFACE

OF any soul that accomplishes its predestined task it may be said with truth, " non est inventus similis illi "; there is no other soul exactly the same in vocation, in God-given gifts, in accomplishment of God's purposes. If in the natural order we can find no limit to the Creator's power, in the supernatural order every human heart has its own special character and can give glory to God in its own appointed way.

Thus, when we take up the lives of the Saints or of the saint-like, we are struck, on the one hand, with certain characteristics which are common to them all; while, on the other, they possess very individual qualities which make it impossible for us to mistake one for the other.

The Life of the late Mother-General of the Society of the Sacred Heart is a notable instance of the manner in which God prepares and fashions His chosen servants so that they shall render homage to Him in a way that belongs to each one alone. Doubtless the virtues of Mother Digby as a religious of the Society which she governed for so many years are to be found in the same, or, perhaps, even in a higher degree, among those who were her sisters, and, afterwards, her daughters in religion. The same spiritual training, the same exercises, the same duties, the identity of community life will have produced, and are daily producing, similar effects in countless souls called by God to the same way of life. But there are two aspects of Mother Digby's life which seem to mark her off as a specially chosen soul, appointed to give glory to God in a fashion not belonging to others.

In the first place, the unfolding to her mind of the compelling truth of the claims of the Catholic Church was a manifestation of God's over-ruling Providence which,

06783'7

if not unique—and we know that God does occasionally manifest Himself thus in a moment of clearest light,—yet was an indication of a very great predilection of Divine Love. The details of her sudden recognition of her duty to submit to the authority of the Church were kept by Mother Digby as a secret between herself and God, but we know enough to see in her sudden and quite unlooked for change an outpouring of supernatural illumination and guidance such as are bestowed only upon those whom their Divine Master destines for great purposes.

Then, towards the end of her life, when she had been raised to the chief government of the Society of the Sacred Heart, God gave her a task calling for more than human energy, however great, and she accomplished it with a completeness surpassing, so far as I know, any like effort at any period of the Church. She was already in failing health, and very frequently suffering acute pain, so that the discharge of daily duties of administration even in peaceful times had become a heavy burden. Then it was that the bitter relentless hostility to religion of the French Government burst upon all the religious congregations of that country. First by unjust taxation, ultimately by proscription and confiscation, their existence was rendered impossible. Their houses were closed, their sisters forcibly expelled, and their property seized and sold. The story has yet to be told of all the misery that was inflicted during those years of continuous spoliation on women who were innocent of any crime, and whose sole aim in life was to love God and serve their neighbour. Upon no Society did this persecution fall with a heavier hand than on that governed by Mother Digby. She was called upon to close no less than forty-eight houses and to make hurried provision for all their inmates. The story of those anxious days told in the pages of this Life show how she accomplished this fresh God-given task. For every house closed in France a new house was opened elsewhere, so that when the work of destruction had been accomplished across the Channel, the Society as a whole could count a larger number of centres than it had possessed in the days of peace. Meanwhile every member of the Society expelled from France had found in other lands another home, like in rule, in spirit, and in daily usage, to the one the doors of which had been so rudely closed against her. Truly, when the task was done, Mother Digby could turn to God and exclaim with humble and grateful heart: "Those whom Thou gavest to me have I kept."

For the religious of the Society of the Sacred Heart this Life will recall many things that they know already, but it will teach them continually, with new emphasis, that the Hand of God that guided their Blessed Foundress is not shortened in their regard ; and that, if they remain ever faithful even in the small things of which their life of self-sacrifice is made up, He will never abandon them in those greater matters which He alone can over-rule.

All, whoever they be, will read the Life of Mother Digby with interest and with profit. It gives us many details, to most only imperfectly known, of recent events in France. It causes to live before our eyes the inner organisation of a great Catholic religious society. It depicts for us one who in any position could have taken a leading place. Above all it shows us a noble courageous woman with all her great natural gifts strengthened and enhanced by the Divine gifts of grace which she strove to use with all her energy. Such a life has in its remembrance a mighty power to lift us to higher thoughts and render easier the accomplishment of whatever task God may have entrusted to us in things both great and small.

FRANCIS CARDINAL BOURNE,
Archbishop of Westminster.

October 12th, 1913.

CONTENTS

CHAP.   PAGE.

I. CHILDHOOD .   1

II. CONVERSION   12

III. IN THE WORLD   22

IV. OUT OF THE WORLD   31

V. THE NOVICE   47

VI. THE MISTRESS GENERAL .   57

VII. THE SUPERIOR   72

VIII. MARMOUTIER   82

IX. THE TERRIBLE YEAR   96

X. ENGLAND   116

XI. THE TRAINING COLLEGE .   130

XII. IRELAND   152

XIII. A WONDERFUL CURE   162

XIV. EVENTS OF TWELVE YEARS   170

XV. REVEREND MOTHER VICAR FOR TWENTY-TWO YEARS .   185

XVI. THE ASSISTANT GENERAL AND THE SUPERIOR GENERAL   206

XVII. DANGERS AHEAD IN FRANCE   221

XVIII. PERPETUAL JOURNEYS   232

XIX. AMERICA   251

XX. THE LAW OF 1901 .   272

XXI. THE BILL OF 1904 .   282

XXII. THE LAW OF 1904 .   296

CONTENTS

CHAP.   PAGE

XXIII. CAST OUT   319

XXIV. CONFLANS, THE LAST FORTRESS   329

XXV. SUPERIOR GENERAL FOR SIXTEEN YEARS   .   .   346

XXVI. THE END   372

XXVII. EPITAPHS   388

XXVIII. SOME FAMILIAR SAYINGS OF MOTHER DIGBY .   .   395

INDEX   399

LIST OF ILLUSTRATIONS

PORTRAIT OF MOTHER DIGBY, 1895 (AGED 60) . *Frontispiece*

CHÂTEAU DE CHATIGNY, NEAR TOURS, 1856 . *To face page* 32

MABEL DIGBY, 1856 (AGED 21) . . . 48

MARMOUTIER, PORTAIL DE LA CROSSE, 1870 . 82

MARMOUTIER, PORTAIL DU MITRE, 1870 . . 96

ROEHAMPTON CONVENT, 1890 . . . 162

ROEHAMPTON CHAPEL, 1890 170

THE HÔTEL BIRON, PARIS, 1910, "*The Deserted Mansion*" . . . . . . „ 328

FACSIMILE OF MOTHER DIGBY'S WRITING . . *page* 345

MOTHER MABEL DIGBY

CHAPTER I

CHILDHOOD

"Don Diego Faxardo, in his 'Instruction of a Christian Prince,' uses the coral growing out of the sea as an emblem of beauty and force, to be a model to kings and nobles. Sprung from the midst of the waves, beaten by the tempests, it grows hard in suffering, and impervious and fit for the most precious purposes of men, whilst the rose perishes at the first blast "—KENELM DIGBY, *Mores Catholici* (Booker, 1831), book I. ch. ii. p. 72.

"Every man is the son of his own works."—KENELM DIGBY, *Godefridus* (Lumley, 1844), p. 213.

MABEL DIGBY was born at Ashford House, near Staines, Middlesex, on 7th April 1835. She was supposed to be dead, and her mother dying. Her father, wild with grief, ordered his horse, and galloped aimlessly across country for hours. When he came home, it was to hear that mother and child were going to live; the baby had uttered a little cry, and the mother had asked for it. Mabel was baptised, but with rosewater, for fear of a chill.

This young mother, as Elizabeth Anne Morse, brilliant in mind as in person, daughter of John Morse of Sprowton Hall, and Bagthorpe, Norfolk, and Abbots Wooton, Dorset, heiress through her mother of the last Baron Haversham, had been destined for some splendid match. Suitors—to John Morse's mind—were not lacking to his daughter, but she fixed her choice upon a very handsome fair-haired young gentleman without a title, and with sporting tastes, albeit she cared nothing for horses, nor he for books—Mr Simon Digby, of Osbertstoun, Kildare.

I   A

He was, by the declaration of Sir John Bernard Burke, Ulster King of Arms, and Principal Herald of Ireland:

"A direct male descendant of the very ancient and distinguished family of Digby, ennobled under the title of Baron Digby of Geashill, Viscount Coleshill, Earl Digby, Baron Digby of Sherborne, and Earl of Bristol . . . rendered famous in history by . . . among others, Sir Simon Digby, who contributed mainly to the success of King Henry VII. at the Battle of Bosworth; by the celebrated Sir Kenelm Digby, styled (for his learning) the 'Ornament of England,' and husband of the renowned beauty, Valentia Stanley. . . . *Deo non Fortuna.*"

The pedigree in the female line goes back to King Edward III. and to William the Conqueror, but discreetly omits Sir Kenelm's father, the accomplished and misguided young Sir Everard Digby, who lost his life for Gunpowder Treason; an ancestor to vaunt nowhere less than in an Orange family. As little account, no doubt, did Ella Morse then make of her Jesuit cousin five times removed, Henry Morse, *pro fide suspensus et dissectus*, at Tyburn Gate, 1645 A.D.

Not the least of Ella Morse's endowments was an indomitable will, and on 7th January 1830, at the age of twenty-four, she became Mrs Simon Digby.

Two sons and four daughters issued of the marriage: Kenelm (1830-1859); Geraldine (1832-1905); Gertrude (1833-1838); Mabel (1835-1911); Essex (1838-1909); Eva (1843-1869).

Mabel's earliest recollections were of death, and beauty, and sport, and the troubles of life. Her sister Gertrude at five years old was dying of scarlatina; she was perfectly conscious, and looked forward with considerable interest to "going to heaven." She made her will and arranged all her toys, setting apart a large portion for the poor, and called for her brothers and sisters to receive their several legacies. No precautions were taken against contagion, and Mabel was lifted on to the bed to take her share; it seemed disappointing, and at three years old she realised her first disillusion. Grief at her sister's loss coincided with these personal feelings. "I remember my sorrow" she said, late in life, "as if it were yesterday."

It is interesting to compare this early death, and the religious atmosphere that surrounded it, with similar losses to Simon Digby's cousin and intimate — "more than a brother," says a contemporary. This was Mr Kenelm Digby, the accomplished author of the *Broad Stone of Honour*, and its companion volumes : a complete grammar of mediæval manners, and a very mine of extensive and cultured learning ; but his most charming production is, perhaps, *The Children's Bower*, upon the infinite charm of childhood, and its insistent virtues : a literary monument to his own two sons, as genuine young heroes as figure anywhere in the *Compitum*.

"I have wished," he says, at the close of the little book, "to arrange, as it were, a vast and imposing procession ; to call forth as assistants at the funeral of this child and youth, both the dead and the living . . . men of all time—things splendid and illustrious in every sphere ; from the pomps of nature . . . to the ephemeral joys of our early dreams. And why? . . . that even one reader should be moved to turn henceforth to the *Children's Bower*, and there learn to love himself less, and others more— to keep his mind unspotted from this selfish world, and his heart more innocent . . . then shall this record be a service beyond the bounds of time, and transcending all the limits of human thought ; . . . there were the strewments, and the songs of requiem." [1]

Intercourse between the Simon and the Kenelm Digbys was constant, and it will presently be seen how profoundly this influence was to affect the mind and character of Mabel.

Mrs Simon Digby had been called by the courtly Charles X. "La Rose Blanche de l'Angleterre." Her portrait — by Queen Victoria's desire — was painted in water-colours by Mr W. Drummond for the *Book of Beauty* of 1844. The children would sit, rapt, gazing at her during the sittings, and wondering whether anything on earth could surpass their mother. She was then

[1] Kenelm Digby, *The Children's Bower* (Longmans, 1858), vol. ii. ch. xxi.

thirty-seven ; but even in middle life Mrs Digby attracted more attention than many a younger beauty.

The picture shows the type of Juno, a commanding face and form, to be rendered by the epithet "handsome" rather than "lovely"; though that word may be applied to an earlier miniature by Taylor, showing the delicate roseate complexion and slender proportions of some twenty years. Both portraits delineate a pronounced aquiline nose, just not too large for symmetry, arched eyebrows, liquid brown eyes, and clustering curls of a darker hue. The younger lady in the miniature wears a splendid yet simple dress of blue velvet, cut low, and with lappets of superb, *point d'Alençon*, part of the Haversham heirlooms.

Opposite the portrait in the *Book of Beauty* is the following tribute to her mind as well as her person ; it had been paid to Miss Morse at nineteen years of age.

LINES ON MRS SIMON DIGBY

By HENRY HALLAM, ESQ. (*Author of " The Middle Ages," etc.*)

Bright be thy path in Beauty's gay career,
And fair the spring of life's just opening year.
Enjoy the hour, while Youth and Hope are warm —
While gleams with rainbow hues thy fairy form ;
And oh ! may Time but shift the changeful scene
For sweeter cares and pleasures more serene,
And those enchanting moments leave behind
The tranquil bosom, and the cultured mind ! (1826.)

Her society was sought by writers whose verses she more than once inspired, and a brilliant circle would discuss with her important questions of the time. She had travelled on the continent, knew six modern languages, understood Latin and Greek, read English literature widely, and possessed the usual accomplishments of the finished education of a woman of her day.

The children worshipped both their parents, and in more ways than one, but it was to her father that Mabel turned with deepest affection, and their tastes as she grew older threw them more and more together.

In 1840 the family left Ashford House to reside near Bath, at Cranhill House, where Mr Simon Digby kept his hunters. A pencil drawing of the time shows the garden front of a handsome Georgian manor. The centre, with a classic portico, rises in an octagon of three storeys; one-storey wings stretch on either side. In front is a broad terrace with stone vases; before this again is a terraced lawn, bordered by shrubbery, and shaded with noble trees. The house, built of Bath stone, has now an added storey. It stands on a hill, and overlooks the city and the Avon valley. Here Mabel Digby must first have learnt to love, as she always did, a scene of natural beauty—a younger love than some elders think.

At five years old she became the mistress of a much loved pony, who would give every sign of delight at her approach. She preferred him even to the pet owl she herself had tamed. She constantly accompanied her father on horseback; he had, unlike the governess, only two rules: she must be ready to the minute, and must *make but one* with her steed. They took long rides together before breakfast on the Downs above Bath, coming home sometimes with a handkerchief full of mushrooms from the sheep-walks, and she rode to hounds with him—the Duke of Grafton's stag hounds—at the age of six. She was attended by an old coachman, and mounted on her clever Exmoor, who, with the excellent gift of his race, managed to keep her with the field, and *taught her to ride*, threading his way through the crowd, and creeping where he could not jump. Moreover, Mr Simon Digby would not tolerate anything that savoured of the rocking-horse. Mabel remembered all her life the stinging touch of his lash on her fingers when it was hard to sit her plunging pony, and she held on a moment by the pommel. He was immensely proud of her spirit; but her mother, whose tastes were confined to literary, artistic, and household matters, looked coldly upon horses and sport.

"What shall I gain by a life of study," says the youth in the old play. "How shall I look my horse in the face?"[1] Mabel shared his opinion, and, when she began

[1] Kenelm Digby, *Orlandus* (Quaritch, 1876), p. 208.

to feel the yoke, sighed out to her mother : "Why must I be educated?"

Mrs Digby endeavoured to convince her daughter of the advantages of mental culture. "And will my education last long?" enquired Mabel after a pause. "It must go on all your life!" The child reflected on this terrible sentence, and took refuge with the more easy-going parent. "They say mama is a 'woman of mind.' Have I got any mind, papa?" "About as much as a pin's head!" was his gay reply, welcomed no doubt by Mabel as parental sanction for her resolute idleness.

The governess had no easy task. Geraldine was tractable and gentle, but the leader, first in the nursery, next in the schoolroom, was always the terrible younger sister. Only the presence of her mother could daunt her. With calm insistence she taught Mabel, and the rest of the children, to *think*, from the age of four upward.

"You did not *think* before that question. Go out of the room, wait a little, then come in and ask again." Thus perhaps was developed the extraordinary power of concentration which enabled this daughter of Mrs Digby to accomplish, later in life, an amount of labour whose sum total and complexity would require, in the given time, partition among ten ordinary heads.

Unconsciously the child was practising already the motto of Crown Prince Fritz: "Lerne zu Leiden." At four or five years old, riding aloft on the shoulder of an uncle who cantered under a doorway, her head struck with great violence against the lintel; from that time to the end of her life she remained constantly subject to dreadful headaches, which nothing could relieve. Here too, Mrs Digby's training was austere: "We must only know by your greater cheerfulness," she would say, "that you have a headache." But indeed this trial interfered but seldom with Mabel's exercises, or even her spirits, so great was then and always her redundancy of life.

She could not be tied to her mother's apron-string.

Her character for deeds of daring became so well established that she was constantly blamed without question for every mischief that arose, nor were her accusers frequently mistaken.   She used the gardener's squirt as the governess happened to pass by, and the two engaged in ceaseless warfare.   The schoolroom party were brought to the dining - room every evening for dessert, when, as often as not, a long indictment for the day's misdeeds, edited by " Mademoiselle " upon Mabel's entry, brought about her summary banishment.   But an old butler would sweeten the exile by a surreptitious store of "goodies"; wherein, being thoroughly human on every side, she found compensation.

Many were her hairbreadth escapes, as when she bounced into an old well in the garden, and hung on by a chain for a space that seemed an eternity, until a gardener heard her cries.   She was locked up in the night nursery on the third floor : but when she was seen from below, sitting outside on the window sill, with her legs dangling, enjoying the situation and the view, the family hastily came to terms.   "That child," the mother said in the hearing of Mabel's elder sister, "will be either a devil or a saint."

Mabel was now and then misunderstood, no doubt. Once, when she should have been waiting for the carriage, she turned aside among the strawberries ; they told tales upon her white frock, and she forfeited her turn for driving out with her mother.   But she had not eaten any strawberries ; she thought the gardener looked tired, and had gone to help him.

The climax of her early troubles came with her younger brother, the chosen comrade of her pranks. She put him in her mother's bath chair, and "took him for a drive"; but the chair passed out of control on an incline ; she could only follow helpless as it dashed along till at the bottom of the hill it overturned and Essex was hurled out and lay quite still.   They carried him home unconscious.

She had murdered her little brother—the nurses said so ; and now it must be brought home to Mabel how exceedingly wicked she had been. That she might never forget it, they set her on a chair outside the darkened room, to take it all in—the hushed voices, the mysterious movements, the dreadful fear that he was even now dead or dying.

Many another seven-year-old of Mabel's strong and passionate affections might have been crushed by this treatment into a state even more critical than that of little Essex, on the mental side. But she sat still, uttering no word or cry ; and a strange strength seemed to bear her up. She realised, probably for the first time in her life, that there was an appeal possible beyond nurses and even parents ; that God knew all about it, and would stand by her, though every one else was against her ; and this great security of mind remained long after the accident was forgotten.

God was again the supreme authority to which she silently appealed, when, hidden behind the window curtain, she overheard her father and mother expressing their anxiety, and perhaps their bewilderment, as to the training and the future dangers of this unmanageable and high-spirited child. What would become of her? . . . what could they do with her? Together with a sort of despair at being such a hopeless case, came the feeling that God alone knew, and could bring help. But at last she could bear the concealment no longer, and came forth with hanging head, silent, self-condemned.

Thus, in one way or another, life never ran smoothly, especially when there was a perfect sister to act as a foil. Geraldine was devout, and read a daily portion of the psalms in a walk between two hedges, which she reserved for her devotions, and on which her brothers and sisters never trespassed. Now and then Mabel in a moment of fervour undertook a similar daily office, and joined Geraldine in the secluded path, but the mood never lasted long. More pressing claims upon the younger sister's attention carried her off again with her brother, until, when she was nine years old, a great trouble came to all the family.

Mr Simon Digby put his hunters in harness during the

summer, and drove them four-in-hand. He had gone out
with the coach one morning; at the bottom of the hill
the team got out of hand, and came into collision with
a farm waggon. He was carried home. At the hall door
Mabel met the bearers with their burden; it fell to her
to break the news to her mother.

He was insensible for days, and blind for long after his
fall. He never hunted again. But, after that time of
misery, Mabel and he were more than ever to each other.
Leaning on her shoulder, he took his first walk to the
stables "to see the old Colonel," the favourite hunter, who
broke nearly everything within reach when he heard his
master's voice again. So a seal was placed peculiarly
upon her friendship with her father.

Mabel's schoolroom studies were intermittent. Her
mother tried to impart to her daughters some of her own
knowledge of languages, and read with them Spanish
and French. But perhaps the most powerful literary
influence ever exercised over Mabel was that of Mr
Kenelm Digby.

He was an M.A. of Trinity College, Cambridge. In
1819, at nineteen years of age, he was converted to Roman
Catholicism. In 1826 he published the first volume of
the *Broad Stone of Honour*. These writings, from the
historic aspect, added considerable force to the great
wave of mediæval sympathy that had been propelled by
the Lake poets and by Scott on the poetic and romantic
side, by Pugin and others on the archæological, before
it culminated, so to say, in the thirties, by the definite
religious teaching of Newman and the Tracts.

Mr Kenelm Digby's household was devoutly Catholic
and Roman. In fact the tone of that family is truly
depicted in his books. The *Children's Bower* has been
treated of already; the *Chapel of St John* is a portrait of
his wife; his own habitual thoughts and conversations
are revealed in the *Broad Stone of Honour* and the rest.

Mr Simon Digby, on the other hand, was an Orange-
man. Roman Catholics stood blackened to his eyes
as deceivers by profession. It did not strike him that
his own horror of the vice of lying could be shared by

any one who did not hold to the national section of
Christianity. Mrs Digby seems to have held the same
views; the children, and Mabel in particular, embraced
them as a point of honour.

Yet the two families were united in the closest friendship, spending together the summer of every year,
apparently, at Shaftesbury House, Kensington, the
Kenelm Digbys' home. How such ties could be, and
they were lifelong, is not clear, but so it was; nor, it
has been noticed, is such inconsistency uncommon with
persons of strong religious prejudice.

The erudite volumes of Kenelm Digby, weighted as
they are with untranslated passages from the ancients and
the moderns, prove deeply interesting to the courageous
reader who makes up his mind, first to begin, and then
to go on. Leisure permitting, he will surely finish; but
of such was neither Mabel Digby nor her father. Her
mother, however, certainly knew well the *Mores Catholici*:
she read aloud with her daughters, and it must have been
thus that the spirit of Kenelm Digby's books so passed
into Mabel that one could hardly have known her, and
have also read any considerable portion of, say, *Tancredus*,
without being struck by the coincidence of its sentiments
with her own fundamental ideas. She was always
possessed by that dual origin of the chivalrous spirit:
reverence for God, and for parents and forefathers, which
forms the quintessence of the *Mores Catholici*. Its pages
are illustrated, here and there, by the " Diggeby " ancestors,
and inspire that pride of family alone which is a spur
to rival its best traditions. Akin to the Digbys' *Deo non
Fortuna* and that very similar *Deo non armis fido* of the
Morses, was Mabel's favourite motto *Noblesse oblige*. Later
on in life she was to give it a sublime extension in the
supernatural order.

But perhaps of no book save the Bible could one say
that it was part of herself. For she was mainly formed,
not by books, but, almost from the cradle, by surrounding
human life.

To return to the forties. Did the perusal of Kenelm
Digby's *Apologiae* for the Roman Church leave no

suspicion in Mrs Digby's mind that it had been, in the Middle Ages at any rate, a tolerable system? Whether or not, no misgiving whatever upon the orthodoxy of Protestantism had so far crossed the imagination of Mabel.

In 1849 Mrs Digby's health began to give anxiety, and the doctor recommended the south of France. The family migrated to that country, spent some months in Paris and Touraine, and then took a house for a term of years at Montpellier. Mabel's childhood was at an end.

CHAPTER II

CONVERSION

" O sun and dulcet air of brilliant France
  What heart will beat that thou canst not entrance?
  Oh yes ! thou dost possess a potent spell
  Though what it is exactly I can't tell."
—KENELM DIGBY, *Temple of Memory* (new ed. Longmans, 1875), canto iv.

AT Montpellier the French aristocracy of the south had gathered together after the subsidence of the Revolution and the return of the *émigrés*. "How can I," says Newman, "an untravelled John Bull, form an idea of the wit and grace of the French *salons*!"[1] Mrs Digby was well fitted to shine in such an assemblage, and her daughters in 1850 were of an age to accompany her everywhere.

Mabel was in her sixteenth year, and very attractive. Her appearance was handsome and striking, but she possessed little of the fleeting charm of youth as youth. Her complexion, without a trace of pink or olive, rather what the French admire, and call *blanc mat*, clear and pale, set off her straight black eyebrows ; she retained the marked and regular features that had been hers at six years old, as can be noted in a pretty but expressionless drawing then executed by her mother. Her nose was straight, her forehead straight and broad, her mouth well-shaped and firmly closed, her hair was brown, she was not above the middle height, and her figure was rather too massive for girlish grace ; but her fine eyes of a deep blue, full of fire and life, her most expressive countenance, the gaiety and vivacity of her talk, the dignity of her manner and bearing, gave an extraordinary charm to an appearance that exactly tallied with her

[1] *Grammar of Assent*, p. 29, 4th ed.

12

character. A Holbein could best have painted her and her mother; a Vandyke, or Sir Joshua, the rest of the family. Geraldine, fair-haired like her father, with fine aquiline profile, was somewhat shy in manner, and, though pronounced beautiful, seemed cold and lifeless by her sister's side. She never exercised the fascination or roused the affection that Mabel easily inspired. But their mother, at forty-four, was still decidedly " the beauty of the family." Her husband made some fast friends among learned ecclesiastics, and by his gay and genial manner was everywhere popular; in this respect, Kenelm and Essex were, like Mabel, their father's replicas. Eva, five years old and kitten-like, with curly hair, completed the group, pronounced by the French a charming one.

Amongst their greatest friends at this time was the Marquis de Castelbajac. Mabel and Geraldine would pay long visits in the winter and spring to his château near Pau. The Marquis was of the old *régime*. His charming daughter Sidonie, then a person of mature age however, made a confidant of Mabel. Another frequent visitor to the château was Madame de Montijo, Comtesse de Téba, with her two beautiful daughters, one of whom became eventually the Duchesse d'Albe, the other Empress of the French. Eugénie de Montijo, a graceful and accomplished horsewoman, would often join in Mabel's rides through the Pyrenees, and confided to her sympathies that troublesome affair, the persistent attentions of young Louis Napoleon, whose "prospects" many thought uncertain. "Fancy the impertinence of the man wanting to marry me!" she would exclaim. This was, perhaps, the " protest in form " before yielding up the fortress; for the marriage was eventually an *affaire de cœur* on both sides, not a mere bargain for a crown.

The old Marquis de Castelbajac enjoyed long walks with this bevy of girls; he always insisted on their ending at the pastrycooks. He noted with amusement the good appetite of the young foreigners, and their appreciation of the confectioner's skill, and would present them on their departure with sticks of *sucre de berlingot* a metre in length.

One day a pedlar was passing by the château de

Castelbajac; he had a quantity of muslin, and the Marquis bought the material and presented it to his daughter and his young guests, suggesting that each should try to concoct for herself the most elegant possible dress. Eugénie de Montijo entered into the competition with as much zeal as the rest, and she, who for twenty years was to set the fashion to half polite Europe, wore for once a garment of her own construction. The young ladies at last, arrayed each in her handiwork, appeared before the Marquis, that he might pronounce as to the most successful; he decided that Miss Mabel Digby was the undoubted victor in this trial of skill. Like her sister, she had had the advantage of her mother's training in the matter.

Mabel, as always, enjoyed gay life under any aspect, but her chiefest pleasure was still the riding expeditions with her father. To his delight, though now and then also to his anxiety, she would choose by preference even a dangerous mount. On one occasion the horse started off at a gallop before she had time to gather up her reins, and she disappeared from view. Two hours afterwards the laughing rider brought him back, perfectly under control. The family spent the spring and summer at Bagnères de Bigorre, and many were the delightful rides for Mabel and her father in and out of the Pyrenees. One day she lost her way completely in the mountains. It grew dark; she shook the reins upon her horse's neck so as to show him he was free. He sniffed the air in various quarters, and then set off rapidly in the direction of his stables; she arrived unconcerned, to find the assembled family and servants preparing to beat the byways in her pursuit. The peasants in those parts, unaccustomed to see ladies on horseback, enquired whether she was a girl or a boy, and would hospitably offer black bread well rubbed with garlic.

Those were happy days. Utterly hidden was the crucible in which the friendship of father and child was soon to be tested.

A strange interest was beginning to encroach upon Mrs Digby's thoughts. So good a French scholar could enter

easily into any topic of conversation ; that of religion was
often interwoven with the rest.

The question of English conversions had, from the days
of the Stuarts at St Germains, excited a deep interest
in the French generally. Their sympathy had been
immensely heightened by the development of the
Tractarian Movement, which was, in 1850, gathering in
its harvest from the successive effects of the Gorham Case
and the Durham Letter. However dim the niceties of the
Anglican position might appear to even well-educated
Frenchmen for the most part, there remained the clear
fact of the illustrious Newman's conversion, and of six
hundred eminent names following closely in his wake,
mostly with forfeit of all that makes life easy. The charming English heretics were therefore watched with keen
attention.

At the close of 1851 the girls noticed with wonder that
their mother would send them out in society with a
chaperone, Mademoiselle de Sainte-Maurice, whilst she
herself stayed at home to study all the evening. Mrs
Digby perceived that the foreign Catholic, seen in fancy
from the English shore, had no counterpart in his native
land. Surprise at this discrepancy led to questioning ; she
asked for books ; amongst others presented was Bossuet's
Exposition de la Doctrine de l'Eglise Catholique. Perplexities
began to clear away, doubt vanished in assent, and early in
1852 she openly declared to her husband that she must
follow her convictions into the Roman Church.

Mr Digby's amazement and anger exploded together in
a fury that he took no pains to conceal from his children.
Scenes of passionate reproach on the one hand, met by
mournful but steadfast meekness on the other, were of
frequent rehearsal. The children began to "take sides."
Geraldine, while deploring the event, sympathised with
her mother ; Mabel took her father's part entirely. Her
brothers followed her lead, but her own attitude was by
far the most pronounced. She declared to her sister
that their mother was doing what in her lay to " wreck the
family happiness," and she began at the same time both
prayer and penance in order to win for her mother light

from heaven upon the error of her ways. The idea of disgrace it was, in reality, that galled Mabel. A sense of the fitting kept her always freezingly respectful, but she withheld from her mother every mark of affection.

Mabel, if self-deceived, was honest, as the severity of her secret penance at this time attests. But whence had come to her these most unprotestant ideas of intercession, atonement, and efficacious suffering? The *Tracts for the Times*, apparently, never reached her, and here comes in strangely the evidence of Catholic notions imbibed from the *Mores Catholici*.

Her father's love centred more than ever in his younger daughter; he confided in her utterly, and entrusted her with the keys of his desk, and the management of his affairs.

Months dragged on, and Geraldine's admiration for her mother's patience led her to investigate the religion for which Mrs Digby was ready to sacrifice so much; both were actually received into it in September 1852, at Montpellier.

As soon as the fatal news reached Mr Digby, he summoned the family into the dining-room; his wife remained at one end of the room, while he went to the other. He told their children that they must take their choice between her and himself. Geraldine was the first to move; she placed herself by her mother. Then Mabel walked over to her father with determined step. " I promise you," she said, "whatever may happen, to remain always a faithful Protestant." She was followed by both her brothers. Eva, seven years old, stood irresolute for a minute, looking from one parent to the other; then she said firmly, "I shall stay with mama always," and joined her elder sister.

Mr Digby set off next day for England, taking with him Mabel and his sons. The boys were sent to rigidly Protestant establishments; Mabel remained with her father as companion and solace.

As might have been expected, the violent emotions she had sustained without any outward betrayal began to tell seriously upon her health. Hardly a month or so

had elapsed before the doctors imperiously prescribed a
sojourn in the south of France for the winter.   Sorely
against her inclinations and his own, the anxious father
compelled her to return to Montpellier, where her reappear-
ance caused considerable sensation.

Her father could not stay far from her for long, so
he rejoined his wife and daughters.   Here a fresh blow
awaited him.   Eight-year-old Eva walked into the
drawing-room, placed herself between her mother and
sister, and seized a hand of each, saying to her father:
" Papa, I want to be a Catholic like mama and Geraldine."
" It is your mother who has put this idea into your head,"
he replied angrily.   " No, papa, I've found out by myself
that the Catholic religion is the best one."   The father
remained dumb with surprise; he placed her in a
Protestant school in Montpellier, where the girls and
the mistress, spying a medal of Our Lady round her
neck, tried violently to tear it off; the child broke loose,
and rushed home with dishevelled hair and dress, still
clutching close her medal.   Then she was sent to a
Protestant family in England, but remained staunch, and
the separation proved more than the father himself could
stand for long.   The obstinate Papist was recalled and
baptized.   On this occasion Mgr. Thibaut, the Bishop
of Montpellier, put a document into Eva's hands; it
conferred upon the priest who baptised her the dignity
of Canon, and she took ever after no small pride, and
he no little amusement, in this bestowal of ecclesiastical
preferment.   The well-known Père Hermann, in an
eloquent allocution to the neophyte, told her that she
must carefully keep from stain the whiteness of her
baptismal robe, for she was now a sister of the Angels.
She could not long remain at this level, though her
peccadillos never compared with Mabel's for number and
weight.   Some time afterwards a learned Jesuit enquired
of Eva whether her robe was as white as ever.   "I am
afraid, father," she sadly rejoined, "that it is already
rather grey!"

Mabel's demeanour at home remained unaltered.   But,

B

save for the forbidden topic of religion, and to all but
her mother and sisters, she could be sweet as summer.
She was popular with other girls, though familiar with
but few.   One of these was Louise de Dagneirolles,
who had taken a great fancy to Mabel, and who became
next year the Baronne de Rolland de Blomac.   Louise
in 1852 had just completed her time of education at the
Convent of the Sacred Heart.   She wrote later of her
new friend :

"There were in her nature such marked features of frankness,
independence and highmindedness, and, on the other hand, so
much delicacy of feeling, keen wit, and openhearted gaiety, that
one felt her influence, without being able to pass into the charm
of a thorough intimacy; she certainly kept one at a distance."

This dignified reserve did not prevent Mabel from
joining with great zeal in her young friend's undertakings.
What is now called "social work among the poor,"
generally introduced, in towns at any rate, among gentle
folk in England not many years ago, has been very common
in France since the close of the worst days of the Revolution.   Before that, even the proscribed and persecuted un-
constitutional clergy received valuable assistance from the
ladies of their country, who gave them shelter, carried
on the work of religious instruction secretly among
the peasants and the poor, keeping up the fire among
the ashes until better days.   At the commencement of
the nineteenth century all this was openly done ; the
religious orders reassembled, fresh congregations were
founded.   Amongst these, later still, were the Little Sisters
of the Poor, who possessed a large foundation for aged
men and women at Montpellier.   They received valuable
aid from the young ladies of the city, who were joined
by the Digby girls.   These were not content with merely
visiting the old people, but took an active part in their
service.   Mabel was particularly energetic, and would
sweep out their rooms, wash up, and work for them.
"She never did anything by halves," said her sister
Geraldine, later.
Eugénie de Montijo was secretly bent upon the con-

version of Mabel, and Sidonie de Castelbajac went upon
a journey to the Curé d'Ars to tell him all about their
English friend. He promised to pray for her. "God,"
he added, "will soon have complete mastery over her
heart."

Louise de Dagneirolles, a fiery southerner, built great
hopes upon Mabel's works of charity. "You will soon
be a Catholic, as we are!" she burst out one day with
the tactlessness of a newly emancipated schoolgirl.
"Never!" replied Mabel with conviction too deep to
make even scorn worth while. Her enthusiastic friend
would, nevertheless, have plunged at once into controversy,
but a dart from Mabel's eyes slew the burning words
upon the lips of the *indiscrète*, whom the ever - prudent
Geraldine, with deprecating glances, now drew aside.

Louise, in St Augustine's words, changed her plan,
but never her design. For its attainment she enrolled
five of her former school companions, with Geraldine
and herself, in a society of prayer and penance. As the
weeks wore on without sign of encouragement, fasts and
heroic practices were multiplied by the militant seven,
and their hopes of victory grew to actual assurance.
Had not Saul of the Acts been obdurate up to the very
last moment? And, ten years ago, Alphonse de
Ratisbonne, a young man of fashion, a Jew, had entered
a church in Rome, with words of mockery, as usual,
upon his lips. Suddenly he had fallen prostrate before
an altar; when he arose, bathed in tears, it was to
declare himself a Catholic. So let it be with Mabel.
The girls decided that she must somehow be induced
to set foot within a Catholic Church. Heaven would
effect the rest.

In February 1853 a troup of musical mountaineers
from the Pyrenees passed to Montpellier. They appear
to have travelled from city to city, out of devotion, singing
only in the churches. Their chant was peculiar; half the
band accompanied the voices of the rest by a humming
sound made through closed lips, producing the effect of
some musical instrument. The age was not one of
excellent taste in music; whatever might now be thought

by a trained musician, of this "powerful harmony," it was reported sixty years ago to the simple folk of Montpellier as "grave, superbe, impressionante." It was a question of hearing this choir only once in a term of years, and the "Chant des Béarnais" was the theme of universal expectation. Geraldine hoped that curiosity at any rate would lead her sister to this extraordinary concert; but it was no such thing.

The "Montagnards" were to sing only once more, on the 17th February, at a grand Benediction, to be given by the Bishop of Montpellier in Notre-Dame-des-Tables. The seven made a plan for that day.

Early in the afternoon they invited Mabel to accompany them for a long country walk, in splendid weather. With the eight went several "mamans"; for young French ladies went nowhere unchaperoned. In returning they passed naturally by Notre - Dame - des-Tables. The Benediction was just beginning, and the "Chant des Montagnards." The girls must positively hear them again! for the last time, *alas*! They all trooped in as if by a sudden impulse. "Vîte, *ma chère*!" cried Louise, taking Mabel by the hand. She followed mechanically; they all pressed up the centre of the church, and the entering crowd closed in as an impenetrable barrier behind them.

Mabel sat down at once defiantly, amid the kneeling congregation. Her sister was at her side. Louise crept up to a position whence she could furtively watch the countenance and attitude of Mabel. She remained impassive. The chants ended; the priest slowly removed the monstrance from the throne; the throng bowed low; Mabel, still seated, threw back her head haughtily as if in protest; the bell tinkled as the Blessed Sacrament was now raised in benediction. In an instant Mabel Digby had slipped from her seat on to her knees and flung her arms across her breast with a clutch that gripped both shoulders. Her face seemed to be illumined; her tearful eyes were fixed upon the Host until the triple blessing was complete, and it was replaced in the tabernacle. Then she sank crouching to the ground, whilst the last short psalm was entoned; she remained bent low and immovable.

The congregation dispersed, not before Mabel's attitude had been widely observed; the seven, all but Geraldine, went away too, in awestruck silence, leaving the two sisters with a single friend. Some one took the news to Mrs Digby that her daughter had fainted. Geraldine relates the rest.

For fifteen minutes she did not interupt this strange trance. Then, touching Mabel on the shoulder, she whispered: "Mama will be getting anxious; let us go home." Mabel rose to her feet, and followed Geraldine to the church porch. Here she placed her hand upon her sister's arm. "Geraldine," she said, "I am a Catholic. Jesus Christ has looked at me. I shall change no more."

CHAPTER III

IN THE WORLD

" But before Eternal Truth had spoken to the wearied spirits of men, who would have sought for felicity under the yoke of servitude, and dereliction, and poverty ? "—KENELM DIGBY, *Mores Catholici* (Booker, 1831), ch. viii. p. 211.

FOR the first time since Geraldine's conversion, the sisters spontaneously embraced in the afterglow of a crisis they felt to be supreme. Geraldine, as they walked home, strove to master the mingled awe and happiness that possessed her. " I tried," she said, "to speak only the language of reason. 'You will have to study our religion, Mabel ; you must settle nothing in a hurry.' 'Give me a catechism,' she replied."

   They resolved to avoid the shock of too sudden a joy to their mother, who was not well that evening, so they retired at once to Geraldine's room. Here an *Exposition de la Doctrine Chrétienne*, perhaps that of Bossuet, lay open. They sat down before it. No sooner had Geraldine read aloud and slowly each separate dogma with its definition and circumstances, than Mabel laid solemnly her hand upon the book, as if she swore to its contents, saying : " I believe." She, so wrapt in objections only yesterday, saw now with unveiled eyes.

   Next morning came the avowal to her mother. She made it with the frank humility of a proud character newly facing truth. But there was no shamefaced self-reserve with eyes averted ; these two, so like in nature, forgiving and forgiven, met in long withheld embraces, where love pent up rushed together again with a mighty shock of joy. "God alone," the mother had said gravely, more than once, in the old days, "can subdue that unconquerable Mabel."

Mabel sought that very day the Bishop of Montpellier. It was he who had given the Benediction at Notre-Dame-des-Tables. He knew from her—so it was conjectured—whatever there was to be known concerning the mysterious message of the day before. On its import, none ever dared to question her directly. But all Montpellier was asking then, as Mabel Digby's friends have since asked more than once: "What *was* it?"

In 1875, a *récit édifiant*, long drawn out, but exceedingly interesting in matter, of the conversion of the Digby family—all under assumed names, of course—was published in the *Messager du Sacré Coeur*, a pious fortnightly, edited by Père Ramière of the Society of Jesus. The proofs were brought to Mabel Digby by her sister, who had herself furnished the matter of the article. Geraldine and her mother desired its insertion. Père Ramière believed it would do "no end of good." Great was the chagrin of Mabel Digby at this unwarrantable breach of privacy. But the thing was published all the same. With her accustomed self-abnegation, she yielded; or perhaps she could not help herself. She is said to have lined out half the article, in which case much has certainly been restored. She destroyed every copy of the magazine she could lay hands upon, and the subject was never mentioned in her presence. Her friends are grateful to Père Ramière.

They turn eagerly to the words of Mabel Digby to her sister: ●

"I cannot tell you, and will never tell you, what I felt in the presence of the Blessed Sacrament. But *Our Lord looked at me*, as of old He did upon St Peter after his fall, and He forced me to throw myself upon the ground in His presence. An interior *voice*, which I dare not and cannot resist, *tells me that I must belong* wholly *to* our Lord in *the Catholic Church*. . . . " etc.

This recital as a whole bears evident marks of a speech put together after the manner of an old historian. Thus and thus, given the circumstances, did it behove Miss Digby to have spoken. In reality, the words in italics—there are no italics in the original—are the sole reported consistently by Geraldine Digby, to several confidants, as used by her sister on the occasion.

The exterior facts of Mabel Digby's conversion have been related at different times, and by many independent witnesses. The extraordinary change instantaneously worked in her is the important matter. What passed within her could only be told by herself, or conjectured by analogy with similar cases, where the subject, like St Paul, has related his own experiences. Alphonse de Ratisbonne, and many other moderns, have given the fullest account of their visions, whether as affecting the senses, or the imagination, or as the direct "illumination of the spirit." Mabel Digby, tradition says, told of hers to only three persons : the Bishop of Montpellier, Blessed Madeleine Sophie Barat, foundress of the Society of the Sacred Heart, who died in 1865, and Joséphine Goetz, now no more, who succeeded her as Superior General.

Between Mother Digby, late in life, and another person, passed, however, some words which were written down almost immediately by her interlocutor. The idea of becoming a Catholic, said Mother Digby, had seized her while she was at Benediction in the Church at Montpellier. She added : "Next day, I asked Geraldine to go back with me to Notre-Dame-des-Tables ; *I thought that happened to everybody.*" "And that you would see our Lord again?" "I never said that," she answered hastily.

"She was reproving me gently for some fault," says another who knew her intimately from 1872 onward. "She dwelt upon the fact that it was displeasing to Our Lord. 'Ah!' she said, as if rapt in some sudden remembrance—'if you had ever seen Him!' —She stopped—I fancied that I had the key. . . . But that is all."

No other facts there are to place before the reader ; all we know is, that whereas she was blind, now she saw. Perhaps she herself could have conveyed little more—save to the expert.

On 19th March—the feast of St Joseph—she turned to the faith of her ancestors. She took the baptismal names of Mary Josephine, and adopted her second namesake as her special patron. The Bishop of Montpellier, who took a paternal interest in "Mademoiselle Meuble," performed the ceremony. The Baron de Sainte-Maurice, her godfather, presented her with "a little book of devotion"—the works of Bourdaloue in ten large volumes. " From which time and circumstance," said Mabel Digby afterwards, "dates my love for the Society of Jesus." Two days later she made her first Communion, and was confirmed, shedding on both occasions abundance of tears; of joy, she said, on the one hand, and, on the other, of contrition for the wanderings of the past.

The change in action and demeanour of the new convert astonished all Montpellier, but her family and more intimate friends could better observe the radical nature of the transformation. She, so wilful, now made her will the servant of others; her tongue lost its occasional sharp edge ; her manner and countenance, their alternations of amenity with haughty reserve. All was peace, and sweetness in the old and virile sense of the word. So say the memoranda of her mother and sister, of Mademoiselle de Castelbajac, of Louise de Dagneirolles, and others. Perhaps a crucial test of her humility is the gratitude to friends whose prayers she thought had won her conversion. Had she heard of those of the Curé d'Ars ? The triumphant *seven* now fearlessly poured out to her their past hopes, fears, plans, deeds, and they were welcomed.

Still, to be the object of public compassion, solicitude, intercessions, congratulations, is hardly pleasant to an independent nature ; to receive alms gracefully is the virtue, no mean one, of a beggar. She thanked her friends with the simplicity of a first communicant seven years old.

A letter of that time bears witness ; its artlessness combines with a certain reserve ; the allusion to Mademoiselle Sidonie's curiosity, delicately evaded, is here put in italics.

Mabel Digby to Mademoiselle Sidonie de Castelbajac.

" MONTPELLIER, *May* 1853.

" DEAR MADEMOISELLE,— I should ask your forgiveness fifty times for having so long postponed my answer to your

kind letter.   You are much too good to me, indeed ; thank
you for the picture you sent me ; I shall value it greatly as
coming from you.

"I fear that, since my abjuration, I have been very
selfish in the midst of my happiness ; the only excuse I
can offer is the impossibility, almost, of expressing to you,
above all in writing, all the graces wherewith God has
filled me ; one is so cold on paper!   But I think of the
day of my baptism, a remembrance that can never fade!
and of Monseigneur's little chapel, where my family and
I have received such benefits.   Then one feels how
powerless one is to thank God for all He has done ; one
can only humble oneself deeply before His infinite greatness, and adore Him in silence.   *You ask me for a faithful
narration of all my impressions on that day.*   That would be
very difficult, for such happiness cannot be renewed here ;
one feels as if in heaven at such moments—there is a
calm that nothing can express ; one knows that all doubt
is at an end, all anxiety over.   But it cannot be
explained! it is a moment that passes quickly, and will
be renewed for all eternity, if, by the infinite merits of our
Lord Jesus Christ I go to see and adore Him in heaven.
Then, indeed, I shall be able to thank Him worthily for all
the favours He has done me here below.   Pray for me,
dear Mlle. Sidonie, with your good prayers.   I owe my
conversion to those of many devout Catholics, no doubt. . . .
If I were to count up all my happy days I should never
end, for now I am allowed to communicate three times a
week ; what a joy!   But my father and my two brothers
are not perfectly happy, for they are not yet Catholics ; we
must hope on and pray always.

"I hardly venture to ask you to give me news of you
from time to time, though that would be such a pleasure to
me.   Goodbye, dear Mlle. Sidonie, all three sisters unite
in assuring you of their sincere and respectful attachment.
—MARY JOSEPHINE DIGBY."

In May 1853 the Digbys left Montpellier for Tours.
Then, as now, the mild climate and historic associations
of that city, and its situation in the "Garden of France,"

attracted many English. But the European reputation of the physician, Dr Bretonneau, residing at Tours, offered the most powerful inducement to persons of delicate health, and Mrs Digby was solicitous for that of Mabel.

The charming châteaux in the vicinity, of Italian inspiration, and planned probably by Fra Giocondo, have recently been the subject of more attentive study.[1] The Digbys presently took one of these at Luynes, near Tours, the château de Chatigny. At each of the angles is a round tower ; one of these was made into a domestic chapel. It was beautifully fitted up and arranged, and the Archbishop of Tours, Cardinal Morlot, secured for Mrs Digby the privilege of reserving here the Blessed Sacrament. Nothing could exceed the reverent care of the sacristan, Mabel.

The Comte de Thiene writes in 1912 :

" I was then but twelve years old ; I was staying with my grandmother at the château de Mareuil. . . . The Digby family settled hard by, at the château de Chatigny ; we visited each other every day. The family consisted of the father, of Mrs Digby, one of the most beautiful women of her time, of their eldest son Kenelm, of a second son, Essex, an officer in the English army, and of three daughters, the eldest, Geraldine, the second, Mabel, with whom you are concerned, lastly, Eva, with whom *I* was concerned, for I loved her tenderly ! "

Her father somehow received less of a shock from Mabel's conversion than from those preceding ; he seems gradually to have drawn near to his wife and daughters ; the happy English home life was resumed at the château, and Mabel rode out as before with him. But his troubles were to begin all over again. Mabel wanted to be a nun.

Her mother, to whom she told everything, with the one reservation already noted, believed that her daughter's vocation was born at the eventful Benediction at Montpellier. Whether or no, her godmother, " la Marquise de X——," says the *Messager*, presented a crucifix to her on her baptism with words that the godchild never forgot. " You

[1] *See* Simpson, *A History of Architectural Development*, vol. iii. Longmans, 1912.

can never love Him enough ; He is the only One to be
loved without danger."

Since that time Mabel Digby cast about for the religious
society best suited to her ambitions.   Which should it be?

Meanwhile, Eva was put to school at the Convent of the
Sacred Heart at Marmoutier.   Apparently conscious of
her charms already, the little girl showed an overweening
inclination to pleasure and frivolity, according to the nuns'
report ; and they set to work to try and deepen principle
in this interesting character.

On the right bank of the Loire, two miles from Tours,
there remained still standing until 1791, the most magnificent group of monastic buildings, save perhaps those of
Cluny, to be found even in France.   Marmoutier, the
Majus Monasterium, is figured in an old engraving of
its plan, belonging to the Collection Peigné-Delacourt.

The Abbey buildings are here shown, arranged over
a ground of some four hundred and fifty feet square, the
whole being enclosed by a high buttressed and battle-
mented wall, with towers at the angles ; towered gates
open towards the four points of the compass.   Within
the enclosure rises a church of cathedral proportions ;
it is connected, by cloisters that enclose two quadrangles, with blocks of monastic dwellings.   This main
group is surrounded by trees, vineyards, and gardens ;
smaller chapels rise up here and there ; farm buildings, workshops, and stables lie nearer the enclosing
walls.

Over the grotto of St Martin, cut in the rock, was made
the matchless Gothic edifice, the pride of all France till
the revolutionary furies seized the revenues, drove out
the monks, tore down the roof, broke up stained glass
and stone work, and demolished as far as could be even
the walls.   St Martin's memory, for a thousand years
hardly second to that of St Louis, seemed in the nineteenth
century to be no more.

But there were some still who remembered the old
days.   In 1847 Mother Barat acquired for her congregation a portion of these hallowed grounds.   The Digbys
often visited the convent, and Mabel was before long pro-

foundly attracted by the spirit of the institute, centering as it does round the Person of Christ.

The well-known Jesuit, Père Barelle, gave a retreat of some days, as is the yearly custom, in houses of the *Sacred Heart*, to the girls at Marmoutier. Mabel joined them. On returning she begged permission from both her parents to enter the noviciate there. Her father was nigh distraught at the request; her mother's dismay was scarcely less, but to her the blow was hardly unexpected. She took time to think it over; reflection gave her relief. Mabel's health was far too delicate for the religious life. The doctors of that part of France were consulted; they fully justified her opinion. More than this, Père Barelle, the director of the retreat, spoke his mind. He had conceived the highest idea of his penitent from the first. Mabel Digby, in moral and mental gifts, was, so to say, one among thousands; and her endowments were of a nature that should adorn rather the world than the cloister. Her vocation for the married state, and that in some influential station, was clear.

Amongst the persistent visitors at the château de Chatigny was the Comte d'X——. A suit that before Mabel's conversion he had feared to be hopeless, he now urged with ardour. In all respects, of age, of character, of person, and of fortune, he could offer a position that many girls might envy, and that her mother, as well as the saintly Père Barelle, thought worthy of even Mabel Digby. The finger of Providence seemed indicated with clearness in a combination of circumstances so favourable.

But her ideals? God inspires them indeed, replied the reverend father, to ennoble us by desires of the highest; but all such aspirations must be bounded by the circumscription wherein His will has actually placed our lives. In lofty but impracticable wishes for a life of greater self-sacrifice, He takes the will for the deed. Therefore did an Elizabeth of Hungary, a Frances of Rome, bow before the wishes of her parents, the advice of her confessor, and the necessities of the case; thus, he might have added, Mary Beatrice of Modena gave way to the command of a Pope; and, to come home, there was M. Dupont, living in

Tours itself, working good through all France, himself—
like St Peter—a married man, and a father.

Mabel found nothing to say.

The Comte d'X—— knew of her hesitation, and of its
cause. He watched with anxiety for the effects of the
counsels employed to persuade her. The mother and the
director gave · him every encouragement; but Mabel's
health, whether from mental strain or no, began to fail
rapidly. Parents and doctors became anxious; the
Comte, terribly in earnest, set off on a pilgrimage to the
Holy Land to win her cure, and the matter of marriage
was for a time in abeyance.

In June 1853 the Digbys were watching from a
window the beautiful and imposing procession of Corpus
Domini slowly advancing through the streets of old Tours.
As, after a long stream of chanting choristers, the Blessed
Sacrament, carried beneath a canopy, and accompanied
with lights and incense, passed below the window, Mrs
Digby suddenly raised her head, and whispered to her
daughter—no one knows why—"Are you still thinking
of becoming a nun?" "Yes," she replied, in penetrating
accents. "Think no more of it, then," said the mother,
"till you are twenty-one." Mabel's health began to
improve with that gleam of hope.

CHAPTER IV

OUT OF THE WORLD

" Our Saviour Jesus Christ is become the chief and eternal king of all the really free, generous, and heroic spirits that exist upon the earth. ' Videmus, et venimus,' is from henceforth the cry of genuine chivalry. ' Procidentes adoraverunt eum ! "—
KENELM DIGBY, *Godefridus* (Lumley, 1844), p. 101.

It seems to have been generally agreed that for the present Mabel must stay at home and get strong. When she attained her majority it would be time enough to decide upon the future.

So she looked round to see what there was to do these three years at Tours. To her former work among the poor she added that for poor churches, and she joined the Confraternity of the Children of Mary of the Sacred Heart to which she had been affiliated in May. These several pious associations assembled monthly to consult upon common action, and to verify results ; in between times the members would meet in groups, at the homes of one or other of them, to work together at this or that.

Reminiscences of these days have been furnished independently by survivors, then girls of her own age. All agree so far, that Mabel Digby was the favourite for the superiority of her gifts in the practical, social, and spiritual order ; that her fingers were the deftest, her sympathy the deeper, her manner the more affectionate ; above all, she was intimate beyond the rest with the writer, who in each case believes herself the friend *par excellence* of Mabel Digby.

Was she already perfect? Mrs Digby declared so, and she was a shrewd observer ; besides, mothers ought to know. Domestic intercourse hardly allows a fault to escape unnoticed. Yet habits, as is trite, must be acquired, and step by step, though ardour would fain proceed by bounds. Mabel Digby owned, says one, "that sub-mission still cost her much." Another says, " she gained not a little by her intercourse with other Catholic girls."

Among her young companions she had at this time special friends, some with whom there could be mutual give and take in a higher degree. The English colony in Tours possessed many well - known converts of the time. There was Mrs Leslie, a lady of real holiness of life ; she is the subject of *Eleanor Leslie, A Memoir*, compiled in 1898.[1] The tale of her conversion, of a recalcitrant husband, and of children won over finally to Catholicism, had much in common with Mrs Digby's own story. The two families entered into a life - long friendship, and Mr Digby, whatever he may have thought of their religion, always gave courteous welcome to Catholic visitors. Mrs Leslie's daughters were like unto herself ; Mary was already a nun, and Charlotte, also minded to enter religious life, was specially drawn to Mabel. But the doctors held out small hope that Charlotte's health would suffice for such an enterprise. She lives yet, but had then accepted their verdict—death, in perhaps a year's time. Mabel Digby envied her fate. Heaven or the cloister appeared the only satisfying alternatives.

There being no immediate prospect of either, she renewed her application meanwhile to good works. Her delicate health obliged her to be less at the active service of the poor ; she gave the more time at home, with her girl companions, to manual labour.

Mabel had fingers that could execute anything and everything in the feminine province, from bread to embroidery. There is in these matters an aptitude to learn, a lightness and dexterity of touch, a delicate finish combined with speed, delightful to witness in the doing and in the result, and which, taken all together, appears a form of genius in itself. Ability just short of this practises a craft, and well, for years ; but is surpassed

---

[1] Stone (Art and Book Company)

CHÂTEAU DE CHATIGNY, NEAR TOURS, 1856.

[To face p. 32.

in it by certain rare persons, "new hands," in a fortnight.

The Digby and Leslie girls met constantly for their common work. Their converse was that of fervent converts; their happiness in the new - found old religion, the wealth of symbolism in its liturgy, the steps by which they had been led into its fold, the obstacles that still held those less fortunate. Sometimes they spoke together of suffering, and as at that time many doctors prescribed painful remedies, Mabel seemed positively to envy Charlotte Leslie any that fell to her lot.

Geraldine Digby had begun to share her sister's aspirations after religious life in the cloister, and both of them now determined to be—and to look—as unworldly as possible. With the enthusiasm, and, as sometimes happens, the exaggeration of youthful converts, they pushed the matter to a rigid puritanism. There is, of course, play for an exquisite taste in the "frock and gipsy bonnet"; this they did not seek. Mabel's riding habit and hat formed her one becoming costume, and most of the money allowed for expenses of toilet slipped through her fingers to good works. Many are the innocent devices for making the hair look richly abundant; she would have none of them; hers was brushed flat on either side of her face with a studied disregard of appearances. In spite of these precautions she exercised a magnetism strong as ever; her charm, in fact, was largely independent of dress.

Mrs Digby was not pleased at this development. She gently insisted that her daughters should make such concessions as her own good sense and knowledge of the world deemed indispensable; she herself was always arrayed with faultless elegance, though the most ordinary attire must have caught distinction from such a wearer. The girls were positively ashamed of their mother's queenly appearance, as savouring of worldly show. This vagary passed away from Mabel later on; but, reflecting on this touch of narrowness, it appears fortunate in view of her later destiny, that Mabel Digby had to spend some

C

years still in the world.   In any case she saw a good deal
of life, and she came to know some very remarkable men.

   Not far from Pau, high up in the Pyrenees, is the
château d'Abbadie, surmounted by a glass observatory.
Here, in the days of her girlhood, dwelt a great observer
of things ordinary and extraordinary in the heavens
above and the earth beneath.

   This was Antoine d'Abbadie (1810-1897) the more
famous of two brothers, distinguished men of science
and travellers in Abyssinia and the Levant.   He is still
a standard authority upon the language, archæology,
geology, and natural history of those regions.   He was
a Knight of the Legion of Honour, and a member of
the Academy of Sciences, to which, when he died, he
bequeathed his estate and astronomical observatory in
the Pyrenees.   The brothers' romantic adventures in
Abyssinia were as often political as scientific.   To their
Irish mother they owed in part their zeal for the faith.[1]
Everywhere they used their powerful influence with the
natives to protect effectually the Catholic missions, which
a considerable fortune allowed them to reinforce with
princely generosity.

   The château d'Abbadie in those days resembled, in its
furniture, and the habits of its master, the house of the
English naturalist Charles Waterton.   Rare animals
were preserved in the grounds, or kept in the house ; the
drawing-room footstools were tortoises, who took a liberty
denied to the unlucky Valerian by the tyrant Sapor :
when weary of pressure they revealed their living condition to the surprised visitor by crawling away.   During
the hours consecrated to research in his study and in
his workshop, only his deaf and dumb Abyssinian servant
was allowed to wait upon *Monsieur*, for an idle word
might rudely jolt a crystallizing theory or frighten out
of memory some timidly approaching clue.   His wife
and sister, highly gifted like himself, and, like him, liable
to the eccentricity of prolonged absences of mind, understood him perfectly, and seconded his labours.

   [1] Their sister, Cæclina, became a nun of the *Sacred Heart*.

His doors one would suspect not easily open to the profane, but, contrariwise, no sharp holly-leaves hedged in his leisure, and he would act as a cicerone to the many whose curiosity led them to his wonderful abode. Here the Digbys had enjoyed a free entry since they first came to France; M. d'Abbadie was devoted to that family, and in special loved young people. Eva was his favourite. Mabel, a student of well-trained human nature, found his goodness of heart, his delicate kindness, his constant self-discipline, his invariable evenness of temper, more admirable phenomena than all his collections could afford. He was, in fact, not merely a devout man, but one of finished virtue.

He himself constructed much scientific apparatus, polished his own lenses for telescopes, and furnished the finest articles of the kind then found in all France to other observatories. As is well known, lenses for optical instruments have to pass in the making through so many different fluxions and processes, some of which occupy many workmen for weeks, others for days, the danger of fracture increasing at every stage, that even before the last is reached, a suitable glass of large size has become rare and costly; then, the lengthy and laborious operation of grinding and polishing by hand must be entrusted to a skilled workman.

M. d'Abbadie, himself such a workman, had at last completed in this way a lens of unusual excellence. Its price had been computed at a thousand pounds sterling. He had received at his house, with his usual courtesy, a tourist — English, alas! — of the unmannered type. Upon the work table lay the precious lens. Without invitation from his host, the visitor took up the lens— and let it fall. It broke. M. d'Abbadie betrayed no emotion, nor did his politeness suffer change. The museum of Dr Buckland was better guarded against persons of defective nursery training by large placards here and there, indited " PAWS OFF!" . . . But . . .

In Tours itself dwelt M. Léon Dupont (1797-1876) of quite other fame. He had been a handsome youth of good family and fortune, educated partly in the United

States, partly in the Collège de Pontlevoy. He shone in
the Restoration Society at Paris as an *élégant*, danced,
hunted, rode, and canoed with distinction, and was known
as the *Marquis des égards*. Mothers were on the watch
for this eligible *parti*. He lost his early piety, though
never his virtue, for his mother shared his home, and
possessed the power that the *élite* of Frenchwomen retain
over their sons. His chief pride lay in his tilbury *à
l'anglaise*, and fine horses, displayed in the Bois de
Boulogne. Passing one day a diminutive Savoyard
sweep, he espied a likely groom for his equipage. The
"innocent blackness," scrubbed, and attired *en jockey*
in the smartest of liveries, with arms correctly crossed,
added a last finish to the cabriolet. One day he came
late, and explained to his impatient master that he had
been attending a catechism class preparatory to his first
communion, given by a youth who with others devoted
himself to the little Savoyards in a certain locality. Léon
Dupont, wishing to satisfy himself of the good faith of
the ex-sweep, drove to the address, and at the hour given
he found M. Bordier surrounded by children, listening
with the most affectionate interest to his words.[1]

Dupont's generous mind drew the contrast between
this zeal and his own idle life, and began to reverse his
course. Yet, even in his worldly days, he had once
sold his tilbury and horses for ready money to pay the
debts of a poor father of a family, a stranger. Now,
however, he applied himself to charity on more even
lines. He became and remained always a member of
the Society of St Vincent de Paul ; after some hesitation
in face of a fancied vocation for the priesthood, he
married, and the delicate health of his lovely daughter
brought him to settle at Tours. She was longing for
the world and its pleasures, just nearing her grasp ; her
mother was no more, and the father watched this gay
butterfly with anxiety. Death carried her off at sixteen
—the greatest grief of his life, save one. But he knew
her to be safe.

---

[1] *See* Janvier, *Vie de M. Dupont* (Paris, Larcher, 1879).

When Mabel Digby first saw him, he was beginning to be an old man. He was tall and venerable, with regular features and high forehead, and of a most sweet countenance; his carriage was noble, his dress suited to his rank, and always scrupulously neat. His manners were easy and urbane, he had the tact and *savoir vivre* of his nation, and its great conversational gifts, but always well under control; he was a patient listener, and full of sympathy; he had numberless friends and of every rank.

After years of research throughout the forties, aided by learned archæologists whom he inspired, and amid unheard-of difficulties, he discovered the original tomb of St Martin at Tours, and his relics, with sculptures of the earliest period, profound in interest, as well as the entire plan and foundations of the original church and monastery. Through him, the Abbey was not impossibly "restored," but its place was occupied by the present basilica finely executed in the Norman style—a national monument. But upon all this volumes have been written.

Together with a saintly Carmelite, Soeur St Pierre, he was just now (1853) instituting the soon popular devotion to the Sacred Face of Christ, as a remedy to the appalling habit of blasphemy then too common in France. In a place of honour on the wall of his drawing-room hung a beautiful painting of the head of Christ suffering. In front was a lamp always burning. The drawing-room was gradually transformed into a place of pilgrimage; M. Dupont's reputation as a thaumaturgus extended throughout Europe; the safety of the city, threatened with inundation in 1856, was set down to the prayers of the "holy man of Tours." He was the simplest, the most unpretending of men; amongst those who came to consult him was William Palmer of Magdalen, then the champion of the Union of Churches. M. Dupont managed to keep abreast of an enormous correspondence with those who sought his advice; he served the poor, and gave large alms; he won men and women from evil life; he was the adviser of great ecclesiastics, of religious, and of laymen. And all this tells

but a fraction of the man and of his labours. When
nearly blind, and in his eightieth year, he would repeat:
"*I thirst to die, and to behold the Face of Christ.*" After
his death, his room was acquired by the Carmelites, and
made a public chapel, the "Oratory of the Holy Face,"
where the lamp still burns.

To Mabel Digby he was a friend after her own heart,
and always a living memory.

All this time she and her sister and Charlotte Leslie
were under the regular training of two adepts in the
spiritual life. The one was their own confessor, M. l'Abbé
Genty, archpriest of the Cathedral at Tours, and Director
of the Children of Mary of the Sacred Heart, at the
Convent of Marmoutier; the other, the directress of the
same Confraternity, Mother Nolan.

The Abbé Genty had been appointed Superior of the
Little Seminary at Tours. He found that establishment
crippled by debt, and he set himself, by the strictest
economy and the entire sacrifice of his own means, to
relieve its embarrassments. Rash or perhaps malicious
persons accused him of squandering its revenues. He
was summoned before Mgr. de Montblanc, Archbishop
of Tours, and his Chapter. M. Genty remembered Our
Lord's silence before His judges, and resolved not to
exculpate himself by a single word. He was in consequence dismissed from his post penniless. Subsequently,
however, his merit came to light, and he was appointed
Canon in the Cathedral Chapter, and confessor to Mgr.
Morlot, Archbishop of Paris.

L'Abbé Genty's character bore marks not usually looked
for in a Frenchman: a deep enthusiasm that maintained
its strong action amid imperturbable calm. He was wont
to say to his penitents: "My child, hurry is quite useless,
even for the salvation of the soul." One day he met
a poor half-blind woman in the cathedral close. Some
sparks from the chaufferette she was carrying had lit upon
her petticoat. "My good woman, you are on fire," he
quietly remarked, extinguishing the flames with his hands.
Then he led her to a convent door, and requested the
nuns to supply for the injured garment.

If M. Genty had borne the crucifixion of the soul,
the cross of dishonour, Mother Nolan had carried yet
another with no less patience. Her mission with the
Children of Mary at Tours had been eminently successful :
she trained young women in virtue, for she was always
an exemplary religious. But what more can be said of
such a life? for it is of its very essence indescribable.

Extraordinary occasions do not make heroism : they
merely reveal its action. Such an opportunity now came
to Mother Nolan. She was attacked by consumption.
Soon the doctors gave her only six weeks to live ; then
a dangerous affection of the throat made it likely that
unless the surgeon were called in she would die in twenty-
four hours. 'Her superiors asked her consent to the operation. After prayer and reflection she decided to endure
it, as, if successful, it would afford her six more weeks of
suffering and work for God. The science of anæsthetics
had as yet made little progress, and in her case it would
have been dangerous to employ chloroform. She was
therefore bound during the operation, as a movement on
her part might prove fatal. Mother Nolan suffered all
in silence. "Madame, you must cry out!" said one of
the surgeons at last. "Monsieur," she answered, "I
have not got the strength ; but please untie my hands,
so that I may make the sign of the cross." Six weeks
later she died the death of a saint, and one of the
surgeons, an atheist, returned to the faith of his childhood. Of Mother Nolan few have not heard, who, after
this, knew Mabel Digby well.

Under three great masters she had now studied,
generally, self-control ; from this humble mistress, the
special and womanly art of patient physical endurance.
The manner of all four is traceable in the formed style
of Mabel Digby's strong but receptive character.

Two incidents of the year 1854, or thereabouts, already
bear this out. For some ailment or other, she had croton
oil applied to her chest. The remedy, left on too long,
owing to the ignorance of the attendant, burnt deep into
the flesh. Mabel made no sign whatever of feeling
throughout. More severe was another experience. She

went again to Pau for a time, and assisted the Sisters
of Charity in their work.   One of them, charged with the
dispensary, concluded from the young lady's demeanour
and devotedness that she must be a postulant; and,
to test her nerve took her to the *Salle des teigneuses*,
whose disease, in the fifties, was treated in an effective
but barbarous manner now superseded.   Upon a number
of hapless children was performed simultaneously an
operation too horrifying for description here, though
St Augustine, in a tougher age, lays down concerning
the martyrs: "What they endured, we should bear to
hear of."   The sights and sounds were not too much
for Mabel Digby's self-possession, whereas a fainting
fit, followed by a nervous attack, was no unusual result
of this spectacle upon beginners.   Great was the disappointment of the Sister on learning that a subject so
promising as the young English lady—even with dis-
count for the *flegme britannique* — was not at once to
be enrolled among the brave daughters of St Vincent.
Not that Mabel Digby was uninfluenced by the Congregation and its noble work.   In fact, her attraction to the
religious life wavered long between the charitable action
of the Sisters, and that other self-forgetting spiritual
activity of the Carmelite contemplatives.

The year 1856 had now arrived, and Mabel Digby had
attained her twenty-first year.   She reminded her mother
of her promise.   The Comte d'X—— had reappeared upon
the scene, his constancy unshaken by delay.   Mrs Digby
suffered cruelly.   The thought of a convent wall of
separation between herself and her daughter seemed
more than she could bear.   And the mother seemed
to have reason on her side; Père Barelle was one great
authority, Dr Bretonneau another.   But Mabel wanted
a fresh opinion.   Père Belfour, another priest of reputation, was to give a retreat at Marmoutier, and she wished
to join it.   Mrs Digby consented.   Did she prime the
father beforehand?   Mabel Digby herself related the
sequel.

A few days before the retreat began he called at the
château de Chatigny.   "You wish to follow the retreat?"

"Yes." "You wish to be a nun?" "Yes. Did my mother tell you so?" "Well, we will settle that during the retreat. But during its course, you must remain alone with God . . . and me. That is, you must not speak to the nuns." "I have not done so, save to the Superior." "That is the very thing to be avoided!"

During the retreat he questioned her. She told him all her mind with perfect frankness. He listened, and replied with calm: "Your vocation to the religious life is certain, supernatural, clear as the sun at noonday." Mabel's heart beat high with hope. He went on: "It is equally clear that you must give it up! This, my child, is the sacrifice the good God demands of you in this retreat. Go and tell your mother you are at her disposal as to M. le Comte d'X——." "And will you, father, take the responsibility of this decision before God?" "I will."

She left him and went to weep within the grotto of St Martin. Returning, she met her friend, the Superior, who was concerned at her tears. Mabel told her tale: the Superior consoled her, and remarked that the excellent father was not, after all, infallible.

Mabel went home; grief began again to affect her health seriously. Mrs Digby felt torn in two. She cast about for some most wise counsellor, and she bethought herself of an illustrious Frenchman who was by many counted almost as a prophet: Père Félix. His words and deeds may be studied in eight or more biographical notices, as well as in a complete *Life* published in 1892.[1]

Célestin-Joseph Félix (1810-1891) was the son of a country innkeeper. He developed from an apt pupil at the Seminary of Cambrai into a distinguished professor. His writings were read on both sides of the Alps; he entered the Society of Jesus; in 1848, at Rive-de-Gièrs, he harangued the agitated and menacing groups of workmen, and they went home quietly. He preached in Amiens Cathedral upon the Feast of the Sacred Heart, 1850; the orator stood revealed, and the Archbishop of Paris chose him to succeed the great de Ravignan in the pulpit of

[1] Tenner, *Le R. P. Félix* (Tequin, Paris).

Notre Dame.   His person has been described as "petit comme rien et laid comme tout!"[1] but this was forgotten when he opened his mouth.   Soon beneath his pulpit sat the most distinguished men of the third Empire, believers or no, political, learned, or literary; hearts were touched, conversions won.   Père Félix had come to know very well the Congregation of the Sacred Heart and its foundress.   It was arranged that Mabel Digby should accompany her mother to Paris; the well-known Dr Bouillet there would finally examine her health, and Père Félix her vocation; Mabel professed herself satisfied.

The mother indeed had the first interview with Père Félix, then Mabel was called in, and in her presence he said: "Your call to the religious life is supernatural and as evident as can be."   So far the words of Père Belfour, and she trembled.   "You wish to enter the *Sacred Heart*: meet me, therefore, at the door of the Hôtel Biron next Friday."   Mabel knew she had won.   Mrs Digby was too great to act disloyally to her daughter; she was convinced at last, and the Comte d'X—— was forced to take his leave for ever.

On the day appointed, the mother and daughter, and Père Félix, arrived at the convent and were received by one of the Assistants General, Mother Prévost.

The career and character of this religious are sufficiently remarkable to deserve a short mention.

The father of Elizabeth Prévost (1784-1871) had enjoyed a good position at San Domingo.   But the principles of 1789 had entered the island, and in 1792 the blacks, taking a liberty enjoyed in Paris, rose against the whites with murder and arson.   After extraordinary adventures, she escaped with her father to France.   One of the first objects that met their eyes was the head of the Princesse de Lamballe on a pike, borne by ruffians through the streets of Paris.   She was educated by her elder sister, an Ursuline nun, expelled by the Revolution, who lived retired at Clermont-en-Beauvoisin.

Here a whole society of *suspects* of every age and rank lived with closed doors after the manner of the early

---

[1] "Small as nothing and ugly as anything."

Christians, and all on an equality of heroism; for the mere practice of religion was a sufficient title to the guillotine, and life was a daily preparation for the death that might rush from an auger hole. Here, with a white dress secretly prepared, and in ineffable joy, Betsy made her first communion. The words *I was created that I might know, love, and serve God, and so save my soul*, commented by the mistress, made so profound an impression upon Betsy, that she went about repeating them constantly to herself, and pondering their significance. Life became a new thing.

Of the company here was one of a famous house, Mathieu de Montmorency, who had thrice escaped prison and the scaffold. He found much recreation in the vivacious talk of the little creole, who had no small share of French wit; but recreation did not enter much into her sister's plan of education. She put a broom into Betsy's hand within a day or two of her arrival, and the idle petulant child, accustomed to be waited on hand and foot by slaves, had at eleven years old to practise assiduously the hard work of a domestic servant, and to learn the care of a household.

Nine years afterwards, Elizabeth Prévost entered the Society of the Sacred Heart. Her great virtue and good sense caused her to be chosen for one post of authority after another; she rendered extraordinary service to the Congregation, till in 1851 she was appointed one of the Assistants General, and Superior of the Convent of the Rue de Varennes. As Superior, her rule was as kind as it was firm, and there is ample evidence that she was always greatly loved by her subordinates.

All this of Mother Prévost makes both the manner and matter of what here follows the more inexplicable, save by the platitude that very wise people are liable, say once in a life-time, to some great mistake.

To return to the interview in the parlour of the Rue de Varennes in 1856. Mrs Digby related the whole case to Reverend Mother Prévost, who, in the presence of Père Félix, thus addressed Mabel Digby in terms that the latter has herself recorded:

"After all that I have heard, you are totally unsuited

to our Congregation.   We have already enough of these
converts—forgive, madame, my frankness—who afford no
hopes of perseverance, and are hardly even instructed in
their religion ; worse, you have no health ! and we require
no more persons sent merely to edify the infirmary ! "

Père Félix was stupefied.   The visitors retired in silence,
leaving Mère Prévost satisfied, no doubt, that she had
performed a strict duty with a firmness that had killed all
false hopes by the most speedy and therefore by the least
painful of deaths.

Records of the early monasteries tell that those who
postulated for admittance were sometimes repulsed.   The
would-be disciple, if of undaunted mettle, would take his
stand outside the monastery door, or the hermit's cell, to
wait through wind and weather for days or weeks, till the
abbot or the anchorite, satisfied of his perseverance and
his humility, would greet him with the kiss of peace,
and the words : " Enter, my son, into the dwelling thou
hast chosen."

Mabel Digby's determination was not less.   Moreover
she had now, in her mother and Père Félix, two champions
of her cause.   They applied to Mother Barat herself : she
meanwhile, had received a letter from the Superior of
Marmoutier over which she paused in reflection.

" MA TRÈS VÉNÉRÉE MÈRE, — . . . The young
English girl of whom I have already spoken, and
whose cause Monseigneur Cardinal Morlot has so much
at heart . . . has a soul highly gifted in prayer
(élevée dans l'esprit d'oraison) and withal an astonishing humility and childlike obedience . . . she is
charming. . . .—VICTOIRE DE BOSREDONT."

The foundress proved herself wiser than the wise.   The
rule of the institute precluded her, she said, from receiving
a postulant immediately threatened with consumption ;
but if Miss Digby's health proved no worse after the delay
of a single year, she might certainly be apt for the life of
the Congregation.   This decision coincided with that of Dr
Bouillet, and Mabel with her mother went to winter at
Hyères.

Here may be inserted two testimonies, given much later, concerning this time of Mabel Digby's youth, just before her entry into the convent.

Father Gordon, for long Superior of the London Oratory, came to know her, and expressed the greatest admiration for her character. "She is a Spartan—a heroic soul," he said, "she has a will of iron, but it is a will that never refuses anything that God may ask." The second witness is the well-known Cardinal Langénieux, Bishop of Rheims. As Curé of St Augustin in Paris, he had been Mabel Digby's confessor during her short sojourn there, and this intercourse he declared, when an old man, to have been one of the chief privileges of his life. "What things I could tell of her!" he said significantly, "if the secret of confession did not bind me!"

She went out still with her mother into society. Mabel's partner in the dance was not infrequently young M. d'Outremont, afterwards a distinguished prelate.[1] Their ambitions were similar, and their conversation grew confidential. "This is the last time we shall meet thus!" he said one evening. "In a month I shall have entered the seminary! And you?" "I trust by that time to be admitted into Marmoutier!"

Her health was greatly improved, and no obstacle to her entry remained but the clinging affection of Mrs Digby, who on one pretext or another kept putting off the evil day. Cardinal Morlot said to her at last: "How long, madame, will you keep God waiting?" "I am ready," said the poor mother. "Go then," he replied, "and conduct your child to the convent."

Her father, as soon as Mabel's determination was made known to him, departed for England, and, in the first burst of his anguish and resentment, sent his wife a formal deed of separation. She and her daughter knew his impetuous nature, and that his moods were wont to change; but there was no faltering on their part.

On 19th February 1857, the day appointed, Mabel made her adieux to the household. The servants thought

---

[1] Vicar of the Cathedral of Tours ; Bishop of Agen in 1871, then of Le Mans 1874. Bellune, *Mgr. d'Outremont* (Tours, Mame, 1900).

that Miss Mabel was to make a rather longer voyage than usual, perhaps for the sake of her health.   Lastly she went to the stables and embraced her horse.   She was not sure afterwards whether or no a tear fell upon his neck.

It was a Friday ; and at twelve o'clock—the hour she had chosen as that of our Saviour's nailing to the Cross— bidding adieu to the valiant mother who accompanied her, she entered the gates of Marmoutier.   To this home of her choice she received from her old friend, Mère de Bosredont, the welcome always accorded to a new daughter, with of course the heartfelt charity common to religious inter- course.   But, underlying the grave and affectionate sympathy of the Superior's greeting, was a more than ordinary respect ; for her penetrating eye had discerned what had been unaccountably hidden from the excellent and capable Mère Prévost—that the postulant carried with her unawares into the Society of the Sacred Heart the ten talents that multiply into other ten.   In that moment of supreme anguish Mabel Digby felt her own gain.   Neither then nor ever did she suspect that she had with herself brought a great gift in return.

By the time that all kindly introductions to her new sisters and her new quarters were completed, it was about the hour when was consummated on Calvary that dread immolation beside which all lesser ones diminish into almost nothing, and human patience at the sight grows strong again.   Mabel Digby made her way to the chapel, to offer up anew what her Mistress of Novices pronounced " the greatest sacrifice that it is given to the human heart to make."   Here would she pour out her soul, and seek consolation from the Hidden God of the Tabernacle.

But hardly had she knelt down upon the *prie-Dieu* when a gentle voice whispered in her ear a request that she would make herself useful by taking at once *une petite surveillance.*

CHAPTER V

THE NOVICE

"Some of them were saints, and rode through the forests with a thoughtful heart, and attended by smiling angels, winnowing the air with their eternal plumes."— KENELM DIGBY, *Mores Catholici* (Booker, 1831), book II. p. 278.

SISTER AMABLE (so she was described in the catalogue of the house) left the chapel at once, and meekly followed a mistress of the boarding-school to the place of execution. The latter, opening the door of a class-room with the words: "You will give the signal, and say the *Veni Sancte*," and placing a small wooden clapper in the hand of Sister Amable, left her to functions entirely novel without more ado or explanation.

Here was a lively set of *Tourangelles* from ten to twelve years of age, who formed the third division of needle-work. They eyed the newcomer with delight tempered by curiosity, promising themselves agreeable diversions from hemming and stitching, as soon as the door should be shut upon themselves and the inexperienced English postulant.

The latter obeyed her directions and clapped the signal. The little girls placed themselves on their knees for the short prayer preparatory to every fresh occupation of the day. There was a moment's pause, for no word of the customary prayer came to the mistress's memory. One imp ran up with a book, and a patronising air ; a second turned round and called out pertly, "The nun always says the prayer!" "With me," promptly answered the postulant, "the prayer will be recited by the best con-ducted child. Begin!" And she motioned the book to the most staid-looking of the set.

Her authority was established. With the keen instinct

of their age, the children felt at once that they had a mistress. She found out from the beginning what she often repeated later, that children in their heart of hearts love to be held, and pardon more easily even severity than weakness. The new postulant erred to neither fault. The little company, to whom perpetual motion was no secret, settled down happily to their sewing, whilst one of the number read a book aloud, ·and the mistress asked thereon some suggestive question, or examined and directed the stitching. The mistress of discipline presently appeared at the door, took in the situation at a glance, and vanished with a pleased smile.

Sister Digby was installed at once as regular mistress of the third division. Mère de Bosredont had rightly believed that her new daughter would show at once a talent for government.

"*How do you do it?*" said a wondering mistress to Mabel Digby later on. She replied humbly, that she would address a prayer to the guardian angel of any child whose aspect seemed to threaten immediate trouble.

But she was always more ready to submit than to command; never, save at the call of obedience, moving a hair's breadth beyond her own office. In all this, and more, her superior recognised one of tried virtue, and was able to trust the postulant from the first, as an already formed religious. Thus, at the end of a single month, in lieu of the usual three, Sister Digby by the vote of the community was pronounced already fit to wear the religious habit and white veil of a novice. Cardinal Morlot examined her afresh concerning her vocation, and her mother giving consent to the clothing, he himself performed this ceremony on 20th March.

Mme. de Malmusse, *née* Lucie de l'Estoile, wrote (19th January 1912):

"... I was educated at Marmoutier, with Eva Digby, of whom I retain a delightful recollection. I was present at the clothing of Mother Mabel Digby in the lovely convent chapel; I can see her now, with a wreath of white roses on her dark hair, whilst Eva, and

MABEL DIGBY, 1856.

Aged 21.

[*To face p.* 43.

Berthe Pascot, another fair-haired child of the same height, carried a basket containing the religious costume to the altar. Miss Geraldine was there, with her mother; we children were much impressed with Mrs Digby's appearance, and *air de grande dame.* . . ."

The house of noviceship was at Conflans, near Paris; owing to Mabel Digby's fragile health, however, it had been judged better that she should stay in Touraine. But Mother Barat was writing in answer to Mère de Bosredont, "Your little Digby interests me," and when Père Félix, whom the foundress greatly regarded, told her that her best novice was hidden away at Marmoutier, she resolved to summon her to headquarters. She could, if necessary, return now and then to Tours for change of air. To Paris Sister Digby was accordingly sent before the end of March.

The city was still ringing with the murder of Mgr. Sibour, stabbed in the Panthéon by an unworthy priest he had loaded with benefits, and whose evil life he had tried to reform. This tragedy carried on but did not close the long list of martyred archbishops. The vacant and perilous post at Paris was now filled by Cardinal Morlot; Mrs Digby had therefore a double reason for fixing her residence in the capital, whither she followed her daughter almost immediately.

At the Motherhouse, 33 Boulevard des Invalides, were gathered round Mother Barat venerable names and well-known in the history of the congregation, chosen companions who had rendered it great services, and who now occupied the highest posts. Passing along the corridors that led to the Superior General's rooms, Sister Digby will have knelt, according to the custom, to kiss the hands of the Reverend Mothers Assistants General, Henriette Coppens, Félicité Desmarquest, and Elizabeth Prévost, the last of whom soon recognised the promise of one whose admittance she had sternly withstood. The novice's downcast eyes will not have noticed the striking profile of Mother Barat's sub-secretary, the daughter of

D

Lucien Bonaparte, Constance,[1] who resembled the first Napoleon in more than features. At thirteen this head-strong child had determined to go off to America and seek adventure with her brother. Sore against her will Cardinal Fesch placed her in the Convent of the Sacred Heart, the Trinitâ dei Monti at Rome. Here she declined to write the given essay, *On my Guardian Angel*, and wished to organize a " game of bandits." After many campaigns she gained the empire over her ambitious nature and turned its ardour to God's service. She won her father back to the sacraments on his death-bed, and induced him to make a public retractation of his conduct. The son of her brother the Prince of Canino, she led by her example to renounce the world; he became a priest, and Cardinal Buonaparte; meanwhile she, at eighteen years, entered the Society of the Sacred Heart.

But "la petite Digby" knew or cared for none of these things. She was pre-occupied with the thought of meeting the Mistress of Novices, Mother Goetz,[2] and Mother Barat herself. With feelings of some dread—for the memory of Mother Prévost's rejection was fresh—Mabel Digby entered the little plainly - furnished room of the "Très Révérende Mère Générale" for a first interview. And the most perfect confidence and mutual understanding was established at once between the venerable foundress of seventy-seven years and the novice of two-and-twenty.

Madeleine Sophie Barat, beatified by Pius X. in 1908, the daughter of a vine-dresser of Burgundy, learned in the ancient classics and in all womanly accomplishments, was the foundress of a society that grew from lowly beginnings in 1801 to number four thousand members and ninety-nine houses at the time of her death. In any one of her several biographies can be studied the mingled strength and sweetness of her rule, her breadth of sympathy and of view, and the great affection and esteem bestowed upon her everywhere.

For the present Mabel Digby was sent to the noviciate at

[1] 1833-1876. Her constant prayer was for the salvation of Napoleon III.; she died on the anniversary of Sédan.
[2] *Life of Blessed Madeleine Sophie Barat* (2nd ed., Roehampton, 1911). For Mother Goetz, *see* pp. 622.624.

Conflans.[1] Here her training fell to one whom Mother
Barat had secretly named Vicar General—or provisional
ruler of the Society at her own death—the Mistress of
Novices, Mother Goetz.

Joséphine Goetz, an Alsatian by birth, was now forty
years of age. At eighteen she passed from the school
of the Sacred Heart, where she had been educated, into
the noviceship, and so might be supposed little conversant with matters of business or of the world. But
this was not the case ; for she possessed so rare a power
of penetration and of memory that she was able to seize
more profit-from ten minutes' experience than the ordinary
mind would gather in a month. Hence she was from
the first occupied with the exterior affairs of the congregation ; and such grasp did she show of intricate matters
that after their discussion with a man of the law, he,
taking her for a woman of fifty, said, " Permettez-moi
de le dire—Madame est parfaitement conservée ! "[2] She
was just twenty years of age.

Her insight into character was also of the keenest ;
in the spiritual life, moreover, she was an adept,
and under this able professor Mabel Digby made rapid
progress.

" It's such a comfort (wrote a young novice under
Mother Goetz) to have some one to look after one's soul
as a Mistress of Novices does, and ours is exactly what
I used to think a Mistress ought to be, immensely kind
and· easy to get on with, but quite capable of giving
a poke when needed."[3]

The noviciate at Conflans, with its daily round of
duties apparently small, its share of menial work, of
sewing, embroidery, music, or illuminating manuscripts,
reading, chanting of Office, mental and vocal prayer,
joyous recreation, instructions on the meaning of religious
vocation, has all been well set forth in the life of Mother
Kerr, above mentioned. In 1857-1859 there were about

---

[1] Where, at the old château, had been signed the treaty between Louis XI.
and Charles the Bold. The place became a hunting-lodge for Louis XIV. After
the Revolution, it was acquired by Mother Barat.

[2] " Pardon my remark—you look very young for your age ! "

[3] *Life of Mother Henrietta Kerr*, 1887, p. 98. Letter to her mother.

eighty novices. All were faithful and fervent — for any
others would be promptly shown the door; but some
left their mark above the rest, and Mabel Digby was
of this number.

Amongst those who ran her very close were Augusta
von Sartorius, who was to be the fourth Mother General
of the Society, and Marcella Digby, daughter of the
writer Kenelm Digby, and a contrast to her cousin Mabel
in many things. From her father she had inherited the
abilities and tastes of a student; she was conversant
with Latin, Greek, and Hebrew. Never did learning
hide itself under a more shy and shrinking exterior.
From her father's books she had learnt to prize the
monastic life above all other, and great was his consternation, when, on asking her whence came her extraordinary
idea of entering a convent, she handed to him the seventh
book of his *Compitum*. Just so had the daughter of
Montalembert pointed to *Les Moines d'Occident*, her father's
masterpiece, as the origin of her vocation; and, like him,
poor Mr Kenelm Digby refused for some time to countenance this concrete application of his ideals. But, in the
end, the timid daughter got her way, and entered at
Conflans a few months after her favourite cousin. Both
had the same exalted standard, and they were permitted
to converse together; more often, however, they gave up
this privilege as an exercise of self-denial.

But of surpassing interest among Mabel Digby's
religious sisters at this time was a family group, Madame
Mallac and her two daughters. This mother of a French
émigré family had lost her husband and her youngest
son in almost tragic circumstances; her eldest daughter
married happily, and she herself with the two younger
girls entered the *Sacred Heart*. The three rivalled each
other in fervour; the mother at fifty years of age would
meekly obey her own daughter as head of some department, and the daughter exercised with equal simplicity
her part of command. Mabel Digby would speak many
years later of the mother, "cette sainte Mère Mallac."
"We had permission," she said, "during my noviceship,
for pious converse now and then. One day I wrote

her a note, signed in the customary way, 'Your humble sister.' 'You are fortunate indeed,' said Madame Mallac, with French *malice*, 'to find yourself already humble. *Je n'en suis pas encore là!*'" (I have not reached that stage!)

Louise Mallac, her daughter, who had recently made her vows, was sacristan, and Mabel Digby, to gain by her example, was put under her. Mother Goetz encouraged an intimacy between them. They were to warn each other frankly of faults and shortcomings.

Mrs Digby's visits to her daughter, never more frequent than the rule permitted, were marked by a spirit worthy of her wide understanding. One day she arrived at an unusual hour; she only wished, she said, for a word with her daughter. "I have just read in Rodriguez' *Christian Perfection* that in monasteries they reprove one another for their faults. Is it so here? What a grace! Profit well by it, my child!"

On 21st November 1857, the fifty-sixth anniversary of the foundation of the Society of the Sacred Heart, its first Mother, whose visits to the noviciate were frequent, spoke for some time to her daughters concerning the course of its history. She recalled once more the difficulties and enthusiasms of old, and the novices never forgot her words. But to none was her last sentence to prove of greater significance than to Mabel Digby, as yet entirely unconscious of her own destiny.

"We have often been despised and persecuted; but this must be so, and I should no longer recognise our Society if it did not bear this mark of resemblance to its Divine Master."

Many years afterwards, Mother Digby described the following scene:

"Our first Mother entered the room one day, sighing deeply. She remained silent, then sighed again. A novice ran up to her in consternation: '*Ma mère*, are you sighing on my account?' 'Yes, *ma bonne fille*, for I must send you away.' Then, all at once, like a flock of birds, we flew together to the feet of our Venerable Mother, imploring her to forgive our sister. Our Mother was silent; at last she said: 'Well, yes, then; we will give you another trial; but you must take your place below every one else, and begin your noviceship all over again.' The trial answered [Mother Digby went on]; our novice is now a professed; we met again last year, and she had not forgotten!"

Mother Barat usually made her retreat at Conflans, and was still in its seclusion when Sister Digby was reading a spiritual book one evening at a quiet hour in the empty chapel. She was startled at hearing a voice high above her, low but distinct, addressing Our Lord in pleading tones. Then there was silence, as if waiting for an answer; soon the colloquy again continued. It was Mother Barat in prayer in a little upper tribune that opened on the chapel. The novice, awe-struck, wished to retire; but, fearful of disturbing the blessed Mother by any movement, and fascinated, too, by the beauty of her communings, she imitated the example of Brother Leo, who from behind a tree would surprise St Francis in an ecstasy. In her book's page she read no more; but, with Mother Goetz's full permission, she continued to visit the chapel at the same hour until the retreat was ended. "I fancy," says one to whom Mother Digby half a century later repeated this occurrence—"I fancy from what she said, that she learnt much not to be told, during those hours of revelation.'

The novices' weekly confessions were heard by experienced confessors. One of these was the famous De Ravignan. He had just addressed the novices collectively in a way that revealed to Mabel Digby, she said, some secret of her soul. No one was usually more sympathetic and indulgent in his intercourse with penitents, but he seems to have divined in her one who could bear sterner dealing. She confessed to some weakness or other. "What cowardice!" was his only comment. These must have been his last words to her, for the great orator died in 1857. Another, Père Gamard, said to her, "*Ma petite soeur*, you will give Holy Church the trouble of canonising you, will you not?" He alluded to the assertion of Pius IX. that a religious who was proved to have kept her rule to perfection was a saint *ipso facto*.

Very different advice was to come presently. The two years of noviceship were nearly ended when the Bishop of Montpellier, her old friend, asked to see her. He had actually come up to Paris on purpose, in the interests of one he so esteemed. "You must leave this place at once!" he exclaimed. "Time was, when I believed the *Sacred Heart* to be a fervent Society. Now I know better! . . ." He proceeded to assure her that he had been told of most condemnable practices. Mabel Digby's answer was not much longer than "*J'y suis, j'y reste!*" Not till later did she know the whole story, a rare one fortunately, but never new, since, in the days of St Benedict, the first faint-hearted monk looked back from his ploughing. The one lax member of the community it was who had left it, and sought to justify her course by calumniating her superior and sisters.

Meanwhile Marmoutier was not without impatience to possess again this precious novice. She had been sent back during the summer heat — so oppressive in the Paris basin — to the "Garden of France" for a time, and in 1858 Mère de Bosredont was not without hopes of retaining her altogether for employment in the school. To these hints Mother Barat replied in her charming but decided manner concerning "notre chère Digby":

"PARIS, 31*st July* 1858.

". . . We must all put ourselves out until our young militia is ready to fill the gaps left everywhere by death and ill-health. You, like the rest, must have patience. Madame Digby will not make her vows till March 1859, and you must not count on her till then. You will be grateful for this delay later on. . . .—BARAT."

In 1858, it was Père Félix who preached the retreat at Conflans. Mabel Digby's spiritual life, its style or colour, was always largely influenced by the man and his words.

"What is the mother-thought of your Conférences in Notre Dame?" his nephew once asked. "It is expressed," he replied, "in the general title of the series,

Progress through Jesus Christ . . . which comes to this :
The nearer we follow Him, the Way, the Truth, and
the Life, the more surely we tread the ways of progress,
either as individuals, or in the domestic or social life ;
and this knowledge and this following are the law and
the criterion as to religion, as to philosophy, in every
economy, and science, and art ; thus are men enlightened
and purified, and this for eighteen years has been the
substance of my preaching."[1]

Not without significance was this quotation preserved
from the retreat of 1858. "He is God, He is Man, He
is also Redeemer ; and, with His head crowned with
thorns, His heart pierced with sorrow, He says to us :
See, it is I, the Christ ; love me as I am ; and then,
our vocation can be thus rendered : like Him, to obey,
to be humble, to sacrifice self always."

These words comprise Mabel Digby's plan of campaign
for the peace and warfare of her life henceforward.

And now her noviceship was over. "I made my vows
in the joy of my heart fifty years ago!" she wrote in
1909 ; and in the month of May she was sent back to
Marmoutier.

[1] *Life*, pp. 188-189.

CHAPTER VI

"'The gardener,' says St Anselm, 'gives space and freedom to young plants, that they may grow and spread forth their sweet branches, and so should masters provide indulgence for the young, who, by oblation, are planted in the garden of the Church that they may increase and bear fruit to God. They ought not to be cramped and restrained by terrors. threats, and stripes."—KENELM DIGBY, *Mores Catholici* [Booker, 1831], book IV. p. 194.

THE new aspirant—so are the nuns of the *Sacred Heart* termed for the five years preceding their solemn profession—was to take up the onerous duties of Mistress of Discipline in the school at Marmoutier; and in this, as well as in her, so to say, social capacity, she was eagerly welcomed back.

But a storm of private sorrow was to overwhelm her own soul at the outset.

Her father, since 1857, had remained in England. His dispositions had already begun to soften upon the subject of his daughter's entering a convent. "If only they would send her to England," he repeated, "I should not mind, and we should meet again." His wife and daughters formed fond hopes for the future. Cardinal Morlot shared them; he always declared the entire good faith of Mr Digby, co-existing with prejudices that had already diminished to a great extent. Mrs Digby had fitted up at her Paris residence a beautiful chapel, wherein she had permission, as at Tours, for the Blessed Sacrament to be permanently kept. Geraldine, after mature consideration, had taken the Cardinal's word that it was her duty to remain with her mother for the present at any rate, and not to follow Mabel into the *Sacred Heart*. In Paris, then, the wife and three daughters ceased not to pray devoutly for the father and brothers.

Now, alas, came the great tragedy of their lives.

It was preceded by a lesser one.   The eldest son, Kenelm, had been placed at a military academy.   Some alarming symptoms of disease appeared ; he went off alone to a specialist, who told him, with cruel inconsideration, that he had but a few months to live.   The shock must have accelerated his end ; in a few weeks he was no more.

The more terrible blow followed shortly.   On 26th October Mr Simon Digby was riding to the railway station at Reading, when he was taken suddenly ill, alighted, and died in the waiting - room.   Thanks to some letter or card in his pocket his man of business identified him, and the intelligence was forwarded to his family.

The Superior at Marmoutier had not read previously the letter conveying the awful news.   By some mistake it was handed to Madame Digby open, when she was in the school, preparing to lead a file of children down a corridor.   A glance revealed its contents ; she continued on her way without sign.   Those afterwards with whom she wept over their similar losses, will realise how strong were the floodgates of her sorrow.

She would omit no point of rule in order to make time for the indulgence of feeling.   Now and henceforward, as she afterwards told, she offered up to God this constant fidelity to duty as a propitiatory sacrifice for her father's soul.   And in a mysterious way she had, later on, an assurance that it was accepted.

Madame Digby was to lose a great friend.   Mère Dumazeaud, the Mother Vicar, arrived shortly, and announced that Mère de Bosredont's services being re-quired in Spain, her place at Marmoutier would be taken by another, Mère Gazelli.   This was made known to the assembled community with much dignity and delibera-tion, and in the finest French, but it all sounded some-what cold to the young novices, who, after the wrench of leaving Conflans, were struck with sorrow at the prospect of this new loss.   Upon the exit of the *Mère Vicaire* one of them turned to Madame Digby, and observed with Scotch frankness : "That is a very dry party !"   A smile was scarcely dissimulated as the

latter made reply, "Sister Cecil, you must never speak
of a Mother Vicar as a *dry party* !"

This was a highly interesting personality, Cecil Kerr,
a daughter of the well - known Tractarian convert,
Constance, Marchioness of Lothian, of whom presently.
By Madame Kerr's talent for music she rendered excellent
service as organist.   Her straightforward unworldliness
of view, sterling self - sacrifice, and keen appreciation
of spiritual things, endeared her to Madame Digby, and
appealed to her strongly, despite the novice's utterly
unconventional and sometimes awkward ways.   One
morning, long before dawn, the Mistress of Discipline
heard a knock at her door.   "Come in! What's the matter,
my dear sister, are you ill?"   "No, but I've been thinking that neither you nor I pray half enough for the
conversion of England!"   And, taking a seat by the
bed, she began to unfold with enthusiasm her ideas on
this vast subject.

In 1861, Madame Charlotte Leslie arrived at
Marmoutier.   Madame Digby and she were delighted to
meet again; the latter, bewildered at the complicated
duties of her new surroundings, had recourse to the
Mistress of Discipline, who set her at once on her feet,
so that her attainments, power of teaching, and self-
possession could furnish valuable assistance.

" Mother. Digby's sweet serenity [says Mother Leslie, of those
years] was never ruffled. She knew how to distinguish between
real faults and innocent blunders ; of the latter there were plenty."

Certain letters were written to Mother Barat by the
superiors, or others in office, at Marmoutier.   Nineteen
of these remain, together with some of the foundresses'
well pleased replies.

". . . Madame Digby is most virtuous [writes Mère de
Bosredont] . . . she is capable of making an excellent Mistress
General . . . Monseigneur (Cardinal Morlot) who is devoted to
our Society, also has the highest esteem for Madame Digby and
all her family. . . ."

Mother Gazelli, very shortly after her instalment,

writes in the same strain time after time, adding (this is the substance of a dozen letters):

"Our new mistresses are beginning to shape themselves well for the school . . . but as for Madame Digby, she knows already the spirit of the *Sacred Heart* and its system . . . she is entirely docile. . . . None could second me better than she does. She knows each child individually; she influences them in a wonderful way. . . . A pupil who wished to leave us immediately, refusing to eat or to study, has been taken in hand by Madame Digby, and now does remarkably well. . . . Madame Digby knows, too, the exact status of each of the children's families; you would hardly believe to what extent they trust her. Her calmness, maturity, tact, spirit of conciliation, yet firmness in the face of duty, make her loved both within and without the walls. . . . She is but eight and twenty, but her judgment and virtue would do credit to forty years of age."

Meantime, Madame Digby's relations with Mother Barat had been continuous. She wrote to her regularly, and as soon as the summer vacations began, the Superior General always recalled her to spend them in Paris. Here the young religious received counsel as to ways and means in every order of things. Further, Mother Barat saw with special clearness any lingering defects in one whom she believed capable of the highest, and she would be satisfied with nothing less. She knew how to rouse any dormant energy by vehement reproach and, by Mother Digby's own avowal, she herself was not spared in this matter. Mother Barat knew how to keep the soul in humility by turning her eyes from what had been done to the far more there was still to do.

It is customary to recall the aspirants to the Mother-house for six months' special probation—a renewal of the noviceship, as it were—before the final vows are taken.[1] Mère Gazelli was loth to spare Madame Digby for so long a period, unless some person of mature age could be sent to fill her place at Marmoutier the while. Mother Barat therefore arranged that Mabel Digby should go to

[1] During this period the aspirants are termed, in the Society of the Sacred Heart, *Probanists.*

the Motherhouse for two months at a time during the summer holidays of two consecutive years, and return in the interim to fulfil her office at Marmoutier. So in great joy she set out in August 1862.

At Paris she met again her friend of friends, Louise Mallac, with whom she had corresponded ever since 1859. No weak sentimentality had ever tarnished the lustre of their intercourse. Indeed, self-sacrifice was carried to a point that may seem excessive. The maxim of Père de Ravignan : " Nature shall not touch me," Mabel Digby and her friend applied here, and in all similar circumstances of life. Not only did Louise now make no effort to renew their exceptional relations, but she agreed with Mabel Digby to give up any correspondence by letter. Each mentioned to a third person the keen sacrifice that this cost her, and spoke of her friend with the most affectionate esteem. They were to meet no more. Louise Mallac had offered her life in sacrifice for the conversion of her brother, who was held back by an unworthy tie from the practice of religion.[1] Soon she was stretched upon a bed of suffering ; her natural impatience of inactivity she gradually schooled into resignation. " Our Lord would gather me as a fruit," she said one day, " but I am yet too green ; He leaves me to ripen on the straw ! " Her early death coincided in time with her brother's return to his duties, followed by his entry into the Jesuit noviciate. As priest he ministered to his own mother on her death-bed.

Madame Digby returned for a time to Marmoutier, wearing the silver cross usual to professed only ; for though no more than an aspirant, she was now to add to the functions, the title also of Mistress General. She fulfilled the duties of Mistress of Discipline as well, until presently another came to assist her in this department. This was a young religious of great promise, Madame Marie Zaepffel, who thus describes her own impressions :

" In March 1863, our Blessed Mother sent me to Marmoutier. Here I found Madame Digby in full activity at the head of a

---

[1] *Vie de Madame Louis Mallac* (Paris, Dupuy), 2nd ed., 1863.

numerous school.   I was struck by her whole attitude; under her rule all went on to perfection.   Parents as well as children held her in deepest regard: 'It is,' they said, 'the iron hand in a velvet glove.'   When I recalled to mind later on this early and complete maturity, I recognised the anticipated portrait of the ideal Professed religious, traced in one of her own letters.   Her self-possession was unfailing; whether she suffered or no, physically or morally, she was impenetrable.   A shrewd and intelligent pupil was wont to say, when the days of her education were over: 'I divined the character of each of my mistresses, with the sole exception of Mother Digby. Her thoughts it was impossible to read!'   Her presence alone sufficed to restore or maintain order; the children obeyed instantly the single light stroke of her well known little brown wooden signal."

In what follows concerning Mother Digby's action in the school, it is not claimed that she originated any system, or portion of the system, she pursued.   In essentials, and even in many details, the education and training at Marmoutier had much in common with all sound Catholic and convent methods.   It is here essayed to dwell merely upon what was salient in her ideas and influence.

Madame Digby required a sense of responsibility and a constant vigilance on the part of each mistress, but she detested anything like spying, any traps to catch a child in a misdemeanour.   " Watchfulness," she repeated, " must be open, wide, and unsuspicious.   We are the guards of princes—for every soul is of blood royal." She was invariably punctual, and demanded the same exactitude from both mistresses and children.   But, if this were all, it were little indeed.   Exterior regularity was but the *sine quâ non*.   Her own influence struck deep within.   She was greatly loved and trusted.   A little English girl remembered her pride in claiming Madame Digby as a compatriot.   The French children insisted that she must be French, seeing how well she spoke the language.   The new comer pursued the matter with warmth, and somehow the word *Waterloo* came up.   Her companions declared that the English never won it!   The Mistress General arrived on the playground to find the Briton with flashing eyes and dress dishevelled, pouring forth in any words that came to mind a torrent of contradiction to a statement so outrageous. Madame Digby was, of course, appealed to by both parties, and set the matter right as she knew how! Many years afterwards she would recall such scenes with keen amusement.

It has been said that she was loved. But she had a horror of the caressing or impassioned friendships to which young people are liable, particularly the more ardent natures, and any attempt to fasten such attachment upon herself was instantly repelled. A child of Turkish race took this sort of fancy to the Mistress General. On pretext of opening or shutting the door, she began to follow her about, and to seek her notice. "What do you want, my child?" Then, seeing her embarrassment, "I hate followers!" (Je déteste les suivantes!) said Madame Digby, as if she meant it, and passed on. The child was cured of her folly by this douche of cold water, but retained a strong and respectful regard for one whom she knew to be her true friend. Respect, in fact, as well as confidence, Madame Digby insisted, must temper all relations between mistress and pupil. Children should neither blame a mistress nor praise her, were it even for her virtue. "Your Mothers," she said with dignity, "are not for your discussion."

She hardly ever scolded, but the thing, if it had to be done, was deliberate, short, and effective; a repetition was never required. Rare was even her phrase of reproof; a look, a nod, now and then a tiny shaft pointed with French *malice*, would carry home.

Given an effectual discipline, two things, as regards this world, made a good school in Madame Digby's idea; strong studies and thorough play. The Superior General gave her an able mistress of studies, Mère Célestine Dufour, who to cultivated talents joined the rarer power of displaying the interest inherent in things of the mind, and of stimulating their pursuit by both teachers and pupils. "You don't manage your children properly," said Madame Digby at another period to a young mistress, new to a class, "because you do not, like such-a-one, take pains to make lessons delightful. Her children are so fascinated that they don't even think of being naughty!" Therefore the Mistress General, herself not much of a reader, would safeguard at her personal inconvenience the time of the mistresses, so that the necessary preparation might precede each class.

The recreations she considered almost as important. How often in later days would she insist upon it that education means formation of character, not only mind, but heart and will. So she took the question of games most seriously to heart. When she first went to Marmoutier, these were of the most unsophisticated description. She saw that there was room for improvement, and when Lady Lothian came to see her daughter, the subject was talked over. Before long there arrived at Marmoutier an ample variety of game - sets for all weathers; amongst them, the newly - invented croquet, now almost despised, but then engrossing. The young religious—nothing loth, especially the novices—were set to work to learn the games themselves, and practised them in the holidays so as to set the children going, and the playgrounds and playrooms became places of delight. When Mother Digby, on holidays, headed a children's band of hide-and-seek, nothing could exceed the valour and endurance of the combatants, half smothered it might be under the hay in her company, or hearing in silence an onslaught of sticks that probed the heap.

But she went to the foundations of things. "Two faults I fear above all others in children: want of straight-forwardness, and flippancy.[1] Such characters have not even the capacity of a cream cheese for receiving an impression!" She would quote a doctor, famous for his skill in mental disease, who assured her that most cases of insanity arise merely from defective nursery training, and that moral education is too late if begun at only four years old. Without going so far as this, of course, she thought certain tendencies, such as sloth and slowness,

[1] "Légèreté."

very difficult to deal with unless corrected in early youth. Faults of the head she dreaded more than those of the heart and will, as less corrigible; the power of loving increases with efforts at unselfishness, a weak will is strengthened by self-sacrifice, but what can cure a radical defect of judgment?

Beneath all other instruction must lie a strong basis of religious knowledge. Herein the children were, of course, grounded every day by the several mistresses in a class of half an hour's duration, but in the application of this knowledge to practice lies the chief task of the head mistress. Every week, according to rule, the whole school was assembled for a short "general instruction," in which she urged the highest standard of action. *Noblesse oblige.* "You are the children of saints!" Personal love of the living Christ was the beginning and end of everything. Piety, devotional rites, were used as a means; but she never over-rated exterior helps, or prolonged them beyond the powers of children. She often quoted a devout but restless spirit of ten years old: "Oh! madame, how well I would say my prayers if you would let me run round the garden all the while!" and the sad complaints of the junior school, compelled to sit out the too-long sermons of the Abbé Darras: "M. l'Abbé never knows how to get to *eternal life!*" [1]

According to custom, in many convent schools, during the novenas preceding all great feasts, the practice of some special virtue or point of rule was made the subject of emulation. Bad marks were a sufficient visitation for faults, while the proficient could gain some special reward on the feast day; it might be to serve the poor, or present them with gifts, or to decorate an altar, or what not. In all this, as has been said, Mme. Digby was merely using the customs and systems of her Society, but she employed them with a master hand. To all this and more the most telling witnesses are the mothers and grandmothers who

---

[1] "Ne sait jamais faire venir *la vie éternelle*!" (with which words it was customary to end the sermon).

E

spoke and still speak of all they owed to a Mistress whose formation they have transmitted to already two generations.

In 1896 a former pupil of Marmoutier made a long journey to see her. "I would go up and down all France to find her again!" she said.

"'Take care (relates another) of the beautiful roses on the path of life. Their perfume attracts us, and we stop to gather them, but their thorns may hold us back from our journey!' So, twenty years ago, she spoke to me at Marmoutier with so much gravity, yet goodness; her words, as they always did, filled me with joy and courage!" "How can I forget (adds a third) her strong lessons at work, at class, or at recreation even! She knew how to transform the dictates of duty . . . into a voluntary impulsion. . . . She entered into all our naïve joys and little troubles, so overwhelming at that age; and the new children, timid and surprised, like birds fallen by chance from the nest, were quickly made to feel at home." "In looking through the pictures given to me by her at that time, I find in each some mention of the Cross. It is 'O Crux Ave,' 'In cruce salus,' or 'Can you drink this chalice with Me?' At seventeen years old, this teaching seemed to me severe. But later what consolation have I not found therein!" (A fourth writes:) "I was sent at four years old to Marmoutier, my parents being dead. I had a little crib near her room. One day I said to her, 'Ah, ma mère, you know my self-love!' 'Yes,' she replied archly, 'I assisted at its birth!'"

The Mistress General is naturally much concerned with the bodily health of the children under her charge; the direct care of ailments great and small, however, is committed to infirmarians under a special Mistress. Marmoutier, for its famous climate, was the sanatorium of the French houses; a superintendent of marked ability was here required. Mme. Digby's talent for sick nursing and general insight into physical conditions could not pass unnoticed by Mother Gazelli, who soon gave her the formal title of Mistress of Health, with orders to train an assistant under her. This charge she esteemed as an immense privilege, and there is but one voice from those who were ever the object of her solicitude. Suffering had long been her own intimate acquaintance, and her tender sympathy soon detected it in others. Who can describe the lightness of her footstep, the absolute noiselessness of her every movement? This extraordinary silence of action indeed she had acquired as a second nature, and it followed her to every place like an atmosphere, but of course in the infirmary it acted in a specially soothing manner. Watch any one of her movements, and you would call it slow; but their number was entirely restricted to the necessary, and, as each told home, her speed of accomplishment was astonishing.

That in sudden emergencies she made no uncalculated movement hardly needs the saying, but it is worth record for those with experience of novices, that even at that stage, new to the functions of scullery maid, she broke literally nothing. Here seems the place to mention the dainty neatness of everything she used or touched. Her work or writing table, her school or infirmary, showed invariably the sort of brilliant cleanliness that shines in a well kept dairy, and the perfect arrangement that charms the eye, and is, even in the humblest surroundings, rightly called beautiful, if St Augustine correctly defines beauty as *the splendour of order.*

But more than all this is, of course, necessary for an accomplished sick nurse. She had been trained technically in this respect by the Mistress of Health who preceded her, Mère Courtois, a former *Hospitalière* ; and she was able to take an active part together with the surgeon when there was question of an operation. More than one preferred her to his own assistants. Her nerve was equal to all emergencies ; her hand was delicate, yet firm and steady as that of a man. She gradually acquired an immense experience.

Tender as was her sympathy for suffering, she was not to be taken in. A little girl—as girls will, sometimes— made herself interesting by fainting away. She was carried up to the infirmary and lay motionless. Mme. Digby with one finger lifted her eye-lid, and inspected the eye. "Get up, my child," she then said quietly. The little actress dared not disobey, and fainted no more.

So much for her main duties; but there were "odds and ends" besides. The music she took to heart; that is, the organ and choir in church. She herself had little taste or attraction for this art, but, just as in the province of studies, and in all else for the matter of that, she seemed to divine a horizon beyond her own ken. She believed that Mesdames Kerr and Leslie were to be trusted in the domain of music, and she saw to it that their taste should prevail. They were devoted to classical music; some offertories and hymns of the kind were played, and received by the community with much good-humoured disparagement. Nowise disconcerted, Mme. Kerr said to Mme. Leslie with determination: "We'll *make* them like it!" And day by day ears were gradually opened till they heard rightly, and the classics actually came into favour.

Mme. Digby was, however, a proficient in the art of illuminating upon vellum; not that she composed original designs, but she copied beautifully, or adapted the old ones. Here she had scope for her power of faultless finish that has its right place in miniature art. Detached leaves and altar cards were thus executed by herself, or under her superintendence, and, though she had never read the *Lamp of Sacrifice,* she would use only the very best material for purposes where the altar was concerned. A little cake of carmine that cost a guinea, most carefully husbanded, saw service for years.

At Marmoutier began two great friendships. Here she first made acquaintance with an Englishman who had brought his little sister-in-law to school: John Hungerford Pollen, the Tractarian convert and artist. They understood one another at once; never were two natures more unlike, save in entire sincerity and high ideals. On both sides sprang up a mutual trust and admiration, a life-long regard. So was it, too, between Mme. Digby and Cecil Lady Lothian, of whom it might have been predicated, as of St Theresa, that she was "fair, wise, and holy." Lady Lothian indeed showed the convent unnumbered kindnesses. She would bring with her English games and story books for the children, and for the nuns, paint brushes, music, or anything else; sometimes as commissions, often as gifts, always the best of their kind. Sorrow the friends little knew of was to draw them together, and they were to work side by side for many a year.

The year 1864 had arrived, and in the autumn Mme. Digby was to be recalled to the Motherhouse to complete her time of probation.

" Madame Digby," writes Mère Gazelli, " is happy beyond words at the thought of completing her probation . . . she is preparing herself for this grace by a greater fidelity than ever to all your directions. She is herself writing to you. . . . Hers is a soul that must be indeed pleasing to our Lord ; she will certainly do great things for Him. The other day an ecclesiastic, seeing her pass by, turned to me and said : ' The spirit of wisdom is in her.' In fact she is in every way a person highly advanced in perfection."

A special Mistress directed the probanists,[1] but Mother Barat, nevertheless, constituted herself sole guide and confidante of Mabel Digby, to the great content of the latter. Again she laid open to Mother Barat her abiding sorrow at her father's loss. Mother Barat replied with an air of confidence : *"He is safe."*

It happened at this time that seventeen deaths by yellow fever had taken place at the house of Louisiana. The probanists unanimously offered to go out there, the whole set of them, to take the place of these workers. " My poor children !" replied Mother Barat, "this would be too many at a time ! Besides, Europe has its needs." To Mabel Digby in private, however, she said these never-forgotten words : " *You will one day go to America. That will be God's answer to you, signifying the safety of your father's soul.*"

The three months drew to a close, and the probanists entered into their final retreat of thirty days that pre-cedes the most important act of their lives. To one who knew her later, Mme. Digby confided this passage from a work of Père Huby, which summed up for her

[1] *See* p. 60.

the great lessons of this period of reflection, renovation. resolution :

"This shall be my portion, Nothingness : to remain underneath ; to see the plans and sayings of others preferred to my own ; to rejoice in being considered without wisdom, without capacity ; to have in fact no credit, no authority ; to love dependence as an empire."

Here is revealed the strong and independent nature, still in combat serene and strenuous, never disturbing the repose of others by the clash of arms within the sound-proof walls of the heart's secret chamber. There is One that seeth.

In her handwriting is a list of persons and causes to be prayed for on the day of her profession. She begs for grace to die rather than commit deliberately the smallest sin ; she asks that she may bring many souls to the service of God ; and, mysteriously, in words under-lined ; *That the truth may shine out, ever more and more, Our Lord knows why.*

Mother Digby related many years afterwards :

"On the eve of the ceremony of profession our Venerable Mother who was speaking to the probanists, stopped short suddenly, and appeared lost in thought. Then she exclaimed : 'My God ! No—never permit that a Judas should be here !' . . . A shudder ran through the whole assembly."

November 4th was the day of Mabel Digby's profession ; she added, according to rule, the vows of devotion to the education of youth, and of stability in her vocation, to those of poverty, chastity, and obedience. Mrs Digby and her daughter were amongst the spectators at the public ceremony ; Mother Goetz suspended the silver cross round the neck of the new professed, Blessed Mother Barat placed the gold ring upon her finger. The venerable foundress was in her eighty-fifth year, and Mabel Digby was never to see her again.

She departed for Marmoutier bearing a sealed letter.

". . . A line, dear mother and daughter, to let you know that we are sending you back your new professed. You will be consoled by her religious spirit ; I trust that the Divine Heart will make use of her, that she will win the hearts of her pupils, and relieve your own burden, my child, for your work at present is heavy. I can say only thus much, for to-day I am busier than usual. Our Digby will be my living letter.

"Adieu, dear mother and daughter, I am yours in the Hearts of Jesus and Mary.—Your mother, BARAT."

CHAPTER VII

THE SUPERIOR

"'Now,' said the king, 'it only remains that I give you the accolade, which I am willing to do; but you must first promise me, that you will, above all things, honour God who made heaven and earth. After that you must swear to follow the lessons and doctrines which have just been given you.' Then answered the youth, his eyes being tearful with devout thoughts, 'this I have promised to do!'"—KENELM DIGBY, *Mores Catholici* (Booker, 1831), book VI. p. 185.

ON 25th May 1865, Ascension Day, the Society of the Sacred Heart lost its venerable foundress; on 8th September Mother Josephine Goetz was elected to the general government. No appointment could be more acceptable to the Society at large; but Mabel Digby's consolation would have disappeared had she foreseen the first official act of her former Mistress of Novices.

Not many days after the nomination of the new Superior General, Mère Gazelli sent for Mabel Digby. "I am going away." "Yes, Reverend Mother?" "And you don't ask why?" "*Why* is such an ugly word." "Well, I am going." "Surely not for good!" "Yes— and who do you suppose is to take my place?" "Since I am to lose you, I do not care." "But—it is yourself! . . . Come!" said Mère Gazelli. She walked out into the garden, sending a message to Mère Zaepffel, in whom she specially confided, to join them in the *charmilles*; *allées de silence*, the monks used to call them, where the branches of great secular hornbeams still meet overhead, like the aisles of a church.

"Mère Gazelli was seated, and she whom her superior used playfully to call 'my only daughter'—for there was none like her—sat by her side. 'Mother Digby in tears!' I cried, in unguarded astonishment and sad concern at a sight so novel. 'It is because she is to take my place!' 'Is *that* all,' I exclaimed in

profound relief—for I feared I know not what misfortune—forgetting
the necessary corollary, our good Superior's departure! Never
can I forget the sight of Mother Digby's face, calm as ever, yet so
full of pain, inundated with tears that flowed down silently; there
was no contortion of feature, no contraction of brow; I read a deep
anguish, joined to an entire resignation."

"Unfortunately," said Mabel Digby later on, half in
jest, to one whom she herself had named Superior,
"unfortunately, one survives these things!"

"The first shock once over," Mother Zaepffel goes
on, "she took up her cross with a brave simplicity.
Together we prepared for the departure of Mère Gazelli."
Mother Digby showed her care in all details down to
the smallest; and the secret of the approaching loss was
kept until presently the Mother Vicar, Mère de Tinseau,
arrived at Marmoutier to effect the change officially. She
was accompanied by two religious of mature age and
experience, who were to act, the one, Mère de Rochequairie,
as assistant or next in rank to the new Superior, the
other as Bursar. Mme. Digby opened the door of the
carriage. The Mère Vicaire eyed her with astonishment,
and then turned to her companions: "How young she
is!" To poor Mme. Digby the accents bore something of dismay; and, as she declared afterwards, she
felt thoroughly ashamed of herself.

It is characteristic of Mrs Digby, that on hearing
that her daughter had been made Superior, she came at
once to see Mother Gazelli. "Has my daughter always
been obedient?" "Yes!" "Then I am at rest about
her."

The community as a whole were now made aware
of Mère Gazelli's departure; it was deeply felt, but all
accepted the sacrifice with submission, and on 30th
September they were called together for the solemn
installation of a new Superior. The rule forbids any
mention of the subject beforehand in private intercourse,
and no word of conjecture had been hazarded as to who
had been nominated. But the venerable appearance of
the new arrival Mère de Rochequairie, and her known

reputation for prudence and virtue, would make her the object of inward guesses. When, amidst profound silence, Mother Digby's name was announced, there was, says Mother Zaepffel, a palpable start of surprise, and a perceptible pause, before the community rose and advanced one by one, according to custom, to kneel and kiss the hand of the new Superior, the youngest of all the professed, and looking much younger still than her thirty years. Most of those who were now rendering homage to Mabel Digby had received her as a postulant, and she had served them as a novice — for a novice is at every one's service. " But her air of calm and courageous self-forgetfulness," Mère Zaepffel goes on, "allowed none to despise her youth.   She bore her painful honours meekly."

That evening Mère Gazelli bade adieu to the community, and last of all to Mother Digby, and departed to fulfil the office of Superior at Annonay. "As she drove away," said Mother Digby afterwards to another who bore the same cross, "I realised for the first time the great loneliness of a Superior. I turned into the house again with the thought that all would have the right to come to me for help, but that I had no one to go to."

Twenty - four hours had scarcely passed when all Marmoutier recognised a new person in Reverend Mother Digby. If the Mistress General requires certain powers in order to order well her little world, the head of a convent needs others as well. Some have commanded battalions, and failed to rule a monastery.

Mabel Digby's portrait was painted, generally, by a witness of this and the next three years.

"She faced her new charge with the loftiness of view that she brought to bear upon every duty, and her temporal administration, as well as her spiritual government, presented from the very first a finished model. Nothing escaped her, outlines or details; she foresaw and regulated all things in a calm that multiplied her power of action. She was incapable of umbrage or suspicion ; she desired to be kept in touch with all that went on, allowing always great latitude to her subordinates, and showing them the frankest

.confidence. Her mind was focussed entirely upon the business in hand; she was unusually ready to take the opinion or even the advice of her subjects, but not before she had listened to the very end, and heard all sides, for few things have but two. She was never (adds another) afraid·to recognise or own a mistake though rarely indeed was she mistaken."

Her attitude with elders was one of affectionate esteem. The aged Mère de Rochequairie made herself a mentor. On one occasion she chanced to visit the common room of the community during the hour of recital of Office. Here were two young nuns playing chess! At the first opportunity the Mother Assistant was found at her Superior's door. Was this indeed *her* doing? Yes, the two having been ill, keeping early hours, and unable as yet to walk in the garden, or say Office with the rest, she had installed them in a well-warmed room for a little recreation before bed-time. The good ancient nevertheless took up her parable. It was not the recreation she objected to, but the scandal of the hour chosen! Mother Digby, taking all blame upon herself, fixed another time for the chess, though, in fact, neither then nor later had she done otherwise than unite two essentials for a guardian of religious law ; never to allow a dispensation needlessly, nor, by unreasoning tenacity to the letter, to infringe the spirit of the rule, or obstruct its action.

None held more than she to the common lot of the house in all things. Owing to her weak health, the infirmarian tried to give her more carefully prepared food, but she would suffer no fare upon the Mothers' table in the refectory different from that provided for the rest. It was impossible to deceive her vigilance. One of the first visits was to the kitchen. "For whom is that?" she asked, seeing a dish better seasoned than usual. "*Ma Révérende Mère*, for the Mothers' table, so please you!" "Place it on that of the eldest lay Sisters, and give their dish to us!" It was for lodging as for food. She would sleep sometimes here, sometimes there, giving up her room to an invalid, or to one who required some special outlook or advantage. A young religious had let fall a complaint concerning her own quarters. What was her confusion that night to perceive that the Superior had changed rooms with her! Nor could entreaties revoke the arrangement. The lesson was a salutary one.

Reverend Mother Digby required of her subjects a certain austerity of bodily habit, albeit she herself walked further than she ever permitted them to follow; nor would she tolerate any hanging back in the path of duty to escape an insignificant suffering. Two lay Sisters were sent one day to the beehives, so famous in that land of flowers. The younger, assailed by the possessors of the honey, and profiting by a temporary absence of her companion, fled altogether from the field of battle. Her Superior deferred all comment until the next day, when she sent for the deserter. "Sister, do you think you did well in running away yesterday? Soeur Agathe remained!" "Ah, *ma Révérende Mère*, Soeur Agathe has a tough old skin!" But the Sister went back obediently, nevertheless. Later on, when the same Sister was attacked by a painful affection in the leg, with what affectionate care was she nursed by the Reverend Mother! The patient bore her suffering bravely, till she drew back one day from some necessary treatment. She was severely reprimanded, and returned valiantly to the breach. Such was the ascendency of Mother Digby, and such the training that she gave.

She herself walked always at the head of the attack. She suffered in silence the terrible and constantly recurring headaches mentioned already, nor was this all; another painful malady obliged her for long to take but a single meal a day, nevertheless she would be the first to help the Sisters at any heavy or unusual work. Only a superhuman energy could prevent her suffering sometimes from reducing her to inaction, and the change of her features betrayed her in spite of herself. To the remonstrances of one in her confidence she said one day: "I have asked Our Lord that I may never be without some pain." But her subordinates found this more than they could stand; and on this point alone they now appealed for redress to the first authority in Paris.

The Mistress General wrote :—

" . . . Our Reverend Mother gives us the example of every virtue, but her state of health is by no means reassuring. She takes hardly any care of herself. . . . She constantly overtaxes her strength, and no one can stop her. An express command from yourself would be useful. . . ."

There was one point to which she felt an almost insurmountable repugnance. This was the giving of a spiritual conference to her community, a duty required of a Superior every fortnight by rule. Her humility made her believe that these conferences were poor and useless, and she would postpone or omit them if possible. But her daughters looked forward with the greatest eagerness to her words, and were grateful to Mère de Rochequairie who would with affectionate playfulness drive her forward to the room, using a handkerchief as a whip, " *Allez, allez, ma Révérende Mère, executezvous !* " " It is all very well," retorted Mother Digby, " but I should like to see *you* do it ! "

Her utterance was remarkably distinct; every syllable pronounced in that low musical voice, never raised in pitch, and never hurried, penetrated to the far end of the largest room ; the grave and simple conferences taught mostly the same lessons of love and suffering, in the varied lights of the feasts or seasons of the year. A tale that served as illustration more than once, had been related to her by a holy priest to whom a little goosegirl, brutally treated by her mistress, had confided her troubles. " I am not unhappy," she said, " my angel guardian sings me such beautiful songs ! The music seems to come from heaven, and the words go deep down into my heart." " Tell me, my child, some words that he sang." " One day he sang about the soul that loves Jesus, and the soul that Jesus loves. Jesus consoles and caresses the soul that He loves — and so it is delightful to be this loved soul — but if she suffers patiently and without complaint, she becomes the loving soul too, and it is better to be the loving one who gives, than merely the loved one who receives." Mother

Digby would ring the changes on *l'âme aimante et l'âme
aimée*.

With all her advocacy of suffering, her joyousness of
spirit was something singular.   She had the keenest sense
of humour, and would laugh till she almost cried over
any absurdity that came to pass.   People with a sense of
fun always found themselves in sympathy with her.   Her
childlike buoyancy, her elasticity of mind perhaps it was
that prevented so great a load of responsibility from
weighing her down, and her gaiety, consciously or unconsciously, overflowed upon all around.   Even in the midst
of the most solemn private interviews, a burst of hearty
laughter would be heard by those waiting outside the door
for their turn.

A healthy expansion of mind reigned over the daily
recreations; but it was in the holidays, and especially
during the long summer vacation, that the family life of
the community within itself had full play.   Truly these
were delightful times.   The mornings were mostly taken
up with study — lessons in Latin, in English, and the
preparation of the several mistresses for the classes they
would teach during the coming year.   There were chosen
readings, extra hours of prayer and of recreation, much
gardening, too; Mother Digby planted many trees and
fruit trees at Marmoutier.   There were walks round
the vast property, and visits to Rougemont, a small
château upon a hill, overlooking a lovely country, and
commanding every part of the abbey grounds.   Here
dwelt Cardinal Richelieu in the days when he was proprietor of the Abbey.   Down the steep ascent are seen
the traces of the zigzag path in stone, by which he
could drive up and down on a low incline.   Sometimes the nuns would sit and work whilst some old
book was read, borrowed from the great library at
Tours, concerning the history of St Martin and the
Abbey, a subject of unfailing interest.   Then there were
the *vendanges*, gay and laborious days of grape-gather-
ing at Rougemont, Reverend Mother at the head of the
party.   During the last week of the vacation the community made the yearly retreat.   " Enter upon it," she

would say, "with a calm head, a large heart, an energetic will."

Their patron, St Martin, who shared his cloak with a beggar, she put forward as a type of the fraternal charity that reigned at Marmoutier. To make her daughters happy was one great means of urging on their progress in the spiritual life.

At Marmoutier was a poor school, with a class of boys under the training of Mère Sciout, herself somewhat remarkable, and typical of the few who, having entered religion late in life, and with the already formed habits of one always her own mistress, need the most resolute self-conquest in the taming of an imperious will and an excitable temper. She had not shrunk from the task, though it had been a long one. Now, however, she equalled or surpassed many who had borne the yoke from their youth. Mère Sciout's tall form, and the beauty of her pale, worn, ascetic features, made her a striking figure among her boys, over whom she had a boundless influence for good. The enterprize was an innovation. The neighbouring *curé* of St Radegonde had been at his wit's end with the impious little ragamuffins who feared neither God nor man. They would fling their caps at the sanctuary lamp, and vie with each other as to who could put it out soonest. Mother Barat had given permission for the nuns at Marmoutier to try their hand with these black lambs. The most stringent punishment permitted is the bestowal of bad marks. Mère Sciout effected their complete reformation, which lasted into man's estate; but their conversion, as may be imagined, was gradual. Apples were still stolen from the *curé's* garden, till he threatened at the Sunday's *prône* to inform Mère Sciout of the fact. The crime was never repeated; a beautiful grape-vine covered the little school-house, and the bunches of grapes that hung within the children's reach were never touched. On Mother Digby's yearly feast-day the boys assembled to present her with all the good marks they had earned; these marks were paid by her according to several merit by money, with which they bought for themselves useful objects. The lads collected from their slender pocket-money a little sum which they presented to the Superior for Peter's Pence. The purse was actually presented to the Pope by the Apostolic Nuncio in Rome, and, to the huge delight of the boys, they received from Pius IX. a message and a blessing in reply.

Long after Mother Digby left Marmoutier she used to get letters regularly from *ses petits gars.* One, still extant, ends by wishing her "the first place in heaven next to Mother Barat."

Many of these boys presented themselves to her years afterwards; they had done well in life.

Late in 1865, Mère Sciout was to pass from labour to inaction. She was attacked by cancer; Mother Digby nursed her with heroic devotedness through the long development of this terrible disease. Mère Sciout died in calm, humble endurance. By her bedside Mother Digby entered upon a first experience in a supreme field now first opened to her charity.

Marmoutier was the sanatorium for the French houses of the *Sacred Heart.* Some very delicate children were sent here; several of them died; and Mother Digby wrote of her sorrow to Mother Lehon, now one of the Assistants General. But no loss was more regretted than that of Cecil Kerr. Consumption attacked her; she struggled on long with buoyant courage, and played the organ for the last time at Christmas. "If you pray to St Martin for me," she said to Mother Digby, "he will take me to heaven. He always gives me what is best!" She died in February 1866; Lady Lothian, heart-broken, bore her loss in her own admirable way, and her friendship with Mother Digby was doubly cemented.

Mother Digby said many years afterwards: "I have assisted at many death-beds in religious life; they have all consoled me, save two. These two were Sisters who had shown obstinacy in *refusing to eat enough.* They had a more difficult time at the end, poor things!" And the Superior insisted upon the moral. "There is hardly a more dangerous form of self-will," she said — which sentence, to those who first made Mother Digby's acquaintance, usually caused surprise. Experience convinced them later of her wisdom.

It is certain that Mother Digby paid the price for her devotedness by the sick and dying ; her health was further weakened. Mother Kenney, who succeeded Mother Digby as Mistress General at Marmoutier, relates an act of immolation whereof the short fierce pain would seem to some more insupportable than the terrible vigils day and night by the bed of Mère Sciout, the poor victim of cancer.

Mother Kenney was seized with a fatal disease of the throat. Tours possessed the best resources of medical science—still, it was that of the sixties. The remedy prescribed was that the injured part should be cauterised with a red-hot metal disc the size of a shilling. The poor patient declared that she could not face this agony. If death were the alternative, let it come. Mother Digby pulled up her own sleeve, and held out her arm. Upon the bare flesh she dropped the red-hot disc, and bore unflinchingly its action. Mother Kenney was strengthened to go through the remedy, and was cured. Of her Superior she spoke ever after as of gold that comes out tried from the furnace. In a conference given in Rome in 1896, Mother Digby compared the soul in prayer to incense, and took as her text: *Ab illo benedicaris in cujus honore cremaberis.*[1] Here, once again, she spoke, as the French put it, *avec le goût de l'expérience.*[2]

[1] Be thou blessed by Him in whose honour thou shalt be burnt.
[2] With the savour of experience.

CHAPTER VIII

MARMOUTIER

"He sleeps to the world of shadows, he will awake to reality : his spirit departs in the calm of innocence, or in the sweetness of penitential tears, and flights of angels sing him to his rest."—KENELM DIGBY, *Godefridus* (Lumley, 1844), p. 158.

THE Very Reverend Mother Goetz, like her predecessor, never failed to call Mother Digby to Paris for a week at least once, sometimes twice, in the year. This exceptional confidence and honour was already causing her to be regarded as one of the great names of the Society, and Marmoutier was not without uneasiness lest she should be removed from thence to fill elsewhere some more important post. In April 1866, and again in July, the Mother General, accompanied by one of the Assistants General, Mother Lehon, visited Marmoutier, and was entirely satisfied with the spirit and order of the house.

Another memorable visit of this time was that of Reverend Mother Du Rousier, who had, in South America, effected results similar to those of Mother Duchesne in the States, and was now returning to her mission.[1] Her accounts fired the religious of Marmoutier with zeal, and Mother Barat's words : "You will go to America," were remembered by Mabel Digby. Every year seemed to carry her life further from their fulfilment.

The holidays began in the usual joyous manner in August 1866. On 14th September, at half-past five in the morning, all felt the severe shock of the earthquake that vibrated throughout Europe ; ten days later a more appalling danger threatened.

The Children of Mary had assembled at Marmoutier,

---

[1] Baunard, *Life of Mother Philippine Duchesne* (Roehampton Press, 1879), translated by Lady Georgiana Fullerton.

MARMOUTIER, PORTAIL DE LA CROSSE. 1870.

[To face p. 82.

as they did monthly, to listen to a conference from the Abbé d'Outremont,[1] and to arrange concerning their good works. Their faces wore a look of anxiety ; they informed Mother Digby that the Loire had risen high in its bed, and that an inundation was expected.

The surface of the Loire is higher than that of the surrounding land. The waters were restrained on either side by strong dykes ; but heavy rains about once in ten years had caused an overflow, and last time the dyke had been broken through on the left bank, the Marmoutier side of the river. Grave fears were entertained for the bridge and for the city of Tours should the dyke give way on the right bank, and there was rumour that the authorities might, therefore, cut through the Marmoutier dyke. The flood meant danger to life, and destruction of buildings, of cattle, and of present and future crops, for the fields and vineyards would be buried beneath a layer of sand carried down by the waters. There would even be a difficulty as to getting provisions at all.

No sooner had the Children of Mary departed than Mother Digby began a general and organized movement. The nuns, lay Sisters, and farm servants, who were entirely devoted to her, a few children also, who had remained for the holidays, set to work each in his or her own department, and the place resembled an ant-hill. The sacristy and church were cleared out; the Blessed Sacrament was removed to an upper storey. Tables, chairs, pianos, and the rest, were seen slowly moving towards the top of the house, until the whole ground-floor was denuded of furniture; the planks recently laid down were taken up and stowed in order in the loft, and lastly the doors of the basement were removed, so as to allow free passage to the water, lest it should be dammed up and enter the house at a higher level. Several secretaries aided the Superior all night with letters addressed to the parents, warning them that the day of re-opening school would be postponed for a month.

Next day telegrams of an alarming nature flowed in. Friends counselled that all should at once take refuge at Rougement. But Mother Digby had her invalids' quarters

[1] See p. 45.

to consider, and kept calmly on her way. As soon as mass was over, all resumed labour, some to gather in the winter stores, others to put the farm animals in safety. The water from the river, having penetrated under the soil, was beginning to rise in the fields, so that where a beetroot or carrot was plucked up, a pool of water would appear, and first the shoes, then the feet and legs of the workers were sucked down into the soil. Two good Newfoundland dogs assisted, uprooting the vegetables, and carrying them, at Mother Digby's bidding, to the place assigned. Mère de Rochequairie, infirm and unable to work with the rest, was perturbed at the thought that all this water near the house must be very unwholesome. Mother Digby found time to fill a bottle with it, and to send it in by a trusty messenger to reassure her. The water had filtered up through the soil, and was clear as crystal. The field was already like a sinking bog when Mother Digby at the last moment bethought her of a goat, whose milk was required for her invalids. She struggled through the swamp and back with some armfuls of cabbages for its food ; then she turned round to join the community in hearty laughter at the sight of Mère Zaepffel, valiantly struggling along with a young donkey in her arms. The cows were the hardest to manage ; their terror made every possible resistance to being driven up the hill. But the sturdy farm - servants worked day and night, and put all in safety. Mother Digby did not sleep. Earnest prayers were offered up by all, and the protection of the Sacred Heart, of Our Lady, and of St Michael, was invoked.

All night she saw the gangs of men by torchlight strengthening the dykes. The Loire had burst through at Amboise, and hour by hour news arrived from Orleans of the expansive mood of Marmoutier's terrible neighbour. By midnight on 27th September the greatest height of the river was expected, and if the waters were to break through, it was computed that within fifteen minutes they would flood the fields and reach the convent. Mother Digby and a few privileged ones were still at work outside ; near her was a bell ; should it sound, the nuns were solemnly commanded to re-enter the house with all possible speed.

The bell did not ring, however, and in the evening all save the Superior and the bursar retired to rest at the usual hour. The lowest storey lay empty and opened to the inrush of the redoubtable visitor. At midnight the river roared with a crash like thunder. There were fifteen minutes of suspense; then the inhabitants of Marmoutier raised their hearts in solemn thanksgiving. The Loire had broken through the dyke of St George, and made furious exit on the opposite side to Marmoutier. Mother Digby with her companions walked out into the darkness, and mounted the levée to judge the situation.

Early next morning she conducted her daughters to the top of the bell-tower; from the opposite side of the Marmoutier bank an expanse of water stretched as far as the eye could reach. The Loire and the Cher were joined, and bore the aspect of a lake.

Thou hast tried me by fire and by water. Mother Digby said afterwards, that having witnessed the inexorable force of rising water, she dreaded flood even more than fire. Her daughters were not slow to attribute mainly to the efficacy of her prayers the providential direction of the inundation, just as the city of Tours put down its safety now as formerly to those of the Holy Man of Tours.

Besides the great public pilgrimage on St Martin's feast to Marmoutier, there were twelve or thirteen hundred persons yearly who visited the place between whiles. Amongst the many distinguished prelates who came as pilgrims to the shrine of the primitive model and patron of French bishops, was Mgr. Dupanloup, Bishop of Orleans, already playing no small part in the strifes of his day. As the author of a great book on education, he took a special interest in the Society of the Sacred Heart. Addressing the nuns and children assembled to receive him and his colleagues, he wished them three patristic blessings: *Sanctitas, Scientia, Sanitas.* On a later school holiday, the children, in a species of masque, personified these three S's, and after each had

made out the best case it could for itself, the palm, as
might be expected, was awarded to the first.

The children were losing none of their excellent spirit,
and perhaps the greatest testimony to the entire im-
personality of Mother Digby's action in their regard
was the way in which they had received her successor,
Mother Kenney, to whom, in 1865, the former resigned
her office as Mistress General. The loss of a much
loved mistress is to young people so overwhelming a
trial, that they are usually more than inclined to pay
her the worst of compliments by avenging her loss
upon the newcomer. The case is all the harder if
the former remains in the house, and the children are
teased by seeing her as it were just out of their reach.
But the girls of Marmoutier went through the trial in a
manly spirit, and were on their mettle to show their
new Mother how strong and true had been their training. Thus she had the immense advantage of heading
from the first a regiment in perfect drill, impelled
by lofty motives, and well forward in the path of self-
conquest. Nor even now was Mother Digby's personal
intercourse with the school infrequent. Even to the
end of her days, she was visited from all parts of the
world by her children of the *dulce domum*, now mothers
or grandmothers as might be, to talk over old days and
seek advice or consolation in the present, and adorned
with pride for the occasion with the old ribbon of good
conduct, pink, green, or blue, the attainment of which
had been so longed for in youth.

The greater part married, and indeed very early,
according to the French custom. They were most of
them Children of Mary, and after leaving school would
attend faithfully the monthly meetings of that Congregation at Marmoutier. At one of these gatherings they were
addressed by Mgr. Mermillod, Bishop of Hebron, another
prelate-pilgrim, and a *quasi* successor of St Francis of
Sales in his direction of ladies living in the world. His
words on this occasion were in harmony with his still
well-known book, *La Femme Chrétienne*. One simile of
this address is not unworthy of his great predecessor.

"The existence of a truly Christian woman," he said, "recalls the sanctuary, in its solitude, with the lights and the incense that burn, the flowers that adorn it; that of a worldling resembles the ball-room. Here, too, are perfumes, lights, and flowers. But what a scene when day has dawned, and the dancers have vanished! The lights have burned out, the perfumes fled, the furniture is disordered and covered with dust."

"So," says Kenelm Digby, "Knight Roland, after a pompous revel, cried out at night with bitterness of soul—where is the feast we had to-day—where is the glory of it?"[1]. And he departed to a hermit's cell. He had drained the cup of worldly joy, and turned from the dregs in disgust.

Others, in their fresh youth, pour it on the ground untasted, as David the cool water from the cistern of Bethlehem, offering it rather to the Lord. In this spirit, nearly every year, one or more of Mother Digby's children of Marmoutier, who were fitted for the life—for she discouraged all who were not—would, on leaving the doors of Marmoutier, enter those of a noviceship, at the *Sacred Heart* or elsewhere. In one case the draught was poured out earlier still.

Léontine D——, who at fifteen showed sudden signs of rapid consumption, remained, by the earnest desire of her parents, at the convent. "I had rather die here than anywhere!" she said to Mother Digby. "Is there anything that you wish for?" "Yes, one thing. Draw my bed near the window, that I may see my dear Marmoutier once again." It was April, and Easter. Silently her gaze wandered from the clocktower at the angle of the old wall, to the castle of Rougemont, perched upon the cliff, against whose rocky face is the entry to St Martin's grotto; her eyes followed the horn-beam avenues, that diverge in various directions, the bowling greens, transformed into so many lakes when the water rises. She looked beyond the scattered farm buildings towards the silver belt of the Loire, visible above its raised dyke, and behind it, between clumps of

---

[1] *Tancredus* (Sherwood, 1828), p. 171.

trees, to the stretch of fields and vineyards, fading gradually from green to blue, until the faint distance melts
into the sky line.   Then she turned away.   " Enough of
earth, now let us think of heaven."   And she that was
ready, entered the palace of the Bridegroom.

Mother Digby remarked many years later : " I believe
that the dying are aware of death when it is actually near.
I was once kneeling by the bedside of a girl of seventeen.
' Do not tire yourself, Mother,' she said, ' I will let you
know when the moment comes.'   And, a few minutes
afterwards : ' Now it is time ! '   Then her eyes took an
expression as if she saw something. . . . And do not the
prayers of the Church say, ' May our Lord Jesus Christ
appear to thee with a gracious countenance ? . . .' "

The grand traditions of Marmoutier shed about
the place such an atmosphere of romance as belongs
to some great university.   The spirit of Kenelm Digby
wandered here and there in every age of the old abbey ;
its chivalrous memories spoke intimately to the heart
of his cousin Mabel.   Over the ruins shone the halos
of a hundred saints, and the very rocks were "full of
voices."   Their words of doughty deeds and of meek
penance were interpreted by her in solemn addresses,
or in more homely converse with her nuns, and with
young scholars of whom Léontine was a type.   Not infrequently were scenes from old histories of Marmoutier
played again by youthful actors on holidays, with all
the spirit of French children, and their hearts "beat
to the heroic song of ancient days."

Here, in the catacombs of the cliffs, St Martin had
hidden and shepherded Christian neopyhtes ; here, when
peace came, he watched and prayed.   Here saints had
nurtured disciples as saintly, and poor hermits trained
up in virtue and learning young and noble scholars,
a crowd of whom learned to prefer the solitary cell and
rough dress to the glories of court and camp.   " Who
would not have had Jacob's hard lodging, there withal
to have his heavenly dream ? " says Kenelm Digby.[1]
Here, in stately abbeys, later on, were bred new genera-

---

[1] *Mores Catholici*, p. 77.

tions that vied with the older, the gifted sons of peasants side by side with the scions of noble houses ; an Aldhelm of Ponthieu, a Baldwin of Flanders, a Hervé of Vitré, the last named of royal blood ; they make a long list, a *Chevalerie du Très-Haut.* Here are seated the beautiful legends of the old chroniclers — the Seven Sleepers, the *sainte ampoule*, the heavenly visions, the maladies cured at St Martin's touch, the leper healed by his embrace, the mariners rescued from shipwreck, the miraculous fishing in the Loire, the fountain that sprang up at his bidding, the blackthorn that burst into flowers in midwinter, the mysterious canticles of unseen angels, the white-robed procession of chanters through the abbey at night, the vision of all Marmoutier wrapped in heavenly flames upon Pentecost day.   All these are poems, even in ruggedest words, but mingled with them here and there are traits that show St Gregory of Tours and a score of other mediæval historians to be not without a sense of humour.   Mother Digby would relate with infinite amusement two miracles wrought by St Martin upon most unwilling subjects.   For once, when the potent relics of the Saint borne in long procession were seen approaching, two cripples made off as fast as they could on their crutches, fearful of losing the lucrative profession of begging.   But, " Fast as they ran," relates the monk,[1] "the grace of Monseigneur Saint Martin went faster still "; and the lame men, before a crowd of witnesses, stood straight again, and were, to the satisfaction of the district, thus reduced from jolly beggars to working men ; for the century of the unemployed was yet far off.

Here, through a hundred perils from barbarians, the monks subsisted, protected by Charlemagne, or by the banner of St Martin, at the sight of which the enemy would often fly.   But not always ; and the monastery had its glorious age of martyrs at the hands of the Normans, and was burned to the ground, and ruined again and again.   Then, time after time, the abbey,

[1] Don Martene, author of *De Antiquis Monachorum Ritibus*, a book well known to Kenelm Digby.

upbuilt by monk-architects and brother-masons, rose
more beautiful than before. Even through the tenth
century it had remained a literary centre, with its
chroniclers, its scriptorium, its scholars that left the walls
to sit in the university chairs of Europe; the sons of
St Martin swarmed out this way and that in France, and
England, and the Levant, and Palestine, to build abbeys
and priories, centres of civilisation, only less famous
than the mother-hive. Round Marmoutier the monks
had introduced their serfs to model farms, and taught
them all agricultural secrets. Here Urban II., in 1095,
with all his court, and accompanied by an immense
multitude, came after the Council of Clermont to
consecrate the Church, when all France was thrilling
to the voice of Peter the Hermit; here, after the
ceremony, Hugues of Chaumont, Emeri de Curzon, and
others, took the cross from the hands of the Pope, and
departed to Jerusalem with cries of *Dieu le veult!* Here,
too, came Callixtus II., and presently the troops of St
Louis, to protect the monks against the robber barons.

Then, alas! rose up the Western Schism—the head
was sick, and the members all began to languish. The
silver cord tying Church to State was broken; the golden
fillet of poverty shrank back, the monks grew lax, and
Marmoutier was ruled by royal nominees, *abbés com-
mendataires.* Richelieu was one. He built Rougemont,
eagle-perched, to survey the monks, their exits and their
entrances. He gave them notice to reform. They rose
in ripe rebellion. They, direct dependents of the Holy
See, to change their ways at the bidding of a mere
Cardinal! The minister repeated his command; they
their protest. He sent away the turbulent novices, and
told the rest that twelve monks of regular life from another
Order—Marmoutier, he added indulgently, might choose
the Order—should join their ranks and show them how to
conduct themselves. The monks gave him more trouble
than the Huguenots. The Cardinal had all the zeal of a
Theresa. He did not succeed.

But there was a leaven working from within. A small
band of faithful monks had lived apart at Marmoutier

through all these troubles, true to its best traditions, and gradually, from this smouldering beneath the ashes, charity grew warm again, until the Terror turned a house of prayer first into a den of thieves, as has been told, then into a desert.   Mother Barat passed through a place of ruined walls and brushwood, to pray in St Martin's grotto.   Urged on all sides to purchase part of the place, she made great sacrifices to do so.   "You are honoured, my dear children," she said, "in being allowed to tread the soil of the saints!"

So the convent was built, a small and modest place at first; and Mère de Bosredont with her community had gone through considerable privations in order to erect an architectural entrance to the *Repos* of St Martin. In this they were aided by generous gifts from many distinguished donors; Cardinal Morlot, for instance, presented the marble altars and bas-reliefs within the grotto, which otherwise preserves its rugged simplicity. The façade was the work of an excellent architect, and presents the appearance of a picturesque fragment of the old abbey.   Mother Digby's devotion to St Martin was quite of a personal nature; in his grotto she had prayed in fair weather and foul, to use metaphor; on the feast day the *Repos* was illuminated, and the children and nuns walked round it chanting hymns with mysterious and beautiful effect.

The flood of 1866 had done considerable damage, though the direct overflow of the river had been averted.   Mother Digby set about maturing a long-formed plan for a new building above the reach of floods.   Besides, the present accommodation was both insufficient and old-fashioned—for not all old fashions did Mother Digby think good.   But the proud centuries were gone that could say:—

"De quel côté que le vent vente,
Marmoutier a cens et rente."

and the resources of the convent had not permitted a further essay in building save on paper.   Temporalities had now improved, and she asked permission, and hoped for aid, from the Motherhouse. This was generously promised, and she was now to try her powers in a new and difficult field, full of proverbial pitfalls for the unwary, ever since the builders of two famous towers got no further than to erect a monument to their own failure.

The first thing to do was to examine carefully the existing structures and the old foundations walls, and Mother Digby naturally had recourse to the archæological and other wisdom of M. Dupont. Their friendship had never slackened, and he was no infrequent visitor throughout all these times. He chose for his visits the recreation hour of the community, thinking thus to spare her working hours, but the nuns did not by any means relish this arrangement.

Just about this time an aged monk, who had been a novice expelled from Marmoutier what time the " Bande Noire " in '93 ravaged the monastery, came back with a companion to visit a spot so dear, and spoke to Reverend Mother Digby of the " treasure of Marmoutier." An old manuscript gave as indication : " a little corridor with a gilt inscription upon wood." Gauthier, one of the farm tenants, whose little dwelling was under the cliff whereon Rougemont stands, called Mother Digby to see a hole in the rock, broken by a huge cherry tree that had fallen upon it. A little corridor was visible, and she went in ; the workmen explored here for a few days, but nothing more was found.

" Presently, however, Gauthier gave a hard blow at another spot ; the rock or door gave way, and opened into a vast hollow. On investigation it was found to be an old quarry, whence had come the stone to build the former abbey, and possibly Tours Cathedral. After having taken an opinion as to the safety of exploring the place, Reverend Mother entered it with any who wished to accompany her. The irregular vaulted roof, here lofty, there so low that one must bend, produced a strange play of light and shade ; the religious with their lighted tapers were reflected in a piece of still water round which they had to pass, between huge blocks of stone in irregular piles. Presently we came to St Gatien's well, upon which we had hitherto looked down from a path at Rougemont high up on the cliff, whence the children delighted to throw down stones into the well, and listen to the strange noises and echoes which preceded the final splash.   The water was open by a natural shaft to the pathway above."

This discovery made Reverend Mother Digby the more eager for further excavations. She borrowed an ancient plan of Marmoutier from the *prefecture* at Tours; together she and M. Dupont marked the site of a number of small chapels now buried, and they took to heart their restoration, if this might be.

One day at recreation she removed the moss from the old well, the lower part of which is built against the cliff.   There were stone mouldings; the workmen, full of curiosity and zeal, plied their pickaxes, and presently was revealed a crypt, containing a tomb. "Ma soeur!" cried a labourer, presently, "venez voir un chrétien non *demanché*!" [1]   This was an entire skeleton; further on were others, in the same position, with their heads turned towards the west. Through the skull of one a huge tree root had made its way. But *who were the proprietaries of these bones?* No inscription gave sufficient clue; M. Dupont was of opinion that the monks of the early times had chosen to be entombed in the rock, near the sacred resting-place of St Martin and his companions. Further than this, *oblivion blindly scattereth her poppy.* "These sacred bones are at peace, here let them remain," said Cardinal Guibert, who came to examine these interesting relics; and Mother Digby had them placed reverently in a common tomb with ancient carvings, revealed by further discovery, and laid the tomb within the grotto of the Seven Sleepers, which was the next to be discovered. Those of St Leobard and St Gatien followed. Hardly a month passed without some fresh revelation of mosaics and bas-reliefs, mural paintings, columns, or tombs. The grottos were each provided with a simple altar and a lamp, and transformed into so many chapels, the walls and vaults being left untouched.

[1] *I.e.* not dislocated.

Thus, by the important additions of Mother Digby, these sacred wells, grottos, and monuments have been emphasized and preserved, so that Marmoutier, shorn of its ancient glories, yet presents a highly interesting whole from the artistic and historic point of view. But the "treasure of Marmoutier" remains buried in that *place of shades, of sleep, and night.* For the expense of further diggings could not be allowed; Mother Digby must concentrate all effort upon the necessary convent building.

The first stone was laid on 2nd August 1867 — the fitting feast of the *Portiuncula* of St Francis—by Cardinal Guibert, with prayer, incense, and unction.

During the two years that the building proceeded, Mother Digby was constantly at the scene of action, surveying everything; the workmen seemed always invigorated by her presence; she appeared conversant with every detail. Her old spirit of adventure showed once more as she walked about the scaffolding unconcerned, and across the open joists. A lay Sister who had "a good head" at these heights often accompanied her. "How many times, *ma Révèrende Mére,*" she said afterwards with proper pride, "I mounted the *scaffold* with you!" Her daughters were not without anxiety at these feats. One day a board tilted treacherously, and let her down between the joists, where she hung by her arms three storeys from the ground. Only her assistant, Mother Vercruysse, was with her (for the good old Mère de Rochequairie had passed to her reward), and the voices of the community were heard below, looking for her at the hour of recreation. How she swung and lifted herself back with Mother Vercruysse's help she could never remember; but when she stood at the joists again it seemed for a moment as if her nerve were gone. "Far be it from any son of chivalry," says Kenelm Digby, "to fancy that fear is on all occasions unworthy of a brave man." She felt as if she could never walk back to the ladders with that empty space below—"*So I had to run,*" she said, in telling the story.

A large statue of the Sacred Heart was erected upon the top of the building, within a niche; the children, arranged upon the terrace in a semi-circle, sang hymns as the statue swung into its place, and the house was completed and solemnly blessed by the Cardinal on 11th November 1869.

The new convent had cost Mother Digby long reflection; how to make use as far as possible of existing constructions, how to combine convenience for the school with facility for religious regularity; how to have nothing done that would not last, while saving all avoidable expense. All this was attained in the plain, unpretentious block that could be called "handsome" only in size. Mother Digby had effected successfully her first adventure in building.

CHAPTER IX

THE TERRIBLE YEAR

" Laetus eris sed mox
Non sine lacrymulis."
—KENELM DIGBY, *Orlandus* (Quaritch, 1876), p. 166.

WITHIN the walls of the Marmoutier all was peace, union
and fervour. Faults there were, of course, but they were
always simply and generously acknowledged and made
up for before the day was out. "Every one is happy,"
writes the Mistress General, "and although the character
and ways of certain persons are somewhat trying,[1] this
does not diminish the family spirit that prevails." So
far, then, Mother Digby's burden was as light as could be.

Cardinal Guibert had shown himself always a benevolent and devoted friend to Marmoutier and its Superior.
His more formal visits have been mentioned, when he was
received by the school and fêted according to the best
of its power; his scarlet robes added to the festive
appearance of the chapel on a first Communion day,
and he would address children and nuns individually
and collectively with the paternal kindness that sits
gracefully on a prince of the Church.

One day arrived his Vicar General, to speak con-
fidentially to the Superior. He seemed embarrassed.
The convent needed a new chaplain. His Eminence
would send his own secretary to fulfil that office; but
Mother Digby must see to it that the newcomer heard
the confessions of no outsiders whatever. He was to
confine his ministry entirely to the school and community.
Moreover, the Cardinal's name must on no account be
mentioned. He trusted the Superior of Marmoutier to

[1] "Quelques caractères difficiles."

96

MARMOUTIER, PORTAIL DU MITRE, 1870

To face p. 96.

take upon herself the entire responsibility of this measure and to make no complaint. His Eminence regretted his own inability to act otherwise.

Shortly after this mysterious warning arrived M. l'Abbé. He appeared highly satisfied at his new mission, and listened to the detail of his functions in regard to the school and the convent. "There are also," he rejoined, "a number of persons from the outside world; I will fix the day for their confessions as well." "I regret," replied Reverend Mother Digby, "that our chapel not being a public one, I could not permit such an arrangement." The priest, with an expression that she never forgot, rose to take his leave. His eyes flashed vengeance.

From the first day he wreaked it in every petty way within his power. Presently, in his Sunday addresses from the pulpit of the convent chapel, he began to speak against Mother Digby in terms thinly veiled. The children and the bulk of the community, good easy folk, impenetrable to the notion that any one could think of passing a slur upon one so revered as their Superior, let alone the time, the place, the office of the preacher, listened placidly, setting down the incomprehensibility of the sermons to the vast learning, no doubt, of the new chaplain. But a few of the elder nuns, whose functions in the house made them, like their Reverend Mother, suffer from his acts, began to couple these with his ambiguous utterances, and in full cry of indignation had recourse to Mother Digby. Her only reply was to impose upon them an unconditional silence.

But all this was little. The unhappy man tried to propagate calumny against the convent outside its walls, with such audacity that even the Cardinal seemed staggered. At last the slanderer found it convenient to retire. "Whom shall I send as chaplain to the nuns!" said Cardinal Guibert. "No one will undertake the post!" "Try M. l'Abbé Juet," the Vicar ventured to say.

M. Juet, an excellent man, had, in fact, just offered himself spontaneously for this duty. He had heard every accusation made against the convent; without knowledge

G

of its inmates, he felt that they must have been maligned. "It can't be as bad as all that," he said. "But I shall soon find out. Anyhow, the situation is interesting!"

He went accordingly, and became the staunchest friend of Marmoutier; he was chaplain for many years, and till his death made no secret anywhere of his admiration for Mother Digby. His predecessor meanwhile threw off the mask, and openly joined a schismatical body. His calumnies died a natural death.

The motives of Cardinal Guibert were later made clear. His secretary had been nominal proprietor of the land, or part of it, on which stood St Martin's Basilica at Tours. It was advisable to gain time; to avoid offending him on the one hand, and, on the other, to safeguard his penitents from erroneous notions propagated through the confessional, for he was suspected of treachery in this respect; but of course open action cannot be taken upon mere suspicion. The Cardinal knew that the nuns would be safe, and would keep him so.

He was always grateful to Mother Digby. She had never complained even to himself. He seems not quite to have realised the price she paid for her inviolable loyalty; but he continued his kindness towards the convent until, in 1871, he was, like his predecessor, chosen to succeed Mgr. Darboy, on the archiepiscopal throne of Paris. Cardinal Guibert took an affecting farewell of Marmoutier, and appeared much touched at a parting gift from Mother Digby, an album with fine illuminations, executed at the convent.

Another member of the Digby family was now to work out her fate in tragedy.

Mrs Digby, as soon as her youngest daughter was of an age to be presented, changed her residence from Paris to London — Haversham Grange, near Twickenham— where Eva made her *début*. She was greatly admired, nor was she indifferent to admiration; a happy and brilliant future was opening before her, when suddenly she was struck like a daughter of Niobe by an arrow shot from an invisible hand. The dart was poisoned, and it

made a double victim. Not until her death was the
mystery so far penetrated by her family : the falsehood
of an anonymous letter, penned by a stranger whose
motive remains to this day impenetrable as that of Iago,
was made known too late to the dupe, the joy of whose
life it had also slain. Eva's heart was broken.

> "As you set it down, it broke,
> —Broke, but I did not wince."

Like the heroine of Christina Rossetti's poem, Mabel
Digby's beautiful sister laid upon the altar of God a heart
that He does not despise. But sorrow had done its work ;
and secret seeds of consumption began to develop with
alarming rapidity.

The whole affection of her family and friends now
centred upon this fascinating girl. Her brother Essex
actually threw up his commission in the army in order to
remain with his sister. Good M. d'Abbadie placed his
château at the disposal of the family, and to save this young
life urged Mrs Digby to allow him at his own expense to
conduct herself and Eva on a journey to the East. But
this the London doctors, who for a time were held in
almost daily consultation, would not allow. Yet they were
hopeful ; her constitution was strong, she had youth in
her favour. Eva herself no longer wished to die. Her
mother took her to the Isle of Wight, then to Rougemont,
which she hired for a time ; here all were in constant intercourse with Mabel. One day, sitting on the lawn, Eva
expressed a desire to play croquet ; her brother ran for
a mallet, but it dropped from her hand ; she suddenly
realised her increasing weakness, and remained nearly
silent all day.

She guessed the truth, and was soon assured of it. She
made the sacrifice of her life into God's hands, and the
saintly Bishop Grant visited and consoled her.

Who can describe the last months at Haversham
Grange, save that surrounded by those she loved
best, and in constant correspondence with her sister
Mabel, Eva lay prostrate in calm serenity, in heartfelt
forgiveness of all injuries, in entire self-forgetfulness,

and without an interlude of a fretful word or a selfish movement.

"MY DARLING SISTER MABEL,—How glad I am to feel that you pray so much for your little sister! Oh, how happy I am! I feel nearer to God than I ever did, and can lie for hours thinking of Him and of glorious heaven. But may be I shall suffer yet more, and I should so wish to please our dear Lord by bearing all patiently. . . . Oh, dear Mabel, what a sacrifice not to see you again! I love you so! We shall meet again in our home up above: I throw myself on the mercy of God; how I long to see Him . . . I can write no more. Adieu.—Your loving sister, EVY."

Mabel sent her in return a picture, within a beautifully illuminated border, representing a young girl sailing in a boat towards our Saviour, who waits for her with outstretched arms. The verses beneath are in keeping with the subject. Eva read them night and morning till the end.

Early on January 28th, 1869, she said: "Jesus! let me come to you . . . What happiness! I am going!" Then, low: "Thanks." It was the last word.

Of such as she it is truer to say, as Kenelm Digby quotes it, that they die in joy, rather than in peace. The poison had indeed been sucked from the fatal wound, and, like that of St Theresa, it had given life to Eva. Her mother calmly placed upon her child's head a wreath of lilies; on her breast already lay the crucifix, and those who saw her then, spoke of a vision of surpassing beauty.

Not long afterwards, Mother Digby was nursing a young novice, who lay very near to death at Marmoutier. One morning she said to her Superior gently: "Why am I brought back to life, when I have been all night in the vestibule of heaven? Two of our sisters, and your own Eva, came to me. Eva told me she was in heaven and had passed there shortly after death. 'Why do you not go and tell our Mother so?' I said. 'My sister,' replied Eva, 'has the strength to do without that consolation. You it is that need it.' She vanished." And indeed the novice to the end was greatly rejoiced and strengthened by this fair dream or vision—quite in keeping with mysterious Marmoutier.

Geraldine and Essex had laid their idolised Eva in her coffin. Her last request to her brother had been that he would study the Catholic religion ; this he had promised, and she offered her life for his conversion. He was, in fact, received into the Church two years later, together with his newly-married wife.

In August 1869, the Mother General carried out a plan she had long matured—to assemble all the Superiors of her Society at the same time for a retreat in Paris. Mother Digby attended accordingly. The heavy burden of government was lightened ; old friends met again, and felt that strength which comes from a tangible comradeship ; important consultations took place, for the air in Paris was heavy with war-clouds ; and words of unusual eloquence again brought forward the great principles that must form a common ground of action. The preacher, Père Olivaint, counted even amongst the Parisian Jesuits as a picked man. His burning words seemed in the light of after events to be reflected in an aureole around his head.

Pierre Olivaint (1816-1871) was the son of a veteran of the first Empire. He inherited his father's military ambitions, and imbibed and retained his Voltairian notions inspite of an education with the Jesuits, which had given him a passion for study, and an extraordinary command of language in speech and in writing. With Frederick Ozanam and other flower of the French youth, he was, like them, persuaded by Lacordaire, at Notre Dame, to be a Christian. He entered the Society of Jesus, succeeded at once as a teacher of youth of all ranks, and devoted himself especially to the working classes of Paris, where with the co-operation of many ladies of the city, he did an immense work, especially as to numbers of young girls, whom he successfully launched in life. Few men better illustrated his own saying : " L'homme supérieur, c'est *l'homme de caractère.*" He was now Rector of the Jesuit residence in the Rue de Sèvres, and his was already a name marked down for vengeance.

The nuns of Marmoutier were in anxiety. Gatherings of Superiors in Paris always meant reorganisations ; but

Mother Digby was safely returned to them after the retreat, and within the convent all went on as usual.

Without, the stillness of France contrasted with the ceaseless activity of her north - eastern neighbour. In January 1870, Bismarck was ready for war. He waited, patient, keen, and cautious, ably backed by Moltke and his military advisers. Not until July came the fateful moment; then the hand of France, adroitly goaded, flung down the glove. Bismarck picked it up, and all Paris re-echoed to the cries of "A Berlin!"

With the faultless precision of a machine, the three great armies of Prussia swung into their places across the open gate of France, between the neutral walls of Switzerland on the south, Belgium and the Luxembourg on the north; while ten or twelve French divisions sauntered up, pell - mell and scattered, each short of its complement of men, provisions, or muniments. On August 1st the nations stood face to face. Next day the French made a step forward, at Saarbruck; Napoleon remained irresolute; the German armies passed the border, and took the part of invaders. Fighting gallantly, desperately, but always in confusion, the French all that month were driven slowly back.

Like a funeral wail, the names of Wórth and Spicheren re-echoed throughout France. The nuns at Marmoutier, in the anguish of these weeks, gathered more frequently round their Superior in the country of her adoption. Few had not a father, a brother, a nephew, at the front or in Paris; all were pierced by the sufferings of their country. "Our Mother knows," says the journal of the house, "how to make us forget or bear our anxieties, and how to make us redouble our prayers for France."

Late one evening, towards the end of the month, the portress announced that an omnibus full of nuns of the Sacred Heart had driven up to the great arched door. Mother Digby hastened to meet them; it was a colony from Bourges. Their convent had been seized by the local government for a barracks or hospital; for in many places the revolutionary party, prompt to fish in troubled waters, had made the pretext of national defence an

occasion to attack the Christian schools. Other parties
of refugees arrived in succession, the nuns from the
eastern provinces, menaced by the Prussian approach,
being forced to leave their convents; the noviceship at
Conflans, situated between the forts of Paris and the
ramparts, was also dispersed. Some found shelter within
Paris, in the western provinces, or at Marmoutier, others
in private houses whose doors were thrown open everywhere with wonderful generosity; such is the curious
contrast presented then, since, and always, by this nation
of extremes.

The soberer spirits of France, and with them Mother
Digby, had long perceived the abyss towards which Louis
Napoleon was blindly marching. "He is sold to the
secret societies," she said, "they have put him up for
their own ends, and when he has served their purpose
they will accomplish his ruin." Her poor friend the
Empress Eugénie, " pale, dressed in white, wearing a
light veil, her beautiful features thin and rigid," says
Villefranche, "passed to and fro like a marble statue,
hardly animated, through the vast deserted *salons* of the
Tuileries,"[1] till on September 4th she left them for ever.
For, with the news of Sedan, the Empire, like the
Campanile at Venice, fell to dust.

Not without a fierce contest with the red flag was
the tricolor hoisted over Paris, and the capital became
the objective of the war. The Government of National
Defence was distracted between the Prussians without
and the Revolution within. The *gardes mobiles* were
filing by to the sound of the "Marseillaise."

Meantime, the nuns at Marmoutier were deep in their
yearly retreat during the first week of September. Mother
Digby had to bear the brunt of the war news almost
alone. On September 8th she told her daughters of
the dreadful anxiety weighing upon their whole Society.
Besides the ties of family and of patriotism, and the
crushing sadness of national humiliation, there was the
fear for their Mother General at Paris. The city would

[1] Villefranche, *Histoire de Napoléon III.* (Paris, Bloud, 2nd ed., 1898), vol. ii.
p. 393.

soon be locked in the enemy's embrace, and Mother Goetz
sternly refused to leave the capital.   What were they to
do, amid the uncertain issues of the war, if the eighty-
eight houses of her Society were cut off from all communication with their Superior General?   The question
of her personal safety was a matter apart.   Higher and
higher was rising the red flood that might soon break
away the dykes.   The '48 with its blood, sacrilege, and
pillage, was to many a personal memory.

Pius IX. came to the rescue.   He added his advice,
almost his command, to that of the Archbishop of Paris.
Mother Goetz with sad heart obeyed, and took refuge at
Laval, leaving Mother Lehon and a small band to hold
the Paris convents, which, if now deserted, would certainly
be lost for ever.

Not a day too soon.   On September 19th, the iron
circle, soon to flash into fire, closed in round Paris,
and the King of Prussia and Bismarck sat down at
Versailles.   Next day Rome capitulated to the three
investing armies ; and, at the heels of the Piedmontese,
a force of between four and five thousand ruffians from
all nations, and gaol birds liberated from every prison
in Italy, poured in through the Porta Pia.[1]   The fame
of their nameless deeds percolated to France, whither
the authors were to follow presently in person.   Men
remembered the *Septembriseurs*, and the carrier pigeons
that Mother Lehon sent out every day were anxiously
looked for at Laval.

The heads of the French Government made their
way out of Paris, and established themselves at Tours.
Thither, on October 7th, Gambetta betook himself as
dictator, having escaped out of Paris by balloon ; and
on the 27th of the same month even the Germans could
scarcely believe that Bazaine had delivered over to them
the largest army of France, with its stores and artillery.
The Metz besieging force was thus set free, and one half
was led towards Tours by Prince Frederick Charles.

It behoved Mother Digby, therefore, to complete her

[1] *See* Villefranche, *Vie de Pie IX.* (Paris, Vic, 1883), p. 328, and The O'Clery,
The Making of Italy (Kegan Paul, 1892) p. 530, footnote, and p. 180.

preparations. She had begun them in August, and every one was now astonished at her foresight. The inhabitants of the convent, eighty persons including refugees, besides the children—for twelve had been returned to Marmoutier in October with wonderful trust by their parents—were housed in the recently completed building, and the old house was arranged to serve as an ambulance for the wounded of both nations. There was now a second Assistant, a German, Mother Filling; her nationality was to prove a useful fact. Fruit and provisions had been gathered in, as far as possible; fodder was scarce; the nuns were picking vine-leaves to feed the cows, and were working hard also at accommodation for the soldiers at Rougemont, which from its commanding position they felt sure would be occupied.

The diminution in the number of scholars had effected a corresponding loss in the income of the house; the nuns must earn their bread after the fashion of St Paul. Mother Digby procured a commission from a shop at Tours for the manufacture of army tents. It was severe work, for the material was thick and hard, to be seamed by hand, and worked with numberless buttonholes. The convent appeared like a factory; Mother Digby cheered the workers by interesting readings, sometimes by conversations, and the enemy would have been surprised at the gaiety that reigned. Each of her daughters was on her mettle to complete her tent per day, and altogether nearly eight hundred were completed.

The country round presented a melancholy spectacle. Day by day peasants arrived, many from afar, fleeing before the invasion, or bringing family treasures that they begged Mother Digby to keep or hide. It might be a cow, a goat, some chickens, or a store of linen; an old couple brought their wedding dresses. A flock of five hundred sheep was led from Etampes, the shepherds had been already thirteen days on their journey, and asked permission to rest at Marmoutier for the night. The sheep were folded in the bowling greens. Other parties arrived with carts and furniture; homeless, making their way vaguely eastward, in fear or sad bewilderment.

Gambetta in October had been hailed by the sanguine as the "Sauveur de la Patrie." Energy he did not lack; the whole peasantry of the Loire basin, ready or unready, he enrolled in a band of thirty thousand men—a man being any one old enough to carry a musket, which some of the poor fellows near Marmoutier, at any rate, hardly knew how to handle. Now and again within Mother Digby's experience, they shot one another. This "army of the Loire" managed here and there, however, to beat back the trained troops of Von der Than, and increased the complication of the war.

The sound of cannon was first heard at Marmoutier, on November 2nd; it continued, but no official news reached the convent. The peasant army and the regular defenders of Tours were trying in vain to prevent the relentless advance of the Prussians. On November 13th the wounded to the number of twenty-three—many mere boys—were carried into the convent ambulance.

The Tours Government had ordained the expulsion of all German subjects from France, and Mother Digby feared for Mother Filling; but, with the Prussian advance, the delegates themselves made ready to fly. Gambetta, and Crémieux with his family, had taken refuge with the Archbishop, before starting for Bordeaux; and Cardinal Guibert paid the nuns a visit of consolation. "Do not fear," he said, "the Republic is my guest, and I will see to it that it leaves my nuns in peace." At the next meal the Cardinal approached the subject, and procured a special exemption for Mère Filling.[1]

With December the noise of battle grew nearer. From Rougemont could be seen the smoke of cannon, and naturally the children were excited. Some German cuirassiers had been killed upon the bridge, and a rain of vengeful shells was sent over the city in return. Those who heard the missiles describe the dreadful whistling of their flight and the hard dry crack of their fall and explosion. The ambulances were soon refilled, now with Prussians as well as French wounded. After a parley with the maire, the enemy withdrew, so that the nuns

---

[1] M. Crémieux became from that time forth a great admirer of the Cardinal.

kept Christmas in some peace, and such of the wounded as were able assisted devoutly at midnight mass.

On 19th January two Prussian columns defiled in good order along the embankment of the Loire. They had come fifteen thousand strong to occupy Tours and the environs. No news from the rest of France could penetrate to the city.

The enemy called presently at the convent. They respected the ambulance flag, which was flying over the building, and on learning that some of the inmates were children, showed themselves courteous and even benevolent. No soldiers were quartered there, and before stabling forty of their horses at Rougemont, they asked permission to do so. Mother Digby had reason to congratulate herself on having refused to listen to the advice to have all the live stock of the farmyard killed and hidden, for though the Prussians requisitioned at their will in many places, and though their remarks as they entered that "there were chickens," made the Mother Bursar to tremble, the farmyard, like everything else, was left untouched. The day after the arrival of the Prussians, Etienne, apparently the only farm servant left at Marmoutier, was sent into the town on an errand. He got no further than the bridge over the Loire, where, seeing the cannon posted, and the men at their guns, he returned and asked to see Mother Digby. "I've been thinking that it is not the intention of Mme. là Supérieure that I should get killed. If the Emperor and the King of Prussia have any quarrel with each other let them settle it among themselves. But what do they make war upon us for?"[1] But Etienne was too deep a philosopher for his times. Mother Digby persuaded him to venture again next day towards the city, wheeling the ambulance wheelbarrow, duly marked with a red cross. He was, nevertheless, relieved of his *charette* by an officer and ten soldiers as soon as he quitted the convent door, and returned disconsolate. Mère Filling, however, quickly

[1] "J'ai réflechi que cc n'est pas dans l'intention de Mme. la Supérieure que je me fasse tuer. Si l'Empereur et le Roi de Prusse ont des différends, qu'ils les arrangent entre eux ; mais pourquoi nous font-ils la guerre à nous autres ?"

came forward and addressed the Germans in their own
language.   She represented that the wounded of both
nationalities were tended in the ambulance.   The good
officer undertook to represent the matter at headquarters,
with the result that not only was the *charette* restored,
but Etienne was presented with a safe-conduct, and so
could wheel whither he would.

On the morning of January 28th, however, he found
the gates of the town strictly guarded, and could not
enter.   The Prussians were angry and agitated, threatening to bombard the city, because the ten thousand rations
a day agreed upon had not been supplied.   Some thought
they had received bad news; perhaps of a French victory.
But no word was communicated until February 1st, when
Mother Digby announced to her nuns that theirs was now
a conquered country.   Paris had capitulated on the 28th,
and the new German empire, soon to be augmented by
Alsace - Lorraine, had been proclaimed at the Versailles
of Louis Quatorze.   But those who lived in Paris guessed
that low water mark was not yet reached in the ebb of the
fortunes of France.

Anyhow, an armistice had been signed; there was
breathing space, and the nuns were thankful.

On account of its excellent situation, Marmoutier had
been chosen for the more complicated surgical cases,
while the town hospital also took in many wounded.
The English committee supplied the convent generously
with wine, medicine, clothing, and, in fact, with everything needed.   In the ambulance rooms Mother Digby was
"magnificent."   The doctors and the military authorities
did not conceal their satisfaction.   They called her
"Madame la Chirurgiènne en Chef."   She was present at
all the operations, assisting the surgeons, and afterwards
dressing the wounds daily with extraordinary skill.   After
the war was over, the authorities at Tours presented her
with a beautiful case of surgical instruments, as a testi-
monial of their gratitude.

The patients, both French and German, were docile
as children under her sway.   They were indeed children.
She presented each on the first day with a piece of rose-

coloured soap, with which they were highly delighted. It seemed an augury of motherly care that would attend to every detail. They wished her never to quit the room they were in.

One evening the infirmary guard sounded the alarm bell. Mother Digby, who had retired to rest, descended in haste. It was on behalf of a poor lad, the calf of whose leg had been shot away, and who was suffering greatly. "*Ma Soeur*," he said, greatly relieved at the sight of her, "very sorry to disturb you, but only you can fix[1] my leg properly!" The leg was "fixed" at once, and he finished his night in peace.

Another leg remains famous in that ambulance. The doctor condemned it to amputation as the only way to save the life of its owner. The latter could not make up his mind to the loss. He talked the matter over with Mother Digby; he was not *dévot*, but now entered into her plans for the preservation of his limb. He was to pray to God with great confidence; she was to persuade the doctor to a delay, and to redouble the care of her dressings. Somehow the leg soon got well, and its possessor never forgot his gratitude to Mother Digby, or her religious counsels, to which he remained entirely faithful.

The patients all declared that when struck on the battlefield they felt nothing but a slight shock. It was in the ambulance that the wound became painful. The poor fellows were made happy as far as could be by every device. Mère Vercruysse arranged singing practice for such as were well enough to join in the hymns. This had considerable success. When the "Te Deum" was attempted, the soldiers found the Latin rather strange. "How pleased one is to meet with some French," one exclaimed, towards the end. "See here — Te *chérubin*, te *séraphin*!"

Those well enough to take the air walked on the bowling greens. Opposite was a post of Germans bivouacking upon the embankment, trying to while away their idleness by smoking, and watching the French play

---

[1] *Virer.*

bowls. Very soon, but without speech, the opposing forces made friends. The French threw over, by way of bombs, apples and little packets of chocolate. The Germans retorted with cigars.

All went merry until a couple of Prussian officers— as they did periodically—came to visit the ambulance. Then the French warriors, fearful of being supposed well enough to be carried off to a German prison, became ill again as quickly as they could. They got into bed completely dressed, or hid themselves here and there. The nuns found one of them, after the visit, still concealed by the side of a tank, into which he was fully determined to jump in case of pursuit. No such disagreeable adventure, however, took place.

One day the portress saw through the *grille* an Uhlan, covered with blood, who begged for protection at the convent. Under the influence of potations, he had assaulted some one in the neighbouring village, had been set upon with knives, and seemed ready to give up the ghost. Reverend Mother Digby washed and dressed his wounds with the tenderest care, and brought him back to life. The German authorities came to demand the culprit, in order to punish him for his misdeed. German discipline was inexorable, and he was to be shot. Mother Digby interceded for the poor fellow with the local officers, and caused Mother Filling to write and implore his pardon from Prince Frederick Charles, the "Red Prince," in person. After some days of anguish the reply arrived ; the Uhlan was permitted to go free at the nuns' request.

Not long afterwards two German officers came to visit a Bavarian whose leg had been recently amputated. The visitors were covered with decorations, and were markedly courteous in manner. One, evidently of the highest rank, addressed himself specially to Mother Digby, inspected the place, showed himself full of admiration for everything he saw, and expressed his respectful thanks to his hostess. After he had taken his leave, the nuns ascertained that this courtly and agreeable visitor was no other than the Red Prince himself.

But for Mother Digby and her nuns the great point

was the influence of religion on the wounded. Very different in this respect was the status of the two nations. In every German knapsack was a map and a prayerbook; in the French one usually nothing at all. Few of the French had practised their religion in any way since their first Communion; some had been infidels almost from childhood. But the realities of war gave them leisure to feel that great natural hunger of the soul for God, and most consoling was the harvest gathered in in this matter. The chaplain said morning prayers in common with the wounded, who were greatly pleased with this exercise, including even the unbaptized editor of a socialist[1] newspaper. All listened gladly to the instructions given to them by the nuns; nearly all returned willingly to the practice of their faith, frequented the sacraments, and promised to be faithful in future. They went to pray at the grotto of St Martin; one, enquiring why the lamp was not lit, and hearing that oil was scarce, gave a franc for this purpose out of his slender savings.

Many of the less seriously wounded were able in a week or a fortnight to return to their post at Tours. They went blithely, yet sorry to leave hostesses so devoted. Their last greeting to Mother Digby, to her great amusement, was, "I wish Madame plenty of promotion!"[2] A "pious" wish to be literally fulfilled.

A young soldier whose leg had been amputated became no better after long nursing. He remained, unlike his companions, taciturn and melancholy. Mother Digby feared that these dispositions were obstacles to his cure, and tried to sound him gently. He drew from under his pillow a small box, and a letter. "It's . . ." he began, "there's a girl. . . . We are engaged . . . and it was to have been after the war. I have written to Her, here's the letter, and here are the little bones the doctor took out of my wound. Will you send them all to Her when I am gone?"

Mother Digby promised, and was liberal with consolation and care. But he felt the hand of death upon

[1] It will be remembered that the foreign Socialist attaches to his creed tenets usually unknown to the English variety.

[2] *Bien de l'avancement.*

him, and turned all his thoughts to prepare himself
with piety for his last passage.   This death and another
were the sole ones at Marmoutier; both were edifying,
and the journal tells of the dying man's talk of heaven,
of the fervent prayers he constantly offered, and of the
crucifix which received his last kiss.   The *curé* of Ste.
Radegonde and his parishioners came with ceremony to
bury their country's defenders with all honour in the
little cemetery of that parish.

On 9th March the Prussians took their departure.
Peace had been signed in the previous month.   But
now came the worst of the war.   Since the raising of
the siege of Paris cosmopolitan vultures from every part
of the continent, scenting the prey from afar, had been
travelling towards the French capital.[1]   They entered
gradually in little bands, to the number of eighteen
thousand.   Seven hundred were escaped convicts; many,
and these the most ferocious, women of nameless trade;
boys and girls were among them.   The streets were
filled with horrible faces and sinister threats.   The last
complement arrived by March 17th and joined themselves to everything that was worst in Paris; all was
now ripe for a revolution of which that city was less
the author than the theatre.

The awful scenes of blasphemy and blood that succeeded from March to May were nearly concerned with
the causes that Mother Digby loved best, and with her
personal friends.   Two emissaries of the Commune paid
a domiciliary visit to the Motherhouse.   Mother Lehon
conducted her visitors through the building.   They
became confidential, and talked with jocose freedom of
their own recent quarters in a convict prison.   They
went into the chapel, where they committed neither
robbery nor irreverence; they sat down in her room,
fingered some *rouleaux* of francs and banknotes, and set
them down again.   Whether by the resolute attitude and
frank tact of Mother Lehon, or whether God's angel
kept mysterious guard, or by both together, the Society
of the Sacred Heart was wonderfully preserved.   As

[1] Lamazou, *La Place Vendôme* (Paris, Douniol 1876), p. 46.

usual, it was otherwise with the Fathers of the Society of Jesus, which has always a place of honour in the brunt of battle. Four of their number, with Père Olivaint, all personal friends of Mother Digby, were dragged with the Archbishop of Paris and other devoted priests and citizens—who had risked their lives every day in ministry to the poor and the wounded throughout the siege — to Mazas and Roquette, whence the convicts had been liberated, to make room for them, and to swell the ranks of the Communards.

May drew on, and the Versaillaise army under Marshal MacMahon broke into Paris on the 21st. The ruffians still at bay behind the barricades, then felt that their time was short. Notre Dame was to be mined, and all the city destroyed; the *pétroleuses*, the furies of modern days, went from street to street anointing the basements with their terrible liquid, and setting it on fire. There was not time to accomplish a hundredth part of the mischief they desired, but, at any rate, the hostages should die. They were taken from Mazas and Roquette to the number of fifty-two, bound two and two, and led a long and dolorous way through the streets. Mgr. Surat, Vicar General, and Ecclesiastical Superior of the *Sacred Heart* in Paris, was shot outside Roquette by a girl of sixteen. Another aged priest, at the end of the procession, was dragged aside and murdered by a woman. But the condemned, in Père Olivaint's own words, " went on their way rejoicing," absolving and congratulating each another. At last they reached the howling mob that was waiting for them. "Let the justice of the people be accomplished!" cried the leader. "Death to the priests!" came the answering yells. For if all the victims were not priests, were they not all the friends of priests? The prisoners were brutally pushed into a walled court, and the slaughter began. Men, boys, and women were the butchers, and these scores of executioners took an hour to accomplish their work, whilst the spectators mocked, and shrieked approval.

"Forgive them," prayed Père Olivaint, "for they know not what they do."

H

And Mother Digby felt the richer for having known martyrs, and envied their fate, and often told their tale.

At Marmoutier, as elsewhere at the Sacred Heart, after the suppression of the Commune, all went on its usual course. In May 1872, Mother Digby, as last year and every year, went to Paris, and the nuns were relieved from their usual anxiety by her punctual return in a week's time as before.

But she was carrying back with her a letter of which she meant to keep the pain to herself until the last moment. She found it necessary, however, to tell her councillors, and began her preparation for departure; but two sharp eyes were watching these unaccustomed proceedings. A charming child of four, too young for school life, had been confided to the nuns, and Mother Digby now and then allowed the creature to play about her room. One day she was startled at hearing the infant repeating to her doll the advice she had heard the Superior imparting to a nun. The *enfant terrible*, sitting in the paper basket under the table, had been overlooked during this private interview. She had seen things as well as heard them, and informed one of the Sisters that "Reverend Mother was packing up." The poor Sister, however, remained discreetly silent.

On 3rd August, Reverend Mother Digby announced her departure to the community at large. She gave to each a little picture on which was gummed a portion of the clothing of the priests massacred by the Commune during the preceding year. She was to start next morning for the Motherhouse. All listened in silent grief to her last words; and, after the carriage had rolled out of the court-yard, betook themselves to the chapel to offer a sacrifice that cost them dear indeed. Returning to the common room of the community, they found a large notice, in her handwriting, pinned beneath the portrait of Blessed Mother Barat that hung there. It bore these words:

"I beg of my dear daughters to say no word that might impair the true religious spirit established here before I came, and that I would transmit entire to her that shall succeed me.[1]   May the love of Jesus Christ be your all!"

And the journal recording these words dares for the first time to speak openly of what Mother Digby had ever shown herself at Marmoutier.

"We are all resolved to follow the counsel of her whose humility, gentleness, and charity, have shone so brightly in this house, the very walls of which she has erected to the glory of the Sacred Heart of Jesus."

[1] The new Superior of Marmoutier was the daughter of Montalembert.

CHAPTER X

ENGLAND

"England was at one time the very land of chivalry and all its heroic exercises. . . . Moult ay ony parler de ceste isle de Bretaigne et l'ay ony tenir a grant chose. . . The city of London, says the author of the *Palmerin of England*, contained in those days the greater part of the chivalry of the world."—KENELM DIGBY, *Godefridus* (Lumley, 1844), p. 17.

ON 17th August 1872, Reverend Mother Digby accompanied one of the Assistants General, Reverend Mother Adèle Lehon, to the convent of the Sacred Heart, Roehampton, then surrounded in every direction by miles of open country south-west of London. Here Mother Digby was already known by report.

Mr John Bridge Aspinall, Q.C., Recorder of Liverpool, a Tractarian convert, an old Rugbeian, whose daughter had been at the Marmoutier school, asked a young lady for news of Mother Digby. "What, you, a child of the Sacred Heart, don't know her?" he rejoined, "but she is the most remarkable woman in that whole Society! It is well worth a journey to Marmoutier to see her." Several religious, too, who knew her, were prepared to give Mother Digby the warmest welcome, but, for the majority, she was only "the new Reverend Mother."

Changes of Superiors, affecting a whole house, or a Vicariate, occur every few years in congregations like that of the *Sacred Heart*. Though accepted with submission, these common experiences are, of course, always felt ; more, perhaps, by women, in whom the home instinct is more intimate, than by men. So, at least, most nuns think. If Marmoutier was deploring the loss of Mother Digby, Roehampton, too, was deeply sensible of a vanished personality of great charm and virtue. Mother Marcella Goold, whose sister Charlotte had preceded herself as

116

Superior of the English· house, was the daughter of Sir George and Lady Charlotte Goold. She had, directly after her profession, filled charges of increasing importance, latterly that of Superior Vicar. She was greatly loved by nuns and children, and by secular persons of all sorts.

At the time of Mother Digby's arrival, the nuns had just commenced their retreat; they were, according to custom, summoned next morning for the installation of the new Superior. All was done in silence, and when the blessing had been given, the meeting dispersed. It remained for each to make Mother Digby's acquaintance in a private interview.

"When I first saw her," says one, then a young novice, of considerable strength of character, and perhaps—like many warm-hearted persons—of prejudice as well, greatly devoted to Mother Goold, and not easy in approval—"when I first saw her calm sweet countenance, the impression lasted me for forty years." "She seemed crushed by an overwhelming burden," writes another. "I wondered whether she could ever laugh again; I soon found out my folly. One visit was enough to gain my very sore heart. That benign countenance drew me irresistibly; those deep eyes read me through and through, and I was happy to be open to her gaze."

Another who appreciated Mother Digby at first sight was a character whose fire, life, and individuality, make it difficult to leave her unnamed, or no more than a name. Anna Kieran (1820-1878) the daughter of an officer, was a typical Irishwoman of the sort that manifests a heart of gold within, and without is perpetually brimming over with superabundant life, in act and word, and with contagious enthusiasm for all that is worthy of it. Behind her conversation was a powerful mind, educated in virile fashion by her own father. Her manner, manners, and frank speech, never wanting in inborn dignity or Irish refinement, were by no means formed upon the French model, and her vehement brilliancy seemed altogether too startling to suit the idea of a nun. But her sterling worth was recognised; she was received into the noviceship and made much progress in solid virtue, though little in outward decorum. On the other hand, her method and order as to the practical side of life were unimpeachable. She was a thorough woman of business, with knowledge of affairs, of household management, of society, and of the world.   She was therefore valuable as Bursar, and, of course, she was the life and soul of all community recreations, where her gaiety stood out against an ever-present background of high thought and strong faith.   Like many of her race she had an instinct of second-sight and strange dreams that were sometimes her providence.

Mother Kieran, versatile, observant, and generous, turned at once, with all the cordial loyalty of her nature, to Mother Digby, who warmly reciprocated her attachment, and found in her Irish wit a source of keen enjoyment.

Resembling Mother Kieran only in his instant adhesion to the new Superior, was the convent chaplain.   His terms of high admiration were all the more telling from an Englishman of his type.

The Reverend John Cunningham Robertson, of Winchester School, and M.A. of University College, Oxford (1809-1873), had been chaplain to the Duke of Buccleuch.   The chance purchase of a breviary at a book-stall set him thinking ; and he seconded Tractarian influence upon all around him, notably the Duchess of Buccleuch and Lady Lothian.

Close upon Mr Robertson's resignation of his chaplaincy, and his conversion, followed temporal misfortunes.   But his courage never failed, and his children prospered greatly in the end.   He himself was ordained, and did immense good amongst the poor at Greenwich and elsewhere, until failing health prevented more arduous duties than those of a convent chaplain.

He appeared scholar and saint combined ; the Catholic priest grafted upon the Oxford don.   Any sudden call for his store of learning, or his humble service for the school, the sick, or the poor, found always the same meek fervour and charitable sweetness.   His daughter became a Benedictine at the monastery of East Bergholt ; here, in conversation with one of the Sisters, speaking of the Blessed Sacrament, he forgot for once his usual reserve, and broke forth into a strain that seemed worthy of St Francis of Assisi; his hearer was filled with wonder at this glimpse behind the veil. Almost his last act at Roehampton was to give extreme Unction to a lay Sister of seventy-three whose death appeared imminent. She speedily recovered, and lived nearly twenty years longer. He himself, though his health was usually good at the time, was suddenly struck down in the convent so swiftly as to be unable to return to the presbytery. Mother Digby nursed him devotedly; and he passed away, as he had lately prophesied, within the week. Many poor persons followed his funeral to the beautiful little cemetery within the convent grounds, where, by special privilege, he was buried according to his wish.

To win hearts was the easiest part of Mother Digby's mission. The Society of the Sacred Heart had a work to do in England, a work scarcely yet marked out, and beset with extraordinary difficulties.

"How I pity you, for coming to live in such a hole!" (*taudis*) said Reverend Mother Lehon, who had seen Marmoutier, on introducing Mother Digby to Roehampton. In fact, the tumbledown and gloomy patchwork of buildings that formed the interior of the house promised no facility for regular observance in either school or community.

Outside, it was a handsome building in the revived Italian style of about 1800, with a semi-circular porch and Corinthian peristyle. There were several fine rooms, some with columned apses, domed ceilings, fine brass work, carved mantelpieces, and walls covered with large mirrors, or painted in "illusion" after the mode of Roman villas of the late renaissance. George IV. had danced in the ball-room, nor was there hint of more hallowed reminiscences until, late in the seventies, arched vaulting of the date of Henry VII. was discovered below ground, giving rise to the fancy that the house had been built upon the site of an ancient monastery. But, as Kenelm Digby remarks, the wholesale destruction of mediæval manuscripts at the time of the Dissolution under Henry VIII., has obliterated a thousand interesting

traditions easily traceable in similar spots on the Continent. These ancient vaultings, and a modern report
of a vision of monks chanting in procession over these
very grounds, form all the evidence available for interesting conjecture. Unlike Marmoutier, Roehampton must
begin a history of its own.

The property of thirty-six acres comprised fields, a farm,
and a garden combining park, lawn, lake, shrubberies, and
splendid timber. All had been planned with consummate
taste. Cunningly devised changes of level, winding
paths, isolated groups of shrubs and trees in varied
species rare and common, with copper, shaded green,
and silvered foliage artistically juxtaposed, revealed the
prospect to the visitor in a succession of partial vistas,
with narrow glimpses of blue distance, so that the whole
extent of the grounds appeared constantly varied, and
indefinitely larger than it really was. Thus was artfully
prepared an ideal English garden-scape, whose triumph
is to seem simply natural, while in front of the house,
and in keeping with its character, was a formal classic
arrangement of statues, fountains, groves, and grottos.
Twenty gardeners had been required to encourage art
and nature and to keep them under discipline.

In 1872, the place had been long emancipated from
their guardianship. The statues had been banished, the
lake halved in size, the Italian garden became a field
of useful grass, and a single factotum, with occasional
help, confined his chief attention to the farm, fruit, and
vegetables. The fine trees, however, and especially the
avenues of great elms and acacia, still made the place
noteworthy.

The best-known private owner of "Elm Grove" had
been Lord Ellenborough, the Indian administrator, whose
too famous wife, Jane Digby, Mabel Digby's own kins-
woman, and sister of the ninth Baron, was in 1872 still
living under an Arab tent. Some sinister tales were
connected with the place on her account, and soon after
her departure it was sold, and, passing from hand to
hand, was put to various uses: a hospital, a Jewish
synagogue, a refuge for one class or another. The body

of the house had become a network of unstable partitions, little rooms, narrow stairs, and galleries.   Two important additions, however, had just been completed in 1872 ; a beautiful chapel, with much elaborate stone carvings, and a few good schoolrooms.   But much more was needed.   Gradual changes were to require indefinitely more thought and personal sacrifice than the once-for-all accomplished erection at Marmoutier.

Had sufficient funds been forthcoming, no doubt the most practical plan and the cheapest had been to pull down and rebuild from the foundations.   But apart from the question of immediate expense, the activity of Roehampton could not be suspended even for months, and accordingly its inhabitants, year by year, made shift in crowded quarters, whilst some portion of the premises was bettered or reconstructed.   So there was a twenty-two years' period of ingenious piecing, alteration, pulling down, and building up, without the waste of a sovereign, a day's work, or a ton of material ; a tale of indefinite patience and assiduous labour.   For Mother Digby could not afford merely to stand by and encourage the workmen, though in this she followed St Theresa's example.   Many a time she headed a gang of novices or sisters, removing a partition, carrying bricks or wood, or variously " lending a hand."

At last the formless dwelling was transformed into a complete and highly organized monastery, with its separate quarters, workrooms, and studyrooms for novices and professed, with its dependencies and outhouses, dairy, bakery, carpenter's shop, wash-house, and printing office. The boarding-school annexed was supplied with all the elaborate requirements demanded or even desired in a secondary school after the modern system ; there was, besides, a separate guest-house and one for retreatants.

The garden, too, spoke for itself, and very soon, by careful planting and improvements.   If it lost the stately charm of cypresses and statues, and if a tree-encircled cemetery raised upon a mound where favourite animals were buried, as if for ancestor worship, under stone monuments recording their merits, were demolished, it gained by a beautiful Calvary, by stone images of saints embowered here and there, and by the trellised shrine of Our Lady of the Lake, a more monastic and no less picturesque character, harmonious to present uses. In all these changes, the spade and trowel, as well as the taste of Mother Digby had a large share.

So much for the outward setting of Roehampton. Of more importance were the inhabitants for whom all this was accomplished.

Blessed Mother Barat, as early as 1802, had ardently desired a foundation in England. Her life records how highly she esteemed the greatness of the English character; how she designed, thirty years before the Tractarian movement had quickened or rather intensified French sympathy, to propagate here devotion to the Sacred Heart, for which alone her Society existed, and how in 1841, despite her lack of resources and of subjects, unable longer to resist the pressure of the Vicars Apostolic and the Bishops, she established at their demand houses in Ireland and in England simultaneously, and actually visited this country.

At Cannington, Somerset, the nuns struggled on for nine years under many difficulties; then, after another essay in Berrymead Priory, near Acton, they removed again in 1850 to Roehampton. Nothing could exceed the kindness and encouragement bestowed upon Roehampton by ecclesiastics of influence, but above all, by Nicolas Wiseman, the future Cardinal Archbishop of Westminster.

The Jesuits gave efficient spiritual aid, and other good services; amongst them were noted Oxford converts: Father John Wynne, Father Anderdon, and many others. The well-known Passionist Father Ignatius Spencer, and Doctor Manning, had preached in the convent chapel; the boarding-school, small in numbers, and still conducted on French lines, had shown excellent results in good manners, moral training, and culture.

But the English mission so far, though by no means unfruitful, had been a record of devoted self-sacrifice, laborious experiment, and slow progress. The English noviceship in 1872 numbered few members. Of works for the poor there existed only an orphanage of fifteen girls, to whom a portion of the house was assigned, and the Children of Mary's Congregation, then so new a thing in England, could not develop without a meeting-place in London itself. Regarding the boarding-school, much of supreme importance was to do, and it must re-open in a month's time. The end in view was a school where future women of this nation should receive a culture and training thoroughly English in the best sense.

Mother Henrietta Kerr arrived at Roehampton at this time. Her health at Rome had given anxiety, and the Italian doctor now prescribed her native air as the best restorative.

In the *Life of Mother Henrietta Kerr* (1842-1885)[1] her personality is completely described. A few sentences will therefore suffice to link her to Mother Digby's story.

Henrietta Kerr left at once upon the memory an indelible picture. She was tall, and the eye was caught first by the distinction of her countenance and carriage, by the delicate aquiline perfection of feature, the blue eyes and Saxon colouring, whose brilliancy gave place during her last years to a transparent paleness. More winning was her ever-changing expression, her well-bred ease and frank simplicity, her cultivated tastes, her tact and sympathy, her earnestness and buoyant energy, all rooted in a noble nature, generously exercised in self-sacrifice even from childhood.

This was not her first acquaintance with Mother Digby. Lord and Lady Henry Kerr passed some time at Rougemont during the summer of 1860; their daughter Henrietta made a retreat at the convent, and there came to know Mother Digby, and to discover her own vocation for the Society of the Sacred Heart. Two such minds were fitted to understand one another. Their friendship was now to become a supreme one on both sides; more-over, Mother Digby saw in Mother Kerr the very Mistress General she desired.

Mother Kerr arrived in September, after the re-entry

---

[1] Second edition, 1887.

of the children for the coming term. The situation was difficult. In the first place, though there was an efficient staff of English mistresses, the ideal English school could never exist whilst so many of the girls, as at present, were foreigners, although a proportion of the latter companionship is necessary to preserve English youth from insularity. To send away children on account of their nationality would be invidious ; to decline new ones, a delicate task. Next, the general unrest that immediately preceded the Franco-Prussian war, and the haste with which, for their safety, pupils had been received, had introduced them at an age too late to begin their formation to school life, which at sixteen should be nearly at an end. The majority were now seventeen or eighteen years of age, young women rather than children. Moreover, they were all deeply attached to Mother Goold, and little disposed to welcome any change. More serious was the fact that owing to the same haste there had not been much enquiry into antecedents, and thus some undesirable elements, unfitted to blend with the education proposed, had found their way into the school.

Whilst these exterior problems awaited the Mistress General, she was also conscious, in her humble sincerity, that her power of rule was not transcendent. " I have not wrist enough," she once said, "for a very hard mouth." She had failed to keep in order the fiery little Italians who had loved her deeply, their mistress in the Trinità at Rome. But in courage and fidelity she was not wanting, and a firm and experienced hand was to hold the reins with her at the start.

It would be a mistaken impression that the school had not been well managed up to this point ; the devoted Mother Goold had effected much good, as has been said, but the present circumstances inevitably brought a crisis ; and such tides amongst young people, unless taken at the flood, may, as Mother Digby well knew, run rapidly down-hill to a low level.

The pupils were soon to give a proof of their spirit. Mother Digby assembled them to introduce the new Mistress General. She announced the holiday, to be accorded then and in future, when the school assembled punctually and in full numbers after the vacations. An elder girl rose to answer in the name of the rest. They begged permission to decline a holiday. It was not possible for them to enjoy themselves in their present state of bereavement. Reverend Mother Digby yielded in the same gracious manner as Charles II. used to the Presbyterians upon their request to observe a general fast on occasion of the Duke of York's marriage with a papist. They were entirely free, she said, to spend the day in study if they preferred it.

But on the occurrence of disrespect to the mistresses, and insubordination, she addressed the children in quite unmistakable words. She had no wish, she declared, for a large school, unless each member understood her duty. Those that did not would be returned to their parents.

Outward order was obtained, and Mother Digby retired, as it were, behind Mother Kerr, though nearly every day they might be seen walking together in the garden in close conversation for an hour. A thaw set in before long, and a "second spring," amongst this "innocent, joyous, and engaging race," to quote Kenelm Digby. Indeed, the school matured rapidly into Mother Digby's ideal. The studies were remodelled; English games, cricket, and the rest, were introduced and popularized as at Marmoutier.

The detail of Mother Kerr's work and influence in the school is vividly drawn out in her life; but nothing need be added here regarding her principles. For Mother Kerr, exercising her own charm, and retaining her own individuality and freedom of action, had been, so to say, the creation of Reverend Mother Digby. The Superior came forward to sustain her Mistress General in any emergency, but left to her the affection of her children, and the entire credit of every improvement in the eyes of the world, and even as far as could be, of the cloister.

"Under this twofold influence," says an observer of Roehampton in the eighties, "the school found itself; keeping the features of its high parentage of the Sacred Heart, before known only as a French educational system, it developed into a thing rooted in English soil downward and bearing fruit upwards."

Reverend Mother Digby's most distinguished and devoted women friends belonged to the Sodality of the Children of Mary.[1] For no sooner had Mother Barat established her institute in England, than English ladies, knowing what the Children of Mary had effected in France, were eager to form a similar nucleus in England, and many Tractarian converts of the mid-century, as eminent among women as Newman and his friends amongst men, had enrolled themselves.

Of these were the fifth Duchess of Buccleuch, who had suffered storm and stress beyond the ordinary in passing over to Catholicism; there was Mrs Craven, the fascinating and devout Frenchwoman of literary fame; and Elizabeth, fourth Marchioness of Londonderry, and Margaret, Countess of Newburgh, who like Lady Londonderry kept her comely stateliness unto old age and white hairs. When too feeble to walk, she still worked assiduously with her hands for the poor, and set aside forty pounds every month out of her moderate income for their service. Latterly her eyes were closed in blindness, and her calm joyousness still increased, till in her ninetieth year she was laid to rest beneath a marble slab in the convent cemetery at Roehampton. Lady Lothian's name has already been mentioned. During the Franco-Prussian war and after it, none laboured more devotedly than she for the succour and consolation of the French refugees. She sold her carriage and horses for their benefit, and turned her London house into a central office. To her after the war were sent in gratitude two superb Sèvres vases by the minister Thiers. It was about this time that she broke her arm. "Surely you ought not to be walking off to early Mass?" said a friend whom she met next morning. "I can't see," she replied with a smile, "why

---

[1] A congregation erected by the Holy See with special privileges and distinguished from others of the same name by the addition of " Prima Primaria."

I should lose my daily Mass as well as the use of my arm?" This most devoted friend of Reverend Mother Digby was frequently elected President of the Children of Mary. She made a retreat at Roehampton for twenty consecutive years.

Of the rest, save one, there can be here but a string of names, as of the "most valiant men" of David, suggesting much to those who knew them: Lady Victoria Kirwan, Lady Denbigh, Mrs Garcia, Mrs Bertram Currie, Mrs Victoria Smith, the Hon. Mrs Pereira, the Marquise de Salvo, Lady Clare Feilding, and many others. Rightly were they called "Children of Mary of the world"; they served two worlds, but never two masters; all that was of woman's work they did, but their praise cannot be loud or lengthy.

One, however, led a more memorable life as the world has it, and leaves a lasting name in the world of letters; like Mrs Augustus Craven, who, in her *Lady Georgiana Fullerton, sa vie et ses oeuvres*[1] erects to her supreme friend and English counterpart, a graceful literary monument.

At a meeting of the Children of Mary in the seventies, their President, Lady Georgiana Fullerton, in her melodious and deep bass voice recommended a maid who had given her satisfaction. "I will not dwell on the fact," added Lady Georgiana with a smile, pointing to her head, "that she makes all my bonnets, for I fear this would add little to her credit!" The bonnet in question, trimmed merely with a black ribbon tied beneath the chin, was indeed of the most modest description, and in keeping with the severely simple dress of the same hue, plainer in fact, than that of any nun or nursing sister. The face framed within the bonnet, had, save for the noble forehead, no pretensions to beauty. Her mild eyes, massive features, long upper lip, and refined mouth, made up a countenance that beamed with goodness and seemed to radiate its own peace outwards — an impression that deepened at every moment in her company.

Georgiana Charlotte Leveson Gower (1812-1885) was grand-daughter of the fifth Duke of Devonshire, and

[1] Paris, 1889, 4th ed.

daughter of the first Earl Granville.   Owing to her father's position as Ambassador at the Hague and at Paris, she had known, there and in London, all remarkable persons for three or four generations.

Her novels were acclaimed by the whole literary and fashionable world.   Newman, Lord Brougham, Gladstone, extolled, *Ellen Middleton* and *Grantly Manor*, and *Mrs Gerald's Niece* converted the first Lord Ripon. For, in 1846, Lady Georgiana had followed her husband into the Church; in 1855 she lost suddenly her only child, her ingenuous and high spirited son, within a few days of his coming of age.   She was not seen to weep.   None dared mention his name before her.   She hung a curtain in front of his portrait; five and thirty years later in her last illness, Father Gallwey reading to her the prophecies of the Passion, came to Zacharias: "*They shall mourn for him as for an only son.*"   Then her burst of tears made him pause, and a deeper light upon the force of the sacred text entered his soul.

But long ago she had stretched out her arms and had turned the whole heart of her bereaved motherhood towards the children of sorrow everywhere, to Europe, Asia, Egypt—where not?   When she could, she was at their personal service day and night, but more often she chose the more useful and self-sacrificing office at the helm, planning, organizing, pushing on the wheels of every undertaking with an impetus that carried it far beyond her personal range.   Small kindnesses she shed in largesse wherever she passed.   Young people drew towards her; every one wanted at any rate to tell her of their sorrows; she won even the worldly to live for others, for, in her plain attire, she still adhered to indispensable "society" duties.   Now and then a blunder was made, and a footman would leave her waiting in the tradesman's hall; but to the observant, nothing could conceal the lady.

Her pen was always at the service of truth.   At Mother Digby's instance she translated from the French of Mgr. Baunard the life of Mother Barat and that of Mother Duchesne; she wrote also another biography: *A*

Child of the Sacred Heart; all three had a great sale in England.

" The following pages of her journal," says Mrs Craven, " are dated from the convent at Roehampton, dear to her as it was.   Madame Digby, Superior of the house, was one of her dearest and most venerated friends. . . ." [1]

Shortly before Reverend Mother Digby's arrival at Roehampton, the Superior General visited her English house.   She was received at Roehampton by the whole body of the Children of Mary, Lady Lothian being at that time President.

Mother Goetz had been struck by the contents of a written address which they presented on her visit to England.   It was a unanimous request that she would establish a house of the Society in London itself, where the Sodality could hold their meetings under the auspices of the nuns, and where they could co-operate with that body in work for the poor.   There was also an earnest demand for the establishment of a day school in the capital.

All this was an echo of Mother Barat's idea.   Mother Goetz promised to give it the utmost consideration, and one of her main purposes in sending Mother Digby to England was that she should negotiate these important affairs with as little delay as possible.   The Children of Mary and many other friends were only too anxious to second her.

[1] *Lady G. Fullerton, sa vie et ses œuvres*, pp. 403, 404.

CHAPTER XI

THE TRAINING COLLEGE

" If the citadels of the souls of the young be left void of pure and noble images, they will be taken possession of by those that are contrary to them ; if not guarded by the bright symbols of beauteous and eternal things, error and death—moral death with all its process of intellectual degradation—will plant its pale flag there. The best guards, Socrates said, 'are the thoughts of men who are loved by God.'"— KENELM DIGBY, *Mores Catholici* (Booker, 1831) book VI. p. 189.

DR WISEMAN, from the year 1847, had constantly visited Berrymead. He encouraged and helped the community in many ways, and substantially augmented the number of pupils by his praise of the education they received. In 1850, the new Cardinal, having in a week of strict closet completed his *Appeal to the English People*, arrived unannounced at Roehampton on 20th November, at eight o'clock on the morning that his great *Defence* appeared in the newspapers. After saying mass, he informed the assembled community of the national ferment that was, for all that any one could then tell, putting his life in danger. " If I must seek safety in hiding," he added graciously, " I shall certainly return here ; for the religious of the Sacred Heart, as I know from experience at Paris and at Rome, have a special talent for concealing persecuted Bishops." He returned for some days on 12th December, and this warm-hearted man, a target for the bigotry of England, was touched almost to tears by the cordial reception of the religious, and by the children's gay songs of welcome. To this visit he made a marked reference in his second *Lecture upon the Hierarchy*.

He came again at the New Year ; and on 20th January, struck to the heart by a sudden blow, he had his greys harnessed at once, and drove to Roehampton to seek its

130

hospitality and its compassion. He had just learned the death of his mother in Italy. The news of the insults and attacks flung lately at her distinguished son had been a grievous blow to her great age, and had doubtless hastened her end. She was reputed a saint, and so great had been her charity that she left no fortune and had even bestowed on the poor the greater part of her wardrobe. In the convent solitude for some days he freely indulged his grief, said masses for her soul, and found that artless sympathy from women and children so soothing to one of his cast.

Equal kindness had been shown by the saintly Bishop Grant, Bishop of Southwark, who was very often at Roehampton, and by his successor, Dr Danell, in whose diocese the convent lay. Mother Digby hoped for as much from the Archbishop of Westminster, Dr Manning, a frequent guest at the Trinitâ dei Monti, and an occasional visitor at Roehampton, where, on the inauguration of the chapel, he preached a magnificent sermon upon the Sacred Heart, his own favourite devotion. The congregation of the Children of Mary had rendered good service in co-operation with himself and his clergy in many ways, but especially in the rescue of poor Catholic children from Protestant schools, a matter he had greatly at heart. Supported by the request of his personal friends, Mother Digby placed before him the following facts.

The Children of Mary, finding great difficulty in assembling every month so far from London as Roehampton, had been accustomed to meet in Lady Georgiana Fullerton's drawing-room, in the presence of the director of the congregation — in 1872 the Rev. P. Gallwey, S.J.—and of several religious of the Sacred Heart. Later on, by the kindness of the Sisters of Mercy, the Sodality had met at the convent, Blandford Square. Permission was now asked to found a convent of the Sacred Heart in the Westminster diocese for a day school, a poor school, and a meeting-place for the children of Mary.

This was granted at once, and in writing, for the objects laid before him ; nor did the Archbishop set down conditions or limitations of any sort. A friend of Reverend Mother Digby's, knowing her wishes, found an available house in an excellent situation, No. 1 Dorset Street, at a moderate price. No other Catholic was bidding for it, and fearful that the opportunity would be lost, this lady purchased it, and placed it at Mother Digby's disposal in November.

On 9th December 1872, Mother Digby wrote to the Superior General:

"The priest of the Dorset Street Parish has just been to see me on behalf of Canon Hunt. You are not more anxious to come, added the Father, than we priests are to have you. There is an immense amount of good to be done; children of every class swarm in the parish, and our schools are entirely insufficient. Canon Hunt wishes you to write this very evening to explain why the house was purchased before His Grace's permission had been asked. The Archbishop had asked the Canon if he really wanted us! The latter replied that he could not be thankful enough that we had taken the house in Dorset Street. 'To-morrow,' said the Father, 'I shall dine with Archbishop Manning, and will try to decide him upon the yes that will bring so much good to our poor parish.' I myself have just returned from London; Lady Lothian tells me that the priests are praying earnestly that Mgr.'s reply may be favourable. Lady Lothian shows the Society an unbounded devotedness."

Lady Lothian to Mother Digby.

"15 BRUTON STREET,
10th December 1872.

"VERY DEAR MADAME DIGBY,—In tranquillity and confidence shall be your repose! I have been to see Canon Hunt. He says that the Archbishop was a little hurt at not being consulted beforehand,[1] but that there will be no difficulties. To punish you, his Grace will probably delay his answer a few days, but meanwhile you may be happy as to the result. All the priests of Spanish place are

[1] As to the purchase of the house in Dorset Street.

delighted! It is as if a load were lifted off my heart!—Your very affectionate, C. LOTHIAN."

These hopes were to prove entirely fallacious. There is here no need to dwell upon the estimable side of Cardinal Manning, and upon the immense work he did for those of all ranks who fell under his influence. He has, to a large extent, been misjudged; and those who love and esteem him feel the want of a wide - spirited biography, that, with due balance, shall win for him a universal admiration. The shadows should not dim the lights upon so great a personality. Unfortunately, his relations with Mother Digby serve but to show the effects of a radical misunderstanding. There is no doubt that he had been misinformed as to the Society of the Sacred Heart; and, as usual, once his mind made up upon any point, he proved inflexible.

The Archbishop now declared that he refused consent to the occupation of the house in question by the nuns of the *Sacred Heart.* There was, not far off, a convent of another order, with a poor-school. He wished that convent to establish a training college for teachers, near their poor-school; and such a house in the situation of Dorset Street was just what he should desire for them. He was willing, however, that the Sisters of the Sacred Heart should found a house for the purpose they desired in any position of his diocese where, in his opinion, "such foundation would be for the spiritual good of his flock."

Mother Digby bowed to this decision, and even offered to relinquish the house in Dorset Street, without payment, to the Sisters whom Mgr. Manning wished to charge with the training college. But, a little later on, he gave her notice that he was no longer willing to have a day school opened by her within his diocese, as such an establishment, he had ascertained, was not required, but poor-schools alone.

The Children of Mary, Lady Georgiana Fullerton, Lady Lothian, and several others, personal friends of the Archbishop, presented themselves for an interview.

Their notes of the meeting chronicle severe reproaches against the Congregation of the Sacred Heart. He would never, on any account, tolerate them. Nothing that the ladies urged made any difference to his attitude; he threatened, moreover, to suppress the Congregation of the Children of Mary itself.

However, he appeared satisfied in the end by Lady Lothian's assurances that Mother Digby was actually willing to undertake a poor-school, and that in any part of the diocese that he should wish. "If so," he said, "I will bless them with both hands." He wrote to her very kindly on 26th January 1873 accepting her offer.

Meanwhile, the Sisters who had been offered the charge of the training college had not, after all, undertaken it; and after some time had elapsed, the donor of the house in Dorset Street sold it.

On 2nd June 1873, Reverend Mother Digby wrote again to His Grace, asking him if he would confide to the Sacred Heart any work that he wished for in his diocese; for she had a considerable sum of money now offered to her by a benefactress, who, however, required an answer as soon as possible.

The Archbishop, on 13th June, asked to see her in person. She went to meet him next day, accompanied by Mother Kerr. He was at first cold, but became gracious. "Let us speak of any works you could undertake." Mother Digby suggested a large poor-school, and annexed to it some locality where the Children of Mary could assemble, the school to be under their patronage. She explained the necessity of this work. He seemed satisfied, and spoke next of an orphanage that would be supported by voluntary contributions, and only temporarily, and to start with, under the care of the nuns of the Sacred Heart. She promised to submit this request to the Superior General, and doubted not of a favourable reply, although the work of an orphanage was not contemplated in the constitutions, and the Congregation as a rule only undertook it if no poor-school were available. "I see now what you want," rejoined the Archbishop. "I will look out for a poor-school in a locality where you can assemble the Children of Mary, and you will add to it an orphanage to help me to save the faith of so many destitute children. You can reassure your benefactress, for I shall send you an answer before the octave of the Feast of the Sacred Heart."

He then informed the nuns that he was about to consecrate his diocese to the Sacred Heart. "I have received from it so many blessings," he added, "and will not your arrival be a fresh one?" He blessed them kindly, and they withdrew.

That year, the Archbishop, indeed, had solemnly consecrated his diocese to the Sacred Heart; and it had been further suggested, at one of the meetings of the Children of Mary, that an English pilgrimage to Paray le Monial should take place. Lady Lothian had undertaken to propose this to Mgr. Manning; the idea was taken up with enthusiasm, and the Catholic pilgrims started with an ardour worthy of the time of Crusades, each wearing on the shoulder a badge of the Sacred Heart, of which seven hundred had been made for the purpose at Roehampton; Mother Digby sent a young girl-pilgrim, whose name was Margaret Mary, to represent the English convent at the shrine of the *Beatà*.

To return to Mother Digby's present business. On 3rd July a letter arrived from Mgr. Manning evading any direct answer. Its tenor showed Mother Digby and her friends that he was still of his first opinion : that the nuns, though desirous of establishing themselves in his diocese, would not in reality work for the education of the poor.

But now a new and unexpected proposition changed the face of affairs for Mother Digby.

To explain it, the compulsory Education Bill of 1870 must be recalled. Catholics were seriously alarmed for the future of their poor children, who, unless schools and teachers were prepared to receive them, would be pushed into the Board schools.

In 1847, a Committee had been formed under the Bishops, to see to the interests of Catholic education ; in 1873 this body was named the "Catholic School

Committee " ; [1] its secretary was Thomas William Allies;
who bore the scars of a hundred battles fought of old
in the Puseyite cause.

With the utmost self-sacrifice, generous donations from
clergy and laity, and the pence of the poor, increased the
number of elementary schools, furnished with all modern
appliances.   But the training of Catholic teachers was not
a mere question of money, and the bishops everywhere
looked to the regulars for this essential undertaking.   The
Sisters of Notre Dame had responded by an admirable
college at Liverpool, established twenty years before,
developing students equal in all ways to those issuing
from the Government establishments.[2]   The supply from
Liverpool was, however, wholly inadequate to the Catholic
demand; and the Catholic School Committee faced the
instant need of another college in the south of England.
What religious institute should be asked to undertake
such an establishment?   Not in any case, said some, the
nuns of the Sacred Heart.   It was not their regular work;
they would hardly be capable of pulling it through, or
rather they would be certain to refuse so arduous and
probably at first so ungrateful a task.   The matter was
put to the vote of the Bishops; that of Dr Ullathorne,
by a majority of one, determined the Committee to offer
the undertaking to the nuns of the Sacred Heart, and to
found the College, with the Archbishop's consent, in the
Westminster Diocese.   Mgr. Manning thereupon wrote
a letter with his own hand to Reverend Mother Digby,
acquiescing explicitly on both these points with the
resolution of the Committee.

The clergy wrote independently to the Archbishop on
behalf of the nuns, and to Mother Digby imploring her to
accept the training college.   " All this has shown us, at any
rate," writes Mother Digby to Paris, " that the clergy are
exceedingly well disposed towards us. "

Not before pause and prayer did she send her answer.
It was quite true that the nuns of the Sacred Heart had no

---

[1] The functions, and others as well, are now performed by the " Catholic
Education Council," established in 1905.

[2] *See* Clarke, *The Hon. Mrs Edward Petre* (Art and Book Company,
1899), pp. 295 ff.

experience in the training of school teachers; moreover, Blessed Mother Barat had been always averse to the idea of Government inspection, competitive examinations, publicity, and possible rivalry. Nor did the special difficulties of the case escape Mother Digby's prevision. On the other hand, the necessities of the times must be considered. To train a number of school teachers to whom Christ should be a personal reality, and to send them forth to leaven thousands in His name, appealed to her chivalrous nature as it would have done to that of Mother Barat. She laid the matter before the altar, and then confided it to Mother Kerr and Mother Charlotte Leslie, begging them not to consult together, but to give her separately their unbiassed opinion. Both agreed that the work should be undertaken. The project was then approved in Paris, and on 13th November 1873 Mother Digby wrote a letter to the Catholic School Committee, offering to undertake a training college; she enclosed it to the Archbishop, with liberty to send it on to the Committee or not, as he wished. He sent it on, in fact, with most warm commendations and praises of the Society of the Sacred Heart; but he did not write to Mother Digby.

As the Archbishop had approved the house in Dorset Street for a training college, Reverend Mother Digby enquired of the owners whether it was still to be had. It was, and as no answer was sent to her application to Mgr. Manning, she wrote to Mr Allies who called upon His Grace. On 1st December the Archbishop verbally agreed to the foundation of a house in Dorset Street—or so at least Mr Allies understood it. He therefore at once negotiated for the house, and sent word to the Archbishop that he had invited Her Majesty's inspectors to report upon it. A few days afterwards, the Archbishop sent another verbal message to Mr Allies to the effect that the latter had made a grave mistake. He (the Archbishop) was, he said, unwilling to take upon himself the odium of a direct refusal; but, in fact, he was resolved not to tolerate the nuns of the Sacred Heart in Dorset Street. Why he could not do so was nothing to Mr Allies's purpose. On hearing, some weeks later, that the nuns

were obediently searching for another house, he notified
to them that he did not after all wish them to establish a
training college in *his diocese*. Mother Kerr wrote to the
Motherhouse that the suspense about the training college
was really wearing out Mother Digby. The letters of the
latter, nevertheless, show her thorough appreciation of
Archbishop Manning's radically noble character, marred
now and then, as it seems, by invincible prejudices. Her
only comment runs thus : " How hard, how much harder
than all besides, it is to bear persecution from the friends
of God ! "

Help came from another quarter. Mgr. Danell
welcomed her most cordially to his diocese of Southwark.
And Mother Digby at once put her hand to the plough ot
the training college.

First, a staff must be chosen ; and whilst some
devoted friends were looking for a site, she selected
her most promising subjects, with Mother Charlotte
Leslie as principal, put before them their new trust,
and inspired them, as she knew how, with her own
enthusiasm.

In her conferences to the staff it is not strange to find
that she was undazzled by the notion—lit up by the movement of 1870—that instruction would prove a panacea for
all the ills of society, a vision which has faded in the
experience of two and forty years. Mother Digby looked
not only to the paths of her future college, but to its
foundations, and they bore inscribed words that she had
gathered from an older source than *The Tamworth Reading-
Room* : " Secular knowledge not a substitute for Religion—
Not the principle of moral improvement—Not a principle
of social unity—Not a principle of action ; "[1] Cassandra-
like warnings that might well have been uttered thirty
years later.

Speaking of the merely intellectual side, " Give the
children power rather than knowledge," she said emphati-
cally to one of the staff. She much preferred the crude,
hesitating answers of children, the result of their own

---

[1] *Catholicus*, 1841. Newman, *Discussions and Arguments* (New Impression.
Longmans, 1911), p. viii.

thinking,[1] to the fluency obtained by drill, or by learning from borrowed sources. "Never," she repeated, "let the solid give place to the showy;" means must not be taken for ends, or visible and immediate results for other than the *sine quâ non* of access to what lay behind and beneath. One master thought, God's service, must be to her daughters beacon and compass in this as in every undertaking, though there would be danger as never before of losing sight of it amid the throng of exterior difficulties.

She set them to study according to the government programmé, and professors were engaged to lecture upon school management, with all the novel paraphernalia of blackboards and diagrams to map out intellectual mysteries, and "objects" to fix the wandering attention of youth. Further, she accompanied the staff to Government Colleges, whose principals obligingly imparted every useful information; but to none were, and are, the nuns of the Sacred Heart under deeper obligations in this matter than to the Sisters of Notre Dame at Liverpool, whose magnificent work and unparalleled success are well known to all interested in popular education. Their cordial charity upon every visit of the Wandsworth staff, and their serviceable hints, made it appear as if the success of the Southern College was to be their own.

Several members of the staff now went up for their examinations, and all passed successfully.

The search for a site proved for months wearisome and futile. Sometimes Reverend Mother Digby herself accompanied by the devoted Lady Lothian, sometimes other of the nuns two by two, hunted purlieus in Deptford, Clapham, Blackheath, and elsewhere, till at last a possible halting-place was found at The Orchards, Wandsworth. It had been a gentleman's place, and was now dilapidated; eleven different owners, each at variance with every other, required separate negotiations; and the sum named seemed prohibitory. It appeared, moreover, that an engagement

---

[1] "We are spending annually millions of money of educational fads. . . . Presumably the object of all education is to make men think for themselves. The dock strikers have not even begun to do so. They follow like so many sheep such of their leaders as possess the gift of the gab."—Rev. W. J. Somerville, Rector of St George's, Southwark, *Times*, 30th July 1912.

had been made to run two public roads through the property. However, these and other obstacles fell, one by one. The price abated to reasonable limits, the engagement for the public roads was cancelled, and early in 1874 the contract was signed.

Many weeks of labour were needed to render the house habitable, and the government grant was contingent on the opening of the college on 1st March. Mother Digby therefore determined to receive the students at Roehampton. The community retired into shrunken quarters, leaving space which was prepared for the staff and pupils of the training college. The latter arrived, twenty - five in number, upon the day appointed, and the work began.

, Prophets of evil were not wanting. The college was foredoomed to failure; the mistresses and available students being alike incapable. Here they spoke sooth. The great reputation of the Northern College attracted the best students, and Liverpool could afford to reject any who had not passed an entrance examination in the first-class. There was talk of obliging all pupils from the south of England to make application of admittance to Wandsworth, but this would have been not only unfair but short-sighted. The girls were more likely to work with heart in a college they had themselves chosen; moreover, subsequent failures would be attributed with bitterness to this compulsion. Hence, second - class passes were the best available for Wandsworth; many of the third were added to make up numbers, for in those days students were too few for the colleges. The pupils were required in three months' time to pass a fresh government examination in six or seven different subjects. The grant was proportional to results.

But these girls were deserving of every help and sympathy. Before entering the college they must sign an agreement (not of course binding in law) to teach for two years at least in a Catholic government school, if they could get an appointment, and they were salaried by the local priest, none of whom could afford more than £40 a year, whereas £60 was the minimum pay elsewhere,[1] and good teachers being then scarce, board schools were willing, and sometimes glad, to engage Catholics.

Accordingly Mother Digby warned the mistresses, while zealously preparing the students for the first quarterly examinations, not to let them be depressed by difficulties. Nothing could exceed the good will of the pupils; and when the first quarterly examinations were over, without waiting for results, she rewarded their efforts.

On 20th June the nuns were to take final possession of Wandsworth. Nothing as yet was in order; the large garden untouched for years was like a jungle; the palings round had been stolen for firewood; a caretaker and his large family still, after weeks of warning, remained installed in the ground floor. After a thousand difficulties the house was evacuated. There were no gates or locks, and the newcomers received a friendly warning not to close their shutters at night, as that would imply there was something inside worth stealing. Wandsworth thieves, however, were not to be deluded by such wiles, and the sight of figures prowling near the house after dark carrying a ladder, and making off into the bushes at the sight of a lantern, induced the nuns to keep watch during the night.

Reverend Mother Digby often came down with a band of helpers, to clean and arrange furniture in each room as soon as it became habitable, and to laugh with the foundresses over adventures that might have furnished forth a comic journal in several numbers.

At last all was ready; the students entered, and the foundations of an elementary school, the practising school of the college, were laid. The inspectors were pleased, but Baldad came between whiles to declare that the school was too small, and Sophar, that Wandsworth would never fill it. They were confirmed in their comforting by the unsatisfactory results of the first quarterly examinations. But Mother Digby held on her course undaunted.

1874 was drawing to a close, and she was aware that

---

[1] Many of the Wandsworth girls then got only £25 or £30 a year, and no apparatus to speak of, in their school.

in February 1875 the number of students must be doubled, and that those in residence would have to teach in a practising school under the supervision of the mistresses. Neither the school, nor the additional rooms now building could be ready in time.   An iron church was, therefore, erected, and the large room hitherto devoted to a chapel was converted into a dormitory ; and galleries were put up on the entrance hall, which served as a temporary girls and infants school.

By hard work, and much individual teaching between classes, the students were got through the examinations without one failure — the utmost that could have been hoped for.   But now came a good omen.

Canon Wenham instituted a competitive religious examination between the three Catholic Training Colleges of England; the men's College at Hammersmith, the women's at Liverpool and Wandsworth.   When the list appeared, it was headed by a Wandsworth student, far ahead of any other candidate, and Reverend Mother Digby was greatly consoled.

She used to appear at Wandsworth for at least some hours every fortnight, when once the college was well started, and no longer required her more lengthy stay. The community took new heart at her words.   " Do not waver before difficulties."   To the staff she said, "Your mothers have borne all those which preceded the foundation of the house ; now do *your* part."   And again : "Cultivate the spirit of thanksgiving, and do your best."

She won the hearts of the students straightway; if prevented from coming to see them, she sent a letter, with her blessing.   She kept the highest standard before their eyes.   They were called to nothing less than an Apostolate in the future, to reach thousands outside the range of their present mistresses.   Nor did she give only fine words.   She would receive the girls for holidays at Roehampton, providing lunch and amusements in the garden ; at every half-year she distributed substantial rewards at the college and in the practising school, and brought on her visits a book for the reading-room, a handsome gift for the laboratory, a microscope, or a spectroscope.   She recommended the Superior to give, when possible, a half holiday at some museum, at the Tower, at Hampton Court, or elsewhere.

Her kindness prepared the way for what was most important to the students.   The Children of Mary's Congregation was established amongst them, serious and sustained self-denial and attention to duty being required for enrolment.   Thus habits were formed, and each character was built up; in this sense the "self-made" woman, Mother Digby thought, was well grounded.   Early in 1877 a striking example was to bring these matters home. A great Inspector paid his first visit to the college.   His advent was not without terrors, but he left behind him peace and a great good.

Reverend Mother Leslie, on the evening of 20th February, made the tour of the house; she noticed a light in an upper room of the infirmary; a student, feeling slightly unwell early that evening, had asked to lie down.   No evidence of serious indisposition appeared, but Mother Leslie sent at once for the doctor.   He came at midnight; it was nothing—nothing at all, a slight cold.   She was dissatisfied, sent for another physician, and watched by the bedside till he came. Julia Fitzsimon made no complaint; she was undisturbed. She was an Irish girl, a Child of Mary, quiet and unobtrusive, and a favourite with her companions.

The second doctor arrived towards morning; he looked grave; it was acute peritonitis, which strode on visibly hour by hour.   The young girl calmly resigned her soul into the hand of God; conscious to the last, and fully consoled by her religious surroundings, she expired about mid-day.

Reverend Mother Digby came instantly to console the house of mourning, bringing a white dress, veil, and wreath, to array the dead girl.   To the students she spoke of the privilege Our Lord had bestowed on them in choosing one of their number to repose so early on His Sacred Heart, there to intercede for all their undertakings.   The Bishop, full of sympathy, and many friends, came to pray by the bier.   The beautiful ceremonies of the funeral service were celebrated by many ecclesiastics in the crowded chapel ; a white pall covered the coffin, followed by the students with candles and white veils as far as the convent gate, where a silent and respectful crowd of poor persons had gathered—a scene and an event altogether impressive, and fruitful with lasting good in the district. The students were bound together by a family sorrow ; the great lesson produced amongst them evident results, and was never forgotten.

How the girls would develop could not be told at first ; but the existence of Wandsworth College would not have been in vain, if only for the help given to numbers of the "submerged tenth" in its environs. The place was then largely one of slums ; the poor in the lower parts of Wandsworth suffered much from occasional inundations of the Wandle, whose unromantic waters overflowed into their wretched dwellings, where drunkenness was the least of the rampant vices, but parent of all the rest. Many children of the practising school were among the most miserable.   "Why hasn't Lizzie come to school to-day ?" The young child replied that Lizzie's father had just murdered her mother, and proceeded further with the why and the how, for criminal life had no secrets for the Wandsworth infant. Many suffered cruelty, as when a little girl injured by falling out of a window, was violently beaten with a strap by her father, annoyed at the disturbance.

But the parents, forced to send their children to school, began to find in the house, the chapel, and the teachers, something that spoke of order and of light. Bread and kind words, at least, were to be had at the door ; there was the spectacle of the First Communion day for their children, dressed in the blue cotton frocks, white veils, and wreaths, that the nuns had made for them ; and the solemn renewal of baptismal vows, when before the altar the little ones, advancing two by two, laid their hand upon the Gospels, and promised anew to renounce the powers of ill, and to follow Christ faithfully unto death ; there was the cheerful breakfast for parents and children afterwards, and the Christmas tree, with substantial gifts for hundreds, young and old. The congregation of the Sacred Heart established for women, and the mothers' meetings, attracted the best, who then sought out the recalcitrant ; for the poor understand how to help each other. Many had never known religion ; others had long ago left off its practice ; many a time the children themselves won their parents to conversion of life and of faith.

Already in 1877 the college was beginning to reap what to Mother Digby was the main reward of all her efforts. Each student issuing from thence had been for a year the head mistress of a Catholic school, and, from the respective managers, almost without exception, came the grateful testimony that in adherence to duty, in devotedness to their children's good, and even in secular efficiency, the Wandsworth students were second to none. This latter question was of great importance to the poor Catholic priest; for the government grant, then but 17s. 6d. yearly per child, was bestowed only upon those who had passed their examinations. The young women themselves, thrown into an arduous and a solitary life, with little surrounding aid or sympathy, continued to correspond with their former teachers, and to find therein a great sustaining power. One at Larkhall presented ninety - nine children for examination, and all successfully, whereas in the preceding year only fifteen out of forty-two had passed. Her school was reported the best in the place, and the children flocked to it in preference to five others, non - Catholic. Another "old student" reclaimed twenty children from Protestant teachers ; she has remained until the present day mistress of the same school.

Devotion to the Sacred Heart was an immense and even a civilising influence. Many of the children proved at first utterly undisciplined ; the teacher, standing before some hundred young barbarians, would patiently reduce them to order, sometimes in a single afternoon.

"I put twenty of the elders at desks on one side (says a letter) whilst I tried to cope with the rest. Talking at once began in the

K

first set as soon as my back was turned. 'Can't you be quiet,' growled a boy amongst them, 'don't you see she trusts us?' And from that moment they remained perfectly good, and they have begun to know what honour means."

Another from a poor fishing village related how her children had each brought their halfpenny for flowers for the church, or to send to the Holy Father; "for most of them, this is a month's pocket money, or the price of that day's dinner, or a hard won profit for some piece of extra work at home." "Now I know (writes a third) why God sent me here, and the work He means me to do." Such testimonies abound; in their abundance lay their interest to Mother Digby; and Canon Wenham's words to the girls in college days, were verified: "that it is not their own high place on the class list, but the discipline in their future schools, that will reveal the good teacher."

Still, the aspect of the class list could not fail to give anxiety to Mother Digby. Every quarter, though by comparison there was a slow and nearly steady rise, the names of Wandsworth candidates, taken as a whole, stood below those of other colleges, and the cry from those who looked no further was that Wandsworth was a failure. Even some of the Poor School Committee took the same view, and their remarks prevented the entrance of some good students.

Her Majesty's inspectors, by personal contact with the place, were not of this opinion. They came announced or unannounced, and were usually benign, expressing astonishment that so much had already been done. Canon Tinling, an Anglican, very kind and liberal minded, gave Reverend Mother Digby many useful hints. His outlook for Wandsworth was not hopeful, and his reports rather disparaging. Yet he spoke with admiration of the self-denying way in which by private resources alone, school wings and additions were building at Wandsworth. He encouraged Mother Digby in her efforts to avoid mental "cram" as far as possible; the staff, he urged, should for the present take few subjects, and develop them well, chiefly the three R's, to which were added Religion and

School Management; in these, at least, the students showed almost from the first invariably good results.

The Bishop of London and the Dean of Windsor came one day on a visit of inspection. "His lordship, a fatherly Irishman," says the house Journal, "said a few kind words to the students on their future mission; he then went to the Practising School, where he showed much interest." Noted Tractarian converts, Fathers Anderdon, Wenham, Richards, Macmullen, and others, were also kind and encouraging inspectors.

But the greatest help of all, and the most powerful encouragement to Wandsworth, in public and in private, came from some of the Catholic School Committee. Every year these distinguished laymen came unfailingly and in numbers to the final exhibition. The Duke of Norfolk, as well as Lord Ripon, presented the students with yearly prizes in money; Lord Howard of Glossop gave a set of games. Lord Clifford, Lord Petre, Lord Henry Kerr, and others, were of assistance in many ways. Every year the Committee presented a vote of thanks to Reverend Mother Digby for her services to the cause of Catholic education, and at a meeting in 1878, the sum of £500 was voted to the College with the view of making up in some measure the loss sustained by delayed certificates.

The first Marquis of Ripon rendered the most marked service by his addresses to the students and to the Committee, and by his efforts to befriend the college, when most it needed help and approval from high quarters. In June 1875 he presided for the first time at the distribution of prizes. The knowledge that so late as the previous year he had been a Protestant, and Grand Master of the English Freemasons, raised curiosity as to what he might say on Catholic education. His actual words might have proceeded from Mother Digby herself.

Education (said Lord Ripon) was a work in which he took the deepest interest. How often was the term used to express but a part of it—*instruction*. Secular knowledge, however skilfully imparted, could not constitute *education*, by which he understood the training of the mind and heart, and the formation of the whole person and character to what is good and great. To combine education with instruction there must be strong moral influence, and the example of real religion, gentleness, patience, firmness, and humility. He then expressed the gratitude due to the Society of the Sacred Heart for undertaking this work of training, and wished it every blessing and God speed.

Accompanied by others of the Committee, he visited the poor-school and was pleased at the prevailing neatness, proceeding then to the students at their cricket. Lord Ripon was delighted at the animation of the game, and the modesty and simplicity of the players. On this head a tale is told. Reverend Mother Digby was speaking to the students in early days upon the duty of self-sacrifice. "And now," she added, "I am going to ask you for such an act; but I fear it may prove too costly." She was answered by protestations. "Well, I want you to put by all your jewellery, ribbons, and lace collars. Our children are always very simply dressed." The girls ran upstairs and soon reappeared in plain black uniform and linen collar. Her smile of approval was felt by all as a reward.

Mr John Hungerford Pollen, and Mr Neill, also members of the Poor-School Committee, were amongst those who gave their time, their personal service, and their good words both to and for Mother Digby, in a hundred ways; and this kindness was deeply felt by Mother Digby with all her force of will and capability of standing alone. Cardinal Wiseman himself was not more touched by the sympathy of friends, or more grateful; but as to Wandsworth she perhaps owed most to the valiant secretary of the Committee, Mr Allies, Treasurer of the Wandsworth College.

His addresses to the students were always marked by delicate tact, and carefully calculated to arouse their understanding and gratitude as to the devotion of their mistresses, their own gain by the education they were receiving, and the nobility of their vocation. None recognized more than he the enormous difficulties under which the College was still labouring, and must still labour, perhaps for years to come. His correspondence with Mother Digby in 1877 will add point to what has been advanced.

"CATHOLIC POOR-SCHOOL COMMITTEE,
22 PORTMAN STREET, W.
27th July 1877.

"MY DEAR MADAME KERR,—Since our visit last month the Training College has been continually on my mind. It is to re-open on the 1st, and I want to tell you an accident which has occurred. Lord Ripon and Lord Petre were resolved to try whether the Cardinal could be prevailed upon to let the new quarterly examinations of pupil teachers in his diocese, take place at Wandsworth. . . . The latter received next day from His Eminence twelve reasons most elaborately drawn up, much indeed in the manner in which an ancient Bishop would have condemned a heretic, for not suffering anything that concerned pupil teachers *to go out of his diocese*. The twelve reasons, notwithstanding their compactness, meant simply that, however great His Eminence's affection was for the Sacred Heart, and his satisfaction that he was only separated from it by 'the silver thread of the Thames,' he did not mean in any way to encourage or support the Training College at Wandsworth. I have mislaid the twelve reasons, but I have given you their *succo*. . . . The declared position of this important personage moves me to say how much anxiety I do feel as to how the Training College can adequately meet some very trying difficulties which are being put upon it. It is not a small one that instead of receiving encouragement and genuine recommendation from the person who could most assist it among the Bishops, it has nothing to expect from him. Secondly, it is a very hard condition indeed to be able to look forward for some years to getting only second or third class pupil teachers for students. . . . Lord Ripon, and I, and some others, know that when the list at Wandsworth comes out with lower classes than at Liverpool, there is good reason for it—but the managers of schools throughout the country look merely at the list, and rate the Training College thereby.

"This is a great trial to the teaching staff, and they need a superfluity of force not to break down under it. What I fear is, that one after another will suffer in their health, and cause perpetual changes, which again are most injurious to the success of a Training College.

"The sum of all above is, that it is a *damnosa haereditas* that Mother Digby in her charity has taken up. But one sacrifice entails another. You have laid out a fortune in money on the place. But how much dearer are the labours and prayers of your teachers. I do not know a more difficult work than that of making these girls fit to pass the government examinations. As Madame Digby is over-whelmed with work at present I thought I would write to you, to say what I feel about the urgent need of lightening the task of your teachers in any way that is possible. I may say that when I looked over last year Mr Tinling's comparative statement of the work of the Teachers at the various female Colleges, I could find none that had so much to do as those at Wandsworth. . . . But, you should have more horses to draw a heavy carriage along a road full of ruts."

To this suggestion of the advisability of increasing the teaching staff, Mother Digby replied by sending amongst others Mother Lucy Laprimaudaye, who passed her examinations at once with full success in every subject, and spent a week at Liverpool to study the management of that college.

Mr Allies received the news with satisfaction, and condoled with Mother Digby next month on the break-down in health of certain valuable teachers.

"You have indeed been severely tried. . . . God will accept the offering of their health which they have made in their labour there, and bless its success in the future. I am more than ever encouraged to hope this by what I have learnt from the Reverend Mother and Sister Mary St Philip in this last visit (to Liverpool). They tell me that they have found it most difficult to find teachers. 'We have tried scores without success.' . . . You will say: what encouragement is there here? My point of view is, that the struggle which Wandsworth is undergoing is not exceptional, but belongs to the very character of a Training College. It is not over even for Liverpool, after twenty years' trial. The real cause of their success is, I cannot but feel, in the extraordinary combina-tion of mental and physical energy and ability in Sr. Mary St Philip, whose mind has directed, controlled, divined what to do and what not to do, for all this period. She has got the measure of the Privy Council Examinations. In answer to my question, 'should all parts of a subject be worked up equally?' she replied: 'One gets to know the mind of the Privy Council.' 'Can you give me a notion,' I asked the Reverend Mother, 'of the standard used for correcting quarterly papers?' 'Sr. Mary St Philip's mind is the standard.' The thing to be desired is to obtain for Wandsworth one who could discharge for it Sr. Mary St Philip's part at Liverpool; and I write this not at all knowing but that you may have already in Madame —— just the right person. . . . I have not myself the least feeling that Wandsworth has not succeeded, and am much pleased at Madame Laprimaudaye's nomination. . . .—Believe me, dear Reverend Mother, etc."

In December, he wrote again to Mother Digby upon a point wherein he differed from his correspondent.

"MY DEAR REVEREND MOTHER,—I have just returned from the Meeting (for the distribution of prizes) at Wandsworth which only wanted your presence to be perfect. It was however a success: I think every one was pleased with the Training College to-day, and it is important that what was said by Canon Wenham and Lord Ripon should be fully reported by the Catholic papers. I was saying so to Madame Leslie; she replied that it was your general principle to keep the outward world aloof. I returned home with five Jesuit Fathers, and they begged me to press upon you Lord Ripon's expression of his wish that what he was stating about the Training College for the South should be made generally known. It is besides desirable that a list of the persons present should be given. Now if you will permit Madame Leslie to supply me with the report, I will take care that it is forwarded to the *Tablet*, and I think that the benefit to be expected for the College from this course should overweigh the principle of concealment of your good works. . . ."

After these first years of difficulty, first-class teachers, who had presented themselves but rarely before 1878, joined the college in increasing numbers, and, in about ten years' time, the whole was in full efficiency. In 1904, Wandsworth being too small a house to contain the staff, students, and school, the whole was transferred with the cordial approval of the Archbishop of Westminster, to Bayswater, to the handsome college of St Charles, which had been built by Cardinal Manning himself.

CHAPTER XII

IRELAND

" Men now say, 'thoughtless youth'; whereas in fact, youth runs wild in super-abundance of thought, and it was to give this culture and direction that the various parts of Catholic discipline were framed and exercised."—KENELM DIGBY, *Mores Catholici* (Booker, 1831), book VI., p. 185.

IN Ireland, devotion to the Sacred Heart, Mother Digby's great concern, had made much progress since 1841. Blessed Mother Barat, in answer to many ecclesiastical demands, had made a foundation of her Society at Roscrea in Tipperary. A second at Armagh was granted ten years later at the solicitation of the Bishop, Mgr. Cullen; and, when transferred to the see of Dublin, he obtained a third in 1854 at Glasnevin, transferred later to Mount Anville, five miles from the capital. These houses belonged to Reverend Mother Digby's vicariate; already in 1872, and nearly every succeeding year, she visited a country which in virtue of her father she claimed as her own. In 1874, she was carrying on side by side with the foundation of Wandsworth another in Dublin itself, where a day-school was soon constituted, and a National school added to hold three hundred children. Later on, owing to a change of locality, the school changed hands, and classes were held from six to nine in the evening at the Convent of the Sacred Heart, for shop and factory girls, to be instructed in catechism and domestic economy; here, too, the Children of Mary held their meetings.

In 1875 she saw with satisfaction the great extension of the works in Dublin. That of the Children of Mary, Cardinal Cullen and his successor had much to heart. Dublin, as he pointed out, offered a vast field to their charity.   They visited prisons and workhouses, and obtained access—not then easy—to the hospitals served by Protestant nurses; there were servants and liberated prisoners to place, girls to rescue, poor churches to furnish.   In times of famine, or political disturbance, whole families were, as in the early eighties, reduced to feed on kelp, and rain had sometimes wetted the peat past burning; a centre was established whence food and fuel were distributed.

Mount Anville, like Roehampton, was formerly a gentleman's place, with the usual additions to harbour the works of the *Sacred Heart.*   Near the house are fine cedars; from a Belvedere Tower is visible the eastern seascape; opposite lies the beautiful country beyond Dublin.   The garden ends in wild woodlands; on one side lies Lord Pembroke's park, where the deer can be watched browsing close at hand.   Beyond the cattle fields, and surrounded by yards and outhouses, where prospers every sort of domestic fowl, is the little house and domain of the steward—a sort of "monastery serf" of the typical Irish sort, who lives with his wife and family in supreme content and faithful service.

But it was rather in the utterly unconventional "wilds of Ireland," where the national character appears more decidedly unchanged, though graven with centuries of history upon a distinct and original race, that Mother Digby found her interest in a country entirely new to her.

At Roscrea, in Tipperary, formerly one of the poorest parts of Ireland, stands a white house upon a hill.   When Mother Digby first visited the place, nearly four hundred little barelegged boys and girls, with the famous Irish eyes and colouring, clad like Gainsborough's "Cottage Children," climbed the hill as the morning bell sounded the hour for class, and scampered down in the evening. The children would press eagerly round Mother Digby as she sat smiling in their midst.

But these are pictures of long ago.   For many years now, these interesting children, whose quickness and intelligence—if those who have taught them as well as other races are to be credited—appears surpassing, have been taught and trained in the most complete of modern National schools ; bare legs are no more, and the Dutch neatness and order of the place and its scholars have diminished the picturesque element.

The country people were especially attracted to Reverend Mother Digby. The women of the convent congregations would come in a body to pay their respects. She would affectionately embrace the more aged, who, beside themselves with joy at such an honour, would raise their trembling hands to heaven, invoke a blessing in the poetic language of their race, and call upon the angels and saints of God to escort her—after a long life, to be sure—with lighted candles to the couch of glory.

Her prayers were sought for any enterprise. "Pray for me, Sister," whispered a youth, on his way to a neighbouring village, as he slipped a shilling into Mother Digby's hand, "I'm going to ask a girl if she'll have me ! " And his suit was no doubt successful, for it is the universal practice to come back and ask for fresh prayers, if the matter in question has not prospered.

Once, just as Mother Digby was going away, a good creature ran up with a mysterious present that she must put into the Superior's own hand. She had chosen the grandest in her power, and displayed it with some pride — six quacking ducks in a basket. There was nothing for it but to carry them off.

Her next journey took her to the north, where there was a more rugged soil to work.

The house at Armagh faces, at a short distance from its walls, two hills, crowned respectively by the Cathedral of St Patrick, and by that other built by the pence of the poor, wherein the religion of the saint, driven from its ancient seat, now finds a refuge scarcely less noble.

When the convent was first established in 1851, a mob was restrained only by force from wrecking its walls, but now the old craters were seen to smoke comparatively seldom. "Is it true," asked a foreigner, after a visit to the parlour, "isn't it by accident that the Irish some-

times fight nowadays, and kill people?" Even the
rumblings of 12th July had in the seventies ceased to
threaten the window-panes; a last victim was the convent
dog, who, rashly running down the street on that day,
was recognised and pelted with stones. The poor animal
escaped with a torn ear, and was interviewed, and doubtless consoled, by the Mother Vicar; he was looked upon
henceforth by the friends of the house with respect as a
sufferer for the faith.

Perhaps the man who most powerfully contributed to
a more harmonious blending of the green and orange at
Armagh, and round about, was its Archbishop, Daniel
McGettigan, the Primate of all Ireland in 1870. His
looks were mild and kingly, and from his great stature
he was surnamed "the Gentle Giant." Even the
Orangemen venerated him, and did him many gratuitous
services, declaring that so good a man "must have
Protestant blood in his veins." He would minister
incessantly to his poorer flock, not infrequently till
midnight, and for five or six hours in succession. He
dearly loved the convent, and often appeared unannounced
among the children, talking to them familiarly, but with
the "word in season" that remains, amusing himself
greatly with their answers. Many were the treats and
surprises that he furnished for the holidays of both
schools, and he gave princely gifts to the chapel; to
all, his generosity was indeed *Irish*, and people wondered
where he found his resources.

He was, perhaps, Reverend Mother Digby's special
friend amongst the bishops; in 1884, struck with
paralysis, he yet struggled to the convent, and talked
to her at great length. Two years later he succumbed,
and was buried by his express wish without a monument,
in the corner of the public cemetery where his favourite
companions, the poorest, are interred.

But until these latter years he was in full vigour,
and looked to Mother Digby's daughters to afford him
useful aid, especially along the lines of education. The
most interesting to the Primate and to Reverend Mother
Digby of all the works at Armagh, was that of the

mill-girls, who formed the night-school in the summer months.

Every morning the sharp whistle at half-past five woke the town, and at six o'clock the mills were in full activity. After a day's work of twelve and a half hours, the girls to the number of about a hundred and fifty, assembled for their classes, and during the four days' yearly retreat they appeared at the chapel for mass and prayers two hours before the mills began.

Their gratitude to the nuns was constant and touching ; they economised upon their poor meals and scanty pence in secret committee, and presented an altar cloth with beautiful Irish lace. Their self-sacrifice for each other was no less great. Many passed the night by the bedside of the sick after a long working day ; during the prolonged frosts they gave their only bed coverings to the more necessitous ; lost or deserted children were adopted even by the poorest ; but more than all was the value the mill-girls set upon their own training. They hunted out their less edifying companions, and persevered until they could attract them to the convent ; many a lasting conversion of life was thus attained.

Through the mill-girls, too, the sterner sex beyond the convent walls is reached. Father and brothers were reclaimed by the national school children, notably the "infants" (technically speaking). Their artless rebukes, or promises, their convinced remark that the angels were looking on, or listening, would often make that space for silence in the soul which must precede a return. "Why don't you pray, father?" said a girl of seven. "I can't." "I'll teach you!" and she clasped her hands together and said simple words which he repeated after her. From that day father and child followed on the same path.

"I don't believe there's a man in the world who can't be managed by a little kindness!" said a nun enthusiastically, after some experience of Armagh. In the Irishman, at any rate, there is surely a deep-laid chivalry that makes him so peculiarly amenable to the influence of women and children for good.

The following portrait and incidents show Mother Digby as she was seen by two of her Irish daughters:

"When I first saw her, she had arrived as Vicar at Roscrea in 1874; we were all in the garden to receive her. From the window of the carriage she threw us a long look: her gaze, when it rested upon me, seemed to penetrate to the depths of my soul; an interior impression said: 'Here is your guide.' From that moment I resolved to open my heart to her completely, and after I had conversed with her for some time, I believe she knew every fibre of it. This visit had an immense influence on my whole life; I felt raised to new fervour and generosity; when she went away, her departure was to me so great a pain that it brought even physical suffering, but I felt withal strong and courageous. How we all loved our Reverend Mother Vicar! She allowed me to write to her at great length, and gave me short answers, but full of advice and encouragement. Once I was in a position of great embarrassment; I knew not how to deal with some one under my care. Ah! if our Mother Vicar were here! I sighed. That night, I dreamt that she came into my room. Oh, Reverend Mother, I cried. I knelt at her feet, and told all my difficulty. She indicated the line of action I should take; on awakening, I followed her advice, and the problem was solved in consequence. . . ."

A novice lay Sister was cruelly tried. She had heard of sad losses in her own family, and was quite resolved to go back to the world. At this juncture Reverend Mother Digby arrived on a visit to Ireland, and the poor child poured out her tale. "From to-day henceforward," said the Mother Vicar, "I will be a mother to you, in place of her whom heaven has taken away. God does not want a divided heart, and He has broken all the bonds that attached you, in order that he may possess your love without reserve." The sister felt her temptation vanish on the instant, nor did it ever return.

In this profoundly interesting country, Mother Digby, then, was constantly sustaining and urging forward her own regiment, so that it bore worthily its proper share in that perpetual work of regeneration for which the Church of God exists and strives.

The journal of her visits shows a constant progress. She left each time some profitable change behind her.

To say nothing of opportune gifts in every department, sometimes a great benefit in bricks and mortar was inaugurated, a chapel, a school, a fresh wing, at others, a partition put up, or a staircase extended, more often some fresh combination that no one else had thought of; leaving every one, without expense, the richer in time and resources; there was always a letting in of light and air, a removal of burdens, and a renewal of vigour in every sense. The number of pupils and of religious vocations continued to increase. She knew not only every lay and choir sister, so to say by heart, bearing in mind their family circumstances, and sometimes an endless array of nephews and nieces, remembered only from hearsay, but she knew, perhaps quite as well, for children are more easily fathomed, every pupil in the Irish houses, with many of whom she corresponded for years. Thus the whole immense family was kept together; for, if love produces union, love depends on knowledge, and knowledge largely on personal intercourse.

But this very union and efficiency was, on the other hand, threatened for a certain period by a serious danger.

As to the Society of the Sacred Heart, a few persons laid down loudly a plan of reform. Ireland must contain her own centre. There must be a noviciate in Ireland, totally Irish, managed by a mistress of the same nation, and giving the *couleur locale* to every subject under her charge. Why not? It is only true to say, at starting, that the idea arose outside the Irish houses, and that the overwhelming majority of the inmates never knew, till the end of their lives, or to this day, that such a notion ever existed. This real union of mind within the English-Irish vicariate made, of course, all the difference to the Mother Vicar.

But to come back to the "Why not?" of the separate Irish establishment. Because, thought Mother Digby, in the Society of the Sacred Heart, as in every large congregation, union means strength, and centralisation is the very hinge of union. In any hierarchical government, the sole object of a partition of authority among subalterns is that a labour too great for a single hand may be shared by several persons, each of whom, unimpeded in her own task, refers its main lines easily to the single head. No other principle has guided the foundation, even of a separate house; in the foundress's time no other motive has sub-divided her Society into vicariates. Italy, for instance, and Austria, were to be ruled by different vicars, not in order to be severally restrained to notions peculiar to these countries, but in order to facilitate the control of the Superior General (that is, of the spirit of the Institute) over each. That spirit is cosmopolitan, and ideas narrowed down to some territorial limit are so far from being a reason for establishing a vicariate answering to that limit, that the existence of such ideas would seem to necessitate a fusion in several directions.

Similarly, there was but one noviciate in the Society until the question of distances and numbers required a second, and later on, a third. The three, however, were each made as central as possible; and to counterbalance the separation, the aspirants, before the final vows are made, are united at the Motherhouse, as has been noted in the fifth chapter. Thus is union, by the constitutions, cemented by every external means that is possible; nor are the main lines of this system, of course, peculiar to the *Sacred Heart.*

But is it important that the girls of each country should receive an education characteristic of that land or nation? It has been considered in chapter x. that the best educators of English girls, for instance, are those who, besides a practical knowledge of what is essential to English training, have the width of mind which comes from personal study of the foreign systems, and that, as far as possible, in the countries themselves. These truisms are only touched upon in order to present the larger question in the full light of all its surroundings. It may be noted in passing, that every superior, and even subaltern, as well as the majority of the subjects in the Irish houses, were in those days Irish women. Outside susceptibilities on this head could not therefore be aroused.

A last important point may be suggested. In a society devoted to active works, these will be well conducted, all other things being equal, in proportion to the fitness of the labourer to his task. Now, here conditions are constantly changing. New foundations are required; new members join and disclose fresh aptitudes; the development of some increases in this direction or that, whilst others are retarded by ill-health, or die; a change of air is required—a gap must be filled up. One such move may necessitate several before the staff of each house is suitably provided; and, though exceptions are numerous, the ordinary changes are restricted to the houses of a single vicariate *inter se*. A mere consideration of a problem in arithmetical mutations will make obvious that the larger number of subjects the richer the choice, and so the more effective and convenient the combinations. *Per contra*, to break up a vicariate, especially a small one, into two, would reduce the efficiency of each (and so has experience shown) to perhaps one tenth or less of its original force. Each, as Mother Barat put it, is "a bird with one wing."

The whole question, therefore, of dividing the vicariate, to the thoughtful and conversant, took the form not of "Why not," but of "Why?" Who, in fact, was asking for a division? Cardinal M'Cabe, so rumour has said: and to be in real or supposed opposition to so erudite and virtuous a prelate and lover of Ireland, was for Mother Digby a most painful matter. At this juncture, Father Thomas Burke visited Mother Kerr, who happened to be in Ireland. The great Dominican was in possession of the Cardinal's mind, and thus reported his sentiments. "His Eminence has no concern whatever in the matter unless the nuns themselves wish it." These words removed a load from Mother Digby's mind.

But she was the last person to urge her own opinion unduly. Her letters to the Superior General at this time show an entire simplicity and submission. By every one in the least concerned in the matter, all that could be said, and all that there was to be known, was laid before the Mother General, to whom each one of her daughters was, as always, free to write in fulness and in privacy.

The Very Reverend Mother Lehon was a Belgian. She consulted her council, and deliberated with all the calmness of her nation. She decided that the status of the vicariate should remain as it was.

Thus did Mother Digby when, in 1893, she laid down her office of Vicar, hand over to her successor a heritage untouched in its integrity. Excitement soon died down, and a grand jury of thirty years has given its verdict in her favour.

CHAPTER XIII

A WONDERFUL CURE

" We should be
With all Dame Nature's laws in harmony,
Never demanding things quite out of season,
As would be overdoses of pure reason."
—KENELM DIGBY, *Temple of Memory* (new ed., Longmans, 1875), canto viii.

VERY soon after Mother Digby's first arrival at Roehampton, she had been invited by first one bishop, then another, to found a convent in his diocese; by Mgr. Chadwick, Bishop of Hexham and Newcastle, Mgre. Cornthwaite and Lacey, Bishops of Beverley and of Middlesborough respectively, as well as the Archbishop of Glasgow.

Lady Lothian had set her heart upon a Scottish foundation. She had promised a large sum towards it, and to disguise her generosity she made this offer under the form of restitution; for the Marquisate, in Reformation years, had acquired abbey lands in Scotland. She wrote several long letters to the Superior General, eagerly pressing the matter, and taking all the responsibility of her own insistence. Her request was refused, for the resources of money and subjects did not then permit an establishment in more than one town, and Brighton had been fixed upon. Lady Lothian sweetly acquiesces, adding:

"*6th July* 1874.

"You have given Roehampton a real treasure in Reverend Mother Digby. Under her prudent rule, Roehampton is an earthly paradise, and there is joy everywhere, amid the crosses. Alas, amongst these is the health of our dear Henrietta Kerr! . . ."

Lady Lothian, therefore, reserved her gift by deed,

162

ROEHAMPTON CONVENT, 1 90.

[*To face p.* 162.

devoting it to a foundation of the *Sacred Heart* in her native land, if made within fifty years' time ; and then, as if Glasgow did not exist, she aided Mother Digby in the arrangements for Brighton, half concealing her aptitude for business, and her tact, under a playful humility. She forgot her seventy years, and worked, gay as ever, under Mother Digby's direction. She travelled about London, or to and from Brighton, packed up and took trouble, and with Mother Digby suggested and arranged a hundred things material or otherwise, upon the scene of action—the little temporary house, to be used till the new building should rise from the ground.

The school grew and flourished ; later on an elementary school was added, and placed under government.

But, long before all this accomplishment, Mother Digby touched for the last time a hand that had done much for the making of Brighton ; the world and she had lost Lady Lothian.

Mother Digby wrote to the Superior General :

"ROEHAMPTON, 14*th May*.

" . . . I have very sad news, a telegram tells me that Lady Lothian died yesterday evening in Rome. . . . Her end was admirable . . . the fatal news has spread everywhere and the grief is universal, so deeply was she revered and loved."

The friends and lovers of Pio Nono gathered round him with the greater loyalty for the betrayals of which he had been the object. Lady Lothian had gone on pilgrimage to Rome in 1877, as part of the English deputation, to carry the offerings and congratulations of Catholics and their homage, on occasion of his episcopal jubilee. She spent a week visiting the well-known shrines. "My joy here is too great for this world," she wrote. On the very day fixed for the audience with the Holy Father she was seized with illness ; the sacrifice she made with perfect patience, and in three days, on

13th May, whilst the bells in Rome were ringing out the evening angelus, she passed to her rest.

Superhuman effort was needed between the years 1875 and 1879, perhaps more than at any other period of her life, for Mother Digby to execute every day her appointed task with a bodily instrument so frail as her own. Despite agonising headaches, and other painful ailments, she would give herself no respite, and at night she slept on an average only for a single hour. Nothing would induce her to take care of herself; for one thing she believed it to be useless.

Mother Kerr used her only resource by writing to the Motherhouse, and Mother Lehon sent positive orders that Mother Digby was to listen to her assistant's advice. In this way Mother Kerr obtained something, but so little that the Superior General wrote again, asking her dear daughter why she did not obey upon this subject, as upon every other. Mother Digby humbly replied, that she thought she had done as she was told; but would be more careful in future. Her standard, however, in this matter, was a low one, and her idea that no care would avail really seemed to have truth in it. The pain and sleeplessness continued. The Superior General, however, was determined to leave nothing undone, and summoned Mother Digby to Paris for the best medical opinion to be had there.

The Paris doctor said plainly that she was threatened with paralysis. The only chance of keeping off the evil was, he believed, the cruel remedy of a large seton inserted between the shoulders. Courageous as she was, Reverend Mother Digby had a peculiar horror of this operation from having seen it inflicted on her pony in days gone by. She did not, however, hesitate to have it carried out as soon as her own medical man, Dr Harper, had agreed with the French physician. By the testimony of the Mistress of health, who stood by, Mother Digby submitted to the incision unflinchingly, and without a quiver of muscle. She went about for the rest of the day as usual. The painful wound, dressed morning and evening, was kept open for many months; she could not be in any position of ease, and slept less even than before.

A Chilian lady paid her a visit at this time, and the nuns were horrified to see her greet their Superior after the mode of her nation, with a hearty accolade upon the back, administered just upon the seton. Mother Digby only laughed merrily, returning the salute in the spirit with which it was given.

The memory of Philip Harper brings into mind a typical physician of the olden days, not in his method or practice, for he was possessed of the highest technical skill in modern surgery, but in his moral weight, charity, and deep religious sense, he seemed to justify Kenelm Digby's opinion, that "medicine is the sister of philosophy."[1] His countenance, though rugged in feature, was not unlike in expression that of Titian's marvellous portrait, said, truly or no, to represent the painter's own physician.

Dr Harper's devotion and gratuitous service of the poor is indeed no rare thing in members of his noble profession; but his wisdom reached beyond the confines of bodily ailment, even to that of the soul diseased. His friends loved, trusted, and believed in him implicitly; his advice, like his alms, was given with infinite tact, and could be followed securely, for he was leech, lawyer, almost "father confessor" in one. The needy to whom he whispered words of hope, turning a wretched death-bed into one of consolation, cannot be counted; but the names, a surprising number, of those succoured by stealth in their poverty, was read in his account book after his death.

Need it be added that he spoke little, and so lacked what some persons consider an indispensable qualification for a lady's doctor, the ceaseless flow of cheery inspiriting talk that goes by the name of a "good bedside manner." He was calm, gentle, never put out, even where a man is usually off his guard—that is, in his family circle—and in spite of a disease borne for ten years, requiring the most troublesome remedies. "His

[1] Tertullian (quoted in *Orlandus*, p. 259).

serenity of character," wrote Father Gallwey, who knew him intimately, "was a sublime endowment."

His scientific knowledge was extensive ; he was urged to write, but constantly refused, for the making of a book would, he thought, curtail too much the time devoted to the "instant need of things."

He rose every morning at five, meditated for an hour, and attended mass at 7 o'clock—the latter he never omitted, even had the whole night been spent in sick calls. He communicated thereat with special fervour if the day were to see an important operation ; but in truth he had at all times the spirit of prayer.

To no one did he speak more freely than to Reverend Mother Digby, and she was well able to appreciate his worth.

She had been, ever since she came to England, at her old post beside the sick bed, and Dr Harper trusted her entirely as doctors always did. A lay Sister, who entered at Roehampton after this time, says :

"I was a simple country girl, from Lancashire, and I knew nothing at all. She formed me to everything in the infirmary. She used to say : 'Now, Sister, do the sheets so, and the bed this way, and get the table ready just like this, for the operation.' In Dr Harper's time she was his only assistant. He was quite happy with her by. In my time I was there too. She was in her white apron, helping like a doctor, tying up the veins and all that. She showed me how to help too. It *was* so interesting, all those operations!"

But Mother Digby, alas, was herself for some time the subject of such painful ministrations. Dr Harper was amazed at her extraordinary courage, and said to the infirmarian, "She is *made* for suffering!" The good doctor would preface the renewed fixture of the seton by a characteristic little sermon upon the profit of mortification, and when it was all over, she would say laughingly to Mother Kerr, "Dr Harper has been assuring me that the more he hurts the more grateful I shall be to him hereafter !"

For all this mastery over pain, Mother Digby's community could not be deceived as to the critical state of her

health.   Armed with warrants from the Motherhouse, they
summoned Sir Andrew Clark, one of the first authorities
in London.   He at once began to share the deep admiration always felt by the medical profession for Mother Digby.
"I should never forgive myself," he said, "if I failed to
prolong so valuable a life."   In 1878 Sir William Jenner
was also consulted.   He prescribed an absolute repose for
two complete years ; at that price he thought Mother Digby
might be cured.   Dr Harper was less hopeful, but also
declared rest to be necessary.   But rest was an impossible
prescription, if she were to remain in office at all.   She
continued much as before ; and the many who loved her
were filled with sad apprehension.   People thought and
said that her time would be short.   She knew their opinion.

In March 1879, a priest who was founding a mission
at Acton called to see her.   She was keenly interested in
his undertaking, and, in order to make up for him a large
parcel, went to a wardrobe, and pulled out too far an
upper drawer of considerable weight, full of church linen.
The drawer tipped over on her head, inflicting a heavy
blow.   Mother Digby, however, continued her occupa-
tions for an hour longer ; she was then forced to lie down,
and to confess the injury she had received.   The doctor
was called in and declared concussion of the brain.   Had
she lain down at once, he said, all must have ended fatally
within a very short time ; her chance of recovery lay in
the fact that she had remained on her feet so long.   Her
self-possession and power of endurance had, this time,
saved her life—so, at least, it was hoped.

The whole house was hushed in agonized suspense.
Everything went on as usual outside the sick-room, but
Mother Digby's daughters crept about silently, as if they
were within it.   As for the patient, brain fever set in,
and the left eye was totally blind ; but this news was
communicated only to the Assistant and Mistress of health,
and to the Motherhouse ; prayer ascended continually from
a thousand hearts.

In fifteen days the fever abated, and the eyesight began
to return ; but with the renewal of consciousness appeared
paralysis of the spine, which deprived the patient of all

power of movement. After four months of energetic treatment, she was able to rise and go about slowly, with much pain and difficulty, on crutches. She was now and then wheeled about the garden in a bath chair, and brought crumbs for the birds. The robins came eagerly to eat out of her hand, and perched on her head and upon her chair.

It was something for her daughters even to see Mother Digby again, but her helplessness and suffering were pitiable. Mother Kerr determined on a crusade of prayer for her recovery. On 12th December that year the Society of the Sacred Heart was to celebrate the centenary of the foundress's birthday. Madeleine Sophie Barat would surely add her prayers to those of her children. The Superior General entered into the plan with ardour, and notice of the novena was given to many houses of the *Sacred Heart*.

Mother Digby declined altogether to join in these petitions. In fact, a fresh access of suffering and weakness set in upon the first day, and on the ninth she became so ill that some pronounced it rash further to besiege heaven. God had shown His will, they said, in a contrary direction; and the prayers offered for her recovery seemed likely to win it for her by the remedy of a blessed death.

On the morning of the feast itself, Mother Kerr entered her room gently at three o'clock, and again at five. Her headache had been acute the whole night, and she said : " I am no better; what a disappointment for the children ! "

Holy Communion was carried to her at half-past six. Mother Kerr was kneeling by the bed. Mother Digby whispered : " If He wills, He will cure me." A quarter of an hour later Mother Kerr and the Infirmarian re-entered the room to dress Mother Digby for mass. " I think I am cured," said the latter with a smile. " Take away my crutches ! " She dressed without any assistance whatever, and walked with quick, firm step to the tribune, where the choir was prepared to execute the choruses of the feast day mass. The organist, petrified like the rest for a moment by Mother Digby's apparition, sat down and

pealed forth upon the instrument the chant of thanksgiving, *Quid retribuam*. The choir joined in with almost
a shout ; the congregation below felt a wonderful emotion.

" Mother Vercruysse [the assistant] left her stall," says the sub-
Mistress of Novices, "and returned in a moment to whisper in my ear
whilst she grasped my arm with all her strength : ' Reverend Mother
has walked to the tribune and is kneeling there perfectly cured.' The
feelings with which that mass was heard were indescribable. I
rushed to our Mother as soon as it was over. She looked full ten
years younger, and walked about with perfect freedom, laughing at
our delight and astonishment.

"At half-past nine, the distribution of the Ribbons of Merit took
place in the school. . . . When Mother Digby walked into the room,
the chaplain actually shed tears ! and the children clapped their hands
and jumped. Telegrams were sent to Paris and elsewhere, and
answers came pouring in all the rest of the day."

The Superior General summoned Mother Digby to
Paris to visit her immediately : she brought her crutches
with her, and laid them in the little room of Ste. Madeleine,
a sanctuary where the venerable foundress had prayed so
often. Whether miracle or not, all poured forth their hearts
in thankfulness to the Giver of all good ; for all were
satisfied that a great and visible grace had been granted
in answer to their prayers.

CHAPTER XIV

> " To have done, is to hang
> Quite out of fashion, like a rusty mail
> In monumental mockery."
> —KENELM DIGBY, *Godefridus* (Lumley, 1844), p. 231.

THE Empress Eugénie, who in April 1881 was staying near Roehampton, sent word to Mother Digby, the friend of her girlhood, that she desired to attend the services of Holy Week at the convent. By Mother Digby's delicate tact, the august and childless widow was received with a deep yet unobtrusive respect and sympathy. As she passed out of the chapel, the children were seen drawn up in the corridor *en grande tenue*; she graciously returned their salute. Her son's recent and tragic fate was fresh in every mind. Tears came to her eyes, as two charming little nieces of Mother Kerr, dressed in white, came forward to present a nosegay of violets, the Napoleonic emblem. Every day she attended the services, weeping often the while. She conversed long and frequently with Mother Digby, chiefly concerning her dead son. "He was the joy of my life," she said, "the sunshine of the house when he was there. He used to go about singing like a bird." And her old friend poured in consolation as she knew how. It was not difficult to find in the purity, goodness of heart, devotion to his country, grandeur of thought, and deep sense of religion wherein this young man had lived and died. Better, perhaps, than the Duc de Reichstadt, he deserved the name of *The Eaglet*.

The noviceship at Roehampton, which in 1872 numbered only three, rapidly became numerous, and numbers who offered themselves for the foreign missions were sent there.

ROEHAMPTON CHAPEL, 1890.

[To face p. 170

" ' May I go to the missions ? ' I asked. 'No! We must wait
till you win your spurs.' 'What are they?' She signified one
point, adding : 'That will keep you occupied till we meet again.' "

This readiness was now peculiarly welcome, and
Mother Lehon's visit to Roehampton in 1880 was the
occasion of maturing a long-formed plan.

A foundation at Sydney had been asked for by the
Archbishop as early as 1847. Mother Barat was obliged
to decline; time after time, however, the request had
been renewed, and notably in 1881 by Archbishop
Roger Vaughan, whose influence at that time was felt
throughout Australia. English subjects had begun to
multiply under Mother Digby's rule, and the Superior
General could now give a favourable answer.

This first migration was an important event in the
history of the Society of the Sacred Heart. The
foundresses had been formed by Mother Digby, and
had lived with her for long ; the separation was deeply
felt. On the eve of departure Father Morris, S.J., made
a moving address in the convent chapel, and few eyes
were dry.

Rome lay on the route of this first colony ; here they
saw Leo XIII. who blessed their enterprise.

The foundresses kept Mother Digby constantly
informed of their doings. They were received with
extraordinary goodness by Archbishop Vaughan who
assured them of the strong basis they would find in the
generosity and enterprise of the colonial character. The
Sisters of the Good Samaritan, worthy of their name,
assisted the nuns of the Sacred Heart in the most cordial
manner.

Archbishop—afterwards Cardinal—Moran who in 1883
succeeded to Dr Roger Vaughan, was in no way behind
in favour and kindness to the convent. His one cry
was that more subjects should be sent. The Bishop of
Adelaide, and several other prelates, pressed for foundations in their dioceses. In 1882 a reinforcement was
despatched to Sydney ; in 1886 a deputation of the
inhabitants of Melbourne begged for a foundation of the

Sacred Heart in that place.   The Archbishop, Mgr. Carr, came on 1st January 1887 to see Mother Digby and to press the matter.   The house was established accordingly in 1888 ; and she lived to see altogether seven flourishing establishments in Oceania.

Many keenly felt losses befell Roehampton in the eighties.   Already in 1879, Mother Kieran, still in the vigour of her age, was suddenly struck down by sickness. She had that special horror of death not rare with persons of her vivid imagination : "I have prayed to die in the winter," she once owned, "so as not to have the pain of leaving the earth in its summer beauty."   She passed away, in fact, before the spring, but all fear had vanished in a perfect trust.

Dr Harper died in 1883.   A week before his death, the hall bell rang in the middle of the night to summon him to a dying woman in the opposite house.   He was very ill indeed, but rose immediately, and staggered across the street ; it was his last professional act.   "I revere him as a saint," said Mother Digby.   She suffered a grievous loss in 1881, in Bishop Danell, to whom Father Coffin succeeded in the diocese of Southwark.   With Mother Digby, the new bishop bewailed his lot, in having quitted the walls of his cloister and his black Redemptorist habit, for the heavy burden of mitre, crosier, and purple.

Mother Kerr wrote :

"On 24th September : Bishop Coffin paid us a surprise visit. He saw each of the novices and community in private, and visited the sick ; then he went to the school." . . . "18th May 1883.   Mgr. Coffin came to spend some days with us, and passed the feast of the Sacred Heart here.   He loves to be surrounded by our children, whose simplicity he enjoys. . . ."

The year 1884 saw the passing of three heroic souls. Mother Digby spoke of them as "our trio."   On 18th January died Mother Lucy Laprimaudaye, who had spent herself in labours at Wandsworth, where she was one of the councillors.   Five months afterwards, Mother Emily Fitzgerald, her Superior, was no more.

Mother Emily belonged to a family group as remarkable as that of the Mallacs.   Her mother, Lady Fitzgerald, and her sister, were also nuns of the Sacred Heart.

Mother Emily Fitzgerald and Mother Laprimaudaye were of the same type of character, turning with contempt, even in early youth, from anything like feminine folly, though their gifts might have made vanity seem almost excusable.   Both won easily a life-long affection and trust, and each possessed the mental and moral energy of a man.   Their influence over the students was immense. "Reverend Mother is astonishing," writes Mother Kerr, "but the tears flow every time she speaks of Mother Emily."

Six months later they were to flow more freely still for the writer of these words.   Mother Kerr died on 1st December 1884.   Lady Georgiana Fullerton, lying on the bed of her last sickness, wrote to Mother Digby :

"I have this moment learnt that the angel of your house has departed for a place where her prayers will be for you a more power-ful support than any in this poor sad world, where she has suffered so much and worked so courageously until the end.   They feared to agitate me by the news, and so the long-looked-for misfortune has been concealed from me for many days.   How many of her dear ones have preceded her to heaven, and will be there to receive this flower of a family of saints, this child of the Sacred Heart! . . . As for me, I could never hope to see her again on this earth ; and, when things are thus, the next world seems nearer to us than the place of pilgrimage where we linger yet.   But, poor Reverend Mother, how I pity you ! . . .   My contemporaries are disappearing one after another, but she ! I thought only of her youth, and I had got accustomed to the prolonged miracle of her existence. . . ."

"You will be greatly surprised, when you have lost Mother Kerr, to find out what she really was," Mother Digby had said more than once to the community. Perhaps the majority of those who heard her were surprised, for they already considered the Mistress General as the personification of holiness and charm.   But it was not until her life could be more fully unrolled to their view, that they realized its spiritual worth.   Mother Digby began, by the advice of Father Morris and others, to collect material for a biography. As each chapter was written it was read aloud to Mother Digby, in company of a few whom she looked upon as the best judges; she weighed all criticisms with the utmost care. The *Life of Mother Henrietta Kerr*, by Mother Margaret Ward, was published in May 1886, and its success was instantaneous.

Mother Errington, her successor at Roehampton, writes to the Superior General: "Cardinal Newman wrote a touching letter of thanks on receiving the book. Cardinal Manning is proclaiming the part he himself had in her early formation, and the gravest Jesuit Fathers in England and France are praising this beautiful life." It should be added, that the rectitude of Mother Errington's own judgment and taste, freely exercised upon the book, gave her no small share in its composition.

On 25th January 1885, Lady Georgiana Fullerton was borne to the cemetery of Roehampton, where Mother Kerr and so many of her friends reposed. Two other graves had been prepared: to that on the left of Lady Georgiana, the body of her son was transferred; and in 1899, her husband, in his hundredth year, was laid on her right hand, on the spot where he had been often seen to kneel, looking up at the life-size crucifix which guards the triple tomb. A marble slab not far off marks the grave of the nonagenarian Lady Newburgh, who, like Lady Londonderry, died in 1884—two more irreparable losses to the Children of Mary's Congregation.

In 1889, Bombay lost its Archbishop, Father George Porter, Jesuit, Rector, and former Master of Novices at Manresa.[1] His character, of a mature holiness, was deeply impressed with British common sense, of which he seemed the impersonation. By its calm and even light, the affairs of those who consulted him always assumed their right proportions. Roehampton owed him much; amongst other things, he had laboured long,

---

[1] He is the author of several books on the spiritual life. *See* also *Letters of Father G. Porter* (Burns and Oates, 1891) to which Roehampton contributed much material.

with Mother Margaret Ward, at an English translation of the rule.   By papal insistence he had, in 1887, put on the mitre, and, like Bishop Coffin, mourned his dignities. As he bade farewell to Mother Digby, whom he had advised so often concerning the novices, he wished her "quality rather than quantity" in their regard.   His lonely mission made such slow progress that to himself his two years' labours showed no result.   The climate, as he foresaw, proved fatal to his health.   But he had, in the truest sense, given his life for his sheep, and that was reward enough.

The year 1890, closing a decade so full of mortality to Mother Digby's friends, was to begin with the death of her mother.

Here is a last portrait of this great lady :

"In 1874, and for a few years after, Mrs Digby Boycott[1] spent the summers at Haversham Grange, her place near Twickenham. She used to come now and again for an afternoon to Roehampton. I thought, as I watched her sitting on the terrace, or in a high-backed chair in the Red Parlour, that few queens could have looked more majestic.   Some people approached her with a certain timid reserve, and few would venture to express a difference of view. It is said that the well-known Bishop of Orleans, Monseigneur Dupanloup, whose ways were of the 'grand style,' became quite shy in her presence.   With her, Reverend Mother Digby was like a child, and would kiss her hand reverently on greeting her."

But Mrs Digby Boycott's stateliness concealed a sincere humility and great tenderness of heart.   Her mind preserved its vigour up to her death at eighty-four. In March 1890, she was interred in Roehampton cemetery, where her grave and its white marble cross have always been kept with assiduous care.   The children of Mabel Digby owe, indeed, a debt of gratitude to her mother.   In April it appeared as if mother and daughter were to rest side by side.

The ways of the French government becoming more and more troublous, a general congregation of the Society was to assemble shortly in Paris.   Reverend

---

[1] Her husband had assumed the additional name of Boycott for a time.

Mother Digby was about to join it when she suddenly fell ill. Peritonitis developed with terrible rapidity, and she dictated the following farewell letter to the Superior General :

"ROEHAMPTON, 14*th April* 1890.

"VERY REVEREND MOTHER, — It is an absolute necessity for me now to ask your pardon most humbly for all the faults of my religious life. Above all do I thank you for the motherly affection with which you have always received me, forgiven me, and believed in my deep and filial love for yourself. We can never thank God enough for giving you as a Mother to our family.

"I thank you once again; and whether Almighty God will deign to grant me some years yet for His service, or whether He means to call me to Himself, I have, I think, no other desire than that of His greater glory, and no other love than that for my mother the Society.

"Bless your poor daughter, Very Reverend Mother; I sign myself with the same joy as before,—Your very submissive and unworthy child [the signature follows in trembling characters] MABEL DIGBY, R.S., C.J."

On 25th April, she received extreme Unction; all the professed religious were present.

"You keep praying for my body," said Mother Digby, reversing the words of Louis XI. on a similar occasion, "but not for my soul!" "Ah! Reverend Mother," replied the Assistant, "it is important to keep them together!"

On 2nd May the tide began to turn; two days afterwards she was able to appear at her window, and to raise her hand in blessing upon the community assembled in the garden below. A few days afterwards she wrote:

"Many thanks, dear Mother and child, for your letter and good wishes. Pray that I may realize Our Lord's designs in leaving me here below, and that every breath may be drawn for His greater glory. . . . I pray often for you. . . ."

Towards the end of 1891 Bishop Coffin died, greatly lamented, and was succeeded by Mgr. Butt in the diocese of Southwark. His relations with Mother Digby will be treated on p. 199. The religious orders of the diocese have indeed at all times been singularly fortunate in their pastors.

Here seems the place to mention the friendship between Mother Digby and the Jesuit Fathers of Manresa House, Roehampton, their counsel, assistance, and many kindnesses. Three Masters of Novices stand out in turn : Father Peter Gallwey, Archbishop George Porter, and Father John Morris. The two latter have been already mentioned ; Father Gallwey is well described, and his relations with Roehampton are touched on in a review of his Memoirs lately published.[1]

"The impression which his whole being conveyed was that of a strong and many - sided nature brought under by great self-renunciation. . . . One thing alone mattered to him, the extension of God's kingdom on earth, and the conquest of souls to His service and love. Everything else was secondary and could be brushed aside."[2]

To these eminent names may be added that of Father William Kerr, S.J., the brother of Mother Henrietta Kerr, mourned at his death in 1913—it is not too much to say—by all Wimbledon, his parish, where he effected an extraordinary good.

About mid-day on 2nd January 1892, a stranger rang the door bell, and said that the joyful sounds of the children at their games left him no doubt that the nuns must be ignorant of news that had cast all England into mourning. They were, in truth, greatly grieved to learn that the young Duke of Clarence and the aged Cardinal of Westminster had been carried off by influenza that very day. Despite the late Cardinal's continued hostility, Mother Digby's sincere admiration for his great qualities and holiness of life had never failed.

When Dr Vaughan succeeded to the diocese, Mgr.

[1] F. Gavin, S.J., *Memoirs of Father P. Gallwey* (Burns and Oates, 1913).
[2] *The Month*, September 1913.

M

Weld, a most devoted friend of Mother Digby, and one who had the idea of a London foundation greatly at heart, took upon himself to sound the new Archbishop on the subject. In June 1891, he returned from his visit greatly depressed. Dr Vaughan had vehemently uttered the whole tale of prejudice that he had inherited from his predecessor. He hardly appeared to heed the assurance of Mgr. Weld, that the nuns of the Sacred Heart would be willing to work for the poor of his diocese.

After the departure of his visitor, however, the Archbishop began to reflect: with his natural impulsiveness, he set off at once, and arrived unannounced at Roehampton. Reverend Mother Digby wrote to the Superior General on 26th June:

"Monseigneur talked much to me of the conversion of England, and became gracious, though he remained cold. He will, I think, rather bear with us than welcome us to his diocese, for his prejudices are of long date."

The nuns spent many months hunting for a house in the poorest parts of the East End, where the Archbishop wished them to establish a school. At last a temporary building in Canningtown was about to be fixed upon.

Suddenly—everything in the matter was unexpected—the idea struck the Archbishop to offer the Seminary at Hammersmith, not suited, he thought, to its original purpose, to the nuns of the Sacred Heart. It was no sooner said than done; and the Society made immense sacrifices to meet his demands. Thus the masterpiece of Bentley in the Tudor Gothic, termed by Oscar Wilde the finest building of the kind executed in the nineteenth century, and seeming to breathe the traditions of an Oxford College in its cloisters and quadrangle, became devoted to the works of the *Sacred Heart* in regard to all classes of society in London. The arms of Cardinal Manning on the exterior of the seminary—surrounded by the beautiful stone work detail of which John Bentley was a master—face towards the large school, added since his time, for the "Children of the People"; and his portrait looks down from the walls of the panelled room where the Children of Mary hold their meetings.

Cardinal Vaughan, as soon as the seminary was purchased, showed a most paternal interest in the new works established there, and above all in the four hundred little boys and girls who receive not only the requirements of a government education, but are rooted in the principles as dear to himself as to his predecessor. Nothing, in fact, could be more cordial than his Eminence, in his visits to both Hammersmith and Roehampton. " I wish for nothing better," he said to Mother Digby, "than that you should make at once two other foundations in my diocese!" "I assure your Eminence," she replied with a smile, "that for the present our Society is at an end of its resources."

Much had to be done in 1892 before the Seminary was fit for its new inhabitants. Many a time, an omnibus filled with nuns, amongst whom was Mother Digby, clad like the rest in working apron, drove over from Roehampton to help in the arrangements. When all was complete, she assembled the chosen community, and encouraged them with her own lofty enthusiasm.

"The law of sanctity is the law of separation; therefore it is that we have these partings and uprootings. . . . You will go in the spirit of faith; you are not sent to *a class of society*, but to *souls*. They are waiting for you; in London there are five millions amongst whom you will work and pray; our going there would be worth while, if only to save a single one. . . . You will feel weariness . . . but, buffeted by sorrows and by difficulties, you will cling the more to principle and to God."

The Superior chosen for Hammersmith, Mother Alice Vinall, tells in her autobiography that she had been for many years in an Anglican Convent at Oxford, under the direction both of Bishop Samuel Wilberforce, and of Doctor Pusey. She made known to both in turn her doubts as to the Anglican position, and received the usual answer, that the only safe course was to remain "in the Church of her baptism." In 1850, during the yearly vacation permitted to the nuns, she returned to

her family, and visited Father Gallwey. She gradually
became convinced that it was her duty to enter the
Catholic Church; her parting with the Superior of the
Oxford convent in 1865 was acutely painful on both
sides. She spoke to Father Gallwey of her wish to
become a nun; he finally sent her to Roehampton in
1879.

"I was at once dominated by the influence of Reverend
Mother Digby," she wrote, and at the age of fifty she
became once more a docile novice. Almost as soon as
professed, she was made Assistant at Wandsworth, and
afterwards Superior in one house after another. She was
typical of what is now called the "old type" of English-
woman — simple, austere to herself, robust in character,
and tender of heart; entirely to be trusted in her judg-
ments and adherence to principle. She was kind and
dignified in demeanour; she had been educated by her
father, an Oxford man, and her accent and language
possessed a university distinctness and precision. Mother
Digby, who seldom openly praised the living, expressed
more than once her entire trust in this devoted daughter
of the Church and loyal servant.[1]

In November 1892, Reverend Mother Digby visited
Rome for the first time. Her feelings may be imagined
by the many whose hearts are as Catholic as her own.
She was one of the three Vicars appointed by the Superior
General to present to Leo XIII., on his sacerdotal jubilee,
the homage of her Society, and its offering of Peter's
pence. The Holy Father admitted the nuns to his private
chapel on All Saints' Day. It was touching to hear his
strong and penetrating voice linger upon the words of
that day's gospel, *Beati qui persecutionem patiuntur*,[2] accompanied by an expressive gesture of the head. After mass
the nuns were conducted to the Throne Room. The Pope
entered, exclaiming eagerly: "Where are the nuns of
the Sacred Heart?" He conversed with his usual animation, but now and then with an accent of intense sadness.
"Pray for me, pray! They are persecuting the Church!

[1] Mother Vinall died in 1906.
[2] Blessed are the persecuted.

They ill-treated the poor pilgrims who came to Rome to see me; they call out, 'Death to the Pope!'" "And we," replied one of the Mothers, "have come with the rest, to say: 'Evviva il Papa!'" "Wicked men," he went on, "are deceiving the young, and leading them astray. . . . I count much on your prayers, but sacrifices, too, are needed. Which of you will offer yourself as a victim?" "All, all!" exclaimed his audience. He left Mother Digby and the rest deeply affected by the interview.

Before leaving Rome Mother Digby visited the seven Basilicas. To make this pilgrimage, said the Cardinal Protector of the Society, was not only a privilege, but a duty, to even cloistered religious who come to the Holy City. She returned to England in time to assist at the jubilee of the English foundation, celebrated at Roehampton on 6th December.

Large numbers of the clergy were present; the purple of the canons, the priests' cottas, the various habits of the religious orders, both men and women, the children's white dresses, the decorations, all wore a jubilee look. A multitude of "old children," from every school generation since 1841, arrived with eagerness to spend the day at their former home. The poor children, and the students from Wandsworth, were present, and a number of children and of nuns from every house of the vicariate, guests of Roehampton during the week, and all things, carefully planned by Mother Digby, passed excellently well.

Father John Morris, a friend of twenty years' standing, preached the sermon, naturally a retrospect of the past fifty years, of which twenty had been dominated by Mother Digby's influence. His discourse was full of feeling, expressed with his customary delicacy; he looked to the future, when perhaps another jubilee, and again another might be celebrated, and dwelt upon the great lesson that the house was but a lodging, wherein to prepare for a lasting home. His words, some months hence, when his voice was heard no more, were recalled with a sigh. The Blessed Sacrament was then exposed, and a statue of the Sacred Heart, the gift of the vicariate, was erected upon the terrace and solemnly blessed by Dr Weathers, Bishop of Amycla.

In the evening, a historic piece,[1] composed for the occasion was produced : the time and place were those of the introduction of the Sacred Heart by Père de la Colombière at the court of Charles II. The little actresses played with feeling and spirit, and John, Hungerford Pollen, whose forte lay in historic costume, assisted at a rehearsal, and gave advice as to dresses and scenery.

After the final Benediction of the Blessed Sacrament, Reverend Mother Digby read aloud, in the name of all Roehampton, an act of consecration to the Sacred Heart, summing up the whole meaning of the day.

"*Most Sacred Heart of Jesus, in union with so many who have loved and served Thee in this home of Thine, we conse-crate ourselves anew to Thy glory and Thy love. For fifty years this house has re-echoed the sound of Thy praises ; it has witnessed the acccomplishment of generous sacrifices. Here lies the hallowed dust of those, who being dead, yet speak to us. . . .*

"*O Lord Jesus, may this house please Thee to-day, as in the past, by our service and our homage. . . . Thou hast promised to bless every place where the image of Thy Sacred Heart is exposed; here it is placed before our eyes. . . . May we all after following in Thy footsteps to the end, repeat, fifty years hence, whether on earth or in heaven, with a new generation, what we utter to-day.*

"*Glory, honour, and love, be to the Sacred Heart of Jesus, for evermore, Amen.*"

Congratulations, besides those of the Superior General, arrived from all parts of the world—from North and South America, and Australia, where so many were found who owned Roehampton for their cradle. Finally, the Papal blessing was telegraphed, putting the seal on a day full of emotion and thanksgiving.

Father John Morris was the leading champion of the English martyrs. With what ability he forwarded the cause of their canonisation can be read in his Life.[2] He

[1] *Maids of Honour*, since published.
[2] John Pollen, S.J., *Life and Letters of Father John Morris* (Burns and Oates, 1896).

would bring to Roehampton most valuable relics of the martyrs, with an engrossing tale attached to each. The Superior of St Mary's Convent, York, a place of eminent historic interest,[1] came to Roehampton at Father Morris's request to hold conferences with himself, and other authorities concerning the martyrs and the promotion of their cause, Mother Digby and the community listening with the greatest sympathy to the narrations of this Superior.

Blessed Henry Morse, of Mother Digby's own family, was naturally the object of her devotion. She possessed a copy of his fine authentic portrait. His career was a romance of chivalric heroism. "Come," he cried, when they told him that his time was near at hand, "Come, my sweetest Jesu, that I may be united to Thee in eternity! Welcome, ropes, hurdles, gibbets, knives, and butchery! welcome, for the love of Jesus my Saviour."[2]

Father Morris, in August 1893, was about to preach upon the text from the Gospel of the Sunday. He pronounced the words : *Render to Cæsar the things that are Cæsar's* . . when an expression on his face told of a supreme struggle within. Grasping the front of the pulpit, with a superhuman effort he completed the great sentence—*and to God—the—things—that are God's*. Then he fell back lifeless into the arms of two gentlemen, who rushed up the staircase, whilst a priest from the altar pronounced over him a last absolution. No words better than his last utterance could have summed up his own life, or that of the heroes for whose honour he had done so much.

The year 1893 was eventful. In October the tomb of the foundress in the crypt at Conflans, near Paris, was opened, with the solemnity exacted on such occasions, before eminent ecclesiastics, the accredited members of the Roman commission. The holy body was found entire and incorrupt, though the coffin, and everything around it, had fallen to pieces in the damp earth. "With what ardour," wrote the Superior General, Mother Lehon,

---

[1] See *St Mary's Convent*, 1886-87 (Burns and Oates, 1887).
[2] Challoner, *Memoirs of the Missionary Priests* (Richardson, 1843), vol. ii. p. 285.

in her circular letter upon the event, "with what ardour did I not promise, as I grasped that venerable hand in mine, that we should all redouble in generous efforts to show ourselves her true daughters!" This letter had been looked for with breathless interest; the preservation of the body of the revered foundress, though not a miracle in the technical sense, was a matter of exceeding joy to Mother Barat's daughters. Evidence of her resplendent virtues was not wanting, and, her cause being officially introduced at Rome, she was now to be known, *ipso facto*, as the *Venerable Madeleine Sophie Barat.*

CHAPTER XV

" ' Tell me, what is your philosophy?' says Sophylus to Euthyphron, in one of the dialogues of Hemsterhuis; to whom the latter replies: 'My philosophy, dear Sophylus, is that of children; it is that of Socrates; it is that which is found at the bottom of our heart, of our souls, when we take pains to seek for it.'"—KENELM DIGBY, *Godefridus* (Lumley 1844), p. 180.

"IT is easier to find three excellent Superiors," Mother Digby is reported to have said, "than a single Mistress of Novices."

This office, indeed, is looked upon in every religious order as one of the most far-reaching in its action. The training given to the novice answers to that which a child receives at its mother's knee, affecting in a subtle way the whole career. Mother Digby, in 1892, had fulfilled this function for twenty years.

Amongst the novices were some capable of a wider influence for good. She had an unerring eye for the fittest, and for the particular bent of each. Not infrequently she saw promise even in awkward beginnings, and where other persons of experience expected only failure. A tiny indication often sufficed. " I can tell," she once said, " a novice's capacity for organisation by the way she serves at table." How many scores of Superiors in the various grades, of Infirmarians, of mistresses in the school or noviceship, owed to her the early recognition of their gifts, and development to the uttermost! But it was their formation to virtue, their rooting in God's love, that she set before all else. If this side failed, her subjects, however useful in outward work, were, as she sadly expressed it, "a disappointment to her."

"Her penetration was marvellous. She saw some one for the first time, whom I thought I well knew. 'She is not frank,' said

Mother Digby to me. I was greatly taken aback; no one had ever held such an opinion. It would have been well had the warning been taken in time. Years afterwards the latent uncorrected fault produced its results. She told me again, concerning a most devout Catholic, that his faith, and that of his children, was in danger. This seemed at the time incredible, but was sadly confirmed. Was this natural insight, or some gift beyond? Other instances I could bring forward, and words of a hopeful nature verified where no one looked for hope. But these, I think, were messages given her from above."

In 1878, Miss Josephine Errington — the niece of Archbishop Errington, who was at one time chosen to fill the see of Westminster — was sent by her director, the well-known Dominican preacher, Father Thomas Burke, to Roehampton. She was at once received as a postulant by Mother Digby. When this first interview was over, the latter said to the sub-Mistress of Novices: "I have just admitted Mother Kerr's successor." The sub-Mistress, knowing what an assemblage of gifts were considered by Mother Digby essential for such a post, and aware that she had been forming another very remarkable person with this view, heard her words with astonishment; but they were fulfilled.

As to secular affairs also, Mother Digby's power of intuition seemed now and then akin to prophecy.

" That will never come to pass," she said of a marriage that had been arranged. No cloud was then on the horizon. But her prevision was fulfilled. "How *did* you guess?" "I do not know," she answered, "I felt it." Such instances might be multiplied by the score.

As to her training of the novices a few testimonies of this time are chosen. Their substance is repeated many times in the reminiscences gathered up after Mother Digby's death. Each of the following paragraphs is by a different hand.

"I came to Roehampton in 1874, with two other novices, and felt at first bewildered by the contrast between our quiet and beautifully regular life at Conflans, and the austere practical training we found here. Instructions on the Rule were always full of profound teaching, and went straight to the heart; but words alone, no matter how beautiful, did not count for much with our Reverend Mother. She taught us by example, and looked to our conduct to show how much and in what manner we understood religious life. We were often sent off, unexpectedly, to work in the house or school; our Mother, in working apron like ourselves, would lead the way, and we helped her to carry bricks, or distemper the walls."

"The recreations with her were delightful. In my day she was active and agile, and would often dart suddenly down a side path, or return on her steps, and thus keep us on the alert. Sometimes she took us to pick up fruit, to clean out the garden drains with our hands, to clear the pond of fish and other creatures when the water was low, to venture on rather uncertain ice, or run up and down steep banks. If any one showed some fastidiousness she was led playfully to overcome herself. 'Those hands look too white!' she said, and their owner at once set to work in such a way that they were soon rough and ready."

"I became a postulant in 1881, and gradually began to feel that tender kindness was not all of her, but that I had a master. Thus she both won and held me; and ever since, this was to me her power and charm. Few persons have been able to move me so much, or so painfully; none, in the long run, to give me so great a sense of security. But the price had to be paid, the self-surrender must be complete, to gain from her what she had to give."

"Her open, absolutely straight ways, made me accept the most unpalatable truths; she could annihilate pride, but showed so motherly an interest, that I left her more grateful and attached than ever. How frankly she accepted explanations if I had been blamed without cause! She trusted me so unmistakeably that I turned instinctively to her in distress. And none was more accessible than she."

" 'You are your own heroine, my child,' she said to me one day, 'but the heroism is completely lacking!' This was somewhat painful, but so true, that I laughed outright—and then she did, too."

"If an outburst of temper revealed defects yet unknown, she would say: 'Are you not glad to be found out?' Or, if I went to her boiling over with indignation about some trifle, she sent me away to do some task, and come back. The wolf had turned into a lamb meanwhile."

To another the following appeal appears to have lasted for a lifetime : " *Will you not be very faithful?* "

"One day I accused myself of a certain fault. She seemed to excuse it, and I said, astonished, 'How can you *understand* such meanness, Reverend Mother?' 'From my own heart, my child,' she answered humbly."

"No one could be more tenderly solicitous in her sick nursing, yet none could teach a more supreme indifference to the body's needs. One of her daughters was in anxiety before an operation. 'Leave yourself to God and your Mothers,' she said gently; and her words acted at once as a sedative."

"She had a great heart, full of sympathy for every human misery and weakness, yet so high above it all in her calm serenity. . . . I required frequent reproof for my many faults, but I never left her room without an intense longing for that higher life of which she herself seemed a most perfect type."

"Eighty-six happier people it would be difficult to find," Mother Kerr had written in 1880 to the Mother-house, "than those under our Reverend Mother at Roehampton." The following sketch, from a single hand, deals with Mother Digby's formation of the young religious under her care, and reflects also her own portrait during the decade of the eighties.

"In the training of young religious, Rev. Mother Digby kept on the same line that Mother Goetz had given her for the noviceship : '*Formez-les moi fortes et surnaturelles.*' She would not let them loiter in the way of perfection, or look a second time at something that grace had asked for. She insisted on self-command even in material things, and exercised us on ladders, scaffoldings, and single planks at any height. 'Go up by those ladders to the bell turret and see how the world looks from there.' She asked me to cross the open joists on the floor of a new building, giving her an arm to lean upon, and adding : 'Give the other arm to Rev. Mother G——' And the least remonstrance at having to maintain two such precious lives in that precarious balance seemed quite out of place. We would have done anything at her word without thinking it strange. All of a sudden would come a check, 'No, you are not able to do that'—some very small thing it might be; and how one winced at the words until it became clear that it was for the health of the *soul* that precaution was taken, and that it was only another string of one's instrument that she had selected to tune. This never lasted long; she would propose some inspiriting impossibility to be made possible, and one had the comfort of knowing that one was not intended for the 'Invalides.'

"Above all, we were not allowed to betray the slightest anxiety about her. Any manifestation of this sort was promptly followed by what the nurses used to call 'something to cry for.' She would do something still more daring to give us courage! When she was recovering from illness, and could only go in a bathchair in the garden, her pleasure was to let go at the top of a long incline and steer herself round the walks at top speed, until she reached the level, and the bathchair stopped of itself. We might run beside or behind, but to lay a finger on the chair was forbidden. Once she chose a winding walk for this exercise, with awkward turns; the chair started with a touch, she was steering, and, as she came to a bad corner, she realised the prospect of an upset. There was nothing for it but to drive straight on, and crash handsomely into a mass of rhododendrons and pæonies which stopped the chair. She enjoyed it immensely.

"'Why do you take more care of my body than of my soul?' asked impertinent youth, curbed in a desire for corporal austerities. She did not generally think it worth while to answer the question *why*; it was an attempt to carry the forbidden fruit of the tree of knowledge, and obedience was a sufficient answer to all curious enquiry after reasons and purposes. But this time she condescended to reply: 'You may have another superior who can do for your soul what I have left undone; but if I let you damage your body it can't be repaired.'

"She would never admit shyness as a covert into which one might withdraw; it was 'no excuse.' Shyness was not an apostolic virtue, it had to be given up; and she would prepare and offer many occasions excruciating to a shy person, for this exercise. 'I don't expect to have to open this subject with you again,' she said, 'you must be thoroughbred in everything.' She would not admit that an opportunity had been lost, and should be merely regretted; one had to go back and begin afresh, which of course doubled the difficulty. But she carried out herself so consistently the advice which she gave to a beginner as Mistress of Novices, that one would have followed her example anywhere. 'Let them see that you are going on to God, and come along with you if they will, but *go on to God* . . . catch at every stick or straw that will help you, only *go on*.' Thus she communicated her own taste for difficulties. '*I want you to be all things to all because you are serving God in the present moment.'*   This is, in a short formula, the summary of much of her teaching.

"What she said of prayer and the inner life was in harmony with all we knew and guessed about her own. 'The only time when we can legitimately take the strain off is in prayer,' she once said ; and all she taught us showed how God possessed the whole of her inner life and thoughts. But all was on the simplest lines as far as her teaching went ; study and imitation, self-annihilation, before God ; He to be all, and everything else to be nothing, especially self. Her favourite words for prayer : '*Tu solus Sanctus, Tu solus Altissimus*'[1] summed it all up, and the other best loved words : '*Per ipsum, et cum ipso, et in ipso,*[2] gave the key to her adaptation of the inward to the outward life. She had great and trustful thoughts of God. To one who found a Retreat by Pere Judde depressing and even alarming in the meditations of the first week of the Exercises, she answered in a tone convinced and convincing beyond any argument: 'But don't you know the heart of our Lord better than that ?' and the words expressed her own experimental knowledge of God's love "[3]

The lay sisters, too, have left their portraits of Mother Digby. Only a few paragraphs are chosen from a wealth of highly significant detail.

"Reverend Mother Digby used to speak of us as 'Our Sisters.' We all knew that our perfection was the great thing she had at heart ; she never let anything pass. When we went to her for direction she would be severe if we had not made the progress we ought, and if there had been improvement she would tell us so with pleasure. Her great wish for us was that we should cultivate interior life, and she used to say that she envied us at our work because it was so easy to be united to Our Lord. If she had been allowed when she entered religion she would have been a Sister. She loved our kind of work. "

"Twice I heard her reprove severely, once a Sister who was careless with the children and once for want of silence."

"One day I owned to her : 'Well, I grumble at little things.' 'Yes,' she said, 'that is the Englishman's way ; he always wants

[1] Thou alone the Holy, Thou alone the Great One.
[2] Through Him, and with Him, and in Him.
[3] J. S.

a little more of this, or a little less of that.   But supposing Our Lord should come to us crowned with thorns ; could we grumble then ? ' "

A cook says :

' "She was my sunshine.   Her very presence calmed us, and put everything straight.   She always said a word of encouragement that took away all fear.   When the ladies' retreat was going on, and we were terribly busy, she would come and say : ' I have made my examen early, Sister, so as to help you,' and then she would set to work.   She would ask you how to do things on purpose, for she knew quite well how to do them herself.   There was nothing she did not know ; she taught me how to make a sauce.   But she didn't mind who she asked advice of, and she'd take it when she got it. The black pots kept breaking and cracking—I don't know why, but I got into great trouble about it, and they said I must go to Reverend Mother.   She said : 'Never mind, Sister, they won't break or crack any more.'   Nor they never did.   Her laugh took away all my trouble—it took away mountains."

" I remember once at our mid-day recreation Our Mother came in with one of the Mothers to see about something in the Sister's room : it happened to be Sister Johanna's birthday (she was ninety), and it had for some years past been Sister Johanna's custom to go and get Our Mother's blessing on that day : on this particular birth-day she had tried several times, but had not found Our Mother in her room, so the moment she saw her come in to the Sisters' room, she darted up to meet her, and Our Mother caught sight of her and darted forward ; they met in the middle of the room and both knelt together for a kiss of peace, and Our Mother would not rise till Sister Johanna did."

" One of our Sisters had received the last Sacraments, and our Mother did not like to part with her, so our Mother went to the chapel to pray; after some time, she came back smiling, and said to the Sister, as she blessed her, ' My child, you will not die this time.'   The Sister lived for many years after this."

" In 1895, when the foundation in Aberdeen took place, I had the happiness of seeing her again in Scotland.   It was at this time I told her that she had come to me one night and told me exactly what to do, in a difficult moment.   She did not deny it."

Mother Digby's love for little children has been mentioned more than once.   This feeling was warmly

reciprocated, and she often took the youngest among
the junior school with her into the garden, and delighted
in their company and conversation. The little ones, too,
have left their portraits of Mother Digby, and must be
allowed to present one at least—the most complete.

"My father having a government appointment in the colonies,
I was of necessity sent to school at a very early age. Thus it came
to pass that, almost in infancy, I was brought into touch with Rev.
Mother Digby. She seemed to find expression for her deep affection
for some members of my family in the lavish love she poured out
upon me. She filled my life with sunshine and happiness. She
not infrequently made herself my playmate; and such a one, I
thought, as understood better than any one else in the world the
joys of hide-and-seek. Countless were the games of cricket I
played in her room, her coal scuttle for wicket, the coal shovel for
bat, and her wool for my ball. Oh! the delight it was to be with
her in the garden, weeding or planting or the like; learning to root
up with a steady gentle pull the dandelions with their long tapering
roots, or tear up as a trial in strength the young saplings growing
out of place. Sometimes I would lure her into the boat on the
pond, and pretend I was rowing her round the world; at other
times she would tell me to bring out my stilts, and, when mounted,
dare me to cross some fence or other obstacle; even to walk through
the pond on them, which feat, however, ended in a drenching and
an attempt at a swim. What would I not have ventured indeed in
order to win 'well done' from her? It was such a word as this,
coming from her, I think, that went further than anything else to
inculcate into us children that fearlessness that seemed a special
gift of hers to inspire.

"Perhaps nothing appealed so strongly to my admiration as her
courage. I had seen her, lying back in her chair, white and motionless with pain, yet no word or sigh escaping her, and as I watched,
I wondered at her endurance.

"I myself had such difficulty in rising early for mass, that
dispensation was readily granted me to sleep on. It was on one
of these occasions that Mother Digby chanced to pass through
the dormitory. The bell for the late risers had gone, but I had
not yet disturbed myself. Gently pulling aside the curtain of my
cubicle, she looked at me for a moment, and then said, as she
passed on: 'How utterly cowardly!' Stung to the quick, my
resolution was made. When my school days closed I could look
back over the intervening years and say that never since that day

had I missed daily mass, unless after a sharp encounter with the infirmarian, before whose authority I sometimes had to yield.

"If Mother Digby could reprove severely—and I might cite many other instances—what sufficient can I ever say of her tenderness? At the time of my father's death, she had my bed moved into her day room, and sent a nun to sleep with me. In the morning when I woke I found Mother Digby sitting by my bed. I would now and again give way to passionate grief; then she caressed me, and spoke of God and heaven and of the father taken from me, in a way that could not fail to comfort a child's heart. 'Rev. Mother,' I one day said to her, 'I think you must be a great saint.' She turned to me and said: 'Promise me you will never say such a silly thing again.' 'But,' I argued, 'if it is true?' She insisted. I went somewhat disconsolate to my aunt next door. 'You must never say Rev. Mother is a saint: she does not like it and says it's not true,' I began. 'Saints always speak like that,' was the answer. So I returned to Mother Digby to throw this new light on the matter. Presently I asked: 'How do people become saints?' 'By being very obedient when they are small.' There was an unpleasant allusion in this. 'I think,' I said after a pause, 'I think I would rather be a martyr.' 'Well perhaps you may be some day, but a *saint* you *must* be.' The words sank in, in a way that seemed to admit of no gainsaying. How often, only God has counted, did that word turn the scale on the side of right and duty in my childish efforts *to be obedient, to be a saint.*

"'How much do you love God?' was a question she often asked me. 'As much as I can stretch,' I would say, holding out my arms to their full width. 'And how much do you love me?' she once added. Nothing less than my widest stretch would do for *her*, I felt, yet I knew she would tell me God's love must be the widest. 'I do not know,' I said after a pause, 'but I can show you,' and so saying I flung my arms round her neck and hugged and kissed and clung to her so tightly that she was obliged to call for mercy."

What light do Mother Digby's letters throw upon her personality? Fifteen hundred business letters, written by her, as Superior, to the Motherhouse, and covering a period of about thirty years, are preserved. There is generally in each a frank detail of the affair in hand, a

N

suggestion of ways and means, a declaration of entire adherence to the eventual decision, a tone of affectionate respect as well as an entire absence of self-assertion. No play of fancy, no poetic power, peeps out anywhere, as they may even in business letters of a writer thus gifted. But a few points emerge : the terseness of the composition, not so easy a matter in French, where ordinary politeness requires a more ceremonious phraseology ; and the invariable evenness of the writing. The firm characters are not beautiful, but each is faultless and legible.

This evenness, say her friends, is the only quality of the writing that in any way recalls Mother Digby. In her youth she possessed a handsome and characteristic English hand, but her mistress of writing in the noviceship asked her to imitate another. Mabel Digby obeyed to the letter. However, a professed judge of calligraphy said of this later hand writing : "The writer must be *generous to a fault.*" Taking generosity in a large sense, the single phrase is perhaps as good a one as could be found to estimate Mother Digby's whole nature.

A few letters, of an intimate nature, to those subject to her, are scattered over the narrative ; others are hinted at. They say much in a few words ; they are strong, like herself, now stern, now tender. More often her answers are conveyed in two or three lines, intense in meaning, written upon the letter that has been addressed to her.

The following are chosen out of a long continued correspondence with an absent daughter. The recipient had left Roehampton ; the change was keenly felt, and Mother Digby replies to a first letter :

"MY VERY DEAR CHILD,—I have read and re-read your letter this morning, and thank our dear Lord a thousand times for its tone, and the disposition it reveals. May He deepen still more that unbounded, unquestioning trust in His directing Providence over you, made known by and through your superiors. Very soon you will see the wisdom of the decision taken, and to which you have already adhered in the plenitude of your will. God is good indeed to you, and in Him do I trust fully for a happy and useful future for you, when you will be *radicata et fundata* in true religious spirit and devotedness.—I am, as ever, and more than ever, in C.J.M., your very affectionate Mother, M. D."

"MY DEAR CHILD,—My wishes for you for the New Year are these: detachment, confidence, and joy, to be obtained by mortification. I want you to live *ad hoc*, where you are; not in past memories or future fears. Am I too ambitious? Pray for me, and believe me ever, in C.J.M.—Your affectionate Mother, M. D."

A young religious had failed completely in a post of some difficulty; she received from Mother Digby's secretary the following letter:

"Reverend Mother says (I write the words at her dictation) that it is little wonder that you failed; for you did not understand how to obey. When humility and obedience are wanting, nothing is to be expected but failure. . . ."

Two short letters from Mother Digby followed in due course:

"MY DEAR CHILD,—Your last letters have consoled me, as well as the way in which you took my correction. Continue always to allow those in authority to tell you what is wanting, what you could do better, and all will be well with you."

To the same.

"I cannot say how pleased I am at my dear daughter's resolutions [upon self-forgetfulness]. But Rome was not built in a day, and you must not be discouraged if N. N. (the name of the recipient) reappears persistently on the scene. Treat her with silent contempt, but do not make a fuss, and soon our dear Lord and Master will give calm and strong peace—His own—that which passeth all understanding. Pray well, and believe me in C.J.M.—Yours devotedly, M. DIGBY, R.S.C.J."

Mother Digby was perhaps better reflected in her

conversation than in her letters.   Her words were sparing ;
in a dialogue she listened with sympathy, and to the very
end, before reply.   It remains to say something of common
recreations during her rule as English vicar.

" Our recreations were so joyous and lighthearted that to come
to them after the day's work was like turning from a dusty highroad
into a delightful wood."

Here Mother Digby's keen sense of humour found
play. She had the Irish gift of repartee ; there was a
touch of the artist, too, in her choice of a theme, as when
she adapted the device of St Louis upon the ring he gave
to his queen : *Dieu, France et Marguerite* : *hors cet anel poing
n'ey d'amour*,[1] substituting other words for " France "
and " Marguerite," or again, when she told her daughters
that they should lie like rose leaves upon their superior's
cup full of cares.   Both these ideas were taken up by her
daughters, put into verse, and recited on her feast day.
The little poems pleased her much.

She would comment on current events, and ascertain
the bent of mind thereon of her audience.   When H.M.S.
Victoria went down with most of her crew in 1893, and the
trial of her captain ensued, she followed the particulars
with exceeding interest.   Captain Bourke, it will be remembered, was blamed for obeying the mistaken order
of his Admiral.[2] She rejoiced greatly at his honourable
acquittal and the emphasis set in the navy upon the great
law of obedience.

Sometimes during the holidays she proposed questions
with some direct, or indirect, spiritual meaning, and
listened attentively to the delightful debates that ensued.
Two of these turned upon " The advantages and dis-
advantages of foresight," and " Does success or failure
do most for the formation of character ? "

Amongst Mother Digby's left hand acts of which the
right hand knew not, was the help given with a noble
liberality to members of her daughters' families.   Here it
is difficult to choose among instances.   How often did she

[1] " God, France, and Marguerite ; beyond this ring I have no love."
[2] Such, at least, was the general impression at that time.

receive a postulant or pupil as "a child of the Society," remitting to a family in somewhat straitened case a part or the whole of the pension !

"Our Mother listened to my brother's sad story with the greatest interest. She gave him an outfit, and strengthened his heart. ' I can never forget your saintly Mother,' he said to me. ' I am going to Confession to-morrow, and I shall never be the same again.' "

"A lay Sister had a nephew, whose one desire was to be a priest, but he was unable to continue his studies through want of means ; one day our Mother sent for this Sister, and with evident joy said : 'My child, I have just received an alms, and I am going to devote it to your nephew's education so that he may be able to continue his studies for the priesthood.' The Sister could hardly speak for joy. The boy pursued his studies and became a priest and a religious."

But, though so generous in aid, she never lost sight of the first Beatitude. A young novice came to her, holding in her hand a letter announcing the ruin of her father. "What can be done now?" "Go at once to the chapel, my child," was the reply, "and thank God for the great gift of poverty which He has given to your family." Indeed, in this case, the numerous sons and daughters did manfully, and throve in honourable and successful careers.

Mother Digby's charity, whether dealt in money, hospitality, personal service, or interest, was not confined to members of her own order. Many a hut in the virgin forests, or the desert, has been turned into a chapel by the gifts of Mother Digby to a passing missionary ; many poor priests received all she had to give, but resources seemed somehow to multiply in time for the next comer.

A lad of fourteen had been engaged to help in the farm of one of the Irish houses, and was the object of many gifts and much kindness from Mother Digby. He took to drink and it was impossible to retain him ; but, on her initiative, a little shop was set up for him, so that he was enabled to earn an honest living. Another youth, a gentleman's son, was ruined by the family bankruptcy. Reverend Mother Digby gave him funds to start and secured his nomination to a post in a South American town where he won the confidence of his employer, and became himself a considerable proprietor.

The lay Sisters have their own tales.

"One of the Sisters told her that she was thinking of some poor families who were perishing with cold. 'My child,' Our Mother answered, 'if a ton of coals would make you happy, go at once and get it ordered.'"

"There was an old Irish woman, who regularly came to the door every couple of months with a pile of very dirty pawn tickets. 'Will you plaze take them to the Mother,' she would say; and when she was reminded that she had asked the same thing a very short time before, she replied invariably : 'Shure, and what's that to do wid ye? Ye just take them to the Reverend Mother.' She then sat down peacefully, knowing well the result. Our Mother would smile and say: 'I suppose she wants me to redeem them for her : see that it is done.'"

Space forbids the extension of the catalogue.

How many orphans did she not adopt entirely? "Your mother is in heaven," she said one dây with indescribable sympathy to four little sisters, pressing the youngest to her heart, till passionate grief had somewhat subsided. She obtained leave to shelter this whole family, whose ages ranged from nineteen years to nine months. Numbers of poor workwomen and others were invited to stay at the guest house for change of air and rest. "It would take pages to tell of her manifold help within my single experience."

But of this enough has been written.

What impression did Mother Digby make upon persons of the outside world?

From all such intercourse she shrank whenever she could; her impulse, in accordance with her own heartfelt humility, was to hide herself from the notice of "great people." She considered herself a discredit to her Society. But who, that did not know her well, would believe this? Her daughters lamented her aloofness. "People don't know her worth!" they said. But even Mother Kerr could not persuade her to "come forward." She would send, in her stead, others whom she believed more attractive, and therefore more likely to win a way to good.

Certainly, Mother Kerr, with her air of facile *bonhomie*, was very easy to approach, or, rather, she met all comers at once on their own ground. They felt at home straightway. But the air of calm and regal dignity, entirely natural to Reverend Mother Digby, and of which she was unconscious, the impression of singular moral greatness, of power in reserve, abashed certain spirits, whilst others, on the contrary, it irrevocably won, even at first sight. Of the latter class were little children, the aged and the poor, the workmen about the place, and very simple-minded persons of all ranks. It may be said at once, however, that owing to the shyness of many English people, her friends were more numerous, though not more devoted, on the continent than in this country.

When, however, feeling a barrier, she believed it right herself to cross it, or when she was approached in the spirit of a child who was neither spoilt nor shy, she hardly ever failed to meet the newcomer and to conquer. Then a lifelong friendship took the place of a cold and involuntary esteem. Men and women of the world or of the cloister resorted to her for sympathy, support, assistance, or advice, in the critical moments of life, as to one large-hearted and generous, disinterested and sagacious, who felt instinctively the principles, and foresaw the issue, in a manner apparently vague, formless, threatening, or hopeful ; nor were these friends of hers, if they called at Roehampton, to be put off with any one else. Such a friend was Mgr. Butt, Bishop of Southwark. On his first appointment to the diocese, he came to make the regular visitation of all the convents there. He was extraordinarily shy and silent by nature, and upon his first arrival he looked and felt, as he afterwards allowed, thoroughly alarmed at his prospective duty of paternal visitation. He ended the day with very different feelings, and from henceforth, like Cardinal Wiseman in the former times, he proposed himself periodically for a few days quiet and solitude as the guest of Roehampton, where he rested in every sense from the harassing cares of his diocese, unburdened himself to the Superior, and even consulted her on various matters.

There were, of course, reasons, well known to all in authority who never turn weakly aside, and whom no fear of unpopularity can paralyse; there were such reasons now and then why Mother Digby was the object of resentful feelings and unjust blame. Rebuke is needed to check at once some growing evil; there are refusals to requests apparently reasonable, when explanation would compromise another; there are measures to be taken, changes to be made, of which not all can see the wisdom. And there is always the critic who sees but the fragment within his ken, and mistakes it for the whole; who believes in his mission to declare what none surely but himself has perceived, and who sets the wheel of rumour fast revolving.

Regarding such difficulties it is not possible to particularise, but an imaginary case, taken from one department of a Superior's solicitude, may cast light upon a single point.

A devout lady thinks herself called to the religious life. She prefers the Congregation of the Sacred Heart to any other. Her confessor believes that such a neophyte will profit the Order; the Superior and Mistress of Novices, after careful examination, feel no doubt whatever that both he and his penitent are mistaken. He insists. How can the Superior tell without a trial? Perhaps she yields; time justifies her previsions; and such of the community as are in office tell her that Philothea, pious, amiable, perhaps talented, is entirely unsuited, nevertheless, to the particular life of the Society of the Sacred Heart. The postulant or novice is sent home; her family are loud in protest. Why was she not dismissed sooner? Why was she not kept longer? Why was she ever accepted? What crime has she committed, that she must go forth into the world branded as a failure? The nuns are arrogant, narrow-minded, unjust, blind to real merit. The lady is a person of position, and they are ungrateful, or she is a social nonentity, and her rejection is cruel. What do the nuns say for themselves? Nothing. Therefore they have nothing to say; but the lady and her friends have much ; and the confessor will consider it a duty to warn all under his influence against that convent, this Superior, against perhaps the whole Order. But the Superior, amid all the clamour, with the suffering it entails, and the good it may prevent, knows that of two evils she has chosen by far the least.

"Without doubt," Mother Digby was wont to say, "it is for the priest to decide whether or no there is in any particular case a call from God to the religious life. But, as to whether the postulant is suited to this or that Order, the Order itself must pronounce."

It once came to pass that, regarding some measure of Reverend Mother Digby's, of a different nature however, Mr John Pollen said to her, with a freedom which their intimacy permitted : "This is said of such a matter. That your reasons are, as always, excellent, I know ; but is it not possible that, through myself perhaps, some satisfying explanation can be given?" She replied in a single sentence, and he understood that there was no choice but silence. He kept her secret loyally, and his reverence for her and his sympathy augmented greatly.

Baroness Anatole von Hügel writes of the years in England :

"I went frequently to Roehampton to visit Henrietta Kerr. There I first saw Mother Digby. I was conscious of a face which one could not forget, though it was then nowise beautiful in shape ; only the eyes seemed *the* thing in the room, and the voice.

"Then, suddenly, there was an anxious illness of some dear one ; and I, with a nursing sister, had the chance to be of use. We were all three together in the Tower rooms, and then my time came for realising Mother Digby.

"She seemed to know all health, all character, even all life ; her touch was steady, noiseless, and unfailing ; and all lay in her mind in order, steadied by the supernatural, and played over by the gentlest, most luminous humour. Nature must have been very strong in her, and feeling ; therefore perhaps it was that one never felt her surprised or shocked by anything she came across. She had long been accustomed to find that God's grace isn't ashamed to take hold of very odd hands. Yet, though so gentle, never easy in her dealings with anything of offence towards God ; only, absolutely unpharisaic. The sense of humour allowed her to be critical, but the presence of God kept the judgment tender. And, indeed, I feel sure that she is watching and judging just the same, from her great seat in heaven, as when sitting on some tidy chair, in some delightful bare room in Roehampton—with Henrietta Kerr and me, if my memory serves me, sitting by on the floor.

"How encouraging she was! Henrietta said, one day: 'Izy has too many ideas.' I can hear the gentle voice and the rippling eyes saying together, 'No—I *like* her ideas!' The pretty word helped me along. Another day, I was sitting with Mother Digby in the garden, and a young girl, with a supposed vocation, came shyly, sweetly, up. That set her telling me of the parents, and how they had written of it, that God had done them a great honour. And I well understood when [Mother] Margaret Ward said *what recreation was*, with her presiding. Those short times, she said, were the perfection of human society—with the sins of the tongue drawn away, yet not a gap left behind.

"I came across but one puzzle. I believe that some over whom her power extended felt her hand too heavy. In one case of which I am thinking, Henrietta Kerr was downright angry for Mother Digby. Yet I know that the hurt one was heroically good. Perhaps the explanation may be that Mother Digby was, in those days, a stateswoman rather than a diplomatist. I suppose that a perfect Superior is both, and I feel as sure that she will have gained that farther step in perfection as the years went on.

"Finally, I think that Mother Digby was the most whole and balanced human being I ever knew.

"To me, in one respect, she and Lady Lothian sat on one throne. Life obliged them both, in their ways, to be women of the world ; I go back to them in thought, and feel how no fibre of either had the least scrap of an 'unbaptized right hand' of worldliness. The mere thought of them strengthens one's hand *to try*. And always, since then, I have known that to be a perfect woman of the world one would have to be in the category of the saints."

This testimony comprehends in its scope that of several others from the outside world.

Were there shades to the picture?

Mother Digby's reproofs were rare ; they were stern.

"She was too strong for diplomacy," says one, "and saw too straight."

To find fault always cost her much, and she hardly

ever did so without an intervening delay. "I am not going on a pleasure-trip!" she said gravely to some one who accompanied her to a house where it was her duty to set certain matters right. And again: "To tell people of their faults requires unselfish courage."

The very calm and terseness with which the reproof was administered made it strike the deeper. But, gathering all the testimonies together, it is not doubtful that those who knew her best, and whom she spared the least, were, without exception, the most sincerely devoted to her; in their boundless trust they even valued her severity.

She did not always detect the incapacity of some for a rebound after her reproaches had "laid them low." A safe plan was frankly to tell her so. Her goodness then redoubled, and one felt more at home with her than ever.

A longer experience of human weakness brought to her a greater forbearance, and the progress, as years went on, was marked.

"She had all the downright good sense of a typical English-woman," says Mrs Abel Ram. "She must have been at first incapable of understanding the waywardness of capricious natures; but, as years went on, she was able to enter more fully into the thoughts and feelings of others, and acquired more and more her wondrous power of sympathy."

That Mother Digby made no mistake is unthinkable; that she made few, and none upon main lines, is apparent to a careful student of her life. That she never fell short of her lofty standard cannot be supposed for an instant; that she had her battle to fight, is hinted in the transcript of her resolutions;[1] that she was sometimes reproved by her Superiors she herself told. But she was a soul of prayer; her strength came from God, and in the power of His food she was walking on day by day, even towards Horeb.

And now the year 1894 had begun. The health of the Superior General had been giving some anxiety. She was eighty-seven years of age, but so great was

See p. 70.

her elastic energy, even of body, that she appeared twenty years younger. She resembled Leo XIII. in this respect, in person as well as in demeanour ; he was aware of this, and sometimes reminded her of it.

On 27th March, a letter from the Motherhouse sounded an alarm ; prayers were enjoined everywhere for Mother Lehon, whose condition was serious. Early next morning a bell summoned all to the common room. A telegram had arrived : Mother Lehon had laid down her burden at last. Who would take it up? Letters conveyed details of her peaceful death ; she had passed through its gates in full consciousness. " It was like the going out of a lamp," some one said, " but a lamp that is suddenly extinguished, and without diminution of its brilliancy."

On 30th March a letter from Mère Augusta von Sartorius, who had been named Vicar General—that is, the *locum tenens* of the chief authority until the election of a new Superior General — summoned a general congregation for 18th July.

On 12th July, Mother Digby gave a conference to the community before her departure ; she recommended to all perfect observance of the rules of silence and punctuality. Next day she started for Paris, leaving behind her some sad forebodings. On 22nd July, the day of the election, solemn prayers were said in the chapel ; and late in the afternoon came the expected telegram. Mother de Sartorius was elected Superior General. There were great rejoicings, save from her own solitary heart. She felt a presentiment that she could not bear this weight for long.

The relief at Roehampton was intense. It would again soon see Mother Digby. True, a new Assistant General was still to name in place of Mother de Sartorius. Conjectures were forbidden, and no word was uttered. Some looks and sighs, perhaps, between the elders, were eloquent. The sittings of the congregation proceeded, and did not end until 12th August.

Two days afterwards the bell was rung, and the community assembled in silence at about half past eight in the morning. The Assistant entered with an open

letter in her hand.   She began it—but her voice faltered ;
before the words were spoken they were divined.   All
who have gone through these moments comprehend that
pain of separation which is indescribable and feels like
a mortal blow.   Mother Digby was lost as a permanent
presence at Roehampton.   She had been named Assistant
General.

CHAPTER XVI

THE ASSISTANT GENERAL AND THE SUPERIOR GENERAL

" The cry of the heralds was always, ' Souviens toi de qui tu es fils, et ne forligne pas.' "—KENELM DIGBY, *Godefridus* (Lumley, 1844), p. 236.

MOTHER DIGBY, in 1894, was entering a new France. In 1872 she had left her post in that country; never had its life shown more elasticity. In a few months' time France was to dismiss the last conqueror from her soil, and to shake from her shoulders the debt of 200,000,000 francs designed to crush her, three years before it was due; a tale unique in fiscal records.

Since then the nation had undergone internally changes more radical by far than the war had brought. Why or how this came about would take a volume to demonstrate. Here follows a brief sketch of the events that prepared the scene wherein Mother Digby was now called upon to play a part.

The temper of the great majority of the French people in 1871, as well as of the party in power — once the Commune at an end — was Catholic. But that party rested upon an electorate divided in allegiance between the partisans of a moderate Republic, and those of three dynasties—Bourbon, Orleans, and Napoleon—each at feud with each. Meanwhile, an Opposition, whose political name was that of an advanced Republic, a party impregnable in unity, strongly manned and skilfully organized, gradually made its way to the front. In 1879, the President, Macmahon, resigned, and Jules Grévy took his place, representing Houses of Government that deflected ever more and more towards the Left.

Morally and socially, the new State was pledged to principles ranging from anti-Christian to atheist in scope, but veiled at first by the euphuism "anti-clerical." No Frenchman was taken in by the term, but foreigners were so; their credulity excited a smile amongst the "anti-clericals" themselves. Mr Bodley's *France*,[1] did much, perhaps, to enlighten English opinion. The political programme of the Left, from 1871 onwards, comprised the separation of Church and State, abolition of the Budget of Worship, the expulsion of chaplains from all public departments, and, above all, the State monopoly of education ; as a corollary, the religious Orders were to be expelled, and here it was obvious to begin.

In 1880, by decree, the so-called "unauthorized" congregations of men, comprising between five and six thousand French citizens, were forcibly ejected from French soil. Then, rightly judging that whoso educates the child is the master of France, Jules Ferry brought in his bill by which all public elementary education must be "lay." "*Neutral*," explained M. Ferry, "in regard to religion ; " in reality, opposed to it.

Still, the Catholic elementary schools, largely taught by the "Brothers" and the "Sisters," more than held their own in the competition with the State "neutrals," just as the Convent boarding schools for girls of the upper classes were filled to the detriment of the girls' Lycées. The power behind the government, therefore, felt that the Congregations must be got rid of.

No less than fifteen bills to effect this object were drafted between 1871 and 1892. But the country would not tolerate the measures, and the ministries that proposed them fell, each in turn.

A more deadly engine had opened fire in 1880—one more difficult to discern in its aim and execution—a masterpiece of statecraft : the Ribot-Brisson law, calculated to crush the Congregations out of existence by exorbitant taxation.[2] This, said an eminent statesman, would be easily effected, for even the most prosperous, within a term of twenty years.

[1] Macmillan, 1898.
[2] The law will be dealt with in a future work, and the expulsion of the orders traced to its causes.

But the legal spoliation would not work at first.   The injustice was exposed ; and most of the Orders remained firm in their refusal to pay.   Neither would the government yield ; in 1894 the law had dressed itself in a new form, no less onerous in reality than the old, and the unpaid arrears of the Congregations had mounted up to an alarming figure.

The Congregation of the Sacred Heart was amongst those obnoxious to the government for more than fiscal reasons.

The philosophism of the eighteenth century had largely affected the Frenchwoman ; and it had been with the object of strengthening religious influences within the family that Mother Barat had been induced to found her institute.

If the decatholization of France had not made more rapid progress, the chief reason, perhaps, lay in the home.   A mother took care that her boy should be a believer up to the time of his first Communion at any rate ; and if, later on, the *fiancée* took up the matter, or the daughter, the chances were that the Frenchman, however wide a circle he might have described, came back sooner or later to his starting point.   So it was, perhaps, with Danton ; Napoleon himself was a case in point, and Chateaubriand, Lamartine, Littré ; as for Gambetta . . . who knows?

These facts were clear in the government eye.   Even under the Second Empire the influence of the Congregations was jealously watched in the matter of girls' education. The university system had attempted from 1800 to 1880 to wrest from freedom of control all the upper education of the young men of France.   The struggle regarding primary education had attained fierce proportions since that date ; all this time the higher education of girls had attracted less attention.   But the subject had been by no means neglected.

On 30th October 1867, M. Duruy, Minister of Public Instruction, addressed to the inspectors of the University a circular desiring them to institute literary, historic, and scientific classes to be delivered to women by the State professors. "In a few weeks," he ended, "the higher education of women will be founded; our three thousand lecturers are ready."

Mgr. Dupanloup, famous for his educational works and opinions, saw what this mobilization portended. In two ably written open letters, *M. Duruy et l'Education des Filles*, and *La Femme Chrétienne et Française*, the author had only to quote the avowals of its organizers in order to show their design: a generation of female freethinkers. The proposed classes were formed nevertheless, and served as a preparation for the Lycées for girls, founded a little later on.[1]

Such was the outlook when Mother Digby was called to take her place so near the Mother General of the Sacred Heart.

.   .   .   .

In 1893, at the time when the foundation at Hammersmith was under arrangement, the Very Reverend Mother Lehon, then Superior General, said to her secretary: "Reverend Mother Digby should have been with us long ago, but she is too much needed in England—now, above all." These significant words were not forgotten.

At the General Congregation of 1st August 1894, the name of Reverend Mother Digby appeared on not a few voting papers; but the majority, as has been seen, bestowed the supreme position upon Mother von Sartorius, and Reverend Mother Digby was chosen to fill the office of Assistant General left vacant.

Her first act was to withdraw from all eyes. Instead of occupying her new stall during the chant of the *Magnificat* that followed by custom, she took refuge in a long tribune overlooking the chapel, praying and in tears. Once the first shock was past, however, no trace of sadness appeared in Mother Digby's demeanour. "What shall I offer to the Infant Mary for her feast

---

[1] However, as late as 1899, the Lycées did not seem to have done their proper work everywhere. "The Préfet of Rouen, M. Hendlé, says that young men can be cured of clericalism in the Lycées, but not young women. The Vicaire, for instance, gives a Catechism class; and the girls find this more interesting than any other."—Robert, *Le Mannequin*.

to-day " (the Presentation of the Blessed Virgin in the Temple), asked one to whom she was accustomed to speak more intimately. "Whatever you think she will like best," was the elastic answer. "For my part, I have laid down Roehampton as a carpet for her feet on the steps leading to the Temple." Without loss of time, with entire self-possession, she set out to fulfil her new duties, the first being the installation of her successor in the English vicariate. She returned to France to make it for the second time, and in the completest manner, her home.

The Hôtel Biron, stretching between the Rue Babylone and the Rue de Varennes, and looking out upon the latter, is now dismantled, and, up to the year 1911, with its grass-grown steps and broken window panes, bore the melancholy aspect of a deserted mansion. In the reign of Louis XV. it had been finely built, and decorated with paintings, mirrors, and carving in the style that bears his name. The property came into the market in 1820. Madame Barat, against her will, for a palatial aspect was a great drawback in her eyes, acquired it for her Society as the only house in Paris of sufficient size and moderate price. Louis XVIII. gave a large sum towards its purchase; Monsieur, and others of the royal family, presented gifts for the school chapel. The foundress had removed the mirrors and pictures from the dwelling rooms, and consoled herself for the still too splendid appearance of the house now arranged for the children of the school by reflecting that the Community were lodged only in the stables and servants quarters.

As the Society grew, a plain unassuming structure close to the Hôtel Biron, 33 Boulevard des Invalides, became the Motherhouse, for the Superior and Assistants General, and the probanists. Mother Goetz had built a third house, 31 Boulevard des Invalides, to serve for a day-school, and for the meetings of the Children of Mary. The three buildings were connected by a large garden.

It was natural to expect that at the Motherhouse should

be found the most remarkable personalities in the Congregation.

Augusta-Pulcheria-Hubertina von Sartorius was born in 1830, of German parentage. When still an aspirant in 1862, the house where she was resident, Blumenthal in Holland, was burned to the ground ; her presence of mind quelled the panic of the children, ensured their orderly exit and escape, and all possible rescue of property. As Superior of Marienthal, near Münster in Westphalia, she faced much petty and odious persecution under the Kulturkampf, her community with all others of the *Sacred Heart* in Germany, at Posen, at Kienzheim in Alsace, and at Montigny near Metz, being banished from the Empire by a special decree of 25th May 1873, based upon a long official indictment of the Congregation for its loyalty to the Holy See, a quality suddenly voted " dangerous to the State." At Marienthal nearly all the lay Sisters and many of the others were German ; yet all were faithful to their vows, and accepted as an honour the condemnation which, for such a cause, drove them for ever from the Fatherland. A collective and public letter from all former pupils of the German houses boldly denied the charge of anti-patriotism, and protested against the decree ; the address was published with sympathetic comments in the *Germania*, Mother von Sartorius adding her own courageous remonstrance to the Government.

In 1884 she was sent to America as Vicar of the houses in Louisiana ; and in 1886, when elected Assistant General, exercised supervision over the American houses, though residing in Paris, where her eyes were, so to say, those of Mother Lehon during the blindness of the latter's last years. Mère de Sartorius's manner matched well with her dignified and winning appearance. A charitable and courteous devotion to all around her was, by common consent, her salient exterior virtue. But the frailty of her health made her office a crushing one, and she herself had declared that her tenure could be but short.

Very different was Reverend Mother Juliette Desoudin, Assistant General, under Mother Barat's three successors, and Mistress of Probation. She can never be forgotten by the many hundreds who for that six months' training had passed through her hands, as at once a marked individuality, and a great model for the special type of her order, able to imprint upon others its first traditions. She was born at Metz, and her frank nature, strong sympathies, sound sense, and wit never at a loss, tasted of her province. A hardy education had fashioned these elements and given her that breadth of mind. and knowledge of the human heart which fitted her to win trust and to form and guide the character of others. All in her was grafted on a robust faith, and dominated by a habit of prayer and the sense that God is here. "I have always thought it so difficult to be a perfect religious," said a naïve probanist to her one day. "Nothing, my child, is more simple; it is enough that we keep our eyes on God alone." She was small in stature, her clear-cut features and blue eyes sparkled, even to extreme old age, with superabundant and ever-varying life. In 1881, at the age of seventy-one, she broke her hip; but despite the predictions of the doctor, she forced herself with incredible energy to walk continually between two tables, and regained her power of motion. Ten years later, she fell upon the terrace, fractured her shoulder and put her right arm out of joint. After months of painful treatment the surgeon told her that the limb could never be used again, but in three weeks' time he was stupefied to find her installed at her writing desk, and carrying on her usual correspondence. In 1894 she was walking slowly with a stick, engaged in all her accustomed work with a vigour that belied her age of eighty-three; she looked, in fact, twenty years younger, and her countenance contrasted strikingly with the calm, unchanging expression of the new Assistant General, to whom she was united by the most affectionate bonds.

Reverend Mother Digby was local Superior of the Motherhouse, looking to its particular concerns, so as to free the Superior General for wider business.

"We were very happy under Reverend Mother Digby at this time," writes one of the community; "she identified herself at once and altogether with France.   It was always *our deputies, our soldiers, our government*.   Each of us felt herself helped and strengthened in the measure and fashion that she needed ; every event, even a trifle, served as a reminder to keep the soul above the things of self."

At the end of December 1894, Mother von Sartorius returned from a journey to Italy.   She was awaited with impatience, and the cloisters were illuminated.   When she arrived, her fatigue was great ; she greeted her daughters, and then went to the chapel, where she suddenly fainted ; an attack which was repeated later in an alarming manner.

The troublous situation of France, in fact, pressed sadly upon the Mother General.   Mother Lehon, twenty-three year her senior, had, by her physical strength, been better able to face the immense responsibilities, and the increasing menace, of the times.

In February 1892, a fifteenth bill for banishing the religious associations from France had been laid upon the table of the Chambre ; however, the Ministry, as always before, tripped over it, and fell before the end of the month. That year the anarchists began sowing death in Paris, Marseilles, and Lyons, by bombs and murderous attacks ; in 1893, the government fell again over the great Panama scandal ; the bomb-throwing continued.   Early in 1894 a dastardly attempt was made to wreck the Chambre whilst it was sitting ; but Vaillant, who threw the explosive, was seized and executed.   Casimir - Périer, a moderate man now at the head of the Ministry, avowed his determination to track down the anarchists, despite the fury of the Left ; then, in June, President Carnot was assassinated, to avenge the death of Vaillant, and Casimir-Périer was elected head of the State.   M. Spuller, the new minister of Instruction and Public Worship, declared formally in the Chambre that "a new spirit" must animate the government in its dealings with the Church.   Cardinal Richard, in his visits to the Motherhouse, spoke of his hopes for France, and of the Christian end of M. Carnot.   The Cardinal had presided over his requiem at Notre Dame, and had witnessed the great Catholic

demonstration at his funeral. " The impression," he said,
" is still profound. France has felt that she is Christian,
and that she must remain so."

Cardinal Richard, now seventy-six years of age, was
a constant visitor ; in the chapel, Rue de Varennes, he
had been consecrated Bishop of Larissa in 1872. His
Roman cast of feature, white hair, and dignity of movement, made him appear, especially when robed in the
cappa magna, the pictorial type of an Archbishop of Paris.
As he moved slowly up the centre of a church the mind
naturally reverted to the dangers of his office, for within
the last fifty years, three of his predecessors had met a
violent death. He possessed to a singular degree the
conversational charm of his nation. He dwelt at this time
upon the increasing number of worshippers at Montmartre,
on the various *œuvres* of his diocese, the progress amongst
the working classes, and above, all, upon the " new spirit."

But its signs proved fleeting. On 15th January 1895
the President resigned, unable to bear up against the
violent attacks of the ultras, and his nerve shaken by
the anonymous letters that poured in upon him, threatening even his life. M. Faure, a man not likely to assume
any responsibilities, was chosen in his place.

No threats, however, could stop the action of Mother
von Sartorius. A new house was opened at Bennebroeck,
near Haarlem, with a school and workrooms, where two
hundred and eighty girls and children soon accumulated.
The interesting foundation of Joigny, in Burgundy, the
home of the foundress, at the house of her father, the vine-
dresser, was organized by Mother Digby ; and in March
1895 she was commissioned to establish a first Convent of
the Sacred Heart at Aberdeen. She went to Scotland, and
set everything on a sure standing. The thought of Mother
Kerr, and of Lady Lothian and her daughter, gave an
added zest to this enterprise. In April she returned to
Paris, and found that owing to the renewed outcries
against the religious orders, the Cardinal had authorised
at the Mother General's request a weekly exposition of
the Blessed Sacrament in the chapel of the Motherhouse.
His Eminence came on 14th April to inaugurate this

solemn crusade of prayer, and to exhort the nuns to confidence. His own optimism was unshaken, and it was indeed shared by all, with the sole exception of the Mother General herself and of Mother Digby.

On the last day of that month, Mother von Sartorius was attacked by pleurisy. Her state was not at first alarming. She received in her room the Assistants General, who came to present beforehand their good wishes for her approaching feast. Next day she was seized by severe pain. "I am suffering," she said with gentle patience, in answer to a question, "but it is for the Society." Soon afterwards she was struck with paralysis; when Cardinal Richard came to see her she did not recognise him, and she received the last sacraments in a state of unconsciousness. There was pathos in the contrast between her condition and the flowers and letters that arrived on 7th May, with presents that would have made her happy as a means of succouring those in misfortune. Early on 8th May the cross was lifted from her shoulders; it fell upon those of Mother Digby. The community assembled to receive the announcement that she had been named Vicar General.

On 15th May Mother Digby issued a letter, recalling, in words full of feeling and dignity, the virtues and example of Mother von Sartorius; the personal regrets of the Holy Father for her loss, spoken at a public audience, were reported, and a general congregation for the election of a new Superior General on 25th August was convened for the 19th of that month.

On 10th August the vicars began to arrive. The congregation opened on the 21st by a *triduum* of prayers, with an instruction preached by the Reverend Père Mourier; 25th August, the Feast of the Immaculate Heart of Mary, one of the two great days of the congregation, was that of the election. "It is indeed a solemn occasion," remarked Leo XIII. at this time, at an audience to the Superiors at Rome, "and momentous for your Society." Cardinal Richard, accompanied by the Abbés Thomas and Lefèvre, entered the chapel at an early hour; after mass, at nine o'clock, the Mothers Vicar assembled in the Salle de

Probation, and the doors were closed.   In fifteen minutes, the election was over, and the Reverend Mothers followed the Cardinal into the Chapel.   Matthieu, the steward, a privileged old servant, and greatly devoted to Mother Digby, had already taken in the situation ; eyeing the procession, he said in a loud, triumphant whisper, "*C'est elle !*"   At the chapel of the Motherhouse, the Cardinal, in the midst of a profound silence, addressed a few paternal words to the nuns, dwelling upon his esteem for the Society.   "Your Mothers have elected as Superior General Reverend Mother Digby.   I have just now told her, with my blessing, that Our Lord would be her companion under so overwhelming a burden."   He then congratulated the religious on the unanimity they had shown.   In fact, with the exception of Reverend Mother Digby's own vote, her name alone had been written down that morning.

After the *Te Deum* had been intoned, the religious all adjourned to the community room.   "It seems to me a profanation to seat myself in a chair occupied by our Venerable Mother Barat, and her successors," said the new Mother General on entering.   "But you will have pity on me, and pray for me."   "We shall all be your Cyreneans by fidelity and affection !" replied Mère Gazelli, Vicar of Italy ; and all protested in the same tone.   "See what good daughters you have !" exclaimed Reverend Mother Desoudin, "they will make your task easy !"   Then all advanced to do homage, whilst the telegraph bore the good tidings to the whole Society. Next day the papal nuncio, Mgr. Ferrata, arrived to congratulate the Society upon the election, which was, he said, particularly agreeable to himself.

She received the following letter from an old friend.

"11 PEMBRIDGE CRESCENT,
LONDON, W., 29*th August* 1895.

"MY DEAR MOTHER GENERAL,—People do not rise to top places of importance without making some noise in the world, and so it happened that on Tuesday morning a kind letter from Roehampton apprised me of your election as Mother General.   I saw the announcement also in the paper (with comments attributing fabulous wealth to the Order!).

"That I am greatly rejoiced and all my family with me, I am sure you will fully believe, though, as I told Mme. M. L., I cannot forget that Paris is a good deal further from London than Roehampton. But, when a kind and sympathetic friend becomes the recipient of a very high honour, and secures the entire confidence of devoted persons in the four quarters of the globe, why then all her friends feel elevated with her, as we all did when we had not one but two Cardinals in our midst. No one can feel more than I do for those (particularly if they are friends) who have to submit their shoulders to new and very heavy burdens; but then, if God calls any one, I consider that He means His work to be properly done, and that He can be depended on for the 'requisite powers!' I am not at all uneasy on that score.

"How seldom people of one country are content to be guided by a native of another! In religious matters there is no real frontier. For myself it is one of my keenest pleasures, when I travel abroad in Catholic countries, to feel this; and I admire the French mothers who have so well pressed the consideration home.

"I shall sympathise with all your anxieties; and I know what some of them will be, and pray for happy issues out of them. —Very sincerely yours, J. H. POLLEN."

The following words of a distinguished French ecclesiastic[1] express the general impression made upon her acquaintance by her election.

"When the maturity, care, and discretion brought to bear upon the election of the Superior General of an Order are considered, no other than a very high idea can be formed of the intellectual, moral, and religious worth of Reverend Mother Digby."

Mother Digby's message to Roehampton in an intimate letter ran: "Tell them to live and to love and to suffer for the glory of the Sacred Heart, in and through our Society; and never let any one come down to a thought of self, which would be too utterly low."

Perhaps no one, save those weighted with a similar burden, could fully realize her repugnance to the dignities and calls of her new post. One supreme consolation she received from those under her—their loyal obedience.

[1] Père J. Fourniers, S.J., Bordeaux, 7th June 1911.

" The Society," she said at this time, " is a well-appointed vessel ; it answers perfectly to its helm."

There was naturally, in the heart of Paris, more communication than at Roehampton between the convent and the outer world.   Independently even of religion, to be educated at the Rue de Varennes was a training highly prized ; and passing over many interesting persons and episodes that came thus into Mother Digby's new life, the Children of Mary stand out remarkably.

Their first meeting presided over by the new Mother General was awaited with curiosity.   Upon her election, certain prejudices—it is difficult exactly to name them— had been current in Paris circles.   But, when the meeting was over, the Children of Mary avowed to each that she had won them completely.

The work of the Sodality in England has been sketched ; that of Paris has a length of record and a prestige even greater.   Lady Georgiana Fullerton for instance, who knew Paris well, obtained from thence without doubt suggestions for her work and organisation at home.

Père Varin, famous in the annals of the Society of the *Sacred Heart*, was the first director of the Children of Mary in 1820 ; under Père de Ravignan in 1848 the Sodality was effectively aided, and Père Olivaint ended by martyrdom his own term of office in 1871.   In 1894, Comtesse Louis de Luppé was President ; her life was steadfast to duty, and worthy of the death that was to befall her in the performance of it.

M. Maxime du Camp, of the French Academy, a sceptic declared, yet envying those who believe, has drawn the hidden career of more than one child of Mary of the Sacred Heart.   Awful as a battlefield when the fight is over are the wards of a great cancer hospital ; yet, unwearied and unrepelled, the reader with M. du Camp accompanies the heroines of charity at their tasks.   Who but a Frenchman, who but he, perhaps, has been able to tell of scenes so appalling, so redolent of mortality, in a narrative so beautiful?[1]

---

[1] *La Charité privée à Paris* (Hachette, 4th cd., 1892), pp. 209-212.

Hospital work is but one branch of the charity of the Children of Mary. Although each town, where the congregation is established, has its own President, there is much effectual combination between the different Presidents, where some important occasion seems to demand it for France, or elsewhere in the world.

Much of their work was not performed under the direct control of the nuns, or confined to the initiative of the *Sacred Heart.* Many of these ladies worked also with the Little Sisters, and the Sisters of Charity; not a few shared in every charitable enterprise of the city. Such was the Duchesse de la Rochefoucauld d'Estissac, who founded at Paris the great hospital of St Joseph, where the sick could have the consolations of religion, when the hospitals were laicised by law; such, the Marquise Gouvion St Cyr, who, in 1870, lifted the wounded from the battlefield of Loigny, and conveyed them to her château, an ambulance directed in the most able manner by herself; the Duchesse de Chevreuse did the same on the field of Patay, where her son was struck down.

But, in regard to the *Sacred Heart*, the most important of all enterprises, whether at Paris or in the provinces, was to gather together children of the elementary schools, by any possible means, and restore to them the religion of which the State had robbed them. Many thousands were undoubtedly thus saved, and others are even now being rescued; thus the work of the expatriated orders was to be largely supplied. But upon these tasks, arduous, self-denying, often thankless, no Maxime du Camp has touched, and the world as such takes little account thereof, save in railleries or falsehoods.

The Children of Mary, married for the most part, were often models in their own homes by lives of prayer and piety, ruling their families as if they had no other concern. Some, however, lived unmarried, and followed charity as a profession—humble pilgrims of the streets, quiet figures, dressed always with something of French grace, and with no touch of the nun or the nursing sister in their costume; of untold help to hard worked priests. Such was Marie Marthe Tamisier, a pupil of Marmoutier, who died in 1910, having initiated the idea of the Eucharistic Congress, now so famous in the Catholic world ; such was Mademoiselle de Curzon, who devoted herself to the instruction of children in Salvador, where she fell a victim to yellow fever after founding two houses for her work that developed rapidly.

In the burning of the Bazaar de Charité, 4th May 1897, perished nine Children of Mary of the Sacred Heart, besides the Comtesse Louis de Luppé, their President. How the ladies who held the stalls, together with the Sisters of Charity, refused to leave the blazing furnace till all the rest had made an exit, is well known. The charred remains of Madame Hoskier were identified by her Sodality medal, engraved with her name ; many trades-men came forward to reveal the secret of her daily walk at early morn, to choose meats and vegetables, which she herself conveyed to the needy. What is here stated shows but a fraction of the deeds of the Children of Mary of France, and only a few among a long list of names.

CHAPTER XVII

DANGERS AHEAD IN FRANCE

" Life therefore, as Aristotle says, is practice, not poetry or invention."—KENELM
DIGBY, *Godefridus* (Lumley, 1846,), p. 183.

At the evening recreation, upon the day of Mother
Digby's election, some verses were recited, commencing:

> "*Ma Mère, vous venez gouverner le navire*
> *A l'heure des périls, heure des grandes eaux. . . .*"

It was indeed the time of "great waters." The
government, unable to force its way along the complicated route of the *Droit d'Accroissement*, now resolved
to try and end the matter by a *coup de main*. M. Ribot
being President of the Council and Minister of Finance,
the multifold levy of the *Droit d'Accroissement* was to be
superseded by a single yearly payment called familiarly
the *Droit d'Abonnement*. But the new tax was even more
onerous than the old; and it was to be imposed, this
time—without a shadow of pretext—upon the unauthorised
Congregations as well as the authorised. Such of the
latter, moreover, as had refused the *Droit d'Accroissement*
were to be mulcted of an enormous additional sum, both
for arrears, and as a fine for their recusancy. To clinch
the matter, all cases sent in hitherto to the Court of
Cassation were cancelled. As far as the Congregations
were concerned, no appeal whatever could be made upon
a fiscal question; the Bill was a Bill of Attainder. All
who wore the habit must face the ruin of their works in
part or altogether; they must stand and deliver their
money or their life.

There was visible hesitation, however, in the Chambre.
The Bill passed in March by twenty-seven votes only,

and went up to the Senate to be boldly criticised by men and journals far from clerical.   An article by M. Reinach in the *Matin* echoed widely; the Ribot law was pronounced " a crying iniquity" by the *Journal des Débats*, and the *Temps* declared it to show neither liberty, equality, nor even toleration.   But the government jogged the elbow of the Upper Chamber, and after some timid protests the Bill became law on 16th April.

All French policy was concentrated upon the Congregations.   What would they do?   Would they yield? and should they?   Friends turned about to help them. Committees were formed; there was that of Catholic lawyers at Lyons, as well as a *Comité Pratique de Protection* at Rouen, to study and apply safeguards for works of beneficence, now, perforce, to be abandoned by the religious.

Sympathy and counsels were not wanting, but it was felt that they must fight their own battle.

M. Goblet having expressed himself, in the name of the Government, deeply shocked at the "spirit of opposition to Law shown by the Catholics," received on the spot a sharp reply to the effect that the assassin usually tries to silence his victim; and when the Minister of Worship applied to the Archbishop of Cambrai to repress some indignant words of his clergy, that prelate replied in an open letter full of dignity that he should make a point of letting his clergy know in private his personal opinion concerning the deplorable laws in question. Cardinal Richard, a little later, addressed a noble remonstrance to the President of the Republic; the Cardinal's example was followed by Mgr. Perraud, Bishop of Autun, and by a general movement in the episcopate.   On the other hand, Mgr. Fuzet, Bishop of Beauvais, publicly advised the religious to submit to the law, in order to avoid greater evils; his words were echoed and amplified in a *Mémoire* by M. Louchet, one of the magistrates who had resigned office rather than carry out the decrees of 1880.   But Cardinal Langénieux, Archbishop of Rheims, replied in words of grave remonstrance to his suffragan, the Bishop of Beauvais; Mgr.

Trégaro, Bishop of Séez, annihilated the counsels of the *Mémoire*; and another pamphlet, *Etude Pratique*, pointed out the disastrous effects of a submission which would abandon to spoliation the pious foundation confided to the guardianship of the Orders and deal a blow to the whole Church in France.

What was the sentiment of the Pope on the subject? The government, far from sure of its position, the episcopate, the French public, all listened eagerly for some word from Leo XIII.   It is certain that every Superior General consulted him in private, and that much pressure was put upon the Pope to induce him to counsel submission to the new law.   Some Congregations would have been glad of his support, to cover what, wearied out, they really wished; a few ecclesiastics asked it; the government itself would have been relieved of much embarrassment.   "Never!" exclaimed Leo XIII. with vivacity, on two occasions at least, "never shall we tell the congregations to submit!   It would be against our conscience to do so!"   But neither would he counsel them to resist.   His high sagacity, as always, left the religious congregations to settle their own affairs.   He remained prudently silent; not certainly for want of resolution, but because he would not hamper consciences by any personal influence whatever.   To each one who applied to him he returned the same answer: "You know best the circumstances of your own congregation; do as you think best, before God, for its interests."   Save on the few matters which are *ex cathedra*, it was his policy, or rather his wisdom, to allow a portion of noble independence to all his sons and daughters.

No pretence is here made of pointing out all the agencies at work, or the side to which the personal feeling of the Pope was secretly inclined; still less is it attempted to discuss or to decide whether resistance or submission was, in general, the better course.   It is now too soon to tell the tale in full; here is set down only the most well-known facts.   None can doubt that the Generals of the Orders, men and women of tried virtue and prudence, took their several resolutions in accordance with the highest motives, and after prayerful deliberation.

Cardinal Rampolla, the Pope's Secretary of State, wrote, it may be said officially, to Mgr. Meignan, the Venerable Cardinal Archbishop of Tours, in his eightieth year, recommending calm and uniform action on the part of all religious superiors in France at this crisis. A congress of Superiors General of the men's congregations met in Paris, and addressed to all the religious communities a circular, expressing their determination to meet the new tax by a passive resistance. The fears of the government appeared in the nervous offers of "facilitations for payment," "suggestions for arrangement," and compromises of many kinds, held out at this time.

Two months later the *Osservatore Romano*, 18th October, published a letter addressed to the Pope by the Superiors General of four authorised congregations, to wit, of the Lazarists, of the Sisters of St Vincent de Paul, of St Sulpice, and of the Brothers of the Christian Schools, declaring that they believed it best to resign themselves, and, under protest, to pay the tax. A good number of the unauthorised congregations followed this lead. Others took a different line. The Little Sisters of the Poor, for instance, who had accepted the law of 1884, stoutly refused the new one. The official *Journal* published the names of those who had yielded, together with the number of the recalcitrant, amongst the latter, the nuns of the Assumption and of the Sacred Heart. The two institutes contracted a special bond of fellowship; the nuns of the Assumption made generous offers to the daughters of Mother Barat, in the years of distress. The financial powers had a further grudge against the *Sacred Heart*; they knew that from its long and world-wide experience, the representatives of many younger Congregations had applied to the Mother-house, where they found advice and encouragement. In order not to compromise either Mother Digby or themselves, some used to come late at night.

On 22nd October the Ribot ministry fell; new

ministers were called to office by M. Léon Bourgeois. He himself took the Presidency of the Council, and M. Combes assumed the portfolios of Worship and of Public Instruction.   In November M.   Bourgeois's ministerial declaration comprised the separation of Church and State; and M. Goblet laid upon the table a sixteenth project of law against the religious congregations.   These were the storm-clouds under which the year was to end.

Mother Digby, already in September, had in a circular letter spoken of the grave situation.   She recommended the matter to the prayers of her daughters, and reminded them that now, more than ever, they must keep their own lives at the highest level of generous self-sacrifice.

Cardinal Richard spoke to the Probanists in the same tone:

"The necessity of houses of education like your own is more and more felt in our times . . . God has been turned out of the schools, and children leave them already sceptical. . . . Your Society was born in this century in order to serve its actual needs, and you have till now been faithful to your mission, and to the intentions of your foundress; remain so to the end!"

This was his farewell before starting for Rome, whither the Mother General, accompanied by her secretary and one of the Assistants, followed on 28th October, in order to obtain the Papal advice and benediction upon her generalate and its undertakings.   She had been informed that the Holy Father would grant her an audience in November.

She paid a rapid visit to the houses of Chambéry and Turin; at Avigliana she was received at the railway station by the Comtesse de Briançon, a former pupil of the Sacred Heart, and a benefactress to the surrounding country, to which she was devoting her life and her large fortune, and who felt at once, and always, a respectful admiration for the new Mother General.   In this wooded and solitary vale between the Apennines, watered by the Dora Riparia, was placed a large school of two hundred children and an *ouvroir*, and, for a time, a noviceship. Mother Digby passed from this delightful retreat to Florence, where she arrived on 14th November.

The nuns there made her acquaintance, or at any rate saw her in the new character of their Mother General. One of their number recorded the impression:

"What struck us above all was her imperturbable serenity in the midst of the gravest pre-occupations. Not a post but brought her the news of some death, illness, or other affliction. 'I received a Job's messenger again this morning,' she said to us; but she enlivened our recreations with a gentle gaiety: 'These are happy moments when I can forget that I am the Mother General!' She spoke to us of the approaching foundation at Venice, and of those demanded at several places, at Athens, for instance. This latter idea attracted her, and all of us; for had not Greece been the land of Mother Barat's early dreams? However, it could not be yet. 'Much good could be done there, but the more urgent anything is, the more we must reflect and combine. Remember the great saying: 'It is pressing—then go slowly! Meanwhile, you may study Greek in your free time! Good-bye, and pray for your poor mother.'"

At the Trinitâ dei Monti, Rome, she dwelt upon the danger of routine in the spiritual life. "By it, we become like the cicerone who stand before the Roman monuments with absolute indifference, explaining them mechanically to visitors." She recounted the visit of the Cardinal Protector, to whom she said: "Ah! What it is to have, all at once, seven thousand daughters! Five or six suffice for the mother of a family!"

Mother Digby paid a memorable visit to the General of the Jesuits then at Rome, the Very Reverend Father Louis Martin, a saintly man, a Spaniard, possessed the extraordinary courage of his race, and the wisdom of its best representatives. He was accustomed to spend two hours every morning, after his time of prayer was ended, standing immovable and alone, reflecting upon the government of his great Company. He received the Mother General and two of her religious with the grave dignity of his nation, and with paternal kindness.

Mother Digby saw the Father General again, and in private. She had serious reasons for consulting his

sagacity.   Like her, he had depending upon him thousands
of loyal subjects; his own, much more numerous, had
been inured to persecution for three centuries, while the
Congregation of the Sacred Heart had been saved there-
from in a wonderful way.   But she foresaw that they, too,
must soon make way against more adverse tides.   Few
then guessed the future, but these two souls understood
one another.   Father Martin seemed to value suffering as
the greatest good.   "Our suppression in 1773," he said,
"brought us only blessings," and whereas there were
in Germany, at the time of the expulsion in 1873, but six
hundred religious, there were now more than double that
number.   He could never pray that persecution should
be averted; on the contrary, he asked Reverend Mother
Digby to set her nuns to pray that his sons might endure
constant trials, and so win the true spirit of St Ignatius.
She, knowing that he had made the same request of
others, answered smiling: "Father, one would say that
you are inordinately bent upon these things!"

When she visited him for the last time, he had
recently endured, without moving a muscle, the amputation of his arm at the shoulder, absolutely refusing an
anæsthetic.   He offered his sufferings ,for the Society.   It
was the time of realisation of all the worst fears for the
religious orders in France, and the sight of his heroic
serenity, in a situation so crucial, gave her new courage.[1]
"The surgeons declared," she said, "that they might
been have working upon a statue! Let us hope that the
generation now forming will not be that which seeks
small comforts!"

On 16th November she was received in private audience
by the Pope.

This year was the one of his special interest in her
nation.   In April had appeared his Encyclical *Ad
Anglos*, inviting the English to religious unity; the
momentous *Apostolicae Curae*, upon Anglican Orders, was
now in his mind, and was to appear in a few weeks.

Leo. XIII. had, shortly before, been thus vividly
described to her at Paris by Mgr. Latty, Bishop of

[1] He died 16th April, 1906.

Châlons, lately returned from Rome, where, as notary of the cause of Venerable Mother Barat, he had conversed familiarly with his Holiness.

" At first sight he has the appearance of an old man ; then, suddenly, his head seems illumined. It is the face of a prophet and of a seer, and with so shrewd a smile and such an expression of goodness as altogether escapes the common portraits of him. His countenance, like his conversation, is full of profound thought, and shows a lofty soul incapable of narrow views ; his large heart looks ever to nothing less than the conversion of the whole world. . . ."

Upon Leo XIII. Reverend Mother Digby relied confidently. She would thoroughly have endorsed the magnificent panegyric of M. Gabriel Hanotaux[1] — a testimony, one may say, of an opponent—to a mind and spirit towering amid the leaders of the century. She urged her Society continually to do faithfully its part though a humble one, towards the Holy See ; loyalty to its dicta permeated every line of the teaching carried on within the walls of her convent, whether to children or to young religious.

In all this, of course, it may be roughly said that every religious order acted in exactly the same manner, and that Leo XIII.—like other Popes, some more, some less—looking upon the Orders as forming a line of guard for the defence of the Church, beheld in each Superior General, even if a woman, the captain, as it were, of some frontier fortress. Personally, too, in his solitary power he felt no small solace in the loyal and unquestioning obedience and sympathy of the Orders, at times when even his supporters along main lines were indulging in animadversions upon particular acts of his, of which the bearing was not visible save to the great agent himself. These thoughts come out incessantly in his interviews and relations with the nuns of the Sacred Heart, more especially with the Superior General ; and for Mother Digby, it may be said that Leo XIII. held her in high esteem. He expressed more than once his trust in her

_____
[1] *Histoire de la France Contemporaine*, pt. iv., pp. 247 ff.

sure insight, and undertook her defence under adverse and unjust criticism; for who, placed in authority, and always staunch to duty, can escape occasional stricture? She, on the other hand, with the Supreme Bishop more than any other, could lose her sense of loneliness; she knew herself and her position to be thoroughly understood; she felt her own cares and responsibilities dwarfed by comparison with those of him who stooped to relieve her burden.

It was more than once her painful duty to face the most strenuous opposition. On one occasion, she thought well to write to the Holy Father, and give reasons for her action. Leo XIII. was conversing with some of the Cardinals when the letter arrived; he read it aloud. One of them, a man of high position and influence, exclaimed: "What will people say!" But the Pope replied: "The Mother General is quite right; for if a religious society does not insist that its members keep their rule in its integrity it will very soon come about that the Order itself will need reform."

Leo XIII. received her for the first time as Mother General with his usual vivacious sympathy and kindness. He spoke of the difficulties in France, and she was consoled by the assurance that in all her plans she was in accordance with his own foresight. "Your Society," he said, "is doing good at Rome, and indeed all over the world." On 8th December Reverend Mother Digby had a second audience, first assisting at the Pope's own mass in his private chapel. She consulted him upon the simultaneous demands for foundations at Venice and Genoa respectively; one only could be undertaken. "Oh, go to Venice," he said, "the good Patriarch will protect you."

On her homeward journey, therefore, after a short visit to the house at Portici, on the very flank of Vesuvius, and to that of Padua, she passed on to Venice.

For some years a little group of the Children of Mary of the *Sacred Heart*, dwelling at Venice, had obtained leave to hold their meetings at the house of Padua; but they were desirous that a house of the *Sacred Heart* should be

founded in Venice itself.   The President, Contessa Mori,
applied to the Patriarch, who charged her to ask for this
favour in his name; he invited the Mother General to
pay him a visit.   At the dinner hour she went, accompanied by two religious.   Here was Contessa Mori,
another guest being the musician Perosi, absorbed in
the problem of a symphony, save when his host recalled
him to the duty of the moment.

The Patriarch showed himself eager to see the foundation accomplished, but Mother Digby was silent.   "Will
the Mother General come to Venice?" asked the Contessa
in Italian.   "Who doubts it!" he rejoined in the same
tongue.   "You will come, will you not?"   But Mother
Digby had visited the proposed locality, and was averse
from turning out a few Oblates, who were still living there.
The Patriarch begged her to come again to Venice and
choose a more suitable spot; he then did the honours of
his palace to the nuns, and led them along the private
passage leading from his apartments to the tribunes of San
Marco.   Here he pointed out and explained the mosaics,
and then charged another prelate to act as their ciceroni
through the Basilica, and to unlock to them all its treasures.

In those days the aspect of the Cardinal was genial,
even gay; he was in every sense the father of Venice, and
seemed to know every one by name.   If a workman had
lost his place, if a baby were ill, the Patriarch was applied
to at once.   He resembled Pius IX. in his ways, and not
a little in feature.   His hold over the municipality and his
moral influence was immense; the majority of the electors
gave their votes, for sheer love, to the Cardinal's candidate.
He saw to it that there was no trickery or coercion at the
ballot; the year before he left Venice to become Pope,
bands of ruffians walked through the streets to attack the
voters, but the Guild of Butchers, armed with their long
knives, made themselves into a life guard, and escorted
their Patriarch everywhere.   Religion in Italy was thus
nowhere more free than in the Venetian territory.   When
the Campanile fell in upon itself, without injuring so
much as a dog,[1] the immunity of the citizens was set

[1] 14th August 1902.

down by them as due without doubt to the holiness of their Patriarch.

At the end of 1896, a convent of the Sacred Heart was opened in the city, at the Palazzo Savorgnan ; Cardinal Sarto's beautiful gondola (a gift from the citizens) was constantly seen, shooting suddenly round the corner, when a friendly barber who lived opposite rushed to the convent door to warn the nuns—" Eccolo ! " All assembled in haste, and the Patriarch soon sat smiling and talking in the midst of a group of children happy as himself. This sight of him, familiar to Mother Digby in succeeding visits to Venice, was later to suffer rude contrast when the cares of the Papacy had clouded him with sadness.

Meanwhile, in January 1896, the foundation had been no more than sketched out when Reverend Mother Digby was suddenly recalled to Paris by the alarming news of the illness of Reverend Mother Desoudin.

CHAPTER XVIII

PERPETUAL JOURNEYS

" Nothing was able to shake him out of his saddle."—KENELM DIGBY, *Tancredus* Sherwood, 1828, p. 179.

THE danger to Mother Desoudin soon passed away, but another cause of anxiety succeeded to the first. Reverend Mother Digby's own health deteriorated so sensibly after a neglected cold that Dr Ferrand counselled her prompt removal to a warmer climate. She therefore arranged to continue the journey interrupted in January, when she had proposed to visit the houses in Southern France.

Her arrival, in any case anxiously expected, was now more urgent, for the fiscal agents, grown bolder, had in December again summoned the nonconforming congregations to pay the impost. In February the amount due was published at eight million of francs; from the *Sacred Heart* alone one million was demanded. Each local Superior felt that she could lean upon the Mother General. But what would be the next move? The "opportunist" government itself was doubtful. Was it safe yet to seize a house as compensation, and turn out women on the doorstep? And which house would it be? Perhaps the Motherhouse in Paris.

Mother Digby set off in a pitiable state of health on 20th February, accompanied by one of her Assistants General, and her secretary. She felt so ill on arriving at Lyons that she thought of stopping there for the night, but arrangements had been made that she should go on to Montpellier, and she had strictly forbidden her secretary to speak of her health at any of the convents they visited. The latter conceived herself bound to obey.

and knowing well that in any case remonstrance on this subject would be useless, she confined her efforts to procuring all possible safeguards for one upon whose welfare so much depended. So the journey was continued that evening. It was nearly midnight when they reached the convent at Montpellier. All had been prepared with the utmost care for their rest and refreshment, but the clock struck twelve, and the Mothers rose from their seats in order not to break the fast before Holy Communion. Mother Digby remained all night thoroughly chilled; she appeared next morning, nevertheless, gracious and calm, entirely at the disposal of the Superior, and intent upon the interests of the persons and place she had come to see. She followed the business as arranged for each hour of the day; her secretary alone, who had been her constant companion, was able to divine the effort necessary to go into the garden as she was requested, in order to examine the façade of the new building. Mother Digby's nights were sleepless, and places so full of memories for her became, owing to the lengthy receptions elaborated with the utmost care to do her honour, scenes of acute suffering and well-concealed exhaustion.

At last, at Quadrille, in the Gironde, she was literally forced to take medical advice, but after a few days' rest she persevered on her way to Poitiers. There her companions, now all seriously alarmed, again sent for the doctor, who said, "Madame Digby, in rising from her chair, or in stooping to pick up anything, runs the risk of dropping down dead!" She knew it. On her return to Paris the anxiety felt on her account was at its height, and the very worst was feared. Reverend Mother Desoudin, loth to believe what caused her so much pain, was convinced at last; and, anxious to obtain the intercession of the whole Society for the sparing of a life so precious, addressed a circular to this effect to the Reverend Mothers Vicar. No sooner had the letters been despatched than Reverend Mother Desoudin herself fell ill again, and lay in extremity. The replies to her circular were therefore actually opened by Reverend Mother Digby, its subject.

"I must be ill indeed!" she exclaimed. And, though the thought of death was habitual to her, she appeared on this occasion profoundly impressed.

One thing she had hoped to do before she died; was it not to be after all? "My first thought on opening these letters," she afterwards avowed, "was: 'What about America?'"

The quasi prophecy of the foundress had always remained in her mind. Almost since the beginning of her generalate she had opened the subject with her Assistants General, but, considering her health, always in vain. Reverend Mother Desoudin now reverted to the design she had always opposed. Perhaps a new and generous sacrifice would win from God's mercy the answer to their prayers. With her eyes full of tears, she took Reverend Mother Digby by the hand. "Promise," she said, "that if Our Lord gives you back your health, you will visit America!" Mother Digby promised.

The immediate danger gradually passed away; but it may be said that her physical strength never again rose to its former level.

She had not believed death to be imminent; and only when it came to this point would she listen to advice on the subject of health. Nor were these intervals ever more than of short duration. No mere feeling of fatigue or suffering could stop her, as long as her almost superhuman force enabled her to move. Far from resigning herself to the doctor's verdict that she was "unfit ever to travel," she was henceforth to spend the greater part of each year in journeys and visits that extended over almost the whole areas of France, Italy, Austria, Spain, the Low Countries, and the British Isles; nor were her horizons confined to Europe. Her precarious state was not, in her view, a thing to hold her back from duties that took a first place; and, as she thought, so she acted to the very end. And, it should be added, even they who lived nearest to her, whose entreaties for "necessary care" she silenced, and who went through so much cruel anxiety — even they were forced to own that her action was justified, not only in principle, but by the event. She accomplished what she set herself to do. All that seemed to be most dangerous she passed through safely, and her life, moreover, always active, was prolonged, in spite of the sad prognostics of those who loved her, into a considerable old age.

At midnight, as the Feast of the Sacred Heart, 12th June, was commencing, Reverend Mother Desoudin left this world. She was happy to die, full of thought for those around her, and conscious almost to the last. It was a personal sorrow for thousands. Reverend Mother Digby, in a circular, announced the loss of "an accurate and faithful witness of our Society's past." The letter quotes Reverend Mother Desoudin's reply to a question upon humility, made at the last recreation: "I have a great liking for religious who pass unnoticed; they do their duty in simplicity and quiet; no one even thinks of saying: 'What humble souls!' But they ravish the Heart of God."

Mother Digby's next circular, on 15th July, deplores a fresh loss, that of His Eminence Cardinal Raffaele Monaco La Valletta, surnamed "Il Santo" by the inhabitants of the Neapolitan territory where he had lived, and reputed such by the Pope himself. He united to his important avocations the office of Cardinal Protector of the Society of the Sacred Heart, and for five and twenty years had rendered to it incalculable services; not the least being his efforts to promote the beatification of Venerable Mother Barat. Mother Digby knew him personally; she asked for earnest prayers regarding the Pope's choice of a new Cardinal Protector, a matter of vital importance to her Society. She was able to announce in October the happy nomination of Cardinal Angelo di Pietro, well known to the Sacred Heart in Rome, as well as in Madrid, where he had formerly been Papal nuncio.

At this time, too, died M. Spuller, the old friend of Gambetta, but the man of the *esprit nouveau* — a loss to the moderate party; and Jules Simon, who had returned to the Catholic sentiments of his youth.

In April the Bourgeois Cabinet fell; that of M. Méline, less extreme, succeeded; but religious policy was

unchanged.   At Tours in May the President was bestowing
the cross of the Legion of Honour upon the Sister
Superior of the Hospice Générale, whilst the Petites
Sœurs, Ursulines, and Carmelites of the same town
were threatened with seizure of their property unless they
paid their arrears within a week.   The crops and houses of
several orphanages were confiscated in July and August,
but no genuine purchasers were forthcoming, and the
inhabitants bought back the whole for a small price and
restored it to the nuns.

So the year passed on in threatening uncertainties,
and Mother Digby made up her mind to continue her
visits to the French houses, when in December her doctor
gave it as his opinion that her passing the winter in
France was out of the question.   The Assistants General
strongly supported the advice, and Mother Digby
yielded.   " It costs me much," she wrote, " to leave the
Motherhouse for so long, and to cause an expense to the
Society when my only wish is to render it all the service
in my power.   The prospect, however, of being in easy
communication with our Cardinal Protector, and still
more with the Holy Father, consoles me.   Communications being now so speedy, I shall continue to occupy
myself every day with the affairs of the Motherhouse,
and all correspondence will be forwarded to me."

On 12th December she arrived at the Trinità dei
Monti.

A special character and atmosphere naturally attached
itself to this Roman visit.   Amongst the pupils of the
Trinità were usually found relatives of the Pope himself.
In 1897 two great-nieces of Leo XIII. increased the interest
he had always shown in the establishment ; he constantly
enquired after their health and progress, and received
them with their mistresses and other pupils familiarly at
the Vatican.   Leo XIII. was paternal even in details.   Gifts
appeared at the convent door at all seasons ; those immediately preceding Mother Digby's arrival this year had
been a calf from his stables, and a swordfish seven feet
long, speared by Calabrian fishermen between Scylla
and Charybdis ; there was a request that the cook of the

Trinitâ would prepare and send back a portion for the Pope's own supper, in order that he might do honour to the givers.

On 13th January he received Mother Digby and five of her religious in private audience. They were introduced into the library as the midday cannon sounded from the Casttel St Angelo. "Holy Father," said Mother Digby presently, "our constant pre-occupation is to pray for your Holiness, that Our Lord may preserve you long for the good of the Church." "But I am already eighty-seven! what an age! The prayers of the faithful give me strength for my heavy charge . . . And France! I love her! I am full of interest for her! But she is sick indeed. The spirit of revolution is working her woe!" "And the want of union amongst the good!" she answered. "Yes," he said and his countenance assumed an expression of great sadness. "They would not understand the direction I suggested. I could have wished for more docility; party spirit bars the way. I have not demanded the sacrifice of ideals, of remembrance, of attachment to the past; they are free to believe that a monarchy is in itself preferable to a republic; but France has herself chosen her actual government . . . all Frenchmen should therefore unite in order to save religious interests. They all seek this or that, and meantime the Church suffers. Thus, as to the Chambres, all should elect deputies who would oppose the evil laws; instead of which they send in enemies of the Church, to crush her. . . . And how go your affairs?" "Badly, most holy Father. The government is demanding of us a millions of francs in taxes and fines." He seemed in consternation, and exclaimed with vivacity "Where are you to find it? You have not got it!" "Most Holy Father, they will sell one of our houses." "By auction?" "Yes, they have just done so for a convent at Avignon; they take out of the price what they pretend is owing, and reserve the rest for future debts." The Pope replied, with a look of compassionate kindness: "But you might have said to me, 'In old days, we used to bring you our offering of Peter's pence; times are changed now, we have no longer the means' . . . and I should have understood . . . but you bring it to me all the same ! . . . Well," he said presently, alluding to the *Droit d'abonnement*, "you have reflected long before deciding not to yield. Now you must trust in God, and rely in all things upon Providence. . . ."

Mother Digby, in answer to his enquiries, went on to speak of Porto Rico, where the house had been partly wrecked by a tornado, and of foundations that she hoped to make in Spain and at San Francisco. Cardinal Mazella was then announced, but the Pope retained the nuns a few minutes longer. " How go the houses of England, your own country? . . . Ah," he said, opening his arms wide, " I would fain embrace England, and bring her back ! Cardinal Mazella is coming precisely on that matter !" His last words to Reverend Mother Digby were these : " *You must* re-establish your health !"—a direction that seemed a command, and was heard with satisfaction by the religious that accompanied her.

At the door of St Peter's they had the joy of seeing posted up the official notice that nothing had been found in the writings of Venerable Mother Barat to oppose an obstacle to her canonisation.

The Convent of Sta Rufina in the Trastevere, the schools, workshops, and refuge comprised altogether five hundred and seventy *Trasteverine* of pure blood, lineally descended, as they boast, from the ancient Romans—a race loved peculiarly by the Pope, and much attached to him. Here, the reception given to Mother Digby aptly consisted of a little piece wherein figured St Gregory the Great and the fair Saxons of the Roman slave-market.

But the most charming of the Roman houses is the Villa Lante. It stands upon the Janiculum. Eastward lies the whole extent of Rome, the dome of St Peter's on the near left, joined by the winding Tiber to St Paul's *fuori* on the right. Reverting to St Peter's, the eye in a second sweep follows the ideal outline of the Alban hills, diminishing to the level horizon of the Campagna beyond St Paul's, whence the long lines of aqueduct lead south-ward into the distance. The seclusion of the Villa suits well a house of noviceship, or of retreat, and Mother Digby passed here the greater part of the winter. She took the opportunity of inaugurating an Italian system of studies, on the model of that at Conflans, for those preparing to teach.

In March she returned for some days to the Trinitâ before her visit to the Austrian houses. But on 27th March she was suddenly seized by a failure of the heart, and lay for some hours between life and death. The doctor was about to recommend that the last sacraments should be administered, when after applying some remedies her heart began to recover its action. She opened her eyes as if from a deep sleep, and looked upon the religious who were kneeling round her inclined chair—for she was unable to lie down—and expecting to receive her last sigh. She smiled and said: "It is not yet time for San Lorenzo!" Next morning she received Holy Communion as if for Viaticum, her daughters continuing to take for her the most filial precautions. What was their astonishment when she called for her travelling companions! "We start the day after to-morrow!" she said. "The doctor considers that I may die at any moment in my chair; I shall therefore run no greater risks in the railway."

She was as good as her word, and set out on 7th April for Vienna.

Her secretary thus writes :

"Our Mother Digby, who loved to pray before the tabernacle, felt painfully the passing whole days without this consolation on her journeys. 'Qui Multum peregrinantur, raro sanctificantur,'[1] she would quote, smiling. 'But,' she added, 'God wants me as a pilgrim! That is enough.' She would rise very early and go to the chapel long before any one else. I lodged near her, and she would use my lantern as she made her way down unfamiliar stairs and passages. At Perpignan, on the borders of Spain, express orders had been given by Mère Ladislas Brzozowska, Assistant and Mistress of Health, to safeguard the Mother General's repose, and all were forbidden to pass near her door before the hour for mass. Mère Ladislas had chosen to sleep in the room adjoining Mother Digby's

---

[1] They who travel much, rarely become holy.

in order to be at her call during the night if necessary. What was the indignation of the Mother Assistant on hearing some one walking down the corridor at a quarter past five! This was too bad. She opened the door silently, and spied a religious making for the chapel; Mère Ladislas followed swiftly, and drew the individual by the sleeve till they were under the gas; there she recognised, to her astonishment, the Very Reverend Mother General, who looked at her with amusement."

The Austrian Vicariate, established in provinces of different and rival races, shows in each house a corresponding interest and local colour, not lost upon Mother Digby even in the temporal aspect. In each school the pieces played in her honour related naturally to the memories or heroes of the place. At Buda-Pesth it was the Blessed Virgin, titular Queen of Hungary since the time of St Stephen, *Magna Hungarorum Domina*; at Prague, St Wenceslaus and Blessed Agnes of Bohemia; there were also folk-songs, national dances, and cries of welcome: *vivat*, *hoch*, or *slava*! All this sound and well-drilled movement was executed with grace and keen delight by scores of little girls on each occasion, awed at first, but soon won by the Mother General's kind and smiling looks. "How good she is!" exclaimed a very young child afterwards. "She saw quite through me, and all my faults, yet she never said a word about them!" At Pressbaum, near Vienna, she thanked the school for their music. "That piece," she said, "helped me to pray." And one performer at least avowed that the words had given her a first light as to the meaning and object of music in church.

Other words of Mother Digby's in different places were jotted down at the time, and appear to have remained with her young listeners in after life. "What is the strong point of this school?" Various answers were given, that pleased her. "And the weak one!" . . . "Keeping silence!" . . . "Ah—but you wish to become strong souls, do you not? When I was Mistress General, I greatly liked my occupation. I had one very difficult child, but she was determined to conquer herself. If she were given a very interesting story she would read on till she reached the most thrilling passage—then she would shut the book and read no more of it for a fortnight! Thus she really attained self-mastery; she had great trials in the world afterwards, and remained always faithful.   But some others leave sacrifices to their neighbour, and hope somehow to get a reflex glory from their connection with that neighbour.   A little girl I knew, who was listening to tales of the martyrs, exclaimed: 'Ah! how I should like to have *a martyred brother!*'"

After the children's exhibitions followed usually deputations from the various sodalities affiliated to the Sacred Heart.   There were Children of Mary; the Mothers of Families of humbler rank under the patronage of St Anne, the work-girls, in some places workmen or miners, and so on.   The addresses of these good people had been carefully composed, the Curé of the village having in one case at least, spent the whole night in finishing touches.   Even the servants, farm-labourers and gardeners, presented themselves with a speech, and gifts, of vegetables, pigeons, or objects they had carved in wood.   They had usually taken extraordinary pains in the decoration of the house and grounds for the first visit of the Mother General; there were triumphal arches, water-jets, flags, lanterns, and what not.   Mother Digby was naturally touched and grateful; yet to be *en évidence* was always in itself repugnant to her, and even the modest pomp and circumstance of a convent school got up in her honour seemed out of place.   These journeys, consoling as they were, and important in preserving unity of feeling and of action in the Society of the Sacred Heart, had their fatiguing side.

In order to complete this general sketch of her travels, the following account of a visit to the Low Countries, though not made until three years later, is here inserted.

In September (1900) she visited the house of Bennebroeck near Haarlem.   Every one in the village tried to do her

Q

honour, and the scene made a smiling Dutch picture of spick and span prosperity.

" A coachman whose ten children had succeeded one another at the elementary school of the convent, claimed the honour of driving her, in the best carriage to be had; the baker brought a box of *dragées* denoting the birth of his fifteenth child, whilst his wife came to introduce their eldest, a young seminarist, an old scholar of the *école*, of which the three hundred and twenty children with happy wide-awake faces surmounting spotless white aprons, lined the avenue as Mother Digby drove in.   Later on, each came up gaily with his or her present : a cheese, a tart, eggs, bulbs ticketed ' Queen Victoria'; 'Prince of Wales,' and the like."

She proceeded to Belgium, and arrived at Bois l'Evêque, Liège, on the evening of October 13th.

" A little English 'Daphne' came forward to present a nosegay, and bid Our Mother welcome in her native tongue. . . . Amongst the many *oeuvres* a particularly interesting feature of Bois l'Evêque is the reunions of the ' Association Ouvrière du Sacré Coeur' which take place there.   The day after her arrival the sturdy Walloon miners and other workmen mustered under the heads of the Association in our large *salon*, to pay their respects to the Mother General, whose hospitality they regularly enjoyed.   Each category had its scutcheon ; on that of the miners is blazoned the old cry *Al ward di Dieu*. [Under God's guard.]   They all make it together before descending 600 metres into the coal-pits ; . . . The men, as well as the choir boys, sang beautifully;   several addresses were spoken, and they offered as gifts a peal of bells and a censer. . . . There were many other receptions and presentations of our Liègois and Liègoises faithful to their old traditions and to the title of their province: *Sancta Legia Filia Romanae Ecclesiae*. . . .

" We gathered round her for recreation, 'Ah,' she said, turning to Mère de T'Serclaes, who was also leaning on a stick, having lately suffered by a fall, ' when we worked together thirty years ago at Marmoutier, we had no thought of arming ourselves with such a weapon ! ' . . . (She gave us her *impressions de voyage*.) . . . 'As I came along, the driver of the fiacre wanted me to admire every monument.   He stopped and alighted; ' Madame la Supérieure Générale, je désire vous montrer l'Hôtel de ville ! ' . . . 'This loyal country is in great delight with its celebrations for Prince Albert's marriage.   In Holland too, they are devoted to Queen Wilhelmina ;

'the little Queen'; her youth is a charm the more. . . I am devoted to Holland.' (And how about Belgium!) 'You fish with the net! Others attempt no more than rod and line. Mère de T'Serclaes says to me: 'Truly, *ma très Révérende Mère*, you are worthy to know Belgium!' As to this country, I share the mind of Leo XIII., whose venerable features light up, whatever his cares may be, when anything calls back the happy time of his nunciature!'"

Leo XIII., indeed, had never forgotten his relations with the *Sacred Heart* during his nunciature in Belgium, that "Paradise of Legates" as the saying goes. At the convent of Jette, near Brussels, he instituted the children's Literary Academy which still exists and is in fact now imitated in every school of the Congregation. He read and criticized the essays, presided at the debates, and awarded Degrees. The highest of these could be obtained only by a member whose essay had reached the maximum of marks, and who had moreover produced some notable work of fine art. This little circle was an agreeable diversion to the learned nuncio, whose health was delicate at the time, and who used to walk for his recreation on the beautiful wooded hill that forms part of the convent grounds; he drank daily of a medicinal well that is found there, and is surrounded by a stone parapet, whereon the Latin inscription now runs: *Joachin Pecci, once nuncio in Brussels, drank daily refreshing draughts from our spring; now he, Universal Pastor, waters us, his flock, by the words of life.*

"At our last reunion she resumed in a few words her teaching. . . . 'Love one another always with our primitive charity, and remain unshakeable in your attachment to our Society! . . . It has not yet gone through its great trial! . . .' 'What will happen,' said Mgr. Pie [1] to me in 1869, 'when all those amongst you who have known the Foundress will have passed away?' . . . The gardener and farm labourers waited for her as she drove off, to present a large gift of flowers. Catching sight of the stable hand, she said, compassionately: 'And I hear that you have had the misfortune to lose a horse!' The good man was touched to the bottom of his heart,—he felt himself understood!"

[1] *See* Baunard, *Hist. du Cardinal Pie*, Bishop of Poitiers (Poussielgue, 1893).

The most valuable part of every visit was the time spent in the interior of the community.   There she saw each one in private; she was liberal of her time, visited the sick, climbing steep stairs if necessary, a thing for her even dangerous.   To the invalids, her understanding and sympathy were precious.   She listened to every detail of an illness, now and then re-adjusted a bandage, or made some change to relieve the sufferer.   Madame d'H——, whose young life was ebbing away in intense pain that nothing could relieve, Mother Digby consoled in other wise.   Her parting words: "My child, I envy you!" shed a light over that life-in-death, and raised it from the plane of meek resignation to that of a lofty enthusiasm.

Reverend Mother Digby returned to Paris on May 30th.   In June, the Congregations were still at bay.   It appears to have been at this time that the *Sacred Heart* at any rate, compounded for the sum claimed by trans-forming it into a debt upon state funds.   Thus, for the present, the houses were saved.   This may be looked upon as a relative victory obtained by a long and steady resistance.

Yet, even now, a fresh storm was gathering.   In December 1897, M. Scheurer-Kestner, a Protestant, tried to get the Dreyfus case reopened.   But the ministry looked upon the attempt as directed against themselves, who had imprisoned Col. Picquart for declaring his belief that the Jewish captain had been condemned upon forged evidence.   The anti-Semites believed that Jewish money was being employed to release a guilty man; France, generally, was indignant that the Generals who had condemned Dreyfus, should be accused of so serious a miscarriage of justice; and the Catholics, in particular, regarded any attack upon the army as aimed at their own undoing.   It would not have been the first circuitous method employed against religion of late; and French soldiers at any rate, had for half a century clung to Christian traditions that lawyers and deputies were dis-posed to overthrow.   General Zurlinden, minister of War, had stoutly defended the Sisters employed for army work, and had obtained their exemption from the destructive tax ; the recent religious funerals of Canrobert and Trochu were a relief after the lugubrious burials of the free-masons, with their emblems of rattling tin, and their chill summons to *leave all hope behind*. It was the Socialists who championed Dreyfus, and Zola, whose "Lourdes' had lately struck many as disingenuous. Exasperated by persecution, the Catholics rushed with all the rest headlong into the fray. In vain the Pope raised a warn-ing voice ; whilst Orleanists and Bonapartists tried what adherents could be laid hold of in troubled waters, sharp eyes were watching, and material for a new and tremendous assault upon the Church—beginning of course with the Congregations — was being gathered up from the *Affaire*.

For the time, however, this engrossed ministerial attention, and there was a lull in the pursuit of the Congregations. But Mother Digby during a visit to Amiens spoke already in the most decided manner con-cerning their ultimate fate. "We shall be turned out of France at no long distance of time," she said. "What!" exclaimed the Superior of the house, her interlocutor, "is it possible! But no one else believes it! Our Bishops do not! . . . see the prayers that are being offered up . . . there is Montmartre! there is Lourdes! . . . And all our beautiful houses!" "God will require us to leave them." "And the body of Our Venerable Mother!" "We shall take her with us!" The one who reports this conversation declares that she herself remained thunderstruck, unable to face the bare possi-bility of the event.

This year Mother Digby again visited Marmoutier. The English lay Sister mentioned on p. 166 accompanied her, and relates the excitement that prevailed amongst the country people as her carriage drew near the village. Its entire population came out to greet her, whom they had seen depart with such regret five-and-twenty years before. A new generation had sprung up to inherit the same affection ; there were crowds of smiling faces, eager calls for recognition, and flowers filled the carriage when it halted. Grandmothers held up their grandchildren,

wives presented their husbands, well-grown men declared
themselves the "petits gars" of old Marmoutier. Gauthier,
the monastery servant, also appeared, now an old man;
he still kept a medal, Mother Digby's parting gift, under a
glass shade on his mantelpiece. As these good folk were
recognised by name, and interrogated concerning each
member of the family, the welcome rose to enthusiasm.
And Mother Digby, to whom the reception of "distinguished visitors" had always its painful side, was
really delighted.

Doctor H—— who had attended the wounded when the
convent became an ambulance in "Terrible Year," was
anxious to renew his acquaintance with Mother Digby.
They conversed long together; when he left, he looked
downcast and thoughtful. He had just renewed a
neglected promise made to her in 1871—that of returning to the practice of religion. The promise was kept
henceforth; he did not long survive this memorable
interview.

Here may be added a similar example of Mother
Digby's influence, exercised during her travels at a
different time and place. She had occasion to call upon
the Countess X—— regarding a house to be purchased for
the Society of the Sacred Heart. This lady, embittered
by family sorrows, had isolated herself even from the
great Consoler. After the interview she departed in a
flood of tears; from that day forth she was faithful to
her religious duties; she lived to mourn Mother Digby's
death with heartfelt grief.

Mother Digby visited again the silent community
who rested under the shadow of the ancient clocktower
at Marmoutier. Here lay many who had been her
daughters in the old days. She went on foot, slowly,
stopping now and then; for the distance was considerable,
and she was at present ill able to walk. Every stone of
Marmoutier cried out to her. Her last act before leaving
it was to enter the chapel, and, kneeling down, slowly
kiss the pavement.

She went on to the convents of Eastern France, amongst

others to that of Chambéry in Savoy, where deaf mutes
are taught by very successful methods to understand
and speak.

She arrived in Rome on December 11th, and that day
week was received with six of her religious at the Vatican.
As they advanced for homage, the Pope called out, " Ah !
Mother Digby, Superior General of the Religious of the
Sacred Heart ! Come ! Come ! I know you well, and am
glad to see you—in spite of the motive. . . . Is her health
better?" he asked of the Superior of the Trinità dei
Monti. . . . "And how goes it in France?" "We have
received as yet only threats. We believe that none will
be executed until after the next elections, so as to avoid
public excitement as much as possible. . . ." "The
government knows well enough," said Leo XIII. "that
we only desire liberty in order to do good, and that we
are neither socialists nor radicals, but moderates. Yet it
shuts its eyes, for it wishes to please all parties !" And,
by an expressive gesture, he indicated the impossibility
of such a programme.

In answer to further questions, Mother Digby informed
him of her intended visits to Algiers, and to Spain. . . .
"Good, good ; you will find there a mild climate." . . .
"And will your Holiness approve of my going to
America?" He appeared startled; he seized Mother
Digby's hand with earnestness. "But your health ! Can
it endure such a journey? the sea-passage? change of
country?" "Most holy Father, I have many houses to
see there !" "And what do the Mothers say?" He
turned a questioning gaze upon the nuns. They
remained silent; he seemed to reflect, and then said :
"You must consult the doctors, and then go, unless it
endangers your life." He added, with immense weight
and earnestness : "God has given you a special mandate,
and He wills that you should fulfil it for as long a period
as possible."

And in this manner Mother Digby felt that a long-
cherished design had now the highest sanction. She
meant to carry it out in the coming year.

The Cardinal Protector heard with interest of her projected visit to Spain, his former nunciature, and laid upon her as a duty to visit first the Santa Casa at Loreto.   She went there in January, 1898, made the pilgrimage with all devotion, and received letters constituting her a "Dame d'honneur" of the Holy House. In 1860 there had been a convent of the Sacred Heart at Loreto, upon Monte Reale.   It faced Castelfidardo, and the religious could follow all the vicissitudes of that most glorious defeat.   The walls of the convent were the last refuge of the papal soldiers, outnumbered ten to one; they ranged their cannon and their cavalry beneath the windows, resolved to resist to the end.   The first act of the victors was to turn out the nuns, and the convent, in 1898, was used as a silk factory.

It was still January when she paid a first visit to Algiers.   The Mediterranean from Marseilles appeared stormy; to those who begged her to postpone the journey she answered laughing: "We have all been wishing for martyrdom, and shall I draw back before sea-sickness? *Duc in altum.*"[1] The bad crossing seemed forgotten when she arrived at the convent, the old palace of Mustapha, with its gardens and palm-trees, and all her interest was on the alert.   The European children, as their holiday treat in her honour, entertained over a hundred little Arabs, brought by the *Religieuses Missionaires de L'Afrique*, who directed the Orphanage.   The French girls seemed fascinated by the long look of compassion cast by Mother Digby on the dark creatures to whom she was distributing clothes.   Such expressions are more striking when they play upon what is called *a strong face.*   "See how she loves them!" whispered the children; and they furtively changed their places that they might observe her countenance, which recalled the *misertus est super turbam*[2] of the Master.

It may be imagined how Spain and the Spaniards, a country and people so unique, so different and characteristic in each province, appealed to Mother Digby.   She visited

---

[1] Luke v. 4.   [2] Mark vi. 34.

her seven houses : Barcelona—where, not many years later, her daughters had to conceal themselves in cellars from the ruffians of the revolution ;—Sarriâ, close by ; Saragossa, Seville, Bilbao, besides two at Madrid, and Chamartin in its neighbourhood.   The school receptions, as might have been expected, were founded upon memories of St James of Compostella, King James of Aragon, and other worthies and champions.

During Mother Digby's stay Queen Maria Christina arrived ; unannounced, in order that no trouble being taken for her own reception, all the honours might be directed to the Mother General.   Every one was struck with the dignified and simple way of Mother Digby's converse and manner with the Queen.   In a land where ceremony still lingers more fully perhaps than anywhere in Europe, the English nun seemed never at a loss.   The Queen saw Mother Digby several times, and told her of many solicitudes.   The war with America was imminent, and the spirit of revolution in Spain was eager for a pretext. " Pray, pray much for the King, will you not? " were her last and earnest words.

"Spain is still the country of faith," said Mother Digby later.   " The street crier calls out at every hour of the night: 'Praised be Jesus Christ!' then, 'Ten o'clock, and fine weather,' as the case may be."

Soon after, there was grave news from the Antilles. The Cuban war had broken out ; Porto Rico and Havana were blockaded and bombarded, the houses of the Sacred Heart at both places were under fire, and all communications were cut off.   Not till August did Mother Digby learn that her nuns at Havana had been in want of bread ; with the news came a tale of wonderful preservation through many dangers.

After the Spanish visits she travelled to Vendée and Brittany, another world *sui generis*.   The children were indeed a contrast to the *méridionales* of Lyons and Marseilles.   Clad in Breton costumes, with dances and folk-songs, they celebrated the granite rocks and sturdy faith of their province, its battlefields, its emblem

the ermine, and motto : *Plutôt la mort que la souillure !*[1]
At Quimper they sang :

> " Oh qu'elle est belle, ma Bretagne !
> Sous son ciel gris il faut la voir
> Elle est plus belle que l'Espagne "[2] . . .

So the refrain ran on, and parallels were drawn
between the Britain of France and that of Mother
Digby. The children were delighted with her pertinent
replies. She said a few words on the battle of life, and
on fidelity to God through times so difficult. They gave
gifts, clothing for the poor made in their free time, and
by their closing hymn called down blessings on the
Mother General :

> *O Vierge, bénis-là quand finit la journée*
> *Dont elle a supporté le poids et la chaleur,*
> *Pour qu'elle soit alors de paix environnée*
> *Fais-là reposer sur ton Coeur.*[3]

As she listened, tears were seen upon her cheek.

At Laval, in April, she found traces of her predecessor,
Mother Goetz ; "where (said Mother Digby) she suffered
so much in 1870. Here was the sanctuary where she went
to kneel when this world seemed too heavy, as happens
sometimes, along the short dark path that men call life."

On April 21st she returned to Paris.

[1] Rather death than defilement !
[2] Ah ! how fair is my Brittany !   Under her grey skies, see, fairer than Spain !
[3] O Virgin ! bless her, at the close of the day of which she has borne the heat
and the burden ; then let her rest upon Thy heart, there to find peace.

CHAPTER XIX

AMERICA

"They find themselves compelled to look around for some great bond of fellowship, which may embrace all who love order and freedom, and light and justice; all men of every climate, and language, and people."—KENELM DIGBY, *Godefridus* (Lumley, 1844), p. 126.

AND now Reverend Mother Digby carried out a long-cherished idea — that of visiting the American houses. No superior General had as yet been able to do so. The Venerable Mother Duchesne, one of the first companions of the Foundress, had sailed with a few others for North America in 1818; where, at the repeated risk of their lives, and through extraordinary hardships, she and her fellow labourers had established the *Sacred Heart* firmly in the New World. Union of mind and heart had been maintained by frequent communication with the Motherhouse, and visitors had gone out in the name of each succeeding head of the Congregation; still, the American nuns repeatedly urged their wish to see the Mother General herself. She had made up her mind; her advisers bowed to the decision, and a circular announced it to the whole Society.

"In face of this grave decision, I recall a certain day in 1864, when, kneeling beside our Venerable Mother, she said to me after a moment's recollection: *You will go to America*. May she now bless her own Society, may she cover by her protection the visits I am about to undertake, and assure their fruitfulness for good. The itinerary subjoined will be followed according to the power that the Heart of Jesus will bestow upon me; this capacity will be for me the indication of God's Will."

She goes on to say that all correspondence and affairs are to be transmitted to her as usual.

On August 6th Roehampton was expectant on the garden terrace.   Reverend Mother Digby was coming to join her English travelling companions.

"At last (says the house journal) we saw Mrs Bertram Currie's carriage drive in at the gate.   As it entered all the bells of the house were set ringing.   The carriage was well hidden under the limes of the community alley; then, as it swept round by the plane tree, we saw our Mother's face smiling at us from the window, and we could not repress a sort of British cheer!—subdued, however, for she put her finger to her lips."

On August 11th, accompanied by the Superior of Roehampton and another religious, and the lay Sister who was her usual companion, she took her departure for Liverpool.

"We must be generous [so ran her adieu] and give always with a large heart.   You must write often to Reverend Mother.   As for the novices [she said with a smile] they should do so every fortnight.   The Cardinal Protector, speaking to me lately on this subject, declared that if novices do not give an account of themselves it is as if some one buys sacks labelled *wheat*, and never opens them to make sure it really *is* wheat!   [As she drove off, she ended] You have all made me very happy!"

It was a solemn moment; she was taking her life in her hand.   Would she leave it in America?

"ON BOARD THE *DOMINION*,
August 14th, 1898.

"So far the passage is not good; there is a strong head wind, so we are losing time.   Our Mother feels it very much, but thanks to all the prayers has stood it better than I should have dared to hope. . . . *Aug.* 17 [the anniversary of Mother Digby's first arrival at Roehampton] Posts have been active since this was written.   She had a great surprise; she liked so much what you sent, and said 'Poor old Roehampton, fancy their remembering this!' then she read out, 'Her children rose up and called her blessed.'   '*Weren't they fools!*' she added. It was dreadful; but so characteristic that I have to tell you!"

Mother Digby's message to England was: "I wish all happiness in the Heart of Jesus to every one in the dear old island home."

She was true to her resolve and advice "not to travel about like luggage." "We are an educational Order," she would say, "and must try and improve ourselves." She watched with real delight the spouting whales, and the glorious colour of a large iceberg that passed by in full view under the sunlight.

"SAULT AU RÉCOLLET, *Aug.* 21.

"Yesterday evening the *Dominion* landed our dear Mother General at Montreal at 6 P.M. . . . The Sault was reached in about an hour, bells ringing and chinese lanterns and a long wooden slope all dressed in evergreens, and the Ensign and the flag of St Patrick side by side with appropriate inscriptions. The Community were there; they sang the Magnificat with variations [such pretty voices] and all felt themselves in heaven. I alone remained on earth, considering the fatigue for our Mother. There were quantities of letters from Canada and the States and telegrams and telephone messages kept coming in."

Nothing could exceed the heartiness of the welcome given her by Mother Digby's trans-Atlantic daughters, the care with which all receptions had been planned, and above all, the eagerness of the religious to profit largely by intercourse with her. "They gaze at her," says the writer of the letters above, "with indescribable eagerness." Her visit began with the seven houses of Canada.

"*London, Ontario, Sept.* 19: This is the fifth visit, and it passes over the house like a great wave of grace, and leaves them all so grateful, and drawing a long breath. . . . And it makes one feel *our* great responsibility, having had her for so long, example and teaching together. . . ."

The course of these visits was always alike, so says the same writer; a little awe and shyness at the first meeting with a Superior General; then a rapid expansion of spirit as it became clear that it was a *Mother* General rather than a *Superior*; and genuine, childlike, heartfelt regret when the short days come to an end.

At Halifax, the much-desired Indians—that race had been the first object of Mother Duchesne's zeal—came to see Mother Digby.

"They wore the native dress, but no feathers. There was the Chief, the Judge, their respective wives, and some grandchildren. Sister R—— implored our Mother not to go near the Chief alone, 'as he might still be a little savage!' He is very gentle, however, but has a watchful eye, the eye that might be something more than fiery if the Christianity in it were extinguished. But he is very good. He sang the *Veni Creator* for our Mother in his own language; seeing that she was pleased, he went on louder and louder with the *Regina Coeli*, and then a *Kyrie Eleison* that might have been heard in the street."

The Vicariate of the western States contained the houses first founded by Mother Duchesne; that of St Charles, Missouri, had become doubly interesting since it was expected that the cause of her canonization would soon be introduced.

"*St Charles, Nov.* 8: I cannot describe to you how the presence of our dear Mother Duchesne seems to be constantly with one, above all in the cell in which she died, now made into a little oratory for our Mother. At one end hangs the painting of the death of St Francis Regis; under it are the table on which Mother Duchesne used to write, her note books, her office book with many prayers in her fine beautiful writing, her crucifix, and—one of the dearest things of all,—her old chair, of which she renewed the seat herself with a bit of cord and buffalo hide. . . . Reverend Mother B—— is determined that our Mother is to be cured here, and she would throw me into the Mississippi if she could discover in the depths of my heart that I do not think it too! but rather that God will continue to give her the daily bread of strength and suffering together."

In the cell of the Venerable Philippine Duchesne, redolent of prayer and self-sacrifice, Mother Digby wrote a letter full of deep feeling. The secret of Mother Duchesne's power, she pointed out, was in a practical

devotion to the Sacred Heart; men were seeking everywhere a means for the world's renewal and reformation,
but only in Christ can it be found. . . . All were urged
to turn this treasure to the highest profit; no one must
think that she had now done enough. Mother Digby
declared her consolation at having experienced in the New
World so perfect a union of mind and heart in the Society
she had been called upon to govern.

"St Joseph (Mo), *Nov.* 13.

"Last Sunday at St Louis (Mo) we saw the past,—the real past.
All the old ladies who could say they were actual children of Mother
Duchesne were invited to come together and be presented to our
Mother. There must have been some sixty or seventy of them, and
our chapel at Benediction was filled with venerable grey heads.
They were gathered together in a parlour afterwards, and our
Mother went and talked to them; there was no address, for no
one was capable of making it; their ages ranged from 75 to 90;
some could hardly walk, and one was on crutches. They looked
with compassion upon our Mother's youth! but they came up
like children to get little pictures from her, leaning on one another,
and each, as she arrived, had some little recollection of Mother
Duchesne: 'I used to sit on the floor by her and she told me
about the French Revolution.' 'I held the pall at her funeral'
(this was one of the blue ribbons). Another, whose humility made
some little resistance, was dragged into the middle by three others
as being 'the first *Prize of Success* at St Louis.' Many said that
the *Life* did not half do justice to M. Duchesne. It was altogether
a very touching assemblage of *relics*."

". . . It was twelve hours quiet journey yesterday from St
Louis; there was an ideal Saturday evening sunset, waggons and
farmers going quickly home in beautiful forest tracks. Our Mother
watched it all; the lighthearted train flourished us smoothly through
the oaks; little round black pigs feeding on the acorns added to the
picturesque and gave salutary matter for reflection."

The Mother General's characteristic disregard of herself appeared often in her decisions about journeys: she
desired that her companions should see as much as possible
of the beauty of the country, regardless of the inconvenience
or possible risk to herself. She accordingly decided to go

from Omaha to San Francisco by Denver, and over the Tenessee Pass, instead of taking an easier route. It was the end of November; many were the prophecies of mishap by those who knew the difficulties of the season. Over the Tenessee Pass, more than 10,000 feet in altitude, it was "madness" to take a traveller with a weak heart; such a one had scarcely lived through the ordeal of breathing the rarefied air; another had been ill for months; a third had never been the same again. Besides, the trains were frequently snowed up at that time of year; and who could tell how long she might be delayed, and what she would go through on the way? Her companions did not set out in high spirits for this four days' journey. But she had made up her mind, and nothing daunted her. The trains for a week before and a week after were snowbound, but hers passed through without a hitch, and arrived half a minute before the scheduled time at San Francisco. She had suffered no inconvenience in crossing the Pass, and was delighted with the glories of the road.

"Did you not admire the splendours of your passage?" said some one to her afterwards. "Yes! but I thought, too, of the rapid train cleaving the air, and leaving no trace behind, and so of my own life."

At every arrival in town, the Children of Mary and the friends of the Convent vied with one another as to the honourable reception and escort for the Mother General and her party; the thoughtful consideration and lavish care could not have been surpassed.

"SAN FRANCISCO, *Dec.* 1.

"At Oaklands, the President of the Children of Mary and others, each with a carriage and pair, disputed as to the honour of driving even the members of our Mother General's party. Of course, she was secured by the President; we were dispersed in separate carriages; the husbands ran about with the hand luggage like railway porters, and everybody's hands seemed full of orchids of marvellous size and beauty.

"Mrs S—— has been so thoughtful, so energetic in doing what she could for our Mother, who wanted to see the new property; this good Mrs S—— waited three hours in an office to bully the officials into letting her take her carriage through the station, across the network of lines, to the train, to save walking: she got leave, and it was beautifully done. The pair of chestnuts found themselves almost between two engines, that nearly touched their flanks; one before them and several behind, all snorting, and all moving, and ringing their big bells; the poor dears reared up in horror one moment at their position, and then, trembling all over, let themselves be threaded in and out by a coachman all coolness. They did the same thing coming back in even more difficult conditions, for it was a crowded hour and beginning to get dark. Our Mother *loved* those two horses!"

Menlo Park, at San Matéo, California, was a foundation of Mother Digby's own generalate; the building had been completed in 1898, and a school was already established.

"When we heard that our Very Reverend Mother was at Maryville, the centre of the Vicariate, our expectations grew keen. We all knew by experience, however, the fatigue that, in spite of all American comfort, ensues from four days and nights consecutive railway travelling, and that she must brave snow and icy weather before penetrating as far as our delightful climate. . . . Her conference reminded us of our duty as foundresses. ' It is Our Lord Himself who has chosen each of you, and called you by name, that you might have the honour and the responsibility of this new foundation. It is you who will establish its traditions: of obedience, of poverty, and of silence. If there are fatigues and privations to be endured, you will remember His words to His apostles: When I sent you forth to preach the gospel, did you want for anything? But they answered Him: Nothing.' . . . Her last advice ran: ' Never waste time. God himself, generous and all powerful, does not give us back lost time!' As she left she quoted St Francis of Sales, 'Those who go, stay, and those who stay, depart with the others.' In deeply moved silence we watched the carriage out of sight, and then retired to the chapel to give thanks for the graces of those short but well-filled days."

"*Dec.* 8: We have been to Menlo Park since I last wrote; such a beautiful place, and such a curious mixture; the style of the house (only one wing built) Spanish, like the old Californian mission houses; it will be a quadrangle with open cloisters. The property is timbered with oaks, quite an English park; the two ranges

R

of mountains are distinctly Californian, such beautiful shapes,
and such changing shades of blue. Flocks of wild canaries come,
numerous as our sparrows, to feed on the seeds of the marigold. . . .
We went by the Pacific shore, and so our Mother saw that ocean
face to face, and thought it so beautiful, so stately and calm. We
could see the seals in the distance coming up on the rocks, and
plunging back into the sea; we saw too some buffaloes in an
enclosure, large and sullen-looking, prodigious in strength. Our
Mother regrets much that the great herds of them are destroyed.
We came home through Chinatown; what a place! could one ever
forget those swarms of faces that look out from cellars and doors
and windows, all stamped with such deep sadness, and some with
such hatred.

" *Dec.* 14: In the Mexican desert.

"The car has no heating apparatus, and it froze very hard
last night, so that I fear our Mother felt the cold. The car was
alas very shaky and she got little rest. This afternoon, at 4.30,
we cross the tropical line. To-day we are in a desert, and we
see little trains of donkeys or mules and Mexicans riding about
in a wild half aimless way, in high pointed straw hats and scarlet
blankets."

In Mexico, Mother Digby half felt herself in Spain
again on account of the deep faith of the people. Everything and everybody was Catholic except the government,
a close oligarchy of " anti-clericals " after the French model.
Many members thereof, however, and the President himself, were altogether liberal, and lovers of freedom. His
wife was an excellent Catholic and a great friend of the
Sacred Heart.

"Every one here from the Papal Delegate downward speaks in
terms of the highest admiration of Porfirio Diaz, the President, and
asks what Mexico will do when he dies. His wife came to see our
Mother, and talked of *Porfirio mi esposo.* Mgr. Averandi, the Papal
Legate, came a second time yesterday; the Archbishop of Mexico
came, and the Archbishop of Puebla, who stayed an hour and a
half—an interesting visit."

Mexico was the only country in the world where nuns
might have been obliged in travelling to put off **the**

religious habit. But the President sent word to Mother Digby that she might dress herself as she would. There were many wandering merchants near Mexico city, selling opals; one of them slipped six into Mother Digby's hand with the words: "Take them; you belong to God!"

"*Guadalajara, Dec.* 20: Guadalajara is built round quadrangles, with cloisters; such weather, neither hot nor cold, and beautiful sun. . . . The foreman of the buildings, when called, comes bounding like a lion from his scaffolding through the orange trees in his scarlet blanket, with eyes terrible by nature but softened by religion; he looks at our Mother with the puzzled entreaty of a big dog trying to read in her face what she wants; it is translated for him; then, if it is a specimen of a fruit from the top of a tree, he drops his blanket, shakes of his sandals, and runs up like a squirrel. . . .

"*Guanajuato, Jan.* 11, 1899: This is such a beautiful place, up in the mountains; for the last five miles to it one must go in muletrams. The Governor, who is friendly, sent his private team for our Mother, and one of his guards in white uniform, with bright pistols, and a belt full of ammunition. The mules took the hills at a gallop. Yesterday our Mother went some distance up the dry bed of a torrent, and enjoyed the beauty and solitude; occasionally, however, Indian heads crop up behind bushes, like Zulus in South Africa but more friendly. The children, too, have good faces; but there are shadows to the picture, and ghastly tales. . . ."

Mexico had memories of the unfortunate Emperor Maximilian; Mother Digby passed before the three simple crosses, erected where he was shot near Queretaro. She was told that he gave money to the executioners not to mutilate his face, in order that his mother might recognize him. Colonel Lopez, who betrayed him, was travelling on one occasion in the same train with Mother Digby; he was pointed out to her; every one shrank away from him, and he was left alone. The Archbishop of Puebla had entertained the Emperor and his wife at his palace, in a ghostly suite of rooms with galleries, curtains and paintings, where some of Mother Digby's party slept for a night.

The Vicariate of Louisiana was next visited. At St Michel were buried the pioneers of the Society of the Sacred Heart in America. A member of the Community there writes as follows of Mother Digby's visit:

"A regular blizzard, a rare thing here, burst over the country. What could we do! our visit to the cemetery could not take place; the whole country round being covered with a thin coat of ice, and our horses were never shod for that sort of weather. 'But why should not I walk?' said our Mother General, and walk she did, though we much feared that she would slip or fall. What was a novelty for Louisiana, however, was an old experience for her. She set off leaning on my arm, and surrounded by most careful daughters. When we reached the cemetery she paused, made a solemn sign of the cross, and then advanced at once to the vault and asked to be shown the spot where Mother Galitzin rests. I was much impressed by our Mother's emotion. What passed between her and those pioneer souls of our early Louisiana mission? . . . Mother G—— drew her attention to the dilapidated state of the vault. She had purposely refrained from repairing it, waiting to know our Mother's wish; she had thought of placing all the remains in one large coffin. Reverend Mother Digby turned round vehemently: 'God forbid, Reverend Mother! No, let each one have a separate box, never mind how small it may be.' What a relief this was to the elders amongst us, a goodly number of whom had lived long years here and known these eminent dead as friends. . . . It was raining as she drove away, and the Reverend Mother took up a patchwork quilt and tucked it round her in the carriage. 'Ah! it was not thus our Mother Duchesne travelled!' said our Mother General regretfully. We watched the carriage till the bend in the road hid it from view and then hastened to the upper gallery, where we followed with streaming eyes but grateful hearts the long line of steam and smoke that marked the tram's course to New Orleans."

The American children pleased her much. Amongst many reminiscences is that of a deputy of six years old sent to represent the school at a railway station; incapable of a set speech, she placed a huge nosegay of magnificent roses in the Mother General's hand, saying, with the directness of her nation: "Here, these are all for you." There was a charming reception in the boy's day-school at Chicago:

"These heroes drew up in a semicircle, heels together, heads erect, large white favours, spotless white kid gloves. Each carried a beautiful nosegay of tea roses or white carnations, and a nice red-brown head made his speech with entire self-possession. Then each boy came up, and knelt on one knee to present his flowers, looking up to our Mother General with respect and awe! She gave them red rosaries, and their delight was great; they nearly flew at a poor newcomer of five years who had ventured to turn his back in returning!"

Amongst the thirty - five school - receptions by the boarding-schools, none seemed to give her more pleasure than the beautiful tableaux at Maryville (Mo).

"All were full of thought and very touching; they related to Mother Duchesne: 1. Ruth in exile from her own country, gleaning in the fields of Booz; 2. Rebecca at the well, turning her back on the riches of Abraham to give water from her own wells to the thirsty camels, typifying Mother Duchesne's dear Indians; 3. The years of her hidden life at St Charles: St Mary Magdalen at the feet of Our Lord."

Then there were the populous elementary or parochial schools attached to each house; the children—over five thousand in the northern continent—anxiously awaited their turn to put on white frocks and see "the Mother President"; no title seeming higher to these loyal republicans. "Such bright happy faces, and such perfect discipline," says the letter. Not the least interesting were the Indian schools of Mexico, and the coloured schools of the Louisiana and Mexico vicariates. At St Michel, Louisiana, men and women and children of colour assembled to receive from Mother Digby medals and kind words. Four generations were present, and she noted the admirable background to the dusky faces made by the white and yellow hangings of the room. Young "George Washington" danced solemnly before her, the rest keeping time with hands and feet, and producing a sort of monotonous music with which his steps fell in. Seeing the Mother General's appreciation the music got louder and louder, and George Washington went on so long that the nuns had at last to beg him to stop.

On March 16th, Mother Digby arrived at Manhattanville, New York, where amongst others very well known to her of the one hundred and ten religious, was Mother Errington, the mistress general. It was Lent, and the Mother General sent word that she wished for a very simple reception; no decorations were placed on the exterior of the house. Immense numbers of gifts, however, had been prepared for her: in church linen for instance, and clothes for the poor. Even the seven hundred of the parochial School had done their utmost, and came with little rabbits, doves, or other presents in kind. Mother Digby had arranged to stay a month at Manhattanville, and to assemble there, first all the Mistresses of Studies of America and Canada in consultation, and then the Superiors for a common retreat. Great was the joy at these prospects.

But, three days after her arrival, Mother Digby fell very ill for a week. The state of her heart gave terrible anxiety; then she recovered, and all her plans were carried out.

On April 29th, Reverend Mother Digby left America. Thus wrote one who was left behind:

" *Manhattanville, April* 29: After early Mass, the children were ranged along the avenue. The day was grey and sombre; its colour reflected our feelings. Our beloved Mother blessed us for the last time. . . . She who suffered the most from this departure was the one who best consoled us. I shall never forget the look of our dear Mother Errington, who, at the sight of my tears, said to me with a sort of indignation; 'Ought you not rather to be thanking God for this visit?'"

Mother Digby thoroughly understood the proverbial enterprize and generosity of the American nation, its appreciation of the good and great. Putting together

her own words to the Americans themselves as they report them at different times, they read :

"She spoke so earnestly of the force and activity of the American character—of American straightforwardness—independence—and loyalty to those in authority. It was wonderful to hear her speak of all our different houses ; she followed the work of each with the same accuracy as if she were its vicar—She rejoiced to find the traditions of the Society so faithfully carried out in this country — She spoke earnestly of the great work done,—and still to be done—Above all, she said, you must make the children supernatural. The tendency of America has been the other way, as might have been expected. The country is still young ; minds are now being more generally cultured, and the supernatural, the spiritual, will follow. Strengthen the faith of the children ; they have not the centuries of faith behind them that we have in Europe, but you must teach them to be strong."

What did America think of Mother Digby? In the reminiscences available, the same words occur many times over. Those that follow are perhaps most typical.

"The Superior General of a great Institute, the fêted guest of thousands who loved her as a mother and revered her as a saint, she spoke and acted with the directness of a child, though with a wisdom that was the admiration of all who were in a position to see its workings.—When she left us at last, we had but one thought: gratitude to God for this gift of her to our Society."

The general Statement that "she passed, doing good," is borne out by a cumulation of traits and benefits quoted, ranging from a parochial school to hold four hundred children, built at St Joseph's, Missouri, for the Bishop, who was unable to meet the expense, and supplied with teachers, down to a passing expression of countenance that, like the material benefits, will probably be remembered by many for a life time.

Certain phrases of hers were specially treasured in America.

" What has impressed me most in our Mother General is the
weight of words that from another might be soon forgotten as
commonplace, but, coming from her lips, were guiding principles
as : Loyalty is a beautiful trait in a character, but there is no
loyalty without obedience — I thank God (she said, with simple
and humble dignity) I have never obeyed man or woman, but
God whom they represented—When I enter a house it is not
the number of children or the brilliancy of the teachers that I
look to, but the spirit of prayer of the religious—To our children
she gave two mottos : *Take always the straight course, come what
will*, and : *Do not consider what the world but what God will say.*
Her last words to us all were: *Be worthy daughters of our Mother
Foundress even unto death !* "

To all this it may be added, that it cost Reverend
Mother Digby very much not to pursue her journey
further into South America, and as far as Australia.
Her heart longed to know each of her religious families,
and her advisers had very great trouble in holding her
back.

Mother Digby arrived at Roehampton on May 12th.

" I only saw our Mother General once, and I was then quite
a small child.   It was upon her return from America with Reverend
Mother in 1899.   We had all been counting the days ; at last we
stood upon the terrace waiting for the carriage.   It was a perfect
day, and we wore white uniforms and carried flowers.   However,
I was put under a cloud for a minute, by my neighbour whispering
to me with great joy and superiority : ' It is *our* coachman and
our carriage that is bringing them ! '   Oh ! how I envied her, and
she had a bouquet, too !   But the carriage turned in at the gates,
and everything else was forgotten.   We cheered and threw our
flowers into the carriage and were nearly wild with joy.   By the
time the house was reached, Mother General was sitting in a very
bower of roses ; she smiled at us, and seemed so amused and
happy.   Then we all flocked to the church for the Te Deum.   We
were told that we nearly brought the roof down with our voices,
and I reflected how dangerous Te Deums of that kind must be.
Then Our Mother General came into the study room very slowly,
smiling and looking at everything.   There were beautiful tableaux,
and verses that I could not understand, but at last it was over, and
we waited for her to speak.   She was silent for a moment or two, as

if she were thinking about us, and she looked at us with her head just a little thrown back.   Then she said, with that wonderful voice of hers 'Children, I have brought you back your Mother.' All eyes turned to Reverend Mother, who was sitting beside Mother General holding her bouquet ; the simple phrase won all our hearts. I could not take in much else of what she said, and I was so fascinated that I did not take my eyes off her face, but watched every movement and the play of her features.   Then I went up and she gave me a picture :—and that was all.   Years after I wrote to the Motherhouse asking for prayers, and my correspondent replied that our Mother General remembered me quite well. The thought of this remembrance has helped me through many a bad moment."

On May 20th Mother Digby went back to Paris.

There the sky was frowning.

On June 23rd, M. Waldeck-Rousseau came forward as President of the Council and minister of Worship. He, Jules Ferry, and Gambetta have been ranked together as men of marked ability in the Third Republic. His programme had long been proclaimed : in 1882 and in 1883 bills of proscription for the Congregations had borne his name.

An attempt was made to rouse public opinion against the intended victims.   Passing over the usual Radical rhetoric, an attack that gained credence amongst the inexperienced, Catholics or no, was made upon the educational system of the free schools.   The teachers, it was said, possessed for the most part no diplomas, and were therefore inefficient.   Their defence was ably conducted : confining the present narrative to what regards the congregations of women, it was pointed out that the primary schools adopted of necessity the government programme, and that the teachers were, since 1882, as they must be, furnished with the *brevet de capacité* ; and that in the convent boarding-schools, which imparted secondary or higher education, the teachers were also usually provided with degrees and diplomas—it might be for credit's sake alone ; for such certificates throw no light on the teaching power of their possessor, and are no sure guide to her learning and mental capacity.

Where the plan of studies proper to any Congregation was considered by experienced head Mistresses preferable to the Government plan, examinations more than equivalent in intellectual value—speaking generally—to those of the Lycées were exacted from the pupils. But it was, in truth, the thousands of children who crowded into the convents of France, "amounting," said M. de Haussonville, "to a plebiscite of parents," that impelled a party, determined to secure a monopoly, to proscribe successful rivals.

Soeur Marie du Sacré Coeur, a cloistered nun of the convent of Issoire in Auvergne[1] had striven in a recent book to discredit the education received by girls in convents. The indictment ran thus: nuns remained fixed in a quiet routine; their teaching was therefore inferior to that of the State Lycées; the convents were in consequence emptying rapidly of pupils; the remedy proposed was the foundation of a Normal School in Paris, to which all religious women teachers must go.

That there was, and always will be, room for improvement in the teaching of religious orders, as well as in that of other educational bodies, is a platitude to all who follow up the periodical conferences of head masters and mistresses concerned with every grade. The question is, how to bring about better results.

The book of Soeur Marie, appearing at this crisis, was a godsend to the partizans of the Girls Lycées. It was reviewed with triumph as unanswerable;[2] it had a re-echo in England.

Leo XIII., always on the watch, entrusted the examination, not only of the volume, but of the whole matter in question, to the Sacred Congregation of Bishops and Regulars.

Meanwhile, the work was effectively judged. The answers cannot here be fully set out. Who does not know that it may take a volume to bring home the inaccuracy of a single phrase of general accusation?

It will suffice to say, that Soeur Marie's well-intentioned

[1] Of that *Congregation of Notre Dame* (not to be confounded with that of Namur, or with other Congregations of the same name), founded by Ven. Louise de Lestonnac.

[2] *Revue de l'Enseignement secondaire des jeunes filles*, July 1898.

allegations were without proofs—for a few individual cases do not amount to proof; that the author was clearly ignorant of the teaching Congregations generally ; that the number of pupils in convents as computed in statistics had augmented steadily from the years 1880 to 1904,—this augmentation being the chief argument brought forward for their destruction ; that Ecoles Normales for the training of religious teachers had already been at work in England for thirty years; that in 1898 they existed in Belgium, Austria, and even in Paris—the Institut Normal de la Rue Jacob.[1]

In March appeared the reply of the Sacred Congregation, addressed to the Bishops of France. The book of Soeur Marie was condemned ; a decision to which its author, and the Bishop of Avignon, who had supported it, submitted immediately. The rest of the Bishops hastened to transmit to the Congregations the Roman reply, and to add to it the expression of their own personal satisfaction.

The Commission "after the most careful enquiries" did full justice to the

"*excellent* services of religious congregations in the *civil* formation of girls, as well as their training in piety and *knowledge*. There was no need of a general measure. In particular cases, reforms, if useful, would be made."

The last words of the Commission expressed a noble trust in the Orders.

"They would not fail in the future any more than they had done in the past; they would, directed and aided by the Bishops, take measures amply calculated to satisfy Christian parents, and to bring up young girls in *the culture* suited to a Christian woman."[2]

This was, in fact, putting the Congregations "on their honour" to leave no effort untried for improvement; and as in education advance is always possible, and as each succeeding generation requires extension or intension of the educational plan to suit the present needs, it was in accordance with the custom of all teaching societies,

[1] The reports of the government Inspectors of Girls' Schools in England do ample justice to the Higher as well as to the Primary education as conducted by religious women.
[2] Romae ex Secretaria S.C. Epp. et Reg. die 27 martii 1899.

and of her own in particular, that Mother Digby convened a gathering of the European Mistresses of Studies. At Conflans, both in private consultation and general meetings, experiences were compared, and changes inaugurated; the literary and historical standard of the studies was to be maintained, while the sphere of experimental science was to be enlarged and made real.

In September Mother Digby made a journey[1] to her houses in the Low Countries; travelling to Charleville, Lille, and Amiens, and returning to the Motherhouse on November 14th.

The Centenary of the Society of the Sacred Heart was to be celebrated on November 21st 1900, in the year that closed the nineteenth century; the *Annus Sanctus* of the Papal Jubilee, a year, too, dedicated to the God-Man by Leo XIII. His magnificent ideal that *all things should be renewed in Christ* was announced by a solemn consecration of the human race to the Sacred Heart upon that very feast, in June.[2] "Are you satisfied, nuns of the Sacred Heart?" exclaimed the Pope, with his wonderful smile, at their next audience—"are you satisfied with what I have done?"

A letter from the Vatican itself was to honour and rejoice not only Mother Digby, but the whole Society that she governed.

"To our beloved daughter, Josephine Digby, Superior General of the Society of the Sacred Heart of Jesus. Leo XIII. Pope. Beloved daughter, Greeting and the Apostolic Benediction."[3]

"The sense of joy which all Catholics experience during the whole course of this present year, on account of the great Jubilee proclaimed by Us, is increased for you

[1] *See* p. 241.

[2] This consecration was suggested in a very mysterious manner to the Pope by the saintly and most charming Countess Maria-Anna Droste zu Vischering, the young Superior of a convent of the Good Shepherd at Porto in Portugal. She died on the eve of the feast, after an extraordinary lifework of good to her orders. She kept intact her love for the Society of the Sacred Heart, the home of her youth, where she had first learnt this devotion as a pupil of Riedenburg, in the Tyrol. *See* Louis Chasle, *Soeur Marie du Divin Coeur* (Paris, Beauchesne, 1905).

[3] *Dilectae Filiae Josephae Digby, Antistitae Generali Sororum a S. Corde Jesu, Leo PP. XIII. Dilecta Filia, Salutem et Apostolicam Benedictionem.*

Laetitiae sensus, quem catholici universi, toto hoc elabente anno, percipiunt ex Jobelaeo magno a Nobis indicto, tibi et Consociationi a CORDE JESU, cui

and for the Society of the Sacred Heart which you govern
by the fact that this same year is the hundredth since the
foundation of your Institute. For in the year 1800, on
the eleventh day before the kalends of December (November
21st), the Venerable Madeleine Sophie Barat, your Mother
and the Lawgiver of your Institute, together with her
three first associates bound themselves by vow to God,
and devoted themselves to the salvation of souls by means
of the solid and pious education of young girls. Small
indeed were the beginnings, such as those very troublous
times allowed. But what increase they have made in the
space of one century! For the small number has grown
to many thousands, and the work and zeal of the Society
which in the beginnings were contained within the sole
limits of France, have reached not only to the peoples
of Europe, but even to far distant and barbarous nations.
Rightly therefore you intend to give solemn thanks to
God, albeit modestly and within the walls of your
enclosure, for this, that in the time which has elapsed,
He has shown such favour to your Institute and has
loaded it with such great benefits. We also approve
this most earnestly as well because the soul which is
grateful to God merits the more the Divine Clemency, as
because the will is urged to work with greater alacrity
by the remembrance of past benefits. But, in order that
We also may add something to your joy, We gladly take

praees, inde quidem augetur quod hic idem annus centesimus vobis est ab
Instituto vestro condito. Undecimo enim kalendas decembres anno millesimo
octingentesimo Venerabilis MAGDALENA-SOPHIA BARAT, Mater vestra
legifera, una cum tribus primis alumnis, nuncupatis Deo votis, sese animorum
saluti addixere, puellis rite pieque educendis. Modica enimvero initia, ut
turbulentissima tempora sinebant : sed quanta, unius sacculi spatio, capere
incrementa! Exiguus namque numerus ad multa milia excrevit ; et Sociarum
labor ac studium, quae, initio, unius Galliae finibus coercebantur, non ad
Europae gentes modo, sed ad dissitas etiam ac barbaras nationes pertingerunt.
Jure igitur eo vestri intendunt animi ut, modeste quamvis intraque domesticos
parietes, sollemnes DEO agatis gratias quod Institutum vestrum, praeterlapso
tempore, tam benigne habuerit tantisque cumularit beneficiis. Nos autem id
vehementer probamus tum quia gratus in DEUM animus divinam sibi magis
demeret clementiam, tum quia praeteritorum beneficiorum recordatione ad agendum
alacrius incitatur voluntas. Quo vero iucunditati vestrae aliquid Nos etiam
adiiciamus, occasionem hanc libenter nanciscimur ut caritatem in Sodalicium
vestrum hisce litteris profiteamur ; ac nova porro incrementa adprecantes, auspicem
coelestium munerum, tibi ac singulis Instituti vestri Alumnis Apostolicam benedictionem peramanter impertimus.

Datum Romae apud S. Petrum die XX Februarii MDCCCC, Pontificatus
Nostri anno vicesimo tertio.—LEO PP. XIII.

this occasion of showing by this letter our affection for your Society, praying for still fresh increase; and, as a pledge of the blessings of Heaven, We grant most lovingly to you, and to each member of your Institute, the Apostolic Benediction.

"Given at Rome from St Peter's on the twentieth day of February 1900 in the twenty-third year of our Pontificate.—LEO XIII. POPE."

Three days before the centenary of November 21st, in every part of the world the former pupils of the Sacred Heart were gathering within their homes of education. Old friends met, to catch the delightful aroma of school memories; indescribable, but how intimate to those who have inhaled it. In the grave corridors and halls of study mothers loitered and chatted, watching their own children keep high holiday; great-grandmothers, who recollected the Foundress, watched the games or the school theatre, unwilling to acknowledge that their own day had been less fortunate or capable. The poor too were feasted, served by the children of the house; all was summed up and vivified in the general consecration to the Sacred Heart, pronounced in each crowded chapel during Exposition of the Blessed Sacrament.

At the Motherhouse everything naturally culminated. In St Mary Magdalen's, the little room of the Foundress, the picture of the Madonna and Child before which she and her companions had pronounced their vows in 1800 was surrounded with flowers and lights; here the religious and the two hundred and fifty children of Mary of Paris, by permission, came in successive groups to pray and give thanks. Cardinal Richard was there of course, and other great ecclesiastics; the Papal blessing arrived by telegram; over against the great cedar, under which Mother Barat had sat with her children, a Wellingtonia was planted and blessed with holy water;—*ad multos annos!*

From one hundred and forty-two convents of Europe, America, and Oceania, poured in the congratulations of nearly seven thousand hearts wherein the *esprit de corps* was unbroken. There were cordial messages, too, from the Superiors of numerous congregations, more particularly from the Carmelites, Sisters of Charity, and other Orders who numbered in their ranks so many pupils of the Sacred Heart. The Fathers of Montmartre, the nuns of the Visitation at Paray-le-Monial were not behindhand, and at the latter place Mass was celebrated for the occasion in a chapel, the gift of the Society of the Sacred Heart.

Mother Digby felt and expressed her exceeding consolation. She allowed no gloomy prognostics to cloud the general joy.

An old and trusted friend of the superior General and her predecessors, Dr Ferrand, her physician, died suddenly on 11th December. Like Dr Philip Harper, his charity and learning adorned his great professional skill ; by rich and poor in Paris he was deeply regretted. He was the initiator of the Society of Christian Doctors, comprising many thousand members ; he was a considerable writer on Cerebrology,[1] and showed—without trenching upon theological ground—the harmony between the laws of bodily structure and the doctrine of an immortal soul. Thus, in an age when it is essayed to arm science against revelation, he did honour to a profession which, needing God perhaps more than any other, is apt—on the Continent at any rate— by confining itself to mere materialism, to shut Him out. Dr Ferrand shared and often expressed the high regard of medical men who knew her, for Mother Digby.

The instability of French affairs detained her in Paris for the winter. The Pope received a deputation of nuns of the Sacred Heart, the superior of the convent of Lille, Mère Catherine de Montalembert, being among them. Her name recalled the eternal strife in France. The former nuncio spoke of his frequent meetings with her illustrious father at Brussels ; he enquired closely of Mother Digby and of her present action.

On the last day of the year, by Papal order, the Blessed Sacrament was exposed throughout the world until midnight, when a solemn Mass ushered in the century.

[1] See *Annales de la Philosophie Chrétienne*, 1896.

CHAPTER XX

THE LAW OF 1901

" In vain Columba represented to him that he ought not to abandon his parents and his native soil. ' It is thou,' answered Mochonna, ' who art my father, the Church is my mother, and my country is there where I can gather the largest harvest for Christ. I swear to follow thee wherever thou goest until thou hast led me to Christ to whom thou hast consecrated me.' "—MONTALEMBERT, *Monks of the West* (Nimmo, 1896) vol. iii. p. 3.

SINCE 1871, thirty-two proposals of law upon the Congregations — disregarding abortive projects — had been actually laid upon the table of the Chambre. Nearly all were illiberal, and penal more or less. But the ministries which proposed them fell, and the Congregations came almost to believe that they themselves bore a charmed life.

M. Waldeck-Rousseau had appointed a Commission to sit upon the question. What was brewing?

On January 10th, 1901, the president of the Council brought his bill into the Palais Bourbon. Its preamble drops all other pretences, and, with a lofty pose of impartiality, bases itself upon the fact that unauthorised societies are *ipso facto* illicit — a theory, indeed, entirely refuted, but repeated still for its plausible sound. "How," asked the great sophist of Geneva, "how can what is *legal* be otherwise than *legitimate*?" And his conclusion follows as a matter of course—though not of logic.

The Bill filled eight pages of print, and contained thirty-one Articles, divided into three *Titres*.

The first Titre, like the exordium of a schoolmaster about to administer public punishment, dealt with generalities. Only the guilty need tremble!

Associations may be freely established; they must conform to certain formalities; they must not be formed for any unlawful object.

272

In Titre II. there was still no mention of religious orders. But they loom in the distance. By Art. 12, *"Associations having foreign administrators, or houses in foreign lands, and whose undertakings may be of a nature to menace the safety of the State . . . may be dissolved by Decree."* Mother Digby occurs to the mind.

In Titre III. the Congregations—the culprits, for whose condemnation all the preceding was but a prelude—enter by name. No need now, as in 1880, for a lengthy veil to the *loi d'exception.*

Art. 13. *No religious Congregation can be formed without an authorization given by law which shall determine its functions and conditions.*

No new establishment may be founded (even by an authorised Congregation) save in virtue of a decree of the Council of State.

The dissolution of any Congregation, or the closing of any of its establishments may be pronounced by decree.

Thus, the Religious alone, and *as such*, is deprived of a natural right. He is an outcast from the law which allows association to all else ; he is permitted no appeal ; he is proscribed irresponsibly ; without reason shown ; by *lettre de cachet.*

Art. 14 *forbids any person belonging to an unauthorized Congregation to teach.*

By Article 15, the Congregation which desires to obtain authorization is required to present to government, every year, exact answers to the most vexatious and lengthy perquisitions upon the personal and pecuniary status, the employment, destination, and action of each member, and the property acquired or alienated by the Order ; there follows a formidable list of pains and penalties by which the smallest inexactitude will be visited. By Articles 16 to 21, it is declared that such Congregations as neglect to apply for authorization under the above conditions within three months' time, equally with those to whom authorization may be refused, shall be *ipso facto* dissolved[1] and their goods sequestrated.

---

[1] There were in France, in 1900, 1517 Congregations, of whom 745 were unauthorized. *Études*, February 5th, 1901.

S

M. Waldeck-Rousseau demanded that his law should at once be brought up for discussion.   And at once the battle began.

From the Comte de Mun on the Right, to M. Viviani on the Socialist Left, men of all parties cried out.   The Bill was an outrage on liberty, a mortal blow to the Concordat. For the Congregations to ask for authorization, was to place themselves at the mercy of some future decree ; and, if authorization were refused, the petitioners would be at once in worse plight than before.   As for the final Articles, they were an undisguised robbery.

M. Waldeck-Rousseau cleared up these "misunderstandings" from the tribune.   His bill was destined on the one hand to benefit the majority of the unauthorized Congregations themselves, by legalizing their condition, to eliminate merely such as were useless, or harmful to the State—rivals, moreover, that the authorized Orders would not be sorry to get rid of.

But would applications for authorisation be accepted? would they even be entertained?   Most certainly ! after a fair examination of each case on its own merits.   He pledged his word for it.   And, as to the property clauses, the members of a Congregation dissolved should, if they possessed no other means of support, be provided with a small life pension out of the proceeds of the liquidation of their lands and buildings ; a portion of the money, moreover, should go to schools or charities kindred to those destroyed with the Congregation.

Thus, gradually, the president of the Council secured reluctant votes.   But there was a strong minority, not to be taken in.   The Comte de Mun, upon Article 14, stood out, as he had done for over twenty years, for liberty of teaching, the grand old theme of Montalembert. De Mun burned still with earnestness, if M. Viviani surpassed him now in youthful brilliancy.   The Right, day after day, spoke as men should speak ; amid perpetual interruptions, and sneers, to cynical faces, to minds already made up.   But, "what a test of courage is this," said a spectator, "none can realize but he who has witnessed it."   The Opposition were playing a lost game, and knew it; yet they disputed every inch of the ground; they seized some wavering consciences, diminished the majority, if they could not control it; they delayed the consummation. Not till the end of March was the Bill forced through by 303 to 224 votes; and, in face of these figures, none could say that even the Chambre des Députés, as a whole, desired the Law. The exhausted Parliament then adjourned till May 14th.

The Congregations and their friends were thunder-struck. Waldeck - Rousseau's portfolio was still firm under his arm.

Of the eighteen commissioners appointed by the Senate to examine the law, twelve had been chosen as favourable to it; the mere name of the president, Emile Combes, was eloquent. For the debate, he demanded two sittings daily. All was rushed through with ruthless speed; the amendments interposed by Admiral de Cuverville, by MM. de Marcère, de Lamarzelle, de Blois, and the rest, were not even discussed; still, they fought on undaunted; the battle raged high. On June 22nd there was a third sitting; late in the evening M. Combes had prevailed; on 1st July the text appeared in the *Officiel*: the law was promulgated.

And now the first statesman of the century, and the greatest champion of the religious Orders, raised his voice ninety years old, in their favour. On July 6th appeared the magnificent *Letter to the Generals of the Religious Orders of France* of Leo XIII. It is their *Apologia*: they are "the elect of the City of God"; their consolation: they are "those persecuted whom Eternal Truth proclaims blessed." The Pope signalized his own profound grief and sympathy at their affliction; he reminded them that he had done all in his power to prevent the evil; he deplored the loss of their services for the Church and for France. He recalled the example of their Founders. "There is a voice," he ends, "ever living, and fraught with new courage, which re-echoes across the centuries: Have confidence! It says; I have overcome the world!"

Needless to say how the letter spoke to Mother Digby's heart, and what the effect it produced when read in each

of her forty-six French convents to the community solemnly
assembled.

Though the Congregation of the Sacred Heart
as a whole was authorized, many individual houses
were not.

The Congregations were in a terrible trilemma. Should
they ask for authorization, and risk a refusal which
meant ruin? Should they choose the cruel alternative
of secularization? Could there be passive resistance?
Before October 3rd at midnight they must make up their
minds: in September the inmates of two hundred and
ninety-three convents had already shaken the dust of
beloved France from off their feet. The Carmelite nuns
of the Avenue de Saxe received hospitality for a time at
the Sacred Heart; first at Paris, then at Jette, in Belgium.
Others were asking what to do? where to go?

Each house of the Sacred Heart had, of course, its
solicitor. His services had been loyal under the pressure
of the financial laws; he was no less keen now to seize all
the justice he could lay hold of. But the meshes were
closing tightly round the Congregations. The July law
held every victim by some claw hidden in the convolutions
of each paragraph, vague with many words, so that its
provisions could ever be interpreted in some new and
unfavourable sense, by a decree, or a circular, the stroke
of a minister's pen.

After long hours of consultation with Mother Digby
at the Boulevard des Invalides, the men of business left
the parlour, time after time, with hopes that seemed to
lessen. "Madame," said M. Boyer de Bouillane one
day, coming back upon his steps, "I have been able to
point out, not what can be done, but what is to be feared.
Everywhere there is a trap that hides a precipice! And
yet it is you that must decide where to place your foot."
"This means, perhaps," she replied on a similar occasion,
"that we must not act at all just now." Her method was
to await some light from the movement of circumstances;
this light was, she hoped, a heavenly signal. "Union
with God," she said at this time, "is to our work what
the rising sun is to a traveller. . . . After a dark night

it lights up the horizon, and its first rays help him to find his way and push on."

She was consulted on all sides by religious of other Orders ; some obtained a dispensation from their rule of cloister for this very purpose.

Cardinal Langénieux, Archbishop of Rheims, and one of the staunchest of all defenders of the Church's rights, came one day to see the community, when the storm was still only a threat. The Superior General was absent. "Many religious vocations, alas !" he said, "are in peril. But as for you, you have nothing to fear. God has greatly loved your Society in giving it in times so perilous, so great a pilot as your Mother General. She is a soul full of the Spirit of God." [1]

The great majority—about five hundred—of the unauthorized Congregations resolved to apply for State authorization. Mother Digby did the same for such of her houses as did not possess it. The demand of the Congregations was supported by a petition from the six Cardinals of France and practically by the whole episcopate, accompanied by the explicit adherence of all these prelates to the Republic.

But the Superior General had come to another decision, more vital yet in consequences ; that of the very existence of her daughters as such.

The journal of the Motherhouse notes at this time a series of lengthy visits that Cardinal Richard paid to Mother Digby in private. Nor was he the only distinguished ecclesiastic who suggested to her a certain course of action at this crisis.

Her unauthorized houses might after all be dissolved ; even the rest were in danger. Were their services to be lost to the country?

There remained the alternative of secularization. Men of weight pressed upon her its advantages ; the heroism, nay the necessity of this course. It is certain, that had she so decided, so would it have been done.

But Mother Digby wavered not. Intact she had received the Society ; so she would have it remain until

[1] *See* p. 45 for his early acquaintance with Mabel Digby.

One should come to demand an account of her stewardship. Each of her daughters should keep the precious privilege of her religious life untouched—without change, even of the costume.

The Society of the Sacred Heart was not, in her eyes, a mere aggregation of trained women. It was a system, a compact body vivified by a mysterious spirit that must evaporate if the vase that held it came to be shattered. Her seven thousand daughters, as units, could not carry on the work of the Society, for they would no longer be *nuns of the Sacred Heart.* Such they must remain ; if not in France, then elsewhere. *Dieu le veut!* And her daughters, of France as of everywhere else, say unanimously that for this decision she has earned their everlasting gratitude.

"You will not abandon your mother General, will you !" said Leo XIII. earnestly to a French religious about this time. She assured him that such an idea was indeed far from her mind. But he seemed anxious to probe the matter, and again repeated his injunction.

Mother Digby's first circular letter upon the subject of the Law is dated September 17th, 1901, and is addressed to the Superiors of the French houses.

"The utmost discretion is to be observed in speaking of the Law, of how it may apply to ourselves, . . . of what we may or may not do under given circumstances. . . . But above all I venture to count upon our daughters, that no one shall yield to discouragement. . . . 'Courage and Confidence' was the first watchword of the Society . . . as long as we are faithful to the rule of our Institute, God will take care of us. . . . But His special care is reserved for the Poor of Christ . . . the true poor, whose is that apostolic poverty content with what is necessary for the body, and tending always to possess less rather than more . . . May this spirit be found when the moment of trial shall summon us to show it to the Church and to the world !"

Prudence was indeed necessary. Letters received by superiors through the post were constantly opened by the secret service department, and the re-closing was not always so skilfully done but that the inquisition was traceable. It was said afterwards to a nun of the Sacred Heart: "I congratulate you all on your discretion! Never was any one able to get hints as to what your Society would do! Would you be secularized? Would you settle abroad? And where? And when? You betrayed absolutely nothing!"

"We betrayed nothing," answered the interlocutor, "for the simple reason that we knew nothing! Mother Digby and all Superiors kept their own counsel, even from ourselves!"

Mischievous gossip, however, may be sown abroad by those ignorant of facts—the more effectively, perhaps, because no bounds are thus set to imagination. Therefore an obedient discretion was laid upon the nuns: not to talk at all upon such matters.

At a convent known to the *Sacred Heart*, a certain liquidator, a very polite gentleman, much grieved at the painful but well-paid office imposed on him of turning the nuns out of house and home and selling their property, asked whether they had no movable goods conveyed away anywhere? The goods would be safest with him, and they could count upon his services. Greatly touched, the Sisters furnished him with the address of a friend, who was harbouring in trust their church plate, so that in some new home they hoped to find, perhaps over the frontier, their poor chapel might not be destitute. Promptly appeared the agents of the law at the house indicated, and the church plate was found, seized, and sold by the liquidator with the rest.

In May (1902) the applications for authorization were still lying for consideration on the tables of the Council of State, when to every one's surprise Waldeck-Rousseau resigned his position. It was owing, some said, to his shattered health; others, to his feeling that the current he had started was running farther and faster than he had designed. It seems clear that the two causes interacted; the ex-minister's life was henceforth embittered by seeing his landmarks swept ruthlessly away.

The new Ministry was formed in June by M. Combes;

he significantly reserved for himself the portfolios of the Interior, and of public Worship.

His ministerial Declaration opened with menace. On June 27th, he made the President, Loubet, sign a decree shutting one hundred and thirty establishments of teaching congregations, and, on July 9th, by circular, two thousand five hundred more. All these houses had been founded previous to the law of 1901, and had re-opened after the vacation upon the solemn word of Waldeck-Rousseau, and the government pledge that that law was not to be retro-active. Another circular stirred up the prefects with threats to carry out its provisions in every province with the utmost rigour.

A feature, new to France since the Terror, was the violent expulsion of women. Madame de la Vallée-Poussin (Soeur Sainte - Claire) superior of the Dames Franciscaines, Avenue de Villiers, Paris, was one of the first brought before the tribunal, as well as eleven Little Sisters of the Assumption at Lyons: a thing last seen in 1794. Their functions, the latter declared, of nursing the sick poor at their own homes, were purely humanitarian, and they declined to leave their posts. Several aged and infirm nuns, amongst others a Carmelite of Toulouse, had already died of the shock of removal, and its attendant hardships.

On August 2nd, at the Palais Bourbon, twenty-six Nationalists and Liberal deputies sent a delegation to M. Combes in protest; the six Cardinals of France and all the Archbishops and Bishops petitioned the President of the Republic in the same sense. On July 27th an immense multitude filled the Place de la Concorde at Paris; the wives of deputies and senators, followed by thousands of mothers of families, traversed the Champs Elysées to present a petition to M. Combes, whilst M. Jules Lemaître in the Place de l'Etoile and succeeding orators spoke, to the cries of " *Vivent les Soeurs ! Liberté ! Liberté !*" In every department where the nuns were menaced manifestations took place ; the populace in many places rose to protect the convents; some held out in siege for a week ; blood flowed, lives were lost, and the

most honourable men by position and character, as well
as humbler individuals, were arraigned before the local
tribunals.   They were frequently acquitted and justified,
and an appeal to the Court of Cassation was necessary
for their punishment.   The columns of the newspapers
in September were, for all France, full of the resignations,
revocations, or suspensions of the maires and adjutants
for sharing in manifestations or resistances, or refusing
to proceed against them.   At Nantes, Lieut.-Col. de
Saint-Rémy and Commandant Le Roy-Ladurie were each
brought before a court martial for refusing to lead their
troops against the protectors of the Sisters.   Five hundred
soldiers were sometimes required to safeguard the police
agents who ejected them.

"France," cried many — and they now repeat it—
"looked with indifference at the iniquities committed
upon her soil."   Are they right?

Dividing France into proportional parts, it may be
said that a sectarian minority was banishing the congregations, whilst an opposite minority that greatly outnumbered the first, was doing its very best to defend
them.   Meanwhile, the absolute majority of the country,
with whom, abstractedly speaking, lay the real decision—
for its collective weight, thrown to whichever side, would
bring down that end of the lever—this absolute majority
was inactive.   One part was held by fear, another by
hopes of place or eminence, a third by infatuation for some
lost cause ; others again by a semi-belief in the fascinating
sophistries of the press, by disgust at a few follies of some
just men and women — more still, perhaps, by weariness
for that all passed effort had seemed useless, by disdain
for the chicanery of politics, or by sheer selfish indifference.
Thus, all these scattered interests and want of interests,
chiefly for mere lack of leadership, either stood aside and
let things be, not deigning even to record their vote ; or
else, with a shrug of the shoulders, obeyed the wires.
The same story repeats itself since 1873.

So far, however, the Society of the Sacred Heart was
hardly scathed.

CHAPTER XXI

THE BILL OF 1904

"During one of the most stormy periods of the French revolution, when all the priests of the department of the Seine and Oise were arrested, pressed together upon waggons, and conducted to Versailles, where they were left without means of subsistence, it was the young who came forward as the ministers of Providence, to relieve their distress. Innumerable young persons were seen hastening to console them, who had prepared them for the their first communion, who were the guides and friends of their youth. Those who had no money brought their bread to share with them ; a young maiden cut off her beautiful hair, and hastened to the prison with the sum which she had obtained for it."—KENELM DIGBY, *Godefridus* (Lumley, 1844), p. 132.

THE menace of French affairs, always present to Mother Digby, by no means absorbed her attention. Chief amongst her cares were those of new foundations. Invitations were not wanting ; in 1896 those from Genoa, Constantinople, Athens, and Brazil were refused or postponed of necessity ; the establishment at Venice in that year has been mentioned ; that of Marseilles, Rue Thomas, in 1897, was later transferred to the Rues des Dominicaines. The war that was troubling Spain in 1898 discouraged any new enterprize in that country, but the desires of Cardinal Sancha for a house of the Sacred Heart in his diocese were fulfilled nevertheless ; a deserted and dilapidated property and house at Godella, Valencia, near the Mediterranean, was put into repair, and the works of the Society in this interesting province began at once to flourish. Menlo Park, California, with now seventy-nine children, and the parish school at St Joseph's, Missouri, which harboured two hundred, have been described.

By the efforts of the Children of Mary at Naples, the Palazzo Balzorano was acquired in 1899, and a day-school opened. The foundresses had been presented to Leo XIII. "Ah, a fine colony for Naples!" he exclaimed. "Cardinal Prisco is greatly alarmed at the satanic efforts there. Men buy children by promising the teaching of languages; they give clothes, money, even a dowry! What can we do? Still, the good Neapolitans keep their faith, and to guard them we must all unite." Between the various schools and the workrooms, over four hundred children gathered, before long, in the new convent; there were extensive *patronages* as well. As soon as the law of 1901 had been brought forward, Mother Digby accepted from Countess Balbo, a former pupil of the Sacred Heart, La Peschiera, with farm and vineyard, between Milan and Bergamo; one hundred and fifteen children were at once admitted into the elementary, and seven into the boarding school. The country population, untouched by the socialism of the neighbouring towns, welcomed the nuns with delight. The Freemason element, more daring in Italy than even in France, had affected the former country as a whole far less.

Since her first Austrian voyage, Reverend Mother Digby had been anxious for another house in Poland. In April, 1901, the *Sacred Heart* was able to acquire land at Zbylitowska Gora, near Tarnow in Galicia. The Bishop of Tarnow favoured the project, and the joy of the poor was extraordinary. The schools soon filled, and, in 1902, foundations at Palma in Majorca, and at Chorillos, near Lima, showed life and growth from the beginning.

Mother Digby's had progressed as usual in the visitation of the European houses since her return from America, save that in the critical year 1901 she had confined herself to France. In 1902 however, her houses there being still erect, she visited England in May; she went on to Ireland, for the jubilee of the convent of Armagh, in June, bringing many beautiful church vestments embroidered by herself. Cardinal Logue celebrated High Mass; Mgr. Browne, Bishop of Cloyne, spoke in his address of the good done to the poor since the foundation of Armagh. The poor gathered together for the day in numbers and in great joy. They well remembered Mother Digby, who was delighted to rest amongst them, passing from one motley group to another. Many were blind; the old servant of the convent supported his steps on a stick ; another old soul, paralyzed, was drawn by a donkey in a barrow.

In May, Mother Josephine Errington, the Mistress General of Manhattanville, New York, in the vigour of her age, was seized by a chill and carried off in a few days. Her last messages were for Mother Digby. The elder girls of their own accord gathered round the catafalque whereon she lay, and there, aloud, before the altar, each in turn with her hand upon the coffin, swore solemnly to be faithful to her teaching. They have not yet forgotten it. In September the faithful servant Mathieu Schüller died at Cherbourg, where he had been sent by Mother Digby for a change of air. The old man's last messages to her were of loyal gratitude and of fidelity. As a boy he had known Mother Barat, and received from her reprimands and rewards; to his pride and joy, he had been one of those chosen lately to give evidence for her beatification. His heart would have broken had he lingered on to see the wholesale destructions in France. Mrs Bertram Currie, another staunch friend, died in April, and John Hungerford Pollen in December. He had made a point of coming to see Mother Digby upon her recent visit to England. They talked together, both seated in one of the circular embrasures above the staircase of the vestibule at Roehampton. "I think your father is simply perfect!" she said, smiling to one of his children when the interview was over.

Mother Digby returned in August to Paris—a contrast to the peace and freedom on the opposite side of the Channel. It would be wearisome to detail the measures that every month or week accentuated a relentless and malignant persecution : delations in the army, religious practice abolished in the navy, crosses removed from cities and broken up, fine and imprisonment visited on priest and layman who remonstrated, the hunting down on some pretext or other of even secularized religious employed by parish priests to help them in their functions. Mother Digby was prepared for what was becoming evident to all : that her own convents would be the next places to be broken into.

Ever since the dire threats had been realized by the children of the Sacred Heart, they had resolved to do violence to heaven by prayers and sacrifices. All through the summer holidays gifts of flowers and candles were sent to the altars of the Motherhouse by such as were unable to visit the chapel from time to time; the others arrived in groups to pray, to sing hymns, with the most touching fervour; so it was in every convent. Heaven has its own way of preserving unshaken an innocent faith, whilst answering its prayers in a mysterious manner. It was actually on the last day of a fervent novena, March 25th, 1903, that two Commissaries of police rang at the door of the Motherhouse, and presented to the superior General a ministerial notice concerning her house at Moulins.

"I do not judge it *à propos* to submit to the Council of State your request for authorization, and I hereby enjoin you to disperse yourselves, and to shut your establishment within eight days. You are, in case of non-compliance, liable to fine and imprisonment . . . (here follow lengthy references to the Articles dealing with pains and penalties).—(Signed) The President of the Council, Minister of the Interior and of Worship, E. COMBES."

The chronicle of events at the Motherhouse throughout the spring tells its own tale.

"*March* 31*st*.　Arrival of Digne Mère M., superior of Moulins; she hands our Mother the key of the tabernacle, and is sent to Conflans for some days rest. *April* 2. Another visit of the Commissaries with notice for Orleans. 3*d*. Mère J. goes to arrange the dispersion. Mère de C. arrives with the plan of new foundation at San Sebastien. The Commissaries notify the closing of Nancy; day school in May, boarding-school in August. 8*th*. Wednesday in Holy Week; the kiss of peace; conference on charity, and union *inter se*, very searching and pressing: the first sign of decadence in the Society would occur on this particular point; if we are faithful to it, tempests outside will stay outside. *May* 1. Two Commissaries notify for Lyons in two months. 3*d*. The children of the Rue de Varennes come to present their good wishes [for Mother Digby's feast] with great delicacy of feeling. They brought branches of lilies. Our Mother said to them, 'Your Mothers will be driven out, but not banished. They will still pray

for France and work for France !'   Some of them asked for a private
audience ; they requested in the name of the school that its expenses
should be cut down to the utmost limits and the money saved be
applied to new foundations.   Our Very Reverend Mother greatly
touched ; she cannot agree to all their plans, but will accept the
salary they may earn by mending their own clothes."

The children of Roehampton, too, willingly gave up
their prizes this year, and the sum saved was forwarded
for the same purpose.   To an address from the Children
of Mary, Mother Digby replied with gratitude for their
sympathy ; she recalls the records of their own past, and
reminds them of what they may still do ; the *Sacred Heart*
if it should be altogether driven out of the country, knew
on whom to rely for effective action, whom to entrust
with their work for God's forsaken children. . . .

On July 17th a heavier blow was dealt to the Orders.
Contrary to the pledged word of the late President of
the Council, under cover of which the law of 1901 had
passed, and whereon the Congregations had relied, M.
Combes signified his refusal *en bloc*, and without examina-
tion, to submit the petitions for authorization to the
Council of State.   There was an outcry about honour
from Waldeck-Rousseau in the Senate, and even from
MM. Goblet and Gabriel Monod.   M. Ribot, another
former President of the Council, and author of the Ribot-
Brisson financial law against the Congregations, accused
M. Combes a little later of reducing all questions concerning the nation to the single one of anti-clericalism.
" *That*," retorted the minister fiercely, " *That was my sole
object in taking office !* "

The unauthorized houses of Annonay, Aix and
Angoulême were the next to be struck.

The nuns, who had been ready to second the Mother
General's wish to continue their schools until the last
moment, found themselves face to face with the gigantic
task of disposing of the furniture, library, and appoint-
ments, of large establishments, and of dismantling the
chapels, within a month ; at Moulins and Orleans, indeed,
the time by a special exception was shortened to one week.

Yet the July law had prescribed a notice of at least fifteen days before the end of the school year.[1]   The Radical papers at Orleans, which affected to disbelieve the new summons, and accused the nuns of trying to excite sympathy by anticipating the day of their departure, were silenced on seeing the ministerial Order placarded in the town by friends of the Convent.   There is little doubt that the *Sacred Heart* was one of those to whom the government bore a special grudge.   Thus says M. Ferdinand Buisson on the 31st page of his *Rapport*[2]

"We must distinguish between the Congregations.   It will be easily understood that a great international congregation . . . a monastic federation, may imagine itself able to withstand the French government, to evade its laws, and to remain in existence in spite of everything, possessing a whole *personnel* devoted to the Order."

There was no mistaking the public feeling as soon as the news of the departure began to spread in the towns.   Everywhere the Bishop of the Diocese or his delegate appeared, in consternation: "I see behind you only ruins," said Mgr. Bonnet at Annonay; the friends of the convent arrived in numbers; the tradesmen, even, were dejected at losing the custom of a large educational house, and being, in some cases, thrown into distress. The fathers of the children of the École held a manifestation at Orleans, and at Moulins eight persons were imprisoned.

Ladies and gentlemen bearing the most honourable names in France, not content with sending their servants and labourers to aid in the dismantling at Moulins, worked themselves the whole week from morning till night with the nuns, mounting ladders, carrying furniture, packing and nailing up bales and cases.   The house presented the appearance of a beehive in full activity; no word was spoken save in control of the operations.   Every day a letter arrived from Mother Digby; she sent down two Mother Counsellors to aid; her sympathy, her presence in

---

[1] Loi du 7 Juillet 1904, Art. 3 §3.
[2] *See* p. 291.

spirit, was powerfully felt.   Suddenly took place a moving scene.   A deputation of gentlemen demanded permission of the Mother Vicar to appear as an armed force against the ejectors.   M. Delahaye, a former deputy, ardent now as he had been in the Chambre, implored: "Let us prove!" he cried to the assembled nuns, "that we know how to defend you! even at the risk of our lives!"   He tried long and vainly to wring a "yes" from the Superior, deeply affected as she was; the workmen involuntarily ceased their labours, and closed round to listen; at last he turned away with tears of grief and anger in his eyes.

The nuns were under the double necessity of preserving their own self-control and that of their pupils, who every-where received the fatal news with a burst of weeping indignation.   They consulted together of their own accord, and subscribed towards the expenses of removal, helping in every way in their power, and renewing at the last their promises of fidelity to all that they had learnt. There followed the last Mass, the well-known hymns, the chant of the Miserere, and of the *Parce Domine*, before the slow exit from the henceforth deserted and desecrated chapel.

At Orleans:

"An immense but pacific manifestion of every Catholic in the city, with the clergy at their head, was to take place; it was hoped that this would deter the persecutors from accomplishing their work. The nuns had not been told of this plan, lest they should be compromised; but the police got wind of it and, by a favourite device, they got down from Paris some hundreds of armed vagabonds for a counter manifestation.   At the sight of these sinister faces the Convent was warned, and the Superior, fearful of exposing her community to a night attack, judged better to withdraw a day before the one fixed.   All that afternoon a weeping crowd, poor and rich, filled the courtyard, and pressed into the vestibule and parlour, to thank the nuns, even to kiss their hands, to beg their prayers."

Often a deputation of citizens accompanied one who read a parting address; at Annonay it was the well-known orator M. Camille Séguin, followed by M. de Gailhard-Bancel; at Le Mans, Maitre Jacquier.   At the latter place, many thousands of people accompanied the nuns, and crowded the railway station ; the cries of *Vive le Sacré Coeur ! Vive Mère Barat ! Vive les Soeurs ! Vive la liberté !* rose, say those who heard it, like the clamour of a great sea.   Not a hostile sound was heard.   But at Moulins, as soon as the train moved off, the demonstrators could not be stopped ; crying, " *Vive la liberté !   A bas les sectaires !*" they repulsed the gendarmes, who tried to arrest a priest amongst them.   They marched to the *préfecture*, where its chief occupant remained prudently invisible, and continued the agitation for a considerable time.

At Layrac, fifty - four omnibus brakes and other vehicles were engaged by the "manifestants"; they accompanied the carriages of the nuns through the streets of the town ; every house door was open, and the inhabitants standing together on the threshold, cried out "*Au revoir ! Au revoir !*"   Six thousand persons pressed around as the nuns entered the railway station, and at the departure sang in chorus with irresistible enthusiasm the hymn *Nous voulons Dieu !*

These scenes of devastation pale, of course, before the instances where the religious refused to quit their domicile. It is not to be doubted that had Mother Digby commanded a congregation of men, she would have permitted this passive resistance ;   she would not, however, suffer her daughters to run the risk of personal violence.

In the middle of this eventful year the death of Leo XIII. had thrown all the world into sorrow.   Mother Digby's relations with him had been constant.   Early in 1903 she found herself again at Rome, and obtained an audience on January 11th.   Her object was to present the homage of the Society and its gifts, on the occasion of the twenty-fifth anniversary of the Pope's crowning—a jubilee thus repeated for the second time in the world's history. The gifts of the Society of the Sacred Heart, and from the pupils, in every part of the world, were arranged by permission of the *maestro di camera* in the hall of the Consistory ;   the children of the Roman houses, dressed in white, lined the room in three rows.   "Where

is the Mother General!" cried the Pope.   He laid his
hand paternally on her head as she knelt before him;
nothing could exceed the affectionate kindness of his
words, his last encouragements.   Then, sitting erect
upon his throne, the aged Pontiff, surrounded by his
Noble Guard, after a moment of silence, commenced
an address of exceeding beauty; in words full of ardour
he extolled a Christian education ; commenting the words
*Adolescens juxta viam suam, etiam cum senuerit, non recedet
ab ea!*

Then, as the children advanced one by one to his
throne, he enquired with keen-edged memory concerning
their relatives, their progress in every detail; "Yes, my
child, here is the blessing you ask for your grandfather;
he is eighty-four, but I am ninety-three!"   Calling again
for Mother Digby, and declining the assistance of his
Guard, he leant upon her arm for the last time, examining
and praising the gifts; "How many happy Bishops and
curés I can make!"   Turning once more, before mounting his *Portatina* : "I bless you with special affection;
Oggi ci avete proprio consolato con la vostra visita!"

On July 22nd, a circular letter to Mother Digby's
daughters communicated to them her grief at his death,
and ensured the suffrages of the whole Society for so
great a Pontiff, and so distinguished a benefactor.

Cardinal Sarto was elected on August 4th : the nuns at
Venice knew him, and rejoiced.   Already on the 29th of
the same month he had admitted to his presence the
religious of the Roman houses, and showed by his words
and bearing a fatherly and familiar sympathy.   In the
consciousness of this encouragement, the Society of the
Sacred Heart was strong to meet the last fury of the
storms in France.

By an act of supreme confidence Mother Digby resolved
to assemble the customary Probation on October 1st, and
the school at the Rue de Varennes reopened as usual.
The children were more numerous than ever before, and
as much may be said of postulants for admission to the
noviceship.   Persecution, as it seemed, gave a new animation to its object.   All within the Convent went on in peace

and order—a contrast to the agitation of Paris outside, for the King and Queen of Italy had arrived; the streets were adorned, and the Sardinian cross surmounted the monuments. Under these gay appearances religious hate was sleepless; at 6 o'clock in the evening of October 17th, a wretch in the open street shot a priest through the head: M. Lebel, returning from his class at the Catholic Institute. Shortly afterwards, the Commissary of Police appeared for the thirteenth time at the Mother-house; whilst a rescript of the Holy Father brought permission for a foundation at Cairo, and several of the nuns were set to study Arabic. In December began the Christmas preparations; a great yearly treat for the sixty little girls of the Junior School at 31 Boulevard des Invalides, was carried out with the usual spirit, and on New Year's Eve the clergy arrived, with many other friends, to offer their good wishes for the year to the Mother General. This was done in sadness and fore-boding, for the question of life and death for the Orders was now to be finally decided. The unauthorized had been wiped out; it only remained to get rid of the rest.

On December 18th, 1903, a commission was appointed to examine a project "for the suppression of Con-gregational teaching." Its labours are embodied in a white pamphlet of sixty-four quarto pages.[1]

This is the *Rapport* of M. Ferdinand Buisson, Député [of the Seine] and president of the Masonic *Ligue d'Enseignement.*

The peroration asks why a new law is necessary; the Government having the right to dissolve any Congregation by decree.[2]

"Because this right seems limited by the spirit of the former law to particular Congregations, as illicit or harmful. Whereas now the question concerns a general principle that Parliament intends to introduce into French legislation. And if," adds the author, later, "it be asked why this principle has not been declared

---

[1] No. 1509. Paris. Imprimerie de la Chambre des Députés, Motteroz, 7 Rue Saint-Benoit, 1904.
[2] Law 1901, Art. 13, § 3.

sooner, I reply, in the words of Jules Ferry: ' The Republic was still too young ! ' "

The first section shows the project to be the point of convergence of all previous legislation concerning the Congregations.

"Could it be supposed that the unauthorized establishments had been rejected merely in order to relieve the rest of over-competition! No! The real motives of that refusal could be applied with even more force to the authorized Orders. The Government understood the matter well; the president of the Council,[1] after having declared at Marseilles that the votes of July 1903 ' had torn the education of youth from the unauthorized' added without hesitation: ' Yet a little time ! yet another effort, and Congregational teaching *will have ceased to exist !*'[2] It is, then, *in the will of the Republic* that we must look for the origin of the present Law."

The accomplished writer[3] (for such he is by style and eloquence) investigates, in Section II., its *object*.

"The law is not only one of combat, but of principle. It must pronounce upon a question of social order; it must establish once for all a legal incompatibility between two ideas that in past ages have been intimately allied: the *monastic* institution and the *scholastic*. This Report is destined to prove that the name *Teaching Congregation* is a contradiction in terms; it forces public opinion to lay aside all secondary considerations, it ignores the voluminous indictments, historic, pedagogic, political, and philosophic, called forth by Congregational teaching for now more than a century; it concentrates itself upon one feature only—possessed by every congregation alike—it is this: they are societies founded upon the triple vows of poverty, chastity, and obedience.
"Such engagements have been characterized from the tribune of the Chambre in words that may now be called classic.
" 'By the first of these vows, that of poverty, the individual is detached entirely from the interests of proprietorship—in other words, from what makes him work for the prosperity of his country. By the second, he debars himself from a second care; that of belonging to and living for a family; by the third, the vow of

---

[1] M Combes.   [2] " *Aura vécu !* " (*Rapport*, p. 6.)
[3] Every sentence of this summary is taken actually from the *Rapport*, but in the translation and shortening the charm is lost.

obedience, he performs an act that seems to me the negation of all human personality; he gives himself to God by rendering obedience to a man.'[1]

"Thus, it is clear, the member of the Congregation is in a state of servitude—not merely mental but actual. And can a corporation of slavery be erected into one of teaching!"

In the third section, the *Rapporteur* brings forward two *motives* that show the justice and humanity of the new proposal:

"The State interferes, first, in the name of justice, to protect the Child. Is this frail being to have its imagination seduced, its conscience terrorized, its intelligence falsified, even at the wish of its parents? [M. Buisson here alludes in passing to the petition of 800,000 fathers of families from every department of France against the present law.[2]] No! The Republic has need of men and women who accept the law of personal liberty, the law of labour, and the law of the family for the propagation and perpetuity of the nation.[3]

"We see men and women, in the flower of youth, or in the strength of age, absorbed by a single aim—that of religion. It is for no other end that they devote themselves to teaching;[4] they have indeed mastered their subjects; they are professors, you would say, of history, mathematics, or natural science. But consider more closely—what is their ultimate object! They avow it! it is to impress the souls of their children! Their influence is unbounded! they have the prestige, the aureole, of consecrated beings; they do all in their power to form these pupils to the image of God and to the liking of the Church. . . . They make, in truth, 'soldiers of a single idea'; so they have been described by the greatest of their orators."[5]

The State interferes, next, in pity for the very members of the Congregations. The orator devotes four pages of portraiture[6] to these

"'atrophied' beings; 'pious to exaltation, docile down to fear, obedient to the borders of passivity; to these *sans-famille*, these *poor* in the hardest sense,' for they have not only given up all they possess, but they have not even the ambition or the power of gaining

[1] Waldeck - Rousseau, Discours au Sénat, citations reproduites dans son discours à la Chambre, 21 Janvier 1901.
[2] *Rapport*, p. 24, footnote.   [3] *Ibid.*, p. 12.
[4] *Ibid.*, p. 14.   [5] The Comte de Mun.   [6] *Rapport*, pp. 15-19.

their own bread by serious labour! Would it not be rational [he continues] to liberate voluntary slaves, even in spite of themselves? At least, a Republic founded upon the *Rights of Man*, shall never, directly or indirectly, sanction a condition unworthy of civilisation and degrading to human nature itself."[1]

At last, the Orders are arraigned frankly for their three vows; they are crowned, before being cast out.

The Congregations are to be debarred from teaching; their noviciates are to be suppressed, their establishments closed within a period of five years;[2]—for this was the very shortest period within which to procure sufficient school accommodation and to train the new teachers required—and their property confiscated to the State.

Again the Catholics made opposition; again they battled for a lost cause with ever the same desperate courage—such as fought at all. But these latter were many thousands, "worthy to be remembered by good men." Only a few can here be named: General Geslin de Bourgogne and General Jeannerot protested, and were consequently deprived, the first of his adjutancy, the second of his command; the remonstrances of the Bishops and clergy were punished by a withdrawal of salary and threats of disestablishment.

M. de Gailhard-Bancel, deputy for Tournon (Ardèche) was one of those determined to stand in the breach, and consulted Mother Digby herself concerning an amendment to the Bill, to save at any rate the Convent boarding-schools for girls, on account of their immense utility in the education of the upper classes. He brought forward much evidence[3] gathered from the teachers, inspectors, and pupils, of the Girls' Lycées, showing the inefficiency of the latter, on their own acknowledgment, for any sound training whatever. He spoke of the Convents of the Sacred Heart expelled from Alsace in 1873, of those of the present day in the colonies, and of other Congregations of women. He persevered in unanswerable arguments,

---

[1] *Rapport*, ff.
[2] It was found necessary to extend the period to ten.
[3] H. de Gailhard-Bancel, Député, "Pour les Pensionnats Congréganistes" Discours prononcés à la Chambre des Députés. 15th ct 23rd Mars 1904. Valence, Imprimerie Valentinoise, 1904.

despite interruptions satirical or insolent. "You yourselves have chosen the education of the religious for your own children!" he exclaimed, in the course of debate. And this was true of many. Such facts, like the minor orders of M. Combes, and the ceremonious first Communion of the little son of the President Loubet, often made the Left benches subject to something more than mild banter in the Chambre. M. Combes, however, cannot, at least since 1902, be accused of inconsistency.

De Gailhard-Bancel was staunchly supported by the deputies de Beauregard, Lasies, and Boutard, by the Comtes de Lajuinais and de Pomereu, by Baron Reille, and by the general applause of the Right. History repeated itself: the amendment was rejected by 305 votes against 235, and in April the Bill as a whole passed the lower House.

CHAPTER XXII

THE LAW OF 1904

" The King was afraid, and went out; but he soon came back : ' Perhaps you think I mean to bestow on you the crown of martyrdom ; but I am not such a fool. But, as it pleases you to live apart from all intercourse with seculars, you have only to go back the way you came, into your own country.' All the lords of the King's following cried out that neither would they tolerate in their country people who thus isolated themselves. Columbanus said that he would not quit his monastery unless he were torn from it by force. Then they seized him, and took him to Besançon to await the further orders of the King."—MONTALEMBERT, *The Monks of the West* (Paris, Lecoffre, 1860), vol. ii. pp. 441ff.

MOTHER DIGBY had not waited until now to make her preparations.

A new feature of the present expulsions would be— not the mere sequestration of property, but its confiscation. In the former case, which concerned the un-authorized houses, lands, goods and buildings were to be returned to the original donors if these could make good their claim, and the moveable property had been looked on as effects personal to the individual. Not always, by any means—less often than not—had justice been done in these respects, for the administration of the property was in the hands of adversaries ; but at present, even by the law itself, total ruin was to be brought upon the Orders. Their goods were to become by the dissolution, *sans maître*,[1] and would thus fall to the state without appeal. By Article 7 of the *Bill*, such members as possessed no other means of support, and were too aged or infirm to earn their living, were to be provided with a life-pension drawn from the liquidation of the goods of their Order. " Their right to this pension," M. Ferdinand Buisson had said in his *Rapport*,[2] " cannot for an instant be disputed."

[1] Without owner ; " unclaimed property."
[2] P. 53. Art. 7 § 3

Article 7 was simply omitted in the *Law*. The matter was left to the discretion of the government.

There were in France at the beginning of the century forty-six houses of the *Sacred Heart*. The schools were crowded with children, the works were in full prosperity, enjoying the confidence of the parents and of the ecclesiastical authorities. Never in the history of the Congregation had all been so fair and flourishing. Its banishment would be, in the ordinary sense, to quote Mother Digby, "an immense disaster." But it need not be said that she looked beyond the impending shipwreck.

For some time past she had been definitely preparing her daughters for sacrifices to come. It was certain that there would be, in the near future, a time of doubled labour, and one of privation in the material order, if the Society of the Sacred Heart was to stretch out its resources to cover as much ground as possible with straitened means. All this must be borne; not endured, but welcomed, as consonant to the rule of poverty.

But there might be a call for far greater self-forgetfulness. Mother Digby knew well the French heart, so deeply rooted in its own soil, so rightly proud of a country that is in every sense the centre of Europe, and whose children therefore are less than other nations prone to seek home and fortune elsewhere. She knew too the weakness of human nature, and her letters from now onward not only display a trust in her daughters' fidelity, but contain practical cautions, anticipations of difficulties, firm warnings; a fore-arming in every direction, lest there should be any rapine in a generous holocaust. Many of the French subjects would be drafted to England, or to English speaking lands. None who knew the world outside could be ignorant of the feeling that had now for some years, from one cause or another, grown bitter against her own nation. The Boer war, the Fashoda incident, the Dreyfus case, fifty lesser things, had swelled the irritation sometimes to fever point. True, in the fraternity of a religious order there reigns a Christian breadth of heart that knows neither Jew nor Gentile— still, if the nuns themselves "drowned all unkindness,"

the same could not be said of their families and friends.
Prejudice dies hard, and hospitable England was perhaps
now paying for her haughty insularity of old.

Mother Digby's letter of July 9th, 1903, quotes the
strong counsel of her predecessor, Mother Lehon.

"Become as . . . Spanish, German, Dutch, English
. . . as the house to which you are sent.   Study the
language so well that you shall, as far as in you lies,
be taken for a child of the country.   Let nothing in you
be out of harmony with the local atmosphere — let
nothing taste of the foreigner.

" Be slow to judge, slow to criticise, slower still to
blame.   Lend yourself freely to the ways and means in
use, and do not try to fashion all things à la Française.

" Forget your country—just so far as not to spoil your
sacrifice by dreams of other shores. . . . Give up self-will,
self-love . . . useless thoughts, imaginative fancies !

"Our All is in the tabernacle—there is our Friend,
Consoler, Spouse—our all.   You are no more an exile
than He ! "

Mother Digby adds only that the word "exile" shall
not be used amongst her daughters.   The expulsées will
find a country and a home everywhere.   The Society
gives to each of its daughters feu, lieu, et travail!

From the very beginning of the year commenced the
packing up of all furniture at the Motherhouse not
absolutely indispensable; the corridors were encumbered
with cases; the Blessed Sacrament was carried to the
Probation room, arranged as a temporary chapel, and the
one it had just quitted resounded with the hammers of
workmen.   The children saw with great desolation the
dismantling of their chapel at the Rue de Varennes
as well.

"To realise Mother Digby's sorrow when the altar of the
Motherhouse was wrenched away, one must have been there, and
seen her seated, silent, during the time that the devastation lasted.
It was a marvel how the mass of marble with its perilous weight was
ever brought down and carried off."

What memories clung to that chapel !   She would,

as far as she could help it, leave nothing for the profaners.
The fittings, here, and in every house : statues, stalls,
stained glass windows, were removed, and given away to
the neighbouring parish if they could not be sent on to
serve for some new foundation ; the nuns defaced the wall
paintings and inscriptions.   It was well that they did so ;
one chapel at least was afterwards to be made the scene
of degrading scandals. . . .

And now a sacred and dear deposit was to be placed
in safety. ‑ One evening — few were in the secret—the
incorrupt body of Venerable Madeleine Sophie in its sealed
coffin was reverently exhumed from the chapel shrine in
the garden of Conflans and transported to the convent
at Jette St Pierre near Brussels.   Mother Digby
accompanied her treasure as far as the railway.   When
the daughters of the Foundress came to know that she
had actually taken the road to exile a wail sounded in
their hearts.   But there was no outward betrayal.   Those
who relate these things have lived them.

"PARIS, *April 6th* 1904.

"REVEREND MOTHER AND DEAR SISTERS, — Since
1901, the year in which the General Congregation was
due, it has not been possible to convoke it, so seriously
has our very existence in France been threatened, and yet
in no precise manner.   It was not therefore possible to
provide for a situation not yet defined, and to settle con-
jectural matters, whilst a further obstacle was the incessant labour required by the position of our dear
houses, first attacked, and then closed.   We followed
therefore the traditions of our Venerable Mother ; we
asked and obtained from Rome the necessary dispensation
for postponement.

"Now that by the Law passed in the Chambre the
Society finds itself dissolved, we desire—in agreement
with our council—to profit by the weeks that must elapse
before the Bill is ratified by the Senate, to call round us
our Reverend Mothers Vicar.   We shall seek, by earnest
prayer, and in union of heart, the light necessary for the
most disastrous epoch, perhaps, that the Society has yet

traversed ; at least in regard to the flourishing establishments, whose creation and impulsion are due to the
labours and sufferings of our Venerable Mother.

"This persecution, nevertheless, so poignant in that
it is an attack upon God Himself through souls
consecrated to Him, seems to strengthen yet more the
religious affection which unites us between ourselves and
with that blessed Society, our Mother,—more to us than
life. . . . The storm that will carry away our houses, and
remove the means of outward self-devotion from many of
us, ensures to us by this very fact the real happiness of
our vocation : for apostles we shall always be if we are
adorers, consolers, victims for souls, and for the glory of
the Sacred Heart of Jesus.

"With devoted affection, I remain, in the Hearts of
Jesus and Mary, Reverend Mothers and most dear Sisters
—Your humble servant,

"MABEL DIGBY,
"*Religious of the Sacred Heart, Superior General.*"

The general Congregation sat during May under the
presidence of Cardinal Richard.

"PARIS, *June 1st*, 1904.

"REVEREND MOTHERS AND DEAR SISTERS,—Yesterday
our fifteenth general Congregation ended in the most
perfect peace. It appears as if the more the spirit of
division and of revolution surges around us, endeavouring
to obstruct the work of God, the more our own intimate
union seems accentuated, as if to fortify us against His
enemies. I have just renewed this experience, and impart
it to you, that with me you may thank Our Lord for the
same grace, before I communicate to you certain regula-
tions judged useful by our consent. . . ."

At the community recreation she said gravely : "A
violent wind is rising. The fruits that are not fastened to
the tree must fall,—to their own misfortune, alas ! But, on
the other hand, it is sweet and touching to bring to proof
our own union even to the confines of the world. . . ."

She spoke to willing hearts at any rate. "My one ray
of joy," reads another note of her words at this time, "is

the obedience of my daughters." And she uttered but the simple truth in declaring that not even the suppression of all her houses could affect her so much as one wilful case of infidelity to the religious rule on the part of any of her children.

The Bill was passing into Law. M. Wallon, the most aged member of the Senate, protested energetically against a measure which "attacked the great mass of French citizens." It passed the Upper House nevertheless on·July 5th, and was signed two days later by President Loubet.

On the 10th, the *Officiel* published a list of executions; amongst them were the schools of the Sacred Heart at Besançon, Montfleury, Laval, Niort, Toulouse, Perpignan, to be shut on October 1st; next day, Amiens, La Neuville, Charleville, Lille, Poitiers, and the three Paris houses were added to the list. Cardinal Richard arrived on a visit of condolence; the day before fifty novices had been sent in small groups, some to Italy, others to Belgium; a number of lay Sisters and aspirants had also gone; most of the probanists were dispersed.

Six experts had already been to the Motherhouse to take note of the garden and the lie of the buildings; on July 14th the Commissary of Police and his secretary handed in the order to shut the Paris houses by October 1st as announced already in the *Officiel*.

On July 23rd the children of the Rue de Varennes presented a touching address to Mother Digby. She gave them each a medal of the Sacred Heart, on which was engraved: *Quis separabit?* Two days later their prizes were distributed to them by Cardinal Richard; they sang Benediction for the last time, and broke up in great grief. The children of the poor had feasted under the chestnut trees; on August 2nd they received their prizes. The parents were present; the Curé made a moving address; the deputy of the quarter of Paris, M. Lerolle, protested eloquently against the law; the applause was loud and heartfelt.

On the 28th the liquidator of the Sacred Heart was named: M. M——. His portrait may be seen on page 161

of "Les Parias de France";[1] the centre of a group of
crocheteurs[2] snap-shotted in front of a convent door in 1901.
The liquidator of a Congregation, M. Lasnier, had already
been convicted of embezzlement and dismissed, but no
suspicion attached to the honesty of M. M——.   He had,
he averred, carried the responsibility of his position to
his confessor.   Could he with a clear conscience fulfil
his office of liquidator?   "Yes," was the reported
answer, "but try to accomplish your functions with all
kindness towards your . . . clients."   "In which case,"
added M. M——, "it might as well be myself as some
one else."   Fortified by these considerations, he rang at
the door of the Motherhouse on August 4th.

"It was about four in the afternoon (writes the portress) and our
Mother was at the post she loved, on her priedieu in the chapel.   I
presented the odious card; when I rose from my genuflexion she
met my expression of countenance with a smile full of courage, that
seemed to say: *I know in whom I trust!* 'Warn Reverend Mother
B.,' she whispered;   then leaning on her stick and my arm, she
moved rapidly to her *cabinet de travail*; there she enquired as to
what had passed at the lodge."

The Reverend Mother Assistant, with a companion
who wrote these details of the interview, received the
visitor. He was dressed with faultless care, and held
his hat in a hand clothed in a new kid glove of pearl
grey.
     "Have I the honour to address the Superior General?"
he enquired, advancing deferentially.   "No, Monsieur, I
am her Assistant."   "Ah, I regret that I cannot see her
in person; I came to present my respects, and to pay *une
visite de convenance* in order to make it clear that I do not
come here as an adversary. You are aware that by the
judgment of the tribunal, I have been named liquidator
of all the goods of your Congregation in France?"   "Yes,
Monsieur, we know it by the newspaper."   "I have
accepted this delicate mission," he continued "in order
to fulfil it with every possible consideration. It is not

---

[1] Boyer d'Agen (Rudeval, Paris, 1901).
[2] Officials who came to break open the doors.

I who have made the law, or voted for it; it is not therefore my business to discuss it. I am simply the liquidator, appointed to safeguard as much your interests as those of the government; I shall accept all your little requests or complaints, and see that your alimentary pensions are properly paid . . . for this, funds of course are necessary; we must therefore *liquidate*. I shall perform my office conscientiously, but with every allowance that I can lawfully make. Thus, most certainly, you will be allowed to carry away your personal effects your books, your sheets, and your beds (if indeed you still have them?) and the inventory that I shall have to make will be a pure matter of form—indeed (looking round the denuded room) *if what I have been told is correct* it will prove neither long nor complicated. . . ."

He begged her to name a convenient day for the inventory. One of the religious went to take orders from the Superior General, and returned with the message that the taking of the inventory being an act that the nuns did not accept, but *must undergo*, it was not fitting that they should fix a day; they left the choice to the gentleman who performed it.

"*Must undergo*!" repeated M. M—— reproachfully, as he took his departure, "what a word, when I have come here expressly to signify my consideration and good will!"

A notary arrived presently, appointing the 8th August for the legal inventory. On that day the community had already gone into retreat; the bareness of the house, emptied long ago of all that could properly be called furniture, made its perfect order and cleanliness the more conspicuous; there reigned everywhere an unbroken silence.

At nine o'clock in the morning, Reverend Mother Digby, accompanied by two of her Assistants General, and two others, supported by her man of business, M. Guyot-Sionnest, with his notary, M. Tollu, and his clerk, M. Thomas, all staunch friends, were already awaiting the arrival of the spoilers in the large salon of the Mother-house, stripped of its pictures. In the centre of the room, facing the door, were seated the five religious, and the faithful lawyers; near the left of the door was placed a round table with seats for the visitors. They arrived; M. M—— with M. N——, his notary, M. L—— his secretary, and a valuator (*commissaire priseur*).

As soon as they were introduced, the Superior General rose to her feet, holding a paper in her hand; her friends rose too, and looked toward her with deference. In a calm voice, slowly, and without trace of emotion, she read aloud the following protest:

"In the name of the interests of which, as Superior General, I am the appointed guardian, and charged as I am specially with this house, I protest with all my might against the spoliation of which we are the victims.

"I affirm once again, and the State recognises the fact as well as ourselves [the notice for closing had actually described the Superior General as 'proprietor' of the Paris houses] our absolute right of property over all the goods of which you are about to take the inventory. Your laws may despoil us, but they cannot alter the fact that this house is ours; whoever the State may place here, they will always be in a home that belongs to us.

"To-day we yield to force against which unarmed nuns are powerless; but we know that the hour of justice will strike, bringing with it the reparation due to what we suffer. For *our rights are imprescriptible*."

As soon as she had ended, she handed the paper to M. Sionnest, and quietly left the room with a dignity that seemed majestic.

The intruders were taken entirely by surprise; they remained motionless whilst she spoke, and their demeanour was respectful. The valuator, who had been pressed into the service, seemed dreadfully embarrassed by his position. M. M—— was evidently struggling to appear entirely unaffected; but signs of perturbation flashed across his countenance. As soon as she had left the room, after a moment's stupefied silence, he muttered between his teeth, "Ah, the Superior General does not even deign to remain to the end!" "The Very Reverend Mother

Digby has nothing more to do here," said M. Guyo Sionnest. "The *procès - verbal* is not yet signed!" went on the liquidator. "It can be taken to her room!" The protest was inserted in the *procès-verbal;* the nuns resumed their seats, the valuator retired into a corner of the chimneypiece, whilst the men of the law closed round the table, conversing in undertones. M. M—— placed himself by the side of M. Guyot-Sionnest, the youngest of the opposition, and whispered several times into his ear. To these prolonged solicitations Mother Digby's friend listened with a smile ; then, looking his adversary in the face, he answered by one emphatic "No!" The liquidator then made the same advances to the elder gentleman, M. Tollu. But the latter turned on him haughtily : "Whom do you take me for!" These were the replies to an offer of M. M—— of "a handsome fee" if either man would come over to his side, or at any rate help in his calculations, less easy to manage than he had expected.

The liquidator did not recover from these rebuffs ; rising from his seat, he declared that he too must leave before the end of the séance ; he must really see his children off to the seaside! Hurrying away, he left the inventory to be taken by his companions, and never again presented himself at the Motherhouse.

He would have been surprised to learn that M. Guyot-Sionnest (who also possessed a wife and family) was one of those who absolutely refused to take from the nuns at this time even his well-earned fees. Truly, M. Guyot-Sionnest did them good service ; he has been paid only by the prayers of the women he defended . . . he is not forgotten. Nor is another, who would make no other reply than the following as to what they owed him : "I have two account-books, one for time, the other for eternity. Your name is inscribed in the second."

On August 10th died M. Waldeck-Rousseau, nursed in his last illness by the Sisters whose existence in France he wished—too late—to save ; on August 12th took place his religious obsequies at Ste. Clotilde.

U

"May God bless this new scholastic year (wrote Mother Digby in September from Paris to Conflans) so strange in its arrangements for our dear children, many of whom come from closed houses; and the nuns, too, have been changed. We are preparing our poor dear houses here for their *clôture* on the first day of next month, and strength will be bestowed on us at the right moment to give them back to God, their sole proprietor!"

The Rue de Varennes and 33 Boulevard des Invalides were now deserted, and life at the Motherhouse, for the small number of professed who still remained there, was passed in privation. Rough planks nailed on to uprights, old school desks, a few chairs too bad to sell or give away, such were the "moveable goods" that figured in the legal inventory. But the real hardship was the want of books and of accessible papers. Most of the archives had for some time been packed up in bags and placed in safety during the day, as was dictated by common prudence; they could be used only in the evening;[1] there were no convenient drawers, writing cases, writing desks, or suchlike; no stores of any kind were kept, letter paper was procured in small quantities at a time; even the clocks and bells had been sent away. Yet the Motherhouse continued to be the centre of incessant business, reference, and correspondence for the whole Society. Far simpler had it been to leave Paris at once, and establish the centre elsewhere on a convenient footing. But Mother Digby was resolved, cost what it might, that neither she nor her daughters should desert their own houses till the moment of absolute compulsion. This was a matter of conscience as well as of honour. The friendly lawyers made use of every flaw in the documents of closing, of inventory, of *procès-verbal*, to apply for delay, or to appeal.

Sixteen of the French convents in July had still the numbers of their inhabitants intact, and their works in even fuller development than usual, owing to the influx

_____

[1] No legal perquisitions can be made after 6 P.M.

of children from the closed schools, while the houses
condemned to extinction this year were sending away
their pupils, amidst scenes of great sorrow. "Two
lessons," said the Rev. P. Boulangé to the children of
Charleville, "you should learn from events so dispro-
portioned to your age: a horror of all tyranny, and an
entire devotion to the Church of God." The nuns left
them, as a parting trust, the instruction in their free
time of the little ones from the *école*; the number of
these latter had been lately augmented by a hundred
and fifty children forcibly deserted by the banished
Sisters of Charity. The *Sacred Heart* at Lille had five
hundred children altogether, in its schools, now to be
closed; the parents of the boarding scholars sent a joint
petition to Mother Digby for the substitution of a school
over the Belgian border, offering to pay the expense of
transit; the translation was actually made—to Lindhout,
near Brussels. Lille, the home of great Catholic *Patrons*,
and of the Catholic Institute—in truth a University—held,
with all the obstinacy of the North, a part to Catholicism,
a part to the reverse.

"Who does not know" (said M. Sellosse, a distinguished lawyer
and professor at the above Institute, in his farewell address to the
nuns, before a large gathering of outsiders who listened in sorrowful attention) "who has not read the sentence in our famous
Declaration of the Rights of Man, *All Frenchmen are equal before
the law !* But to you are denied the rights that in every free
country are granted to all but criminals. . . . It is written, that
None can be molested for his opinions ! religious or otherwise : . . .
and you are driven out . . . because you have engaged yourself
until death in the service of God and your neighbour. . . . It is
written, that *Property is inviolable* and that *No one can be
expropriated without a just indemnity*—and to-morrow this house
will be put up for auction; to-morrow will begin the operation
called, in the dulcet language of the law, '*liquidation*,' but termed
by a minister of justice *legal brigandage.*"

Dr Duret, in the name of the parents, spoke also :
"Adieu, *Mères religieuses.* Your flag is Liberty of
Teaching—you will carry it beyond the frontier—it will
produce a potent race for France." The Comte de

Montalembert, deputy of the *Nord*, drove off the Superior in his own carriage : "Vive le Sacré Coeur ! Down with godless education !" burst from a great crowd as the nuns disappeared.

On August 27th arrived at the Motherhouse the Superior who had just been expelled with her community from Laval, bringing to Mother Digby's ear her tale of the last few days. When the nuns had quitted the house, some one painted up on the main door in huge letters : *Stolen property !* A crowd gathered together to applaud the inscription, which the occupier of the house tried long and vainly to efface.

The plan of action after the break-up of the schools was generally uniform. On the first notice of expulsion generous buyers came forward almost everywhere, and carried off—running all risks from police emissaries— flooring, doors, panels, furniture ; the dismantled house was then committed to the care of five or six guardian nuns ; within these walls, stripped of gas-fittings, with straw palliasses for beds, a tallow candle stuck into a bottle for lighting, a single stove, an old chair or stool apiece, packing boxes for tables, the nuns lived on, with one chamber alone decently appointed as a chapel. Broken window panes and loosened tiles were not mended or replaced, and, as winter drew on, and the wind blew unimpeded down long corridors and large rooms of which the doors had been removed, the cold was sometimes bitter.

In several places robbers prowled about, and tried to break in ; at Toulouse the faithful gardener provided himself with a revolver, and kept constant watch ; for he had found a sharp poniard, with a ribald song, dropped by the thieves when pursued. At Perpignan a band of gipsies pillaged the garden, cut down wood, and stole the fruit and vegetables, so that the nuns were for a time in distress ; but poor neighbours brought them eggs and potatoes. A washer-woman said : "Come to my house ! we have bread enough !" At Calais the nuns, anxious to save all possible expense, obtained leave from Mother Digby to make lace for a shop in the town.

The guardians took up any work that came to hand. They assembled the children of the *écoles* for daily instruction. The *gamins* of Calais, for instance, did not even know there was a God. The local Children of Mary helped in this work, as also in arranging the houses for retreats given to various classes ; amongst others to school teachers, many of whom were secularized nuns, full of gratitude to find themselves once more with their fellows, and treated with sympathy. They gathered up fresh courage to carry on their difficult mission, so necessary for France.

In this manner the guardians remained within their walls, despite all efforts to oust them, short of expulsion by force. At the end of October three personages presented themselves at the convent door at Toulouse ; they came to visit the building, they said, which was to be turned into a military hospital. On the nuns declining to open the doors, the visitors were filled with polite astonishment. Doubtless the sisters did not know in whose presence they were. It was *Monsieur le Maire! Mons. l'Inspecteur de l'Académie! Mons. l'Architecte de la ville!* But the proprietors, unabashed, repeated their refusal, and the distinguished individuals took their departure without having set foot beyond the vestibule.

In a good many places the nuns were obliged to appear before the tribunals. "Do you still form part of the Congregation of the *Sacred Heart*?" "Yes." "Why have you not quitted the house by the day notified?" " Because it is our own! "

When all that law could do for delay had been done, the nuns remained in the house until the last day legally permitted. On the day ensuing, the officials arrived— where the district was anticlerical, punctually ; in the contrary case, later. They would then deliver the first summons to depart. Of these there must be three ; intervals between them were delayed or accelerated according to local dispositions. At the third summons the day fixed for expulsion by force was notified to the nuns, who, on the preceding evening, commenced their immediate preparations for departure. Friends usually turned in to aid, and procured waggons or carriages; at dawn or before sunrise the vehicles were driving off; the house door was locked by a trusty workman, who flung the keys into some thicket in the grounds, and then scaled the wall himself to call an adieu to those who had educated his wife, his children, and perhaps himself.

At Charleville, after the nuns' departure, the liquidator wandered round the closed building, unwilling to damage the property further by breaking in without necessity. The men about the place refused to give him the smallest information. After three days vain attempts he burst in by a small door, and found himself in face of a dangerous enemy, the watch dog, who naturally flew at the house-breaker and doubtless paid for the fidelity with his life. The poor beast had followed the carriage of the departing nuns for a long way; he had been given to the gardener, but had run away again, and made his way somehow into the enclosure, to resume his post of guard. The liquidator offered 60 fr. per month to one of the convent labourers, reduced to poverty by the nuns' departure, and the father of seven children, if he would simply act as keeper of the house; he absolutely refused.

There was no surrender anywhere. And, in a land like France, where now thirty-four years of persecution under form of legality had largely wearied out even protest, and where the comfortable salve to conscience, the formula "Legal is lawful" was beginning to be consecrated, so much so that even practising Catholics were found to preach submission to the nuns in language suitable to our English James I.—in France, if anywhere, was the example needed of conscientious resistance, at all costs, without compromise, through years it might be, of privation and hardship. The Orders, and Mother Digby with the rest, were clinging to a sacred trust.

The doings of the *Sacred Heart* in Paris and the provinces, faithful to orders received from headquarters, had not escaped the vigilant eye of M. Combes, who was heard to declare angrily that he would find means of punishing "the proud daughters of the humble Mother Barat" who still ventured to resist him. But Mother

Digby would never endure to hear the minister's name pronounced with indignation. "He is God's instrument!" she answered quickly when some one exclaimed against him. "We must pray for him. God's ways are not our ways." . . . "M. Combes can but destroy our houses" she wrote, about this time. "Persecution will unite us all more than ever; we shall be the stronger and more fitted for our work."

It must now be seen where the nuns already driven out were going to.

Mother Digby had resolved that whenever a tabernacle or school closed in France, a fresh one should open elsewhere for the same worship and the same teaching. The establishments of 1901 and 1902 have been enumerated and sketched out ; her journeys since that date, her letters and negotiations, had had the same object in view. Several foundations refused in past years for mere want of subjects could now be accepted. There were many parents of France able and anxious to retain the education of the *Sacred Heart* for their girls, provided they need not send them too far outside the frontier. But there were of course innumerable difficulties every way that seemed to carry as many cross questions as a monster game of chess. It is not in all parts of the world that French workers are more acceptable than English ; further, convenient ground near France was in many places occupied already by teaching Orders ; there were, too, aged or infirm religious for whom charity demanded care in removal and choice of climate ; more serious was the real or affected alarm of foreign governments at the prospect of extensive immigration of nuns into their borders. Most distracting of all was the short space of time within which all these changes and arrangements must be accomplished for two thousand persons, whom Mother Digby had resolved to provide with home, chapel, subsistence, effective work, and spiritual succour.

For every house about to be closed, or dismantled— perhaps several in a week or month—it was necessary to decide upon the destination of each of the nuns. Their long list of names was laid out upon the old school writingdesk in Mother Digby's little bare room, and was the object of many hours' assiduous study. She pondered on the age, health, character, aptitudes, knowledge of foreign languages, family circumstances, of each individual in turn; she did her utmost to place each in the situation best suited to her, to remove or soften the painful accompaniments of each sacrifice. The infirm and venerable religious who had spent their years and their strength in the service of the *Sacred Heart* were the first to be considered. She descended to details. "We will send her to such a house," she said of one, "where there are plenty of flowers; they will brighten somewhat her old days." And she took every affectionate precaution that the journeys should be undertaken under favourable conditions. As she well knew, there would be plenty of inevitable suffering left. At Poitiers, for instance, Mère de Vandeuvre, who was very ill, was carried out from the house in 1904; she was obliged to traverse France in this state, and died shortly after her arrival at Jette. In all cases there was transportation for life. Mother Digby knew by experience what was meant by a double expatriation; she felt it already at the prospect of leaving France; a country that she had, almost sternly, made her own. But she trusted her children, as they trusted her; and this was an immense alleviation on both sides.

One category of her flock might otherwise have felt sad anxiety. To say nothing of the unfortunate religious of some smaller congregations, deprived altogether of their convent homes and flung perforce upon a merciless world, some being reduced to mendicity—many other Superiors had, by dire necessity, or as a matter of prudence, dismissed the novices; and, in certain cases, the lay Sisters. Heart-rending scenes and tales there were throughout France in these years. But whatever privations might come, the nuns of the Sacred Heart had cause for deep thankfulness that they were, one and all, saved the most terrible of all banishments to the religious heart in this world. "As long as there is a crust left" said Mother Digby to a young postulant, fearful of her fate, "we two will share it!" She made the same reply to the mother of a novice, who had questioned her on the subject : " Madame, as long as there is a morsel of bread, your daughter and I will eat it together ! "

The days at the Motherhouse were passed in perpetual suspense. Members of expelled communities arrived in succession, to receive fresh orders, consolation, and encouragement. The post brought news of the travels of the liquidator to the provincial houses. Many French children of the Paris house were beginning their school year at Brighton. The police called at the deserted 77 Rue de Varennes to see what was going on ; two days later they arrived at the Motherhouse and delivered their first summons. But M. Guyot-Sionnest had spied a legal flaw in M. M——'s document, and lodged an action against him promptly. In this sort of way the autumn drew on.

But, all this time, the example of the Mother General, her unfailing trust, her letters, the consciousness of the one spirit pervading the whole Society, made the daily recreations as happy as usual, both at Paris and *en province*. All who have experienced it, know the zest of hardships borne in common for a worthy cause ; and the small unforeseen adventures of a makeshift subsistence added gaiety to the little company still entrenched behind the walls of the French convents.

And now must be shown what hospitality had been found beyond the frontier.

In the middle of the year 1903, Mother Digby had opened in Spain another house of the Sacred Heart at Barcelona (Calle San Pedro) ; others at San Sebastián, and at Larrauri, not far from Bilbao. These three houses harboured at once the nuns already expelled from the south-west of France, and a considerable number of their French pupils. Las Palmas, in the Canary Islands, which owed much to the efforts of two former pupils of Roehampton, received another colony ; while for the religious and children from south-east France the Society acquired the Villa Sartorio, at San Remo, and a house at Palermo in Sicily. Cardinal Callegari lent his episcopal villa at Luvigliano, near Padua, and showed most fatherly kindness. In all these places the schools began to fill

at once, and other works to prosper. At Albano, an
hour from Rome, at Trinità, near Fossano (Cunéo), and
at Le Cioché, in Piedmont, small villas in primitive
country places served as temporary refuges for groups
of nuns, who undertook what works they could amongst
the poor. The *personnel* of Le Cioché was soon transferred
to Rivoli, near Turin, which served as a noviceship and
a house of studies.

At Mirandola in Tyrol, a day school was begun,
near the existing convent of Riedenbourg, Bregenz;
Goodrington, once a hospital for Nelson's sailors, on the
red rocks of the Devon coast at Paignton, now sheltered
another party; foundations at Cairo and at Malta received
their contingents of French religious, joined to an English
main body. The last two houses soon showed large and
flourishing schools; that of Leamington, in Warwickshire,
though mainly English, required of course French teachers.
Sydney, in Australia, developed a branch house for a day-
school; here too there was scope for European workers.
By the end of 1904 four other houses had been acquired:
Bonchurch, Isle of Wight; Cartagena, Spain; Lake
Forest, near Chicago; and Tijuca, Rio de Janeiro—the
first foundation of the Sacred Heart in Brazil, and the
forty-second of Mother Digby's Generalate.

Regarding their banished sisters, the whole Society of
the Sacred Heart laid itself under contribution. The walls
of the old convents responded to Mother Digby's appeal
" You will widen yourselves out, will you not?" to receive
the newcomers for good, or for a time. Furniture had
been carried away from the deserted French houses;
this was supplemented by gifts from the convents that
were nearest, and who supplied a body of helpers, often
former pupils, to prepare the new houses, with every
delicacy of feeling and attention. Secular or ecclesiastical
benefactors often did much, as has been shown; the
inhabitants everywhere came forward to give a kindly
or a cordial welcome to the nuns. Truly they had cause
for nothing but thankfulness.

But nowhere in all the world were they better received
than in the Low Countries. The *Sacred Heart* was already

known there; in Holland by the convent of Blumenthal,
and of Bennebroeck; and in Belgium by those of Jette
St. Pierre, Brussels, and Bois l'Evêque.

At the Abbaye de Flône, on the Meuse, in the province
of Liège; at Fontaine l'Evêque, an ancient *seigneurie*,
still possessing its thick walls and four great flanking
towers, and Gothic chapel of the thirteenth century; at
Lindhout, in the suburbs of Brussels; at la Ramée, a
Cistercian abbey near Jodoigne despoiled at the Revolution; at Wetteren, the Château of Count Vilain XIIII.—
who had been the host of Mgr. Pecci, the nuncio of 1850
—and at Antwerp, the nuns of the Sacred Heart from
Northern and Central France found homes. These were
nearly all ecclesiastical properties, wrested from their
rightful owners during the great Revolution: "Black
Lands" as they are still called in Belgium, for they are
supposed, like the abbey lands of England, to bring
ill luck to secular possessors. Whether or no, the nuns
met with nothing but heart-felt congratulations and
welcome from rich and poor on the soil of Belgium.
The scenes of the installation of each new convent of
the Sacred Heart, amusing from the naïve simplicity of
the excellent inhabitants, were deeply touching to the
banished daughters of France, and those who experienced
the reception were not tempted to smile. It was similarly
conducted everywhere. The Curé would bring a deputation of youths, maidens, and young children; from another
quarter appeared the President of the Catholic *Cercle* of the
workmen; a body of villagers stood round; the president
read an address, a little child made a carefully prepared
speech, highly applauded by all the rest; lastly the Curé
took up his parable, the theme being that the nuns,
banished in hatred of religion, and desirous only to do
good, were eagerly welcomed to Belgian soil, whilst
Belgium was the gainer. Emotion grew general, the
children struck up a hymn, the good people shook
hands with one another, a photographer on one occasion
came forward to perpetuate the groups! The Superior,
in a few grateful words, would thank her new friends,
and promise that her community should do all in its power

for the little ones entrusted to them.   Then the furniture,
brought up from the railway at the instance of the Curé
by the waggons of the villagers, arrived at the convent,
and sturdy arms and cheerful faces volunteered unlading
and unpacking.

At Ostend, King Leopold II. showed himself greatly
interested in the establishment of the nuns in three
connected villas by the sea.   He "hoped that the
religious of the Sacred Heart would do good widely";
he came several times to see how the repairs were
getting on ; Princesse Clémentine was constantly on the
spot; she knew Jette well, and was no doubt the cause
of much of her royal father's interest.   At Ostend was
soon opened an establishment of "guest-pupils," where
young girls pass in relative liberty a transition stage
between the schoolroom and the time of "coming
out."

The Belgian Premier, called to account in the
Chambre by some of the Left concerning invading
hordes of clericals, the "outcasts of neighbouring
countries," replied that he had no concern at all with
any one's tenets.   Providing the teachers did good work,
whether they belonged to Congregations or no, he was
ready to employ them, even in the government schools.
And the King, to whose ears complaints arrived, replied
in a similar strain.

Belgium from that day to this has found herself
none the poorer for her generous hospitality.   How
far her preservation in recent Socialistic disturbances is
the natural result of Christian education is an interesting
matter for conjecture, and for comparative statistics.   In
any case, her chivalrous welcome to many homeless
women has earned her their ceaseless gratitude.   Nowhere could the seventy-fifth celebration of Belgian
Independence have been more prompt or hearty than
in the convent schools whose teachers had found here
a second fatherland.

Nor has Holland been less kindly.   At Niméguen,
the Society of the Sacred Heart purchased a house from
some Ursuline religious who had just obtained leave to

return to Germany, their own country, and a convent of the Sacred Heart was founded later at the Hague.

Mother Digby wrote to Luvigliano (after the expulsions of 1904):

"My great desire to write had to be restrained by the pressure of business . . . Send me news often, dear Mother, of yourself and your daughters; of your installation, of what works among the people may be possible at Luvigliano. . . . Tell me of your Cardinal, and of everything.˙ I hope that my parcel will furnish you with means to make the people around you happy! It is filled with little things that do good, and give pleasure at the same time. You must ask me, *chère et digne mère*, for more, if you need it. . . ."

"She had sent off (adds the recipient of the letter) a bale of pieces of woollen stuff, calico, and other objects destined for alms. She had always that art of giving which doubles the price of the gift; indeed, she usually forestalled all requests. I had asked her what rule I must follow in endeavouring to succour a ruined family; she replied to the question, and added: "That I may have my own share in this good work, I enclose a small maternal offering . . . Do not thank me for it; my purse belongs to Our Lord, and to my daughters who may all dip into it."

On December 3rd these words occurred in Mother Digby's conference to the community: "We are waiting for God and His reign. This life is but an advent; a combat, and an expectation." Two days later she started for Rome with one of her Assistants. To a second who, owing to her ill-health was unable to accompany them as had been arranged, she wrote from the Trinità dei Monti:

"I enter your room discreetly, my dear Reverend Mother, to let you know our lamentations over the trials that keep you from our Roman joys! . . . Above all be prudent, — wait a few days, and then join us, stopping at Turin; then you must rest here *for good* as the children say. It seems to me that Conflans was going on well, each one at her duty! Count on my compassionate affection in the Heart of Jesus, and say a

thousand affectionate things to . . . whom I miss so
much, as well as . . . etc. . .."

On Christmas Eve Pius X. admitted to his presence,
for the first time, Mother Digby and four companions.
They were conducted to his private study; "*Oh, la Mère
Générale!*" he said in French, and without allowing time
for the customary genuflexions, he invited them to be
seated on five armchairs forming a semi-circle round his
bureau. "How go your affairs in France?" "Worse
and worse, Holy Father!" His face wore a look of deep
concern. "Has the government confiscated your houses?"
"Thirty already are either shut or condemned; fourteen
hundred religious have departed for other countries."
"You are doing as the Gospel bids you: 'If you are
persecuted in one city, flee to another.'" . . . "Thirty-six
new foundations have been made to compensate these
expulsions." . . . "Very good!" He went on to talk of
religious freedom in the States and Canada—he enquired
with interest upon every matter concerning the Society
for nearly half an hour. "Pray for me," he said, in a
low voice as he presented his ring to be kissed.

Reverend Mother Digby was received also with
benevolent kindness that same morning by the Cardinal
Secretary of State. She felt with profound gratitude that
even the loss of Leo. XIII. had not barred the fulfilment
of the promise: *I will be propitious to you at Rome.*

CHAPTER XXIII

CAST OUT

" ' Where is now your fortress?' When he laid his hand on his heart he answered, 'Here, and one whose strength will laugh a siege to scorn.' " — KENELM DIGBY, *Godefridus* (Lumley, 1844), p. 7.

ON January 15th, Mother Digby, at the Trinità dei Monti, began her yearly retreat. The Blessed Sacrament was transported to the shrine of Mater Admirabilis, reserved for her sole use this week, and as usual everything was organized to ensure her complete tranquillity. But this was soon attacked by ill news from Paris. On January 18th, M. Combes, foreseeing his forced resignation at no distant date, hastened to sign the death-warrant of four hundred and sixty-six more religious establishments, and among them were seven of the *Sacred Heart*.

"You are staying some time at Rome?" Pius X. had enquired in the audience on Christmas eve. "Till the end of January, Holy Father." "You must stay at least till the spring, and you must visit me again before you go."

She came on February 12th to assist at the solemn assembly in which the Decree was promulgated proclaiming the virtues of the Venerable Mother Barat to be heroic. Three Cardinals, and many prelates and secular persons, were present; at 11 o'clock the sovereign Pontiff with his Noble Guard entered the Hall of the Consistory; in front of the papal throne places were reserved for Mother Digby, and a certain number of Superiors of the Sacred Heart from all parts of Europe.

The Holy Father listened with marked attention to the reading of the Decree, and to the address from the Postulator. Finally he himself began his speech. His

319

countenance, now too often heavy with sadness, appeared radiant, and he spoke with animation. After sketching in a few words the career of the Venerable Foundress, and the persecutions she had undergone :

"My dear daughters [he continued, addressing the party in front of him] do, you, the children of Mother Barat, raise your hearts, in confidence and consolation. . . . Do not fear ; . . . she, your first Mother, stands before the throne of God to implore for you grace and courage to walk in her footsteps under like difficulties. . . . I will now bestow my blessing upon you, and upon your whole Institute."

And Mother Digby with her daughters knelt and bowed beneath the extended hands of the Pontiff. He conversed with them afterwards in his private library, till the cannon sounded mid-day from the Castel St Angelo, when they retired, but with exceeding great joy.

But of the cause of the Venerable Foundress, which now for years had absorbed so much of Mother Digby's thoughts, cares, and correspondence, more must be related further on.

She left Rome February 27th, and on her way visited San Remo, where the school and community of Aix had taken refuge. Her presence spurred on what was already prospering. From the condemned house of Marseilles she went on to Avignon, still on its feet and in full work. On March 14th she drove through the gate of 33 Boulevard des Invalides, to find the community still standing before the storm. The months had been besprinkled with calls from *commissaires* and *huissiers*, demanding explanations as to why the Motherhouse had not been evacuated on 1st October last. But M. Boyer de Bouillane lodged a counter-summons against M. M—— for illegality in his nomination as liquidator, there being a law that the interested party should be allowed the option of refusing him. M. M——, embarrassed, withdrew his summons ; the nuns presently lost their case in this matter, but there ensued three months delay, with latitude of appeal. Later on Mother Digby appeared—at the Motherhouse—before the Juge d'Instruction, M. André, concerning the continued occupation of the house at Quimper; M. André was polite; it was, besides, a great condescension to come and interrogate Mother Digby on the spot, for she had been summoned to the Palais de Justice. But M. Boyer de Bouillane had represented the state of her health. The affair terminated to her advantage by an *alibi*. So things hung on, but always in uncertainty.

Geraldine, Mother Digby's only remaining sister, Countess of the Holy Roman Empire, and Canoness of the Royal Chapter of St Anne at Munich, died on July 12th in the seventy-fourth year of her age. She had years ago given up her dear wish to enter religious life for the sake of Mabel, whom she singularly loved; for both girls, it was thought, could not leave their mother. Geraldine's patient days were filled with good works; she was very silent, always quiet, always self-devoted; the deafness of her latter years did not alter her gentleness of temper, or promptitude in personal service. There is little to say about this holy uneventful life, contrasting curiously with the chequered existence of her cloistered sister, Mabel, which it takes a volume to relate. Geraldine is buried by her mother's side in the cemetery at Roehampton. Mother Digby had taken a great fancy to the following lines, found in an old English missal, and had them printed on her sister's memorial mortuary cards.

> For ah! the Master is so fair,
>   His smile so sweet to banished men,
> That they who meet it unaware
>   Can never rest on earth again.
>
> And they who see Him risen afar
>   At God's right hand to welcome them
> Forgetful stand of home and land,
>   Desiring fair Jerusalem.
>
> Praise God! the Master is so sweet;
>   Praise God! the country is so fair,
> We would not hold them from His feet,
>   We would but haste to meet them there.

The Clémenceau ministry was to prove no gentler than the Combes. Ten more houses of the Sacred Heart were soon to be abandoned perforce.

X

On September 7th, 1905, at 11 o'clock at night, arrived at the Motherhouse the last guardian of Beauvais ; on the 23rd, the Assistant of Marmoutier ; both had shut their respective houses, and appeared before the tribunal. A basket of beautiful fruit and flowers was brought to Mother Digby from the garden of the latter house which she loved so specially. "Ah," said the bearer, "if they had left you at least that soil of the saints!" A smile was her only reply. The Superior of Montpellier arrived in March, 1906. Five thousand people had pressed round the expelled religious at the railway-station, and their train moved off to a tremendous cry of "*Au revoir!*" The superior went on to Jette St Pierre, and laid the key of her tabernacle on the place where rested the body of the Foundress.

In July, 1906, the beautiful house and grounds of Le Vernet, Perpignan, were to be sold by auction ; no Catholic would bid, for to do so would be sacrilege, and speculators rejoiced that the property must go for comparatively nothing. At this point the Bishop of Perpignan stepped in and secured the whole ; he then asked Mother Digby's leave to retain it for his seminary. She was only too glad to acquiesce. The chapel, at her bidding, and at considerable expense, had been dismantled ; for here and at other places she had had scaffolding erected to remove objects exposed to irreverence. She now restored the whole at her own cost ; the Bishop in his gratitude dedicated the chapel to the Venerable Mother Barat.

An incident at Marseilles is also characteristic of Mother Digby. Just before the closing of the convent, Rue des Dominicaines, a working man, in dress and appearance, rang at the door and handed in an envelope ; without waiting for an answer he left the house at once, pulling the door to after him. The guardian opened the missive ; it contained a note for 500 francs. She wrote that day to Mother Digby to know what to do with the money. "Give it to the Rev. Fr. R——, a Jesuit," was the reply. " It will make some compensation to the Society for our present impossibility to perform certain services, as hitherto." The Father in question expressed his gratitude for this charitable gift, made too at a time when things were going hard for the Society of the Sacred Heart; he added, smiling, "Providence has allowed me to learn in an indirect manner the name of your benefactor; curiously enough, his object was to compensate you for all that you have hitherto done for the Jesuit Fathers."

On December 23rd, 1905 she was on her way to Rome for the seventh and last time. She wrote to the Assistants General in Paris:—

"FLORENCE, *Dec. 22nd*, 1905.

"Christmas is near, and I must send you each and all my most affectionate wishes, asking Our Lord and His Mother to render to you a hundredfold your care, labour, and zeal for the Society which counts upon you to supply for all that is wanting in your mother, unworthy as she is. To-morrow evening we shall have saluted St Peter's, and seen the windows of the Vatican, where the Vicar of Jesus Christ lives and suffers. You will be with us, my beloved Mothers, in Rome, just as I am with you at the 33. That last Wednesday when we said goodbye to each other seems lost in the distance. What then will be the joy of meeting! May Our Lord's heart have you in its lodging; and do you, my dear and Reverend Mothers, forgive my faults and innumerable shortcomings, which I regret from the bottom of my heart! In one respect however I cannot do better: that of any increase in my deep affection for you in C.J. . . . ."

Pius X., Mother Digby's great consoler, was now himself in more need than ever of consolation. The measure separating Church and State in France had been promulgated on December 9th. Her New Year's letter from Rome on January 6th begins and is largely taken up with the sorrowful subject. "They say," she wrote again, "that the Pope is now never seen to smile, and that the Sacred College is in consternation! Need I say with what fervour our little Motherhouse at Rome joined in prayer with the solemn consecration made at Montmartre, in the name of all France."

On January 10th, Pius X. received Mother Digby with other religious, as before, in his library. He seemed surprised and profoundly touched at her gift of Peter's pence. It could not, alas, be as considerable as usual, for the Society was much straitened. "The Holy See is poor," he had said to her last time "poor to a degree that I could not have believed possible. It imitates its Founder, who had not whereon to lay His head—yet He did not die of hunger!" He conversed of all Mother Digby's affairs, and prospective foundations.

In 1906 she planned or followed up foundations at Granada, and at Puerto de Santa Maria, in Spain ; Wellington, New Zealand, and the training college at St Charles' Square, London. Reverting to the state of her health, wonder arises as before at the activities she faced. She had been suffering more than usual, and her counsellors wrote to an English doctor, a friend of old days. He replied :

"I am grieved to hear your account of Mother General, and I am afraid I must agree with you that there is little or nothing to add to what I wrote in 1902 . . . (He adds a few suggestions.) . . I do hope for the sake of others that her valuable life may be spared ; but for herself, life must be dreadful."

Her courage, however, prevented it from being so.

"Our Very Reverend Mother came to the Community (at the Trinità) January 20th, 1906, when her retreat was over; she thanked us for our prayers, and assured us that her retreat had been an ideal one. Never did she look more serene, more penetrated with the peace of heaven ; it was the last time we were to see her here. When we bade adieu to her a few days later, it was with a feeling of unusual sorrow. For we knew she was about to start for Spain in a state of health that was causing our Mothers considerable anxiety."

She travelled during the lulls of the legal attacks upon the Motherhouse. Some months ago she had been to Belgium ; in February she set out for Spain, staying for a day at the forlorn house of Toulouse, to the great joy of the guardians, just before their expulsion. On the 26th she arrived at San Sebastián.

" 'I was anxious to come and tell Spain (she said) how grateful I am for all that the houses here have done for the Society, and for the sacrifices it has made in order to come to our relief!' She spoke of prayer, which conquers the heart, and of suffering, which alone can subdue the mind and the will. . . . She quoted the words of Father Martin, that great Spaniard, to herself: 'I feared for some time, when I heard that prayers were being offered for my recovery, but when I felt the pain coming back, I was at rest.' At her request there was no singing at her reception, for the whole Society was, so to say, in mourning; she talked to the assembled children, first in the boarding school, then in the elementary, and seemed much attracted by the expressive Spanish faces. She was moved by the large numbers of the last named school, crowded into too narrow a space. 'You must begin to build at once!' she said; adding: 'the expense will be my affair.' As she drove over our rising ground, the amphitheatre of hills and the ocean opened out in a great panorama to her contemplation; leaving us as watch-words *Generosity, Fidelity*, she set off for Bilbao."

At Madrid,

"Queen Maria Christina came for a long interview with our Very Reverend Mother, and talked long, with the greatest *abandon*, and with a confidence that seemed to bring relief. 'You will pray for the King, will you not?' repeated the Queen Mother, as at the last interview in a suppliant tone, as she retired."

On May 21st, Mother Digby went on from Barcelona to Avignon, and next day returned to the Motherhouse.

Three great catastrophes in the physical order had visited her houses in 1906. In April, the terrible neighbour of Portici, which stands west of Vesuvius, between the volcano and Naples, began to mutter threats, and on the 6th at midnight an appalling detonation shook the convent for some seconds. From their windows the nuns perceived that the whole crater had blown off, whilst a fan of flame ascended to the skies. Floods of lava poured down towards the south, and a hail of cinders and clouds of dust descended upon Portici; the parents took away their children, and the Superior sent away the bulk of the community, as part of the roof seemed likely to fall in; she and a few others remained in the safer part of the building, sharing their last loaves with some poor people who remained in the village. A file of soldiers, with their captain, guarded the place from robbers, who prowled about in the continual darkness. About May 1st the great nocturne ceased; the nuns would have reassembled their schools, but the house proved to be irreparably injured by the weight lodged upon the roof. It could not then be rebuilt, and Mother Digby decided, with great regret, to abandon it altogether.

On April 19th rumours came of the destruction of San Francisco by earthquake. Mother Digby was in an anguish of suspense; not for a week could the telegram arrive with the word "safe" to reassure her concerning the communities at Menlo Park and at Franklin St. They had escaped all personal injury through days of imminent peril and extraordinary chances, and amid scenes of indescribable woe. The two houses had been wrecked by the shocks. On August 16th Valparaiso in Chili was totally overthrown by another earthquake of awful proportions, and the worst fears were entertained for the convents there and at Santiago. But the lives of the religious were shielded, and their property not so greatly injured.

"Our Mother General said to us at recreation : 'The Society is being tried by persecution in the Old World; and in the New, the forces of nature have caused grave disasters. We have lost property, but not one life, from which I conclude that our Lord wants us to be poor, but not diminished in number!'"

Her letter at this time says: "Our Father has given us liberty of spirit: we see how few things are necessary, and how we can be as happy as when we had all in abundance."

On December 17th, the Cardinal of Paris, now eighty-seven years of age, was expelled from his palace, for the government, having broken the Concordat, was now laying hands on ecclesiastical property. The news of this deed brought twenty thousand persons together to escort their Archbishop to the hôtel which M. Denis Cochin placed at his disposal. The carriage was unharnessed in the court of the palace and drawn along by General Charette, his Zouaves, and a hundred others ; the accompanying multitude defiled slowly like an army in perfect order, chanting the Credo, the hymn " *Nous voulons Dieu*," and shouting at intervals " *Vive Pie X !*" " *Vive le Cardinal!*"   From the windows of the Mother-house the nuns were watching the great procession as it passed along ; Cardinal Richard looked up, and raised his hand to bless them ; the cortège stopped, and cries arose of "Vive les Soeurs !"   "Vive le Sacré Coeur !"

In March, 1907, Mother Digby wrote to her Vicars :

"Although the fate of the Motherhouse still leaves us in anxiety, I do not think I ought to postpone my projected visit to the ten houses of Austria."

She started therefore with her usual companions and reached Kienzheim on April 1st ; on her way to Riedenbourg in Tyrol she noted again the great wooden crucifixes by the wayside, roofed in so as to form a shrine. The peasants sculpture these expressive figures with only a pocket-knife. They showed her the trunk of a tree on which the head alone had as yet been carved. "That is what you have to do with the souls of your children !" she said. "You must bring Him out, and not yourselves !" She passed on to Vienna, then to Pressbaum. She was able to spend a week at Grâz, and another at Prague ; but here she was seized with bronchitis, and, to the great disappointment of the four remaining Austrian convents, as soon as her strength permitted, was obliged to make her way back to France.

By June 19th the convents of Marseilles, St Ferreol (Besançon), and Avignon, were deserted ; those at Quimper, Chambéry, La Ferrandière (Lyons) and Quadrille (Gironde) would be so in a few months' time at most, and it was certain that the long agony of the Motherhouse must end soon. The police in July gave in the first summons to depart. On the 15th the great cedar planted by Mother Barat, and under which she loved to gather her little ones round her, was cut down by Mother Digby's order. Her Assistant, eighty-two

years old, gave one long, deep sigh as she heard the
crash of its fall. The second summons followed shortly,
and the faithful lawyers gave warning that the third
might be expected any day. It came on August 7th.
Any one now remaining would be expelled by force
in four days' time. On the 9th, Mgr. Amette, the
coadjutor of Cardinal Richard, came to express his own
regrets, and those of the Cardinal, now very infirm.

Early next morning the last Mass was said, and the
last Host consumed. The nuns in small groups drove
off at successive hours, some on the way to Belgium,
others to Conflans. All was grave and silent; the date
of departure had been withheld from outsiders, and there
were no witnesses. At five o'clock Mother Digby and
her Assistants met in the vestibule. Every one else was
gone; the house was empty and desolate, spotlessly clean
and neat in every part. On the wall opposite the hall
door, a sheet of paper measuring some six foot each way
had been pasted up for some time. The Superior
General now pulled off this covering; an inscription
was revealed, painted in large black letters, and strikingly
legible to whoever should next open the door. These
were the words:

"The Superior General of the Religious of the Sacred Heart,
expelled by force from the houses of which she is the legitimate
proprietor, and despoiled of the goods which belong to the Congregation, protests with all the power of her soul against this sacrilegious
violation of her rights. She reminds whosoever it may be that shall
take possession of this property, that, by the mere fact, he falls
under the sentence of *major excommunication* which cuts him off
from the body of the Church, and that absolution from this penalty
can be granted to him only by the Pope, after restitution of the
goods usurped, and reparation of the harm effected."

Mother Digby and her companions watched the façade
of the deserted house till their vehicle had carried them
out of sight in the direction of Conflans.

THE HÔTEL BIRON, PARIS.

FORMERLY CONVENT OF THE SACRED HEART, "THE DESERTED MANSION," 1910.

[To face p. 328.

CHAPTER XXIV

CONFLANS, THE LAST FORTRESS

"Chivalry knows not the Word Tomorrow."—KENELM DIGBY, *Godefridus* (Lumley 1844), p. 107.

WHEN the Superior General alighted from the omnibus, she found the whole Community at Conflans assembled to receive her, but—by her desire and their own feeling—in silence. The great noviciate which she had entered fifty years before was now empty of novices. She proceeded to the chapel, where the Blessed Sacrament was exposed; and, as she knelt immoveable, her daughters imagined her laying down upon the altar in spirit the keys of the houses she had defended to the utmost, and taking up those of the last stronghold upon French soil.

Two days afterwards, Cardinal Richard made his way over from Paris to offer Mother Digby his sympathy; a touching mark of kindness from one now so feeble in body. He spoke afterwards to the assembled community, as was his wont in old days; they were never to see him again. He died five months later (January 28th, 1908) in his ninetieth year.

On August 13th the faithful Célestin, the servant of the Rue de Varennes, went off to Paris to get news of his "dear houses." He returned depressed. The walls were covered with placards advertising the three "immeubles" and the gardens. The incomers had been narrowly watched since the nun's departure by neighbours, who declared that the first delegate of the liquidator had turned pale on reading the inscription that stared him in the face. Next came a set of char-women to clean up the house; they sent a message to

329

their employer that there was nothing to do there! it was all "clean enough to eat your dinner off the floors!" Now, however, many of the rooms were already let as lodgings to workmen and shop-girls, the great doors were open to all comers, and dirt and disorder reigned in every part.

Two hundred children assembled at Conflans on October 1st for the new scholastic year; they came from many different houses now shut, but in common they showed an entire family spirit, and a cheerful readiness for inconvenience or change. They entered with sympathy into the situation of their mistresses, and showed delight that Conflans was now the Mother-house. On the feast of St Stanislaus, patron of noviciates, they prepared a musical reception for the Mother General with much delicacy of feeling, and of which the actuality was impressive. They recited an appropriate dialogue: *Au pied d'une ruine*; the decorations were simple and artistic. The children were arranged in close groups, according to the house they had quitted; this was represented also by one out of a circle of adoring angels. Another beautiful tableau was arranged on Christmas day. An image of the divine Infant lay in a manger made of wood from Mother Barat's cedar; the Blessed Virgin offered her Child to the whole world, whilst personifications of the different countries held out their arms to receive Him. Deputations of former pupils from Paris came with gifts of flowers and clothes for the poor at Christmas, to renew their promises and good wishes. Mother Digby expressed herself to the community as exceedingly glad of this evidence of stability in "Our Mother Foundress's work."

Reminiscences of her conversations at this time show how deeply Mother Digby felt the woes of the Church.

"The ravages made by Modernism were now beginning to be felt. 'Pray for priests' she said earnestly one day. 'This new error afflicts the Holy Father most deeply.' She engaged a learned ecclesiastic to give a series of lectures upon this subject at Conflans.

Another sorrow was the profanation of churches throughout France, whether by confiscation or robbery.   It was a great joy for her that several of her houses had become seminaries."

Sometimes she spoke of the nuns of dispersed Congregations who had taken refuge with us for a time, and had shown the utmost calm and dignity.

"One of us asked a holy Carmelite what she had felt like on leaving her convent.   'Oh ! I don't hold to the walls ' she answered, ' as Our Lord doesn't seem to trouble about them ! ' "

Mother Digby would talk also of the Congregations secularized perforce, whose fate had been foreseen with the utmost cynicism in M. Buisson's *Rapport*[1] and of others who secularized themselves freely.

"As for ourselves (she added) it was the moment to repeat : *Je maintiendrai !* "

On February 11, 1908, a telegram to Mother Digby announced another ruined house and a fresh series of wonderful escapes. Fenham Hall, Newcastle, had the night before been gutted by fire.   The flames cut off two of the dormitories from the staircase ; the mistresses in charge lowered their children one by one to the ground, a distance of twenty-five feet.   The children themselves, coolheaded and silent, knotted the sheets together.   Then the nuns got down, the last only just in time, clinging to the ivy.

[1] M. de Gailhard-Bancel, in his *Amendment* (*see* p. 294) upon which he had consulted Mother Digby, had taken M. Combes to task for his coarse raillery :

"I shall not refer again, M. le Président du Conseil, to your toast at the Hôtel Continental, where you thought fit to jest upon the dress and personal appearance of the men and women whom you were about to proscribe.   You might be excused on account of the well-known warmth that accompanies a banquet." (Divers exclamations.)

The speaker then turned indignantly upon M. Buisson :

"But I shall not forget, M. la Rapporteur, this passage from your report, which, with permission from the Chambre, I will read :

"'Think of the hundreds of little teaching Congregations of women, who are the objects of the present Law.   Each of them is composed of twenty or thirty nuns ; they have mostly but a single house. . . . As soon as their convent is dissolved, the little group of women are dispersed ; each will earn her bread as best she can, clothed in secular dress, the only one she may now wear. . . . They will regret their convent, but they will accept, not without tears, doubtless, the command of the Law ' " [*Rapport*, p. 31].

"Woe to those" cried M. de Gailhard-Bancel, "who make women weep ! " [*Amendment*, p. 22].

The year 1908 was in one sense to be the most important yet reached in the annals of the Society of the Sacred Heart, for its Foundress was now to be placed upon the altars. It remains to be seen what steps Mother Digby had actually taken towards this goal of her wishes.

The Cause of the Beatification had been formally introduced in 1879. Owing to the exceptionally long life of the Foundress and her sixty-three years of rule, with the business and intercourse with the secular and ecclesiastical world following on such a position, her acts had been open to a cloud of witnesses, whose testimony to her extraordinary virtues furnished forth what is termed a very rich cause, but a most laborious and lengthy one for this very reason. Fourteen thousand of her letters, and many other documents, must be considered in every phrase, and the favours obtained by her intercession referred to medical evidence, and then sifted and examined by a competent body of canon lawyers.

The seeking out of documents and witnesses, many of whom were scattered in different parts of the world, had necessitated many years of patient research. Mother Digby had had her great share in the multiform correspondence necessary, and in perseverance through perpetual obstacles of one kind or another and long delays.

The methods of Rome are proverbially deliberate and cautious; the number of canon lawyers are few to meet the overwhelming number of causes constantly pending, and it is necessary to follow up the dilatory, and to remind the forgetful as to many minutiae, each one essential to success in a matter beset with legal safeguards. In all this, however, the Postulator of the Cause showed the greatest energy, and the most encouraging sign was that his zeal and that of his colleagues seemed to grow in proportion to their knowledge of the Foundress.

The death of Leo XIII. had been deeply felt, if for no other reason, because he had introduced the Cause of the Venerable Mother, which under his pontificate advanced rapidly — for Rome. Pius X. showed himself no less friendly, and his promulgation of the Decree on the heroic virtues of the Venerable Mother has been mentioned. In

1906, he noticed that the name of Mother Barat was not upon the list of causes to examine that year, the reason alleged being the great press of business now occupying the Congregation of Rites. "Leave her a little place!" rejoined the Pope. This was accordingly done; and the last of the three necessary sessions preceding the final one took place on September 4th of the same year.

Throughout her Generalate Mother Digby never lost sight of this matter of the Beatification. She held it constantly before the eyes of her daughters, more especially from 1900 onwards, when the first of the three public sessions was held by the Congregation of Rites at Rome; she continually asked the prayers of her Society for the end in view, and utilised the thought of the Venerable Foundress to maintain the love and practice of her rule.

On January 1st, 1908, a letter from the Superior General announced that the Decree permitting the solemn Beatification of the servant of God would be promulgated by the Holy Father that very month.

"MY DEAR REVEREND MOTHERS AND SISTERS,— Having read your good and kind wishes for the coming year, I must, in sending you my thanks, share with each one the joy of the whole family in the events which will make the opening year blessed above others.

"Jubilees and centenaries come round in their course by the mere lapse of time, but we see before us an event without parallel in the history of our Society: the Beatification of our Venerable Mother. How many trials and uncertainties, how much labour and prayer have prepared the way for this solemnity! . . . What a succession of graces and virtues in her life! . . . Holy Church is now about to fit the keystone into the arch, and reveal to the admiration of the faithful this masterpiece of the love of God and of the correspondence of His creature. Her sepulchre will be glorious." . . .

The crypt at Jette St Pierre was adorned on the morning of March 27th, Feast of the Five Wounds, with lilies, palms, and lights. Outside it, the ecclesiastical tribunal had assembled in order to examine the relics of the future Beata; opposite the officials were stationed the community and novices, several Superiors from various countries of Europe, and the Mother General. Amongst the workmen was the trusty Joseph Robinot, who had assisted in the first burial of the Venerable Mother, in her exhumation in 1893, and in the removal of her coffin from Conflans to Jette in 1904. Much suspense was felt as to the condition in which the body would be found; when examined fourteen years ago at Conflans it had been found whole and incorrupt. Would it be now disjointed? or even reduced to dust, as had been ascertained in the case of all other bodies removed from the same vault at Conflans?

The ecclesiastical authorities, the sacristan, the medical men, the workmen, took the customary oath one by one upon the Gospels. The representative of Cardinal Mercier, Archbishop of Malines, then read the legal document concerning the translation of the coffin four years previously, comprising its exact description, together with those of the seals affixed to the stone. The prelate declared the excommunication incurred by any one carrying off a portion of the relics, the seals were next verified, and the workmen began operations. Three quarters of an hour elapsed before the cement of the sepulchral stone yielded to the strenuous blows; when the marble was raised at last, the partitions of the tomb were revealed in perfect condition, and the coffin could be seen just as it had been deposited four years since.

" How our hearts beat [said one present] as silently the object of so much reverence and expectation was hoisted into our sight and deposited on a *brancard*, draped with white satin embroidered in gold. As we escorted the bearers to a room near the cloisters arranged for its receptions the hymn *Jesu Corona Virginum* was joyfully entoned ; . . . and we could repeat in truth : *Her children have risen up and have called her blessed.*"

It was now midday ; the precious burden was placed on a table covered with red damask. The Superior General and eleven other religious were admitted into the chamber with the doctors and the ecclesiastical tribunal. After due formalities, the outer coffin, confined with iron bands, was opened; the cover of the leaden case was then cut away, and the third within, of wood, carefully unscrewed. The happiness of the nuns may be divined on perceiving, beneath the silken veil, now in rags, the form of their first Mother clearly indicated. Not a bone was disjointed, nor did the faintest odour exhale from the great relic, raised without difficulty by the doctors, who were full of admiration, and placed upon a table, where all could now contemplate it closely, unchanged since its sepulture in 1893. The head veil was in tolerable preservation; the rest of the clothing was covered with mildew; the iron chain and beads of the large rosary had turned to a hardly recognisable mass of rust; the silver cross and gold finger ring were naturally intact; not less so was the body itself, compared by one present to a carving in ancient oak. The features retained their majesty and characteristic shape, the limbs even a certain flexibility, so that when Mother Digby with her assistants proceeded to remove with tenderest care the decayed garments and to put on fresh ones, the arms could be raised, and the venerable head inclined slightly forward for the adjustment of the cap and veil.

"How I prayed for you all [said Mother Digby afterwards to her daughters] whilst I held between my hands the head of our venerable Mother! I asked that not one of you should be wanting in full and generous response to the sacrifice of expatriation."

One great *lacuna* in the memorials of the Foundress had certainly been remedied by Mother Digby as far as could be. Mother Barat, as is well known to all readers of her life, had steadily refused to have her portrait taken. Thus her daughters were deprived of a consolation possessed by almost every other Congregation founded since the fifteenth century at least. Mère Marie Dufour d'Astafort, who had known her very well, retained a complete impression of her features, which she often described. Though unpossessed of proper artistic training, Mère Dufour had inborn talent, and Mother Digby desired her to attempt the modelling of a bust. Trusting to the inspiration of her Superior, Mère Dufour set her powers to work, and produced a portrait that met the general approval and even admiration. The Italian artist M. Gagliardi chose this bust as the best guide for his painting of the Venerable Madeleine Sophie ; for a "court portrait" as it may be termed, must be suspended during the Beatification, and its solemn unveiling forms part of the ceremonial. Other copies have been made of this bust and painting, and these have superseded former attempts, and remain by far the most satisfactory representations of the Foundress.

On May 24th two hundred nuns of her Society were present at the solemn Beatification of the great Mother in St Peter's at Rome. Mother Digby had fully intended to go. She wrote to her niece only some weeks previously : " I am going to Rome for the 24th of May." But the doctors absolutely prohibited the journey, and she acquiesced. Some one expressed to Pius X. the deep regrets occasioned by this absence. He replied : " Yes, for her it is an immense privation ; but *her virtue is at the height of this sacrifice, and worthy of the crown thus bestowed upon it.*"

One cloud hung over the school at Conflans : the closing of the house this very year. But friends had been unceasing in their efforts to obtain a delay. Mgr. Amette, the new Archbishop of Paris, visited Conflans on the last day of July. The children, who hoped against hope, and had been sent home for the holidays, had reassembled in order to receive him ; at the end of the séance he announced that he was bringing with him the legal permission that gave the school another year of life. The explosion of joy was unmistakeable. It was shared by the young Orleanist princesses, daughters of the Duchesse de Vendôme one of whom had lately stayed at Conflans to make her first Communion. They came on December 8th to carry their lilies in the procession, as often before, and were delighted to be at the *Sacred Heart.*

In March, 1909, it seemed as if the dreaded moment had arrived when yet another link with the Foundress would be dissolved. Mother Digby fell dangerously ill with bronchitis. M. Geoffrey de Grandmaison, who at her instance had compiled a popular life of Mother Barat, visited Conflans to read his proofs to the Superior General, and found her unable to see him. She recovered, however, before the end of the month ; he came later, and submitted to her his work with the most courteous modesty ; it made an excellent impression, and was published shortly afterwards.[1]

Next month Mother Digby made good the words : "Her sepulchre shall be glorious."

As a crowning consolation to all the daughters of the Foundress, the Postulator of her Cause, considering the perfect condition of her remains, referred the matter to the Pope, who decided that no portion should be removed, and that the clothing alone should be distributed as relics.

The intact body, therefore, was laid beneath an altar in the chapel at Jette on April 28th, with due ceremonies, at which Mother Digby was present. It was enclosed in a decorated gothic chase of brass, of modern Flemish design and fine workmanship, with plaques of coloured enamel, each different from the rest, let in upon the roof. The sides are panels of open work, and the one facing the spectator can be withdrawn, so that the body of the *Beata*, dressed in the habit, is clearly visible through a plate glass. The face and hands are covered with a silver mask, exactly modelled to the form beneath, and carefully painted to the likeness of one that may be dead or merely sleeping.

The shrine, ever since its deposition, has been the goal of great modern pilgrimages.

The children of Conflans took an eager delight in all the stages of the Beatification ; they presented to Mother Digby a magnificent reliquary of chased silver to contain relics of the Blessed Mother Barat. As the day of Blessed Madeleine Sophie's anniversary approached, the stream of pilgrims went on more continuously ; two thousand visited the shrine on May 20th, and the feast on the 25th was celebrated in all houses of the Sacred Heart with

[1] Grandmaison, *La Bienheureuse Mère Barat* (Paris, Lecoffre, 1909).

great solemnity. At Jette the enthusiasm naturally centred; many visitors arrived; the Duchesse de Vendôme and her two daughters were received by Mother Digby in her chair which she was still unable to leave. Telegrams of congratulation poured in from everywhere; together with the news that the sale by auction of the Paris houses was placarded on the walls of the capital that very day.

The keys of seven more tabernacles were laid upon Mother Digby's table between 1907 and 1909. There remained Mustapha, at Algiers, which by the official interest of friends was permitted to survive till the summer of 1909. At Conflans, the household in 1907 crowded into close quarters to make room for fifty superiors, who were now gathered round their Mother General to make in common a last retreat on French soil.

Conflans was a place of perpetual passage for those departing to the missions, and luggage labelled for all parts of the world was stored in the vestibule. The Spanish, Belgian, English, French, American bands arrived successively. Those who stayed were inspirited by the free and cheerful exits in any assigned direction. Some of the French lay Sisters had never quitted their houses before; many had been at Laval, for instance, thirty or forty years, and on leaving saw a railway station for the first time. "Where are you going, my child," asked the Mother General of one just arrived. "I don't know at ·ll, ma très-révérende Mère, but it is written on my trunk·" "That reply," said Mother Digby afterwards, "is as our Mother Foundress would have wished." The Mother General superintended the departures, with last words that cannot be forgotten.

During her stay at Conflans, twelve new foundations were undertaken: in Belgium, at Strée-les-Huy, and Tournay; another house at San Remo, as well as at Alexandria, Auckland, Rio Janeiro, and Lima; at Monterey in Mexico, at Springwood, in Australia, and at Seattle, Washington State. One from the latter house writes:

"This foundation was her doing, and our Reverend Mother wrote to ask her for a special blessing on the foundresses. Our

Mother's answer ran: 'May the Sacred Heart of Jesus bless your going out and your coming in; may It be your Treasurehouse, the Home of your hearts in time and in eternity.' She herself was our temporal treasurehouse, certainly. And she loved to hear of her *Benjamin* foundation, her 'growing American Son,' as she termed us; she let us know how she enjoyed our letters, with amusing accounts of the Indians; and of her interest in our initial difficulties. We never realised all she was to us in help and encouragement till she was gone."

The convent at Tokio was the first effort of the *Sacred Heart* in the far East; but to the observer of the times, no foundation perhaps was of as deep a significance as that of Santa Fé di Bogotà. Columbia, the youngest son of the Church, was to compensate her in some sort for the eldest daughter that had cast her off.

On September 15th, 1907, General Jorge Holguin, who at the recent Peace Conference at the Hague had represented the Republic of Columbia, bore to Conflans a mission from its President, General Rafaël Reyes, who after long civil war had given peace to his country and had signed a liberal Concordat between his own State and the Holy See. The government of Columbia was "desirous of giving young girls *a Christian education*, and thus to secure for them a *love of their country* and of *family life*." Moreover, generous offers were made towards the expenses of transit and of first installation.

"The house of Bogotà will be born at the foot of the first altar of our Blessed Mother," said the Superior General; as at early dawn on November 13th she said good-bye to the fourteen foundresses of various nationalities, who sailed from Cherbourg that evening. They were met at Puerto Columbia by the son of General Holguin, and by the Minister of Public Instruction, who —shade of Jules Ferry!—became at once the patron of the nuns. He presented them with a blank cheque on arrival, saying: "It is not the minister, but the friend who offers it!" He remarked with pride that Columbia was now the only government in the world frankly Catholic. The civil authorities had begun the new year in the Cathedral by a solemn *Te Deum*.

Almost at once the temporary convent harboured nearly one hundred children in the boarding-school and two hundred in the elementary; that is, more than they could conveniently hold before building.

The conversations at Conflans naturally turned much upon foundations, prospective or actual.

" I am asked for several in South America " said Mother Digby one day. " What are the means of transport to the place in question?" I enquired. A long enumeration followed . . . ending with " And then, three days on horseback! "

Speaking of changes, she said again: " We must never be *local*, either for persons or places. . . . And, after all, Europe is our town house, and the rest of the world our country house! "

Pius X. had talked to her with keen and familiar interest about Palermo.

" What stood so long in the way of your opening the classes there?" " The Provveditore, Holy Father; and that for months; though we forwarded at once all the necessary papers." " That is because Sicilians are not like the rest of the world—not like the *Continentals*, as they call us. I had to seek long for an Archbishop to suit them. This one? *No!* That one? *No!* At last I chose Mgr. Lualdi, pious, learned, and prudent, and they are satisfied! " " Holy Father, he has been our best protector at Palermo."

Apropos of providential circumstances in this connection, she related :

" A lady had offered me, as well as Mother Goetz and Mother Lehon before me, 250,000 francs for a house at Palermo. Somehow the undertaking could never be made to succeed; the money was disposed of elsewhere by the owner, and not till then did the foundation spring into being, as if of its own accord. I wondered why God did not seem to want that money; some time afterwards I learned that the husband of the lady in question had made his fortune by the slave trade. . . . [Again] The Bishop of Guadalajara, after having given us a spacious house, and visited me, in spite of his condition of great suffering, concerning the foundation in that place, was struck shortly after by the hand of death. He had not had time to legalize what he had done for us, and was already supposed to be unconscious, when of a sudden he opened his eyes, demanded his papers, signed them, and died a few instants later."

But, when all was said and done, Mother Digby, if only for want of subjects, was unable to comply with one-third of the demands made from all parts of the world for new foundations. The labourers were all too few for the harvest. Yet, if fresh fields could console her for the loss of the old pastures, the former were no less in extent. But here the Mother General perceived a danger.

"N'est ce pas que c'est mieux de *fonder* que de *fondre*, ma très-révérende Mère?"[1] asked some one playfully, in allusion to the dissolved houses.

"Our expansion" she said "into so many distant places, demands—commands—fidelity to our traditions, that even to the utmost boundaries we may lose none of our primitive spirit."

But a letter of January 18th, 1909, treats this subject more fully, and carries it on further.

"The Beatification was the central point from which graces radiated throughout the whole world—graces of conversion, signal favours, helps, consolations of every kind, and a devotion to our Blessed Mother so widespread and so ardent that we cannot but conclude that great power of intercession and attraction for souls has been granted to her. We cannot fail to see that this Beatification of our Foundress falls just at one of those critical moments of our life when the interests of our whole future are at stake. We are approaching the time forecasted by Mgr. Pie[2] at the close of our general Congregation of 1874, when all those who had lived with our Foundress and held from her the traditions

---

[1] "Is it not better to *found* than to *dissolve*?"
[2] Bishop of Poitiers, and afterwards Cardinal.   *See* Baunard, *Histoire de Cardinal Pie*, 5th ed. (Poussielgue, 1893.)

and spirit of our beginnings shall have passed away. The Society is not a machine, set up to work on a mechanical principle, it is a body, a living organism whose periods of growth have each their point of departure. Now will be a moment of acute peril, when life itself is threatened, as at Amiens in the early years and again in 1839; again, during a period of tranquillity, without strain or shock, a great development will take place, as in 1818, when the Society took its first distant flight [to the New World]. The time at which we have now arrived has been foreseen, for, as Cardinal Pie pointed out, every Religious Order must go through its turn. Our Society was singularly blessed in the long life granted to our Blessed Mother Foundress; thus was postponed to the farthest possible limit that critical moment when a generation that has not seen or known her must take upon itself to uphold the first traditions and primitive spirit which she gave, and hand them on to the future."

The following impression of Mother Digby belongs to this period. The writer, a man of the world, still young, with a high repute for mental gifts and culture, and for the experience given by much travel, is the son of one of the Presidents of the Argentine Republic.[1] His sister, Me. Victoria Avellaneda, to whom he was tenderly attached, had entered the Society of the Sacred Heart some years previously; a step he had much resented. He asked for an interview with the Superior General, and wrote thus to his sister when it was ended:

"I have just come from Conflans, where I have seen the Mother General, and I am still under the impression made upon me by that highminded woman. I remained for an hour under the spell of her conversation. . . . She spoke of the Cause of Beatification of Mother Barat; and all the while I was thinking that the Society of the Sacred Heart would give yet further work at Rome. Yes, I confess that the impression made upon me by the Mother General is ineffaceable—it is that of a saint. I have seen and listened to

---

[1] M. Marco Avellaneda is now Envoy Extraordinary and Minister Plenipotentiary of the Argentine Republic in Madrid.

many persons during the course of my life, and of my long travels, but there are two that I shall never forget: Leo XIII., and the Superior General of the Sacred Heart."[1]

To this account may be added the following incident that took place before she left Paris.

"I induced my husband to call on Mother Digby at the Boulevard des Invalides. . . . He paid the visit rather under protest. At that time he was as far removed as possible from any religious sentiments, refusing indeed to have the subject mentioned. Mother Digby, with her wonderful tact and calm, succeeded in turning the conversation from the question of medical men (he was far from well) to the healing of the soul—with the amazing result, that after half an hour's conversation only, my husband exclaimed on leaving the house, 'I have *never* seen such a remarkable woman! She has quite decided me to go to London to see Broadbent, and to Roehampton to see a priest.' Which he did on the following day; and, within six weeks, he had been baptized into the Church."

And now it was time to say good-bye to France. The venerable Superior General of the Sisters of Charity, the *très-honorée* Soeur Kieffer, nearly paralyzed, made her way painfully to Conflans, being resolved to give the Mother General of the *Sacred Heart* one more proof of her sympathy. They had suffered together for the same cause and with the same serenity, and now they were not long to be divided.

In June, on the Feast of the Sacred Heart, came two hundred Children of Mary to bid adieu; on the 30th Mother Digby gave the dear children of Conflans their watchword: *Ferme pour résister, patient pour souffrir, constant pour persévérer.* They presented a beautiful statue of Joan of Arc for the future Motherhouse at Brussels, and dispersed in tears. The Community departed gradually

---

[1] "Je viens de Conflans où j'ai vu la Mère Générale, et je suis encore sous l'impression produite sur moi par cette femme supérieure. Je suis resté une heure subjugué par l'onction de ses paroles. . . . Elle me parlait de la cause de la béatification de la Mère Barat, et pendant qu'elle en parlait je pensais en moi même que la Société du S. C. donnerait encore bien de l'ouvrage à Rome. Oui, je l'avoue sincèrement : l'impression que la Mère Générale a fait sur moi est une de celles qui ne s'effacent jamais ; celle d'une sainte. J'ai vu et entendu bien des personnes dans ma vie et dans mes longs voyages ; mais il y en a deux que je ne pourrai jamais oublier : Léon XIII. et la Mère Générale du Sacré Coeur."

throughout July; crowds of persons in great sadness— five hundred on one day—beset the convent for a last visit. Little children were held up at the door for a last word and look. There were hundreds of friends on the 18th from Charenton and the environs of Paris, to read an address. "You will not forget France!" it ended, piteously. They could not tear themselves away. Mother Digby gave to each a memento; they came up one by one and without delay, yet the distribution took nearly an hour.

To her Niece.

"S.C.J.M.

"CONFLANS, *July 28th*, 1909.

"I was so glad to get your letter with news of your journey and safe arrival in. . . . I write surrounded by every sort of luggage, for we leave this on Friday when we are turned out of this house, where I made my noviciate, and my vows fifty-two years ago in the joy of my heart. Who would have thought it would have come to this! We have now twenty-two nuns on sea, and how bravely they started for Japan, Brazil, New Zealand, Australia, Buenos Ayres, the U.S. and so on. Pray for them, and for your poor old Aunty Mabel who loves you dearly."

As she went out of Conflans on the last day of the month, holy neighbours, the nuns of the Good Shepherd, in great affliction, lined the passage.

The place was not left desolate. The Blessed Sacrament remained; Conflans was to pass into friendly hands. But Mabel Digby had quitted the soil of France for ever.

J.Djm,   Conflans July 2-1909

How time flies! here we are
at the Feast of the Visitation while
you will soon be in route for
Cologne & at the end of this month
we shall alas have left France
& now, listen—we shall meet
Dieu aidant, in Brussels on
your return from Germany!
Is not that, for me at least a nice
perspective! Our poor dear
children left us yesterday
in tears and grief, tho' a hundred
& more will follow us & begin
school again after the holidays
at one or other of our houses
in Belgium or Holland. The
Mother-house, ours I mean.

CHAPTER XXV

SUPERIOR GENERAL FOR SIXTEEN YEARS

"And one night in a dream I heard a voice crying: . . . You shall soon go to your own country! the ship is ready!"—KENELM DIGBY, *Orlandus* (Quaritch, 1876), p. 153.

MOTHER DIGBY was now in her seventy-fifth year, and had been Superior General since 1895. During this time her ideas and her lines of action had on the whole been confirmed rather than modified by experience. In her new position she was carrying out the same principles as before, but on a larger scale ; she had shown more clearly what those principles were, as well as what she was in herself.

" Most of all remarkable was her love for the Society. After she came to govern it, this affection, deep already, grew stronger. It was devotion as to a living person great and worshipful, and deserving of all her loyal service. Probably the admiration not unmingled with awe which she had always felt for her own mother, made her capable of that particular kind of reverent and humble allegiance." [1]

"Cardinal Lambruschini read our Constitutions three times," she not unfrequently repeated, "and each time he felt his admiration grow. 'Above all, let not a comma be changed !' he said." Enough has been related of her fidelity in this respect, her solicitude to maintain unity through more than one crisis, and during the increased expansion of late years.

In upholding this allegiance, her words were often touched with chivalry.

"War is declared ; the enemies of Jesus Christ are in battle array, and we belong to the great opposing army."

[1] J. S.

346

" Ne jamais baisser pavillon ! "

" In England, an officer is cashiered by these simple words : ' Her Majesty has no further need of ——'s services.' What a disgrace if this were said to us ! "

" To suffer is an honour.   It shows we are no longer privates, but have risen in the army of the King ! "

In fact, while holding sentimentality a capital bar to a religious vocation, she valued above all other the service of the heart.

"Characters which are ruled by intellect alone can never have the zeal, the fire, the devotedness that is all our life." . . . "If disunion ever began in the Society, it would be, first, by disunion of minds ; that of hearts would follow." . . .

In connection with these ideas was her dislike to the spirit of criticism, which, like a want of frankness, appeared to her sufficient reason for refusing to receive a postulant.   One presented herself with the first named fault, who yet seemed to unite every desirable gift, and none doubted of her admission.   But Mother Digby declined her, and had no reason to repent the decision.

The Superior General was more resolved than ever to admit none merely, or chiefly, on account of useful talents.

" The real treasure of our Society is valiant and prayerful souls ! " she said.

"A postulant had been refused for several reasons, but insisted nevertheless, and tried to move heaven and earth in her own favour. She made every sort of promise, and finally deputed her director to intercede for her.   M. le Chanoine started on a journey of sixteen hours, and was received with great respect by Mother Digby.   He laid bare the object of his visit.   Our Mother replied in a few words that she didn't consider Mlle. de —— called to our Society.   He put forward in turn her good health, her intelligence, her superior education, and her fortune.   ' What reason,' he repeated, ' have you for refusing her?'   ' I do not think she has a vocation for our Society.' . . . A pause ensued.   Then M. le Chanoine rose to go ; he addressed her on parting with perfect courtesy, and seemed to have at last understood the situation."[1]

---

[1] Reverend Mother Digby's secretary.

The duties of a Superior General put no obstacle to Mother Digby's zeal for the souls of her daughters, which she followed up with remarkable insight. She reserved to herself, at the Motherhouse, the direction of those to whom the general government was confided, and replied without delay to their notes.

Few words, but measured, constituted her direction. Once she waited a whole month before making an observation suggested to her by circumstances.

" From this concentration an additional force was added to what she had to give of her own great wealth. She did not talk much ; but how precious were her words in throwing light, in giving counsel, in lifting up anything that slackened or drooped, in opening new horizons." [1]

"Of moods and petty difficulties she made light, but when the stress had grown too strong, one word from her would uplift and strengthen. After a period of acute struggle and with the immediate prospect of a life-long separation from her before me, I (a young English religious) felt my self-control giving way, and I instinctively turned into her room. I could not speak, but she said all that was needed. 'Feel you must, my dear child, you would not be human if you did not, but go to the chapel, there you will find help and strength.' And with her blessing, calm returned."

To another in similar plight, Mother Digby said, affectionately :

" Ne vous reprochez pas de ce que vous pleurez ! . . . Et bien, je le comprends . . . Quand je mourrai, vous verrez combien je vous aiderai. . . . Laissons venir l'avenir â Dieu. Ne restez pas trop longtemps sans venir me voir ! " [2]

" On the eve of profession (continues the young English religious), she gathered us all together and spoke to us with a certain sternness that made us all hold our breath I think. After recalling to our minds the seriousness of the obligations we were about to take upon ourselves, and all that they entailed of self sacrifice, she implored us

[1] J.S.
[2] Do not blame yourself for your tears ! I understand them ! When I am dead, you will see how I shall help you. . . . Let the future come—from God. Do not remain too long without coming to see me !

in God's name to turn back *now* if we were not ready to go all lengths in God's service."

" The reins never slipped in her hands.   Authority was sacred : it represented God to those under religious obedience, and however contemptible she seemed to herself personally, yet she never abdicated that sacred responsibility." [1]

"There were circumstances (writes her secretary), when she believed herself bound to reprove with great firmness ; and her secretary, whilst writing down the messages she dictated, could not avoid an inward tremor, wondering what would be the effect produced.   Far from taking offence, however, the offenders never failed to reply in the spirit to which the reproach had appealed. 'What a blessing to know the truth!   How I wish I had realised it sooner !'   Amendment followed, confidence was reciprocal, and our Mother seemed to respond at once by a special affection, and kept up a correspondence that maintained her children in the right path. Avowals always found her indulgent ; not so, however, any want of frankness.   One felt throughout that it was the honour of God that moved her, and this raised the reprimand above the ordinary level."

Different superiors write :

"Superiors were sure to find in her support and help, advice in doubt, the friend to whom everything could be safely said, and who understood down to the most intimate difficulties.   She might have experienced every situation and every sorrow "—"She knew human nature well, more and more as life went on, I think ; and she pitied its weakness "—"She encouraged those who needed it ; she did not quench the smoking flax, and she demanded this gentleness towards their subjects from all superiors : ' Plants open to the sun !'"

"She herself reflected and prayed, long sometimes, before coming to a decision, but having done so, she did not change, whatever the difficulties, real or apparent, raised by those who surrounded her. This was a principle that she recommended to others."

Mother Digby to a Superior

"SCJM.

"MY DEAR REVᴰ. MOTHER AND NOVICE !—Your letter has been a silent reproach to me for many a day, and I regret also that I could not answer it sooner.   Yet I wished

[1] J.S.

to do so, and to beg of you to give yourself *much more* to your duties towards God and towards your community than to the works of the house, especially the dear schools. These last you will help much more efficaciously through and by means of your nuns than by your own self-devotion.

"More than ever you must become an interior soul, to be God's representative to those around you ; thus the presence of God in which you must live will give you a certain, even exterior, dignity which will turn souls instinctively to God. I know you love all the souls confided to your care and chosen by God to be with you, but please be strong patient and kind to all! A poor Superior is 'hounded' all day long and on all sides, but the last daughter who comes with some tiny, insignificant matter has the right to be received as lovingly and helpfully as the first, is it not so?

"So now, my dear old novice will start afresh upon the lines of those excellent resolutions which I most thoroughly approve.

"When you see her, give my very kind remembrances to your sister and her daughters. How many children has —— and where do —— and —— live. I pray for them, and for poor ——.

"God is giving many graces to your Vicariate, and prosperity to my dear ——.

"Pray for my many needs, and believe me ever in CJM.—M. DIGBY RSCJ."

To another Superior.

"Yes, my dear Reverend Mother and old Novice, you shall sometimes hear from me, and I count upon your making good use of the faults found in your late government at —— by avoiding them elsewhere. In your present mission, my dear child, you must be motherly, and kind, but always uphold our Rule, our enclosure, and so on. Pray much, read the rule, constitutions, decrees, and put all your trust in God.

"Ever believe me in Corde Jesu. Your devoted Mother who asks your prayers,—M. DIGBY, R.S.C.J."

To a young superior.

"Vous voilà donc, ma bien chère Mère, 'chargée et responsable de vant Dieu' selon que le dit votre règle. . . . Ce n'est pas une marque de confiance dont on remercie (comme le font quelques jeunes supérieures de nos jours) mais dont on tâche de prévaloir pour se dévouer aux âmes. . . ."[1]

To another.

"Oui, chère et digne Mère, je souffre avec et pour vous du fardeau qu'il a fallu vous imposer ; charge si redoutable, il est vrai, mais Notre Seigneur voudra bien la porter avec vous . . . Vous trouverez ci-joint le portrait du Supérieur qu'un Saint (Grégoire de Nazienzen) a tracé. . . ."[2]

It was necessary to live with Mother Digby in order to realize her goodness of heart, and to what extent she strove to make others happy. Many pages might be filled with tributes to her generous liberality ; first, towards her own daughters. The families of many of them were assisted — with the greatest tact and discretion—by an annual sum. When Mother Digby was visiting a certain house, a young nun confessed herself a prey to silent grief on account of her brother's debts, for which his family would not be responsible. Mother Digby paid them. Again, a brother greatly wished to come to his sister's profession ; the Mother General somehow learned that he could not afford the journey. She herself defrayed the expense, and offered moreover to pay certain debts involuntarily incurred, in order that the joy of meeting might be undiminished.

"Are we not mother and daughter?" she said to another who did not know how to thank her.

[1] "Here you are then, my dearest Mother, 'responsible before God,' as your rule says ; . . . You have not received a mark of confidence to be acknowledged with thanks (as some of our young superiors have done of late) but a trust that you should use for the service of souls." . . .

[2] Yes, *chère et digne Mère*, I suffer with and for you on account of the burden you must carry : a redoubtable office indeed, but Our Lord will bear you company . . . I enclose the portrait of a superior traced by a saint (Gregory of Nazienzen) . . .

"Would you allow me (a Superior addressed Mother Digby) to spend a certain sum in buying a new harmonium for our church, the old one being almost useless? Our Mother drew her needle through her work, and looked at me silently for a moment. 'No my child, you will not buy that harmonium, I will give it to you!' And on my writing table next morning I found a cheque for 1000 frs."

But, open-handed as she was, and always the first to yield the point upon any heritage that seemed necessary to the families of her daughters, she was yet indignant when, as sometimes happened, a real injustice was done to the Society. However, she pitied rather than blamed a religious who did not understand her duty upon this point. Mother Digby lived to see in all instances the actual accomplishment of her own prediction: "The money that should be given to God never enriches the family that withholds it."

Gifts of money were not all, nor the greatest of her kindness to her children's people. She brought to bear that forethought and delicacy of feeling that makes precious much that has no market value.

"I shall not easily forget the gratitude of my dear old father" says an American, "when I was sent to a house as near him as possible, he being too feeble to travel far."

"An old and infirm lady, finding herself in Paris, called on Mother Digby in order to thank one who had shown great kindness to her daughter, a nun of the Sacred Heart. Our Mother received her with attentive courtesy, and the visitor ventured to ask the très-révérende mère to approach the window, in order that her features might be clearly graven in the memory of one who regarded her with so much gratitude. Mother Digby with a smile moved at once to the required position, and the aged lady after gazing at her fixedly for some time, retired, enchanted with her interview. This lady was my mother."

"Mother Digby was incomparably kind and full of feeling in family sorrows, and in writing on these occasions seemed to know by intuition the very word that no one else would have found, and which set the whole thing in a heavenly light. She was lavish in the masses she gave for our dead, and they all seemed to be her own people.   Here are extracts from such letters:

"God's holy will be done," is what rose to my lips on reading your letter at 11.30 this morning, and now Mother T.'s telegram has just come, saying that he is with God and with your father and mother. You know all I feel and would say . . . this is the last rending of the last family tie.   For H. I feel sure that God said to him: 'Come with me that thou mayest rest secure with me in Jerusalem.'   Three quarters of me shuddered at what God allowed for him, but I am wrong, for his soul is safe and we must be all joy."

Her goodness did not of course stop at the members of her own religious family. Her liberality to priests was well known, and was constantly called upon. The Digbys had been great benefactors to the Maduré mission ; it had received considerable gifts from Countess Geraldine up to the time of her death, and Mother Digby kept up this tradition. An important missionary journal, and a letter from the much-tried mission of Adana, also speak of the Superior General of the Sacred Heart as a "great benefactress."

But upon this subject and upon her multiform kindness to the poor there is only space for one characteristic example. A young mother and her infant looked insufficiently fed. Mother Digby sent for the husband, and made her observations, accompanying them by a letter which opened to him a great Paris dairy. And mother and child henceforward got visibly stronger.

Far beyond all this however went forth Mother Digby's succour into the wide world. To many she acted the part of the good Shepherd, who seeks and saves the wanderer, weak, perhaps, rather than perverse, and sadly torn in the brambles of life. Years of patience on her part, of long and what seemed fruitless effort, won the day nearly always even against those who seemed of set purpose insensible. But then, at last, what a joy for Mother Digby!

z

Amongst the most considerable of her capacities **was** that of transacting regularly and without fault an extraordinary amount of affairs and correspondence.

"The persecution that threatened our Great Seminary at Besançon, (wrote the Father concerned in its management) was the occasion of my approaching Reverend Mother Digby upon business matters. Her broad straight mind, supernatural views, and generous heart, greatly facilitated my task, and her name is inscribed amongst the benefactors of the Seminary."

Two powers acquired in early youth came to her aid : attention and concentration.

" Nothing (writes her secretary) could distract her from the matter in hand. She read all letters through, once only, and then possessed so thoroughly the contents of each, that, days afterwards, the mention of the writer's name sufficed to recall a detail even trifling."

But this is giving too poor an idea of her memory. She would retain, in talking to any one of her daughters, and this after the lapse of many years, all the names, circumstances, and location, of the various members of her family ; not unfrequently, details that the individual in question had really forgotten.

At different times, knowing the weight of her daily post, certain of her daughters who had belonged to her community thought best to omit the yearly feast day letter that they had never failed to send before she was Superior General. But, amongst the hundreds of letters that arrived, the omissions were observed and felt by Mother Digby. She would send a message to the house where the defaulters resided, to ask "What had become of them?" And they, needless to say, then gladly resumed their old custom.

However serious the business in hand she would laugh heartily over children's letters, or over certain eccentric locutions. For she retained a certain invariable freedom of mind ; abstraction was unknown to her, save sometimes in prayer.

"Her concentration was as determined in time as in scope; one thing, the thing of the present moment, occupied her whole attention. And this was perhaps a partial explanation of how she carried so much without being overburdened. Her mind went wholly from one thing to another, so that she was never entangled in after-thoughts of anticipation. Thus, two hours after her election as Superior General, she sent for one of the Vicars to examine under the microscope the head of a particularly fine mosquito which she had killed, as if she had not a care in the world."[1]

Thus, too, she found time and energy to finish off completely all that she undertook; but her genius for order, neatness, and perfection of detail, has been described already.[2]

"Ne serions nous pas heureuses, vous et moi [she said to one who understood her] de donner notre vie à Dieu? Donnons-le Lui goutte à goutte dans chaque petit devoir!"[3]

In accordance with her extraordinary discernment, she sometimes gave decisions that appeared unaccountable, but they were justified by the event.

"She had named a religious, Mme X. to be sent to a far-off country. It must first be said that Mother Digby knew her well, her circumstances, and her great desire for this mission. The time for reflection must be short, and the reply came from the Mother Vicar by telegram: 'Health of Mme X. an obstacle, but Mme Y. ready to take her place.' Mother Digby, after a few moments' pause, telegraphed back: 'Send both!' These two excellent subjects are still working in the most efficient way on that mission, with every prospect of doing so for an indefinite time."

Such instances of the above were of course rare.

"'They say that the climate of —— will be bad for my health, [said a young German], but I beg of you to send me all the same. They want a German subject in that house!' She looked at me kindly and fixedly. 'Never, dear child, would I send you to a place where your health would suffer! Another generous soul will be found to take your place!'"

[1] J. S.   [2] *See* p. 67.
[3] Should you and I not be happy to give our life to God? Let us give it to Him drop by drop in each little duty.

She once said: "Which is the best thought, the first or the second?   The first thought gives usually our special bent; the second gives a view of the whole matter; the third, if good, is often identical with the first."

Mother Digby valued highly the counsel of others—not only of wise, but sometimes of very ordinary persons.

"When one learns from outside (the convent) some unfavourable criticism—say of the school, it is unwise to disregard it.   There may be exaggeration, but there may be a little fire behind the smoke."

The influence of the Superior General over children, no longer so directly or so often exercised, of course, was yet far-reaching in its effects.

When she visited her various houses, several schools that were passing through a difficult phase, and giving serious anxieties to the mistresses, were completely transformed by the sole influence of Mother Digby's presence, and a few talks that she had with the children. She conquered by her kindness; these little souls all of a sudden blossomed out, promised to amend, and they were as good as their word.   She was claimed as Honorary Mistress - General in several countries, and childlike letters kept her in touch with all the progress made.   These, amid the multiplicity of her correspondence, never remained unanswered.

She took pleasure in some charming traits of children's faith that were reported to her.   A child at Seville, entering the confessional for the first time, thus introduced herself: "I am Maria Joaquina, and you are Jesus Christ!"   "That," commented Mother Digby, "is a great thought."   She would repeat, too, the instance of a child of eight in the parochial school at some American house, who, merely by repeating the catechism she had learned at the *Sacred Heart*, converted her father, mother, grandmother, and seven brothers and sisters.

"One day I related to our Mother the naïve reflection of two little sisters that remained with us during the holidays.   'Didn't ma mère X amuse herself very much at the Motherhouse?' (For, to the junior school, the Motherhouse spells surprises, bonbons and presents) 'Perhaps you think she spent her time playing hide and seek!' 'Perhaps she did,' answered Henriette, 'with *le bon Dieu*. But then one would always lose!' 'Not at all' cried Catherine 'He is everywhere. And if He hides Himself, we say *I know you are there!*'"

In connection with the children should be mentioned, one of her first cares in their regard—the studies.

"Teaching [she said] is not an addition; but belongs to the very essence of our Constitutions."

Although she was neither learned in the ordinary sense, nor widely read in the literary, she was exceedingly shrewd as to the training of teachers, and apt to judge instinctively of their educational powers. But she was ready to listen to the opinion of competent persons, to make concessions, to own that she herself had been mistaken, as of course happened now and then, and to yield in consequence.

Thus, as early as 1890, she began to require the mistresses of the boarding schools to pass examinations at the London University or elsewhere. These, of course, had from the first been undergone by teachers and students at the training colleges; the degrees and diplomas were a sort of exterior guarantee of proficiency, to reassure persons who realise no other.

As to Mother Barat's plan of studies, she spoke always with the deepest admiration of its secure foundation upon intellectual principles, and of its elasticity. In the periodical outcries for new methods, new subjects, improvements of all sorts, and especially from 1870 onwards, she experienced with constant satisfaction, that a careful examination by competent judges of each sound educational theory, apparently novel, showed such a theory to be already contained whole and entire in the legacy of the Foundress. All that was required from time to time was an expansion here, and a limitation there, regarding the subjects taught, and adaptations suited to the ever-changing conditions of the day.

She often presided at the meetings of young teachers

under those who trained them, at classes given publicly for the sake of criticism. The studies were never allowed to languish for want of revision, any more than they were permitted to dry up by the fancied necessity of cramming. Examinations, government inspection, lectures from outsiders by specialists in some expanding science, all was used in measure; she was generous in providing the best books, scientific apparatus, and modern pedagogic appliances.

But, to make the mere passing of examinations the be-all and end-all of the classes, or of the training of mistresses — this she always steadfastly resisted, and against the strenuous opposition of persons of repute. Slowly public opinion came round to the view that she herself held; slowly but surely certain boarding schools within the British Isles, whose numbers had been thinned for many years on account of Mother Digby's action, began to fill again, some almost to overflowing, for the very reason that had seemed at first almost to endanger their existence.

And the last General Congregation she ever held, in 1910, was mainly concerned with a general revision of the studies in every country.

What can be said of Mother Digby intellectually? She had a poor opinion of her own intelligence, and would quote her father's words to her in childhood:

" You have a head,—but so has a pin ! "

Save in as much as the work of her Society was concerned, she was unmoved by " pure letters." Her attitude is thus explained by the one who knew her best.

" She set no limits to the gift of self to God, and in that gift she saw a great sacrifice as possible, and therefore to be offered, without hesitation or recall. It was the renunciation of all intellectual interests that were not directly connected with God. She literally determined ' to know nothing but Jesus Christ and Him crucified.' In many another case this might well have been a fatal mistake, a mental suicide, or at least an illusion that would have stunted the whole growth of mind and character. But in her case there was certainly no stagnation of life, and one can only suppose that she made an offering acceptable to God. It was as though she resolutely though unconsciously, specialised in another direction. After her conversion, God and the spiritual life, and the means of union with Him, occupied her thoughts, and when she entered the Society and had to take its double spirit of prayer and work, her second book became that of human nature. She made a study of children in the years that she was employed in the school, of novices and nuns later on ; she knew the world outside through her varied intercourse with all kinds of persons under a wide range of circumstances ; and year by year she added experience to her instinctive penetration, and acquired greater skill in dealing with every variety of character. She would never have cared for a long solitary walk or journey; but everything that turned up became living to her in the mind of some companion affected by the sight or the event." [1]

Some books, however, for their spiritual bearing, she read assiduously. First and foremost was her Latin Bible, which accompanied her everywhere, and which she knew familiarly, in the truest sense "by heart." A few words from it were the frequent subject of her daily meditation. Passages from the Old and New Testament illustrate her conferences ; they are interposed in a way quite original to herself, and thought out for the occasion. The Liturgy, too, she loved, and much of St Bernard and of Bossuet. To one who asked for a list of her favourite books, she gave, in addition to those above mentioned :

"The Imitation of Christ (the last Chapter of Book III. is my favourite), the Commentary of St John Chysostom on St Matthew ; the Letters of St Ignatius Loyola ; Father Nieremberg on the Holy Eucharist ; Rusbroeck ; some chapters of Père Valuy upon government ; parts of Father Faber ; the writings of St Jeanne de Chantal, that woman of rare good sense, and Bourdaloue, my old friend, never to be known too well."

The beauties of nature and of art did not find her indifferent. She possessed an instinctive perception of what is artistically right ; her taste, too, had been trained by her mother, and she always detected and valued original work—but this is no common quality. Her fine microscope—provided that she could now and then call

[1] J. S.

upon others to admire — was a great relaxation, and so were beautiful gardens and views.

Her speech at common recreations was always appropriate, and calculated to draw out others; it was essentially conversation, give and take; but she listened far more than she spoke.   Now and again she would propound questions to discuss, as she used to do in England.

"Which would you prefer, and why: a saint to see your own soul clearly, or you to see his?

"There is a gift of *reading well*.   Some people can read above themselves, others on their own level, others again beneath them; what do you mean by each?

"Of these three little words, *but, if, why*, which is the most pernicious?   [She herself answered: The *but* is diplomatic, the *if* commercial, but to say *why* is to take hold of the forbidden fruit, as in Eden.   So this latter is the worst!]

"How can we best know some one, by her thoughts, words, or actions? supposing only one of these can be thoroughly understood?

"What kind of character profits most by education?

"What do you mean by independence?   Is it a good thing?

"What do you mean by 'doing your best?'"

These questions had been carefully prepared, but her casual words, the result of observation and of insight, were often highly suggestive.   They lose much detached from their context, and in translation from the French.

"We must try to be agreeable to God, as well as useful—for even His enemies are this!

"People physically weak are those that make the most noise.   They have not strength to put things down gently!   It is the same in the moral and spiritual order.

"Two classes of persons are often in a hurry: (1) the habitually slow, who have to make up for this by occasional rushes, (2) the lazy, who want to finish, so as to be at leisure to rest.

"Which do you prefer, the mountains or the sea?— The mountains, because they are stable.

"You wish to 'offer up your life' to gain such or such

a grace? But your life does not belong to you. You have given it to Our Lord long ago, and it has been accepted. You mustn't try and take it back.

"There are certain religious who say on leaving a house: 'I am leaving my heart with you all!' But what are these people going to do without hearts, and what are these hearts travelling about without owners! We must really take our hearts with us wherever we go.

"The *Ego* must never be the captain of our little boat.

"We must treat the *ego* as a negligeable factor.

"What prevents people from becoming saints is the EGO. . . By dint of living with it, we find it charming, and we end by loving it most tenderly!

"Père Barelle once lifted up a little girl on to the table. 'Whom do you love, my child?' he asked. 'Moi! j'aime *moi*!' replied the infant. He put her down again. But she was only saying frankly what many people do without owning it!

"What is the difference between *the hidden life* and *the quiet life*? The latter is: Don't disturb me! the former: Seek the eye of God alone.

"Faults are better than deficiencies in a character. Give an example of a deficiency? A want of tact or judgment. How supply for it? By charity, humility; above all, *silence*. All the success of Napoleon III. was due to his silence. It was held to mean unutterable things!

"Le silence, c'est la patrie des forts!

"Keep silence, and you keep everything.

"To be a good missionary you want nerve, but not nerves.

"We are moveable, not immoveable property.

"Where there is change, there is life; we change house, and the stagnant waters are moved. What a blessing it is to be cosmopolitan!

"I prefer to find, inside the bursar's safe, too little rather than too much. Have we left all things for our Lord, in order to be troubled with money cares? He is pledged to provide us with necessaries.

"We must live *au jour le jour*; if we want anything, we can get it for the asking, but we should not store up, say, bits of pencil, or anything else.   Though indeed collections of all kinds are now fashionable. St Francis, who loved animals so much, did not care for *ants* !

"Il ne faut pas que l'humilité reste pour nous *une belle étrangère.*

"Just see how difficult humility is to human nature. We are always looking for 'a proper pride,' and we pitch upon *esprit de corps.*   Well, a true esprit de corps we must have—call it a love of our Society, and we cannot have too much.   But, what we must beware of, is placing ourselves above any one else whatever.

"Look always at what is best.   Those who do the contrary remind me of the *chiffoniers* of Paris, whose life is spent poking among rubbish.   Two of these folk amused me one day.   I was sitting in a carriage waiting for a lady who was travelling with me.   There came up a *bonhomme*, whose attire was not to be touched with the tongs, followed by *une bonne femme*, his worthy compeer. And the gentleman, pointing to the object of their desires, the dustbin, said with true French politeness: 'A votre tour, Madame!' 'Après vous, Monsieur!' replied the lady, in the same tone."

It was noticed that as long as Mother Digby lived in England, she had, at the recreations, given little digs at the national failings.

"The Briton is self-conscious.   Some one passes by; *Here I am* is the Englishman's first preoccupation.   *What am I to do?* comes next.   But by this time it is too late to bow."

Her love for England was intense, and even these harmless shafts ceased after she left it.

Her sense of humour was as keen as ever.   "I have never been so often to the comedy (she said one day) as since I have been Superior General.   It is true that there is sometimes tragedy as well!"

Sometimes a want of tact supplied her with entertainment.   A person whom she had met on her travels wrote to her frequently afterwards. "The more I reflect," said this simple soul, "the more I see that I am *exactly like you!*" "If so," added Mother Digby, "how I pity her!"

Like the principles of her government, Mabel Digby's own character had undergone development, but not change. Her strength of will, her supernatural habits of mind and heart, had dominated but not altered the elements beneath; rather, what was best in them had become more prominent.

One who knew her well writes:

"Originally it must have been a fearless, proud, rather solitary nature, blended from two strains. From her father came the genial side, the heart, the gay courage, the joy in life; from her mother the queenliness, the governing power, the force of will, the penetrating judgment, the fastidiousness, which, curbed by grace, became hard to please only for what touched God's honour."[1]

In startling contrast to a striking exterior dignity that seemed to point out one born to command, was the self-contempt that could have found no place in the "Magnanimous Man" of the pagan philosopher, and that had come from measuring herself, not with others, but with God, and from a study of One who bid us learn from Him lowliness of heart.

"Self-contempt was her own mode of magnificent humility. Hers was too strong a nature to be self-effaced. But what would have sounded from another unreal and exaggerated, what would have seemed, not humility, but arrogant scorn for something inconceivably base, came from her with the ring of perfect truthfulness and conviction as an overwhelming contempt for herself. She genuinely thought herself the most despicable of God's creatures. When she thought fit to express these views it was worse than useless to rejoin or try to stop her. This only made her hit the harder, and her ready wit and quick repartee never failed to secure the last word at her own expense. Silence was best—but how hard to keep!"[2]

At recreation she naturally took a lighter tone, but

[1] J. S.   [2] J. S.

if occasion offered by some incautious word redounding
to her own credit, her way of turning the tables was
inimitable.

She was highly amused at the opening words of an
address from a good countrywoman, who spoke for her
fellows, beginning: " *A Madame La Supérieure Générale
actuellement régnante* ! " This being recalled: " When I
was first named Superior," added Mother Digby, " one of
my old pupils at Marmoutier, wishing, no doubt, to add
to my former title, began her letter : ' Ma chère et *indigne* [1]
Mère.' No epithet ever pleased me more ; it had a savour
of wholesome truth ! "

Allusion being made to the dangers of her travels in
America : " It was necessary for me to come back to the
Motherhouse, in order to hear of all the perils I had
passed through ! " Was it not true that the horses took
fright at such a place, and nearly upset the carriage?
" On the contrary, nothing would induce them to move
on ! " " Fear, anyhow, is a sentiment unknown to you,
ma très-révérende Mère." " I beg your pardon, I am
afraid of mice ! "

Some one asked in the course of conversation, whether
a certain learned Jesuit, very aged, still retained all his
faculties. " Certainly he does," replied Mother Digby,
but added immediately : " Perhaps not, however ; for he
asked me for my photograph ! " Finding the latter object
on the writing-table of one of her daughters, quick as
lightning she tore it up, exclaiming : " How can you
keep such a horror in front of you ! "

She was fond of the expression *Brother Ass*, as used
in the mediæval lives of the saints, to signify the body,
and adopted " The Ass " as her own sobriquet. But
here, of course, as in the following passage, there was
a mixture of fun and earnest.

" Our dear Mother General would say dreadful things in her
humility, (reports Sister R.[2] who attended her in her infirm years)
' Now Sister,' she said, ' when you come to call me in the morning,
you are not to say ' O Reverend Mother, you really oughtn't to

---

[1] " Digne " is an ordinary addition to a Superior's name.
[2] *See* p. 166.

get up for Mass after such a bad night,' or anything of that sort; but just this : *The beast must get up ! ! !* '"

In answer to the question "What was Mother Digby's characteristic virtue?" "It was not any one virtue in particular, but a general greatness that impressed me." This was the ordinary view taken by those who had followed her general action in any way. Some distinguished Frenchmen seemed to grudge her to the "devout female sex." *She ought to have been a man!* they said. But, in written reminiscences furnished by those intimate with her, perhaps the most frequently recurring point is her *love of suffering.*

Her power of enduring pain was always extraordinary, as has been sufficiently dwelt upon ; and her severe bodily penances could not escape the notice of those who lived with her. But these were necessarily far less than the cross of perpetual infirmity laid upon her since 1896, which up to 1909 had increased more and more. She was powerless to get into a carriage, to walk, to do many other things without help ; she was subject to constant pain, privation, and dependence upon others.

Further, she came not only to endure suffering serenely, but positively to love it ; for suffering was a means to a great end. "Physical pain helps to bear moral," she said. Moreover, both give efficacy to prayer, and fellowship with Christ. "Our great regret at death," she said again, "will be, not to have done all we could for God. . . . How glad we shall then be of this life's tiny pin pricks !"

Once, when she was in great pain, some one asked her: "Would you not like to die now?" "Oh no! there is too much still to endure!" And, during the French crisis: "If our Society were not persecuted through hatred of God, it would be a happiness to suffer."

But Mother Digby had fought her way steadily to this result.

"Yes, I do indeed love suffering [she said to another who came to her in grievous plight]. You ask how to arrive at that! Oh, we must practise much, we must give ourselves trouble, make efforts, ask grace insistently, . . . What pains I have taken to reach it? Well, once, for instance, I wrote the name of Jesus on a little paper. I begged of Him the strength to suffer until such an hour. Then I began again. . . . One must cry out in prayer (she answered some one else), one must beg. Your poor old mother is like you! Often she needs a steam engine behind to push her on!"

More frequent still are the testimonies to her constant serenity. They are, in fact, universal, from those who have mentioned her at all. But then this exterior calm was obvious to all.

"That lady has the peace of heaven in her face! [exclaimed an old woman who passed her in a corridor]. Her very memory by its serenity makes me again serene [writes some one else]. She seemed to me [says the Revd. John Wynn] when I saw her in America, considering her bodily weakness, to subsist almost by a miracle. I found her, nevertheless, amid her crushing solicitudes, calm and serene; she entered into the smallest details of the American houses as if she had no other care."

And her secretary for seventeen years:

"Nothing was more easy than intercourse with our Mother. What she was one day, that she was all the year round. Want of sleep, physical or moral pain, made no change. As one entered her room, one was greeted always with the same kind smile. Her rare self-mastery kept her exteriorly impassible in the face of matters however unforseen, and she redoubled in gentleness before contradiction or painful words. She lowered her voice and spoke slowly, without vehemence. That of her interlocutor dropped at once. The quiet goodness with which she received a torrent of words from a priest on one occasion, who came to pour out his indignation because a young religious had been returned to her family, won him over completely. Impertinence (and sometimes she had to endure it) made her smile, although her delicately sensitive nature and perfect manners made her conscious of the smallest shades, and she felt keenly any want of *convenance*.

"She was meek and patient under garbled reports, ignorant criticisms, false accusations, imputation of evil motives. 'Let us follow the straight line' she would say. 'Sooner or later all must come back to it.' Many a time she took upon herself disagreeable responsibilities, not her own, and bore the brunt and the consequences. Her respect for the reputation of others made her silent even before her council concerning faults that it was not necessary to divulge. Twice, at least, she, so loyal herself and frank, endured treachery. She would not believe it until, in the first case, it was revealed by evidence; in the second, by an avowal. Pardon followed, and forgetfulness of the wrong."[1]

In December, 1895, she visited for the first time the house at Portici.

"The first words she addressed to me" says the Superior, Mother Macchi, "were these : 'Do not be afraid! I come with no hostile intentions!' I assured her that all were, on the contrary, filled with joy at the thought of her visit. She replied, with a touch of sadness in her tone: 'In some quarters they are afraid of me, and I feared that an echo of this feeling had reached you.'"

To some one else, years later, she said :
"Vous, au moins, vous n'avez pas peur ; cela m'étonne. Vous êtes si à l'aise avec moi ; je vous comprends, et je sens que vous me comprenez aussi."[2]
There was the touch of : *Will you also go away?*

"She was sensitive to this thought (writes her secretary) and felt deeply when she perceived in any way that something in her own conduct, or some false report, was keeping hearts at a distance from her. Perhaps this feeling exists unsuspected in most strong natures."

Her very dignity of manner, too, as has been mentioned already, was to some people awe-inspiring.
"C'est un amiral à son bord! J'ai un peu peur, moi!"[3] said a prince of the Church, Cardinal Labouré, who felt for Mother Digby, nevertheless, a great admiration.
Her own straight ways and love of truth led her to

[1] Her secretary.
[2] "You, at least, are not afraid, and this surprises me. You are quite at home with me ; I understand you, and I feel that you understand me also."
[3] She is an Admiral on her own deck ! I'm rather afraid of her myself."

attribute the same to those she dealt with ; her rectitude was sometimes mistaken for hardness and from her very willingness to sacrifice herself, it was concluded that she was indifferent to the feelings of others.   " She never stooped to coax towards the better course," say several.   Who knows?   Perhaps now and then a greater condescension would have won over certain more timid or self-sensitive natures.   As Mother Digby advanced in life, she herself realised this more clearly, and acted accordingly.   Indeed, some who had ample experience of her action, declare, that towards the end of her generalate, it had acquired a perfect mildness.

Enough has been said to show, that while she had an immense power of winning love and confidence, and won it actually from thousands, she was met here and there by coldness and resentment.   But it is not possible to doubt that this attitude existed only in a relatively small minority of cases ; perhaps she herself did not realise their fewness.   To this should be added, that no one who knew Mother Digby well is to be found among their number.

But who, indeed, can please everybody?

"She confessed to a natural strain of melancholy.   She foresaw rather the painful than the fortunate.   During her long sleepless nights, there were many anxieties that occupied her far more before God, certainly, than the success of her personal action, or the material prosperity of the Society.   She would sometimes ask: What colour are your early morning thoughts, pink or black?   Hers, I believe, were not rose-coloured." [1]

The secret of her serenity and strength amid trials from within and from without lay in her spirit of prayer.

By prayer she was anchored in that trust in God without which her natural fearlessness and strength of will could not have sufficed.   *When I sent you forth, have you wanted for anything?   They say to Him, Nothing!* She quoted this at a crucial time.   Of such times, the gravest, she avowed, was the occasional persecution by

---

[1] Her secretary.

the friends of God. But even this could not make her swerve from a step that she thought it right to take.

"In two lawsuits brought by two religious who wished to force the Society of the Sacred Heart to re-open its doors to them, she was obliged in one case to oppose persons high in ecclesiastical and in secular authority, and, in the other, to bear the action of a tribunal little versed in the customs of religious orders. This latter condemned us; but our Mother appealed from it, and with entire success." [1]

From all parts of the world the same thing is constantly repeated:

"Of her prayer, of the supernatural leaven, I can only say that I seemed to see and feel it at all times. She appeared in all things moved by a hidden power, the body being but the instrument."

"Nearly everyday (relates her secretary) as soon as she had examined the afternoon post, our Mother rose, saying: 'Now I am going to see my *Bon Dieu*. Can I go? Is there anything else?' 'No, *ma Mère* but it is only ten minutes to four; you will be a long time in the chapel.' 'Long!' Her expression said enough. 'I can take a good hour. If you want me, come and fetch me.' And, whatever cares were pressing, she looked radiant, and as if passing into another world. Sometimes—but with what regret!—I was obliged to disturb her in her stall. She was so absorbed in the presence of God that she seemed to come back from a far distance to answer me."

The Sacred Heart, the Blessed Sacrament, was her great devotion. She loved to surround and adorn the tabernacle with all that was most beautiful. Inside the door she put some precious stones that had been given her; she did not care for any but natural flowers upon the altar; she was generous in illuminations and lamps, and provided liberally for new chapels in distant missions. [2]

"Two words (she once said) sum up for me the mystery of the Eucharist: *He was subject*, and *He was*

---

[1] Her secretary.   [2] Her secretary.

silent." And, in one of her conferences : *Jésus est tout seul au fond du sanctuaire, et seul Il veut fixer le coeur et les regards.*[1]

Several instances are on record of her visitants from another world. "Is —— in heaven?" some one asked her, earnestly. There was a pause. "Yes," replied Mother Digby, "but she has suffered much." All cannot here be told, but other examples could be given.

"When I was Mistress of Novices at Roehampton, Reverend Mother Digby being Mother Vicar, it happened that my second brother fell very ill and was in danger of death. He was in Ireland at the time. He was gay and pleasure loving, but a practising Catholic. He had been given over by the doctors. Reverend Mother Digby asked for the prayers of the whole house for my brother's cure. On a certain morning the whole community at Roehampton were to offer their communions for him. That very morning he became suddenly better, and in a short time he was quite well Shortly afterwards he came to Roehampton to see me. I took him into the chapel for a short visit. He then said to me : 'On the morning when I suddenly got better, I had a strange vision. I am quite sure that I was not dreaming, but perfectly conscious. I was somehow in the very chapel I have just visited, and I watched all the nuns going up to Holy Communion. As soon as the priest took the Host from the ciborium, and was preparing to communicate the first religious on the left of the altar rails (that is, Reverend Mother Digby) I saw a brilliant ray of light strike outwards from the Host, and in that ray all my sins were written so that in an instant I knew them all, or rather I seemed to see them all. As soon as she had received Holy Communion my sins disappeared instantly from the ray; and there came to me an inward knowledge that another year's life had been granted me.' My brother henceforth appeared most devout and saintly. At the end of a year I received news that he was again dangerously ill. One day, at a few minutes to one o'clock I was on my way to recreation as usual, when our Mother Digby met me : 'Go my child,' she said, 'to the chapel, and pray for the soul of your brother, who has just died.' I did not doubt that a telegram had informed her of the event. Later in the afternoon it was my duty to act as portress, and I soon brought up to her a

[1] "Jesus is alone in the depths of the sanctuary, and He would draw our desires and our hearts towards Himself only."

telegram that had arrived. She opened it : it announced the death of my brother that very day at *a few minutes before one.*" [1]

" At the time of the visit of Oui Very Reverend Mother Digby at Poitiers, in 1896, the whole Community was persuaded that she had received some very special grace. She went often to pray in the little chapel of St Stanislaus, next door to the chamber of our Blessed Mother Barat. One day her prayer lasted an extraordinary length of time. Reverend Mother du Chélas, then superior, became anxious, and went to the chapel ; our Mother Digby was quite unconscious of her presence. When she returned to her room very late indeed, Mère Du Chelas ventured to ask her if she had seen our Blessed Mother Barat. ' One does not speak of these sort of things,' was the only reply she could obtain." [2]

But, all this time, life itself was a burden.

" She had seen we know not what, and it made her long with a great and ever growing desire to be dissolved and to be with Christ. Only once I saw a wave of the opposite current pass across her mind. The loveliness of a Californian sunset between two ranges of mountains, the wonderful light and air and colouring gave a heightened sense of life, and she said : ' It made me cry after Benediction, to see it all so lovely, and to think that in a few years I should be gone —wasn't it foolish ? ' Only for a moment, and then she was herself again, *patient with life because of the desire of death.*" [3]

[1] M. B.   Related about 1903.
[2] Related by M. du Chélas.   [3] J. S.

CHAPTER XXVI

THE END

"'You see me a stranger and traveller in this place, and therefore, on this road of pilgrimage bury me.' Then raising his hands and eyes, he said, 'O Lord Jesus Christ, who hast made and redeemed my soul, I deliver it up and commend it to Thee, that it may be numbered among the elect souls of Thy redemption.' So he died, and the people buried him by the side of the royal road. . . "—KENELM DIGBY, *Mores Catholici* (Booker, London, 1831) book I. p. 208.

THE new Motherhouse is at Ixelles, a suburb of Brussels, and stands back a little from the street. It is a plain conventual building of red brick, with white stone facings; a garden at the back, secluded by a high wall and a row of trees within it, occupies a space about seventy yards wide and four times that length. The two small rooms of the Superior General, on the second floor, may be seen as they then were, with the same simple and indispensable furniture as in Paris. There are a few prints and pictures on the walls, and a crucifix; and a little vase of flowers in front of the statue of Our Lady upon the writing desk. Some of these objects are precious, for they have been used by Mother Barat. A little windowless anteroom holds cupboards for books and papers, and opposite the door of this anteroom is that of the antechapel, a few yards away across the corridor.

Left of the antechapel, as one faces its entrance, is a small parlour; to the right, the little chapel of the Crucifix. On entering the antechapel itself, a door on the left hand opens into the chapel of the Relics. The main chapel itself is now visible through an open screen before its entrance; in front of this open screen, just to the right of its doorway, is a low wooden priedieu. Here, within the precincts of the antechapel, but in full view of the altar, Mother Digby was wont to kneel from seven in the evening till the hour for recreation struck half an hour later. That priedieu still keeps its position.

On December 2nd died the last remaining of Mother Digby's brothers and sisters, Captain Essex Digby, a devout Catholic. She writes to one of his daughters:

" S.C.J.M.

" Tues., 7th Dec., 1909.

"MY OWN DEAR—If you only knew the number of Masses—prayers that so many kind friends are offering for Father you would be quite happy about him ; and indeed can we doubt the love of Our Lord for his soul? And what a beautiful death, thinking of every one save himself! I am so glad you have the last lines, evidently meant for you, and so you were one of his last thoughts."

On December 13th there was great joy. Mother Duchesne, the apostle of the Sacred Heart in America, one of the first companions of the Foundress, was declared Venerable in Rome, upon the introduction of her Cause of Canonisation. Mother Digby had for many years followed up the collection of evidence here, as for Blessed Mother Barat, and was to the end occupied in the advancement of both Causes.

The Probation, transferred to Jette upon the French expulsion, had been re-established at the Motherhouse.

A probanist writes :

" Our Mother's joy at the return of the General Probation to the Motherhouse was great. No detail of our life was too small to be of interest to her. We all felt that we were constantly in her thoughts, and almost daily some message that would give us pleasure reached us from her, something of interest to read, some gift that would recall the traditions of previous years.

" On Sundays we had recreation with her. She used to walk slowly into the room, place her stick against the wall, and then turn to us with a smile that told us how glad she was to see us. Sometimes, before she sat down, she would pause for a moment, and look at the eager faces turned towards her, as though questioning the future. Once she spoke her thought aloud, and said to the Mother standing by her : ' Qu'est ce qui va sortir de cet apanage ? ' [1] During those half hours she gave herself wholly to us. Leaning

———
[1] What will be the outcome of this addition ?

slightly forward, her hands joined on the table in front of her, she seemed to look, not only into the eyes, but into the mind and heart of each. I think few thoughts were hidden from her. A picture of our Blessed Mother Foundress hung in front of her, at the further end of the room; inspired by it, apparently, she often spoke to us of the saint she had known so well, of earlier days of the Society, and of all that would deepen in us the spirit of our vocation; then an earnest look, that went above and beyond us, would come into her face. Letters from the distant houses were often read, to which she added much by living touches of her own. One wished that those labouring in far lands, and often under great difficulties could have heard with what interest and tenderness she spoke of them. When mention was made of such as had suffered in the Society or who were still suffering, I was often struck by her tone of love, veneration, even envy.

"When I now think of Our Mother, it is usually as I remember her on five or six occasions when I met her coming out of the chapel, at half past six in the morning. She rose from her stall, as a rule, after Mass, before anyone else in the chapel had moved. I opened the door of the antechapel, the door leading to her room, and then instinctively stepped back out of her way. She walked very slowly, leaning heavily on her stick, her head bent, her eyes fixed on the ground a little way in front of her; there was a look on her face I never saw there at other times, a far away look, that was almost a light. She seemed quite absorbed in prayer, and I felt sure she saw nothing around her, and did not know that anyone was near. She passed along into her room, and then as silently as possible I closed the outer door after her. I know that in those moments I was privileged to see a saint alone in prayer with God."

In January, 1910, it was evident that a crisis of physical suffering was not far off.

"I went to see our Mother in her room, and held the girdle she was crochetting, whilst she tried to undo a knot in the cotton; it was then that I noticed her swollen hands, and realised how ill she was. She was wonderfully kind and gentle, as I spoke to her of my retreat; but my thoughts were really more of her than of my election. Her face was full of suffering; she looked weary, and it was an evident effort to speak. She had been in the same state for many weeks past. There was an eruption on the leg, the pain and irritation of which deprived her for nights together of sleep, and of the possibility of rest, but she let it make no change in her long day of work and of prayer. She came as usual to the recreations. At times she had acute pain in the head and neck, which betrayed itself with each movement, and yet how often she turned, smiling graciously, to those on either side of her. At one of these recreations she was too ill to speak; she only looked at us, and her eyes usually so full of depth and light, were dull. I shall never forget it; I wondered how she could be there at all. As I look back to this time I know it was my privilege to see something of what a saint will endure and suffer for God."

On the first Friday, February 4th, Mother Digby was taken very ill. The doctors were summoned in consultation. As soon as they had gone, Reverend Mother B——, an Assistant General, went in to Mother Digby: " Ma Mère, do you wish for anything?" "Yes! I wish to sanctify myself!" "Well, le bon Dieu offers you the means. To the sick he sends his priest with the Holy Oils. . . ." "I understand!" answered Mother Digby with a smile. "Whenever you like, send word to the ordinary confessor; I will get ready."

At eight o'clock in the evening the whole Community accompanied the Blessed Sacrament to the door of their Mother's room. She received It, and Extreme Unction, in a state of perfect calm and lucidity.

Next day, she said only: "God is good, immensely good. I desire heaven, but I am prepared to live on."

On February 10th Mgr. Legraive, Bishop Auxiliary of Malines, who had just assisted at the profession of the probanists, gave Mother Digby after the ceremony an absolution *in articulo mortis*. She had suddenly fallen into a state of syncope. The doctors looked upon the case as desperate. The fears and anxiety of the whole Congregation were at the greatest pitch; it was resolved to begin a common novena to obtain a cure through the intercession of Mother Duchesne, newly Venerable.

Little Nelly Hilson, daughter of one of the doctors called in, was much occupied with the state of the Superior General. She woke up one morning, went to her father, and said: "I dreamt that our Mother General was cured,

and not by you, but by God, the best doctor of all!"
"He can do what I cannot!" said the father. The
novena ended; there was no change; a second one was
begun, and on February 28th there was a slight ameliora-
tion. "This is a miracle!" exclaimed Dr Hilson.

Here may be recalled what was observed on a former
page: the admiration always felt by medical men for
Mother Digby. They spoke of her one to another, and
for this reason, before she arrived at some house for the
first time, she found herself already well known to the
local doctoᵣ

On the first Friday of March she was again in her
chair.

To her niece.

"SCJM.

"MY VERY DEAR CHILD,—Here are the first lines since
I am allowed up, and they will assure you of my love
and the union of prayer which never ceases between us.
And after the many trials the Sacred Heart of Our Lord
sends you and us comes the good news about —— and
——. May He be thanked for all His mercies. Dear
Father's intercession is being felt, now he is with our
dear ones in the Eternal Presence. What a sorrow that
I have missed going there! and by so little, as they tell
me. However, it will only be somewhat deferred—at
my age hopes are almost certainties.

"Tell —— my joy about him, and how I trust and
hope he will be worthy of the Digbys of old, the R.C.
ones, of good and learned type. Give me all you know
and hear about the family, please. Each day I pray
for you.

"I am rather sad at coming back to this 'lower world
of ours' as Doctor Rouse used to say—but can thus still
suffer and help to gain souls for our dear Lord.

"Pray for your loving old AUNT MABEL, R.S.C.J."

Preparations for a new foundation at Vancouver now
occupied her attention. She followed up every detail
with solicitude; chose the sacred vessels, and sent the

foundresses this watchword in her own handwriting: *This is my command, that you love one another.*

In a letter convoking the 16th general Congregation in August, she says: " We have turned a new page in the history of our beloved Society. It has passed through heavy trials. . . . On the other hand it is extending itself widely through foreign countries, and the requests for foundations far exceed what our resources of subjects and funds at present allow . . . . We have already the happiness of seeing some preliminary steps taken for the canonisation of our *Beata* . . . and the sessions of the second process in the Cause of the Venerable Mother Duchesne are to begin this week.

"These marks of God's protection . . . are a call to thanksgiving on our part, . . . and to a renewal of fervour. . . . Humility and charity are our life. Our first Mother knew this. . . . When these virtues are found together in our soul, then the spirit of our Society flowers forth in perfection, and something of the gentle royalty of Jesus Christ passes into it. . . ."

She develops these thoughts in the manner most persuasive to her daughters, and concludes:

" I cannot end this letter, dear Reverend Mothers and Sisters, without expressing my gratitude . . . for the prayers offered for me. . . . It is to these prayers that I owe the recovery which enables me to take my part once more in the work so dear to us all. I cannot deny that it is a regret to have been so near to the goal and yet to have returned ; I count on your continual prayers to sustain me in whatever work God will yet allow me to do with the remainder of my life, for His glory, and for the Society to whom I owe it, and to whom I shall devote it to the end.

"Renewing the assurance of my unalterable affection. . . ."

The work of this Congregation upon the studies has already been referred to.

She wrote to her niece about this time:

" How time flies ! at my age specially ; but also we

are nearing the great day of meeting our dear Lord, whom
alone I wish to love and serve to the end.   Pray that I
may do so less unworthily—and with kind remembrances
to ——, each and all,—Ever in Corde Jesu, my dear child,
your loving AUNTY MABEL, R.S.C.J."

And she said to some one else: "Two things stand
out as one grows old : the shortness of time, and what
waste anything is that is not done for God."

"The last visit I ever paid to my Aunt at Ixelles (wrote her
niece) and the last time we were ever together, was on Jan. 18th,
1911.   I asked her to tell me all about her conversion.   She
answered: 'Don't you think, when our Lord gives a great grace,
the secret is between Him and oneself?'   That same evening I
got round her to write in a prayer-book for me.   She had a
special dislike to write in any book, but she wrote these three
lines :

> *Patience—God knows.*
> *Resignation—God sees.*
> *Hope—God remembers.*
> *Pray for Aunty M."*

May arrived, and her feast day, and the joyful holiday
succeeding it.
A week later she again perceived the advent of a
dreaded yet longed-for visitant.   After looking over
a letter she had written, and correcting it, she said to
her secretary : "You see I am not mistress of my handwriting.   I am beginning to be as I was in February
last year."   To a suggestion from her Assistant that she
should see Dr Huyebrechts, she returned a gentle
refusal.
On May 15th she held a council with her Assistants
in the morning, although, as her secretary from long
acquaintance perceived, she had a headache.   She was
the first to arrive at the one o'clock recreation, which that
day was particularly joyous.   One of the Assistants
General related a dream she had had.   "I thought,"
she said, "that our Lord came to me in the garden.

Seeing Him, I cried: 'Lord, wait, I beg of you, whilst I call the Community together.'" Mother Digby smiled: " I believe," she said, "that in such a case I should have forgotten my daughters!"

She was occupied with business that afternoon until half-past six. Her secretary then asked: "Ma très révérende Mère, when will your next circular be ready to go? Not this week, perhaps?" " We shall see," she answered, almost gaily.

"So our Mother [writes one who knew her best] went through the last day of ordinary life until the evening. Knowing so little that it would be the last; a little more gay than usual, they say, and doing every little thing as she always did it, and as it should be done."[1]

At seven o'clock she went to her usual place on the priedieu in the antechapel. Only the sacristan and a single adorer were to be found by the altar at this hour. Twenty minutes later, both heard a dull sound as of a fall behind them. They looked about; Mother Digby was lying upon the ground near her priedieu. Here she was struck down, before the same Presence as at Montpellier fifty-eight years ago.

She was carried to her room. The doctors, summoned by telephone, ascertained congestion of the brain and paralysis of the left side. To their queries she replied: *I am rather ill, but I am content with all God does.*

At half past nine the Reverend Fr. Schurmans arrived. After some seconds passed alone with her, he said: "You have put yourself into the hands of God?" *I hope so!* "And you will all that He wills?" *Yes! all, all!* He then administered Extreme Unction, and she offered her hands spontaneously for the holy Oils.

To the relief of those who were watching, she seemed presently to sleep. Later on they feared that she had closed her eyes to open them no more. But the end was not yet imminent.

Next morning telegrams carried the sad news to each

[1] J. S.

vicariate ; prayer was now unceasing in every house, and adorers went in turn before the Blessed Sacrament ; nor did the others, whilst going about their usual duties, forget the quiet room at Ixelles, and the prostrate form. A precious telegram with the Papal blessing was placed before her eyes, but they did not open. " Your eyes are always shut ? " *They are raised to Heaven.*

No one spoke much to her ; now and then they repeated short or ejaculatory prayers.

" Here is Mother B. . . . " *She is welcome ; you don't know what care they are taking of me !* " You are near the blessed Sacrament." *That consoles me.* " And the Carmelites of Bruges are praying for you." *Thank them.* For the slightest service rendered she would say : *You are too good !* She declined anything to drink, but when told : " The doctor orders it," she took it, without hesitation.

In her illness of the preceding year she had said to Sister R——, the English sister : " Don't ever speak to me of food, Sister ; whatever you bring me I will take." " And I could never get her to say what she liked," added the Sister, " or what she could take." It was the same now. Her Assistant asked : " Would not this be more convenient ? " *We must not seek the more convenient.* " What then ? " *What pleases Him most !* . . . " Is not that less uncomfortable ? " *The beast is always trying to find comfort !* " Ah, there cannot be much comfort when one is so ill ! " *Oh yes ! there is the seeking for ease, and that we must diminish.* . . . " This is heavy," some one remarked, trying to arrange the coverlet. *Yes,* she replied, thinking her office was spoken of ; *yes, a burden, but Jesus bears it with us !* . . . " We tease you by our enquiries ? " *Oh no ! no !*

Throughout all these days there was not a movement that expressed either annoyance or suffering, not a preoccupation about her government, no care or misgiving of any sort, not a contraction of her face ; all was dignified and serene.

Sister R—— who knew well her favourite English invocations, began " Jesus, Mary, Joseph, I give you my heart" . . . at the second invocation her voice was choked by a sob. Mother Digby finished the prayer of her own accord: *Assist me in my last agony.* The Sister continued presently, repeating the Memorare and the Anima Christi. "What prayer do you like best?" *The Suscipe.* After a silence, and as if she had been saying it to herself, she pronounced the closing words: *Give me thy love and thy grace . . . this is enough.*

Quite spontaneously, she was heard to exclaim another time: *How good is our Master!*

On Wednesday the 17th, appeared a revival of strength, and a ray of hope. "If Almighty God would only keep her for you!" said one of the doctors, "her intelligence remains so lucid, that, paralysed as she is, she could still render you the greatest services."

On Thursday the 18th she was able to communicate. "Would you like to receive our Lord?" *O yes!* and she seemed to enter into deep recollection. But it was to be her last communion, and the hopes of her recovery soon died away.

"Reverend Mother, would you like —— to be sent for?" This was her most intimate and trusted amongst the Superiors now in England. But the answer came without any hesitation. *We must not do anything extraordinary.* For Mabel Digby henceforth her own oft-repeated watchword was to be literal: GOD ALONE!

The Superiors of all the Brussels convents came this afternoon to receive her blessing. Some one kissed her hand. "Ma Mère, what do you wish for your daughters?" *That they should belong to our Lord! . . . ever more and more!* "And for the whole Society?" *The same! . . . and that they should be always united . . . so they are . . . but more and more . . . always more!*

Next day her words came with much greater difficulty. In response to invocations of the Sacred Heart, she murmured: *Yes, Thy love, and the glory of Thy Heart!*

"Your head pains you much?" *O yes! but that does not matter.* "We wish we could relieve you." *You cannot . . . Can we call this suffering? What would you wish, my child?* "That God would make you better!" *There are things which He prefers!* "What?" *That we should suffer! Our Lord loved suffering!* "And you too love it!" *His will is always ADORABLE!* The emphasis was her own.

Sister R—— was kneeling by the bed, and felt moved to an imploring inward prayer that she might see her Mother's eyes once more, for they remained fast closed. As if in instant answer to the mute appeal, the eyes opened, and met those of her child and guardian by a last long look. "Reverend Mother," said the Sister, "you wish to go to heaven?" *Yes, very much.* "Our Lord will receive you with great love." *Yes, I hope so!* "Will you give me a little message for the Sisters?"[1] After a pause, *They must be humble and devoted, everything is in that!*

That evening she was restless, far into the night, and frequently made the sign of the cross. On Saturday morning her strength was greatly lowered; the confessor came to give another absolution *in articulo mortis,* and round her they recited the liturgical prayers for the dying. She murmured the responses; her beads still slipped one by one through her fingers. All that day the room was full of peace, and like a sanctuary; the Mothers succeeded one another in prayer by her side.

"Do you bless all your daughters?" *Yes!* "And all your children?" *Yes!* "All our works?" *Yes!* And a large sign of the cross with her right hand seemed to embrace her whole great family at all points of the compass. "When you are in heaven you will pray for the Society?" *Oh yes, Mother, most certainly.* This was particularly distinct. Her crucifix was presented to her and the Five Wounds named in turn. At the last named: *Oh yes, the sacred Side!*

She was now silent. Later on, quite spontaneously, without any exterior circumstance to evoke it, came her last word:

ALLELUIA!

Very early on Sunday morning, May 21st, began the final conflict. Again her children recited by her bedside the prayers for the agonising. They perceived that she

[1] The Lay Sisters.

united with their invocations, and when the chaplain came at about seven o'clock to give her a last absolution, she attempted once more to sign herself with the cross. In the chapel, before the Blessed Sacrament exposed, the rest of the community remained in ceaseless intercession for their Mother, as she strove through the long and painful hours in calm, and ever-lessening strength. A little before a quarter to eleven the breathing became slower; there were a few distinct sighs, the last very gentle, and then she appeared before God.

The body was laid out in the little parlour to the left of the chapel, with candles and a crucifix. Visitors began to flow in, bringing magnificent flowers; persons of all ages, of the world and of the cloister, succeeded one another without interruption, and touched her hand or the bier with the utmost reverence. All were astonished at the peace, happiness, and beauty of her countenance. It seemed to increase with every hour, and a little child exclaimed: "Why do they want to bury the mother General? It would be much better to put her in a chase, like the blessed Mother at Jette! She has a crown of roses and a lily all ready!"

A telegram bore the news to the whole Society, and by the evening came back the messages of sorrow. Friends arrived from France and Germany for her solemn requiem.

And now the Assistants General decided upon a painful sacrifice in favour of England. There was no private cemetery at Ixelles, and they thought it fitting that Mother Digby should find her last repose at Roehampton, where she had worked so long.

So, on the afternoon of May 24th, the whole community at Ixelles assembled on the terrace, and watched the mourning carriages out of sight. An English and a French religious, and the faithful Célestin, were to accompany the treasure to its home in England. At the Brussels station was a company of friends, and a group of trusty and devoted miners from Bois l'Evêque to help in the transport; nothing could exceed their care and reverence, nor was that of the officials less. A railway

compartment had been draped with black and silver; here
was placed the case containing the coffin, and near it two
high priedieux.   The journey took long; a special engine
brought it into Ostend at last, and here another deputation
of friends and pupils was waiting.   It was not far from
midnight when the boat sailed with the precious case.
At Dover there was a thick fog, and the horn sounded
at intervals; eight sailors with great respect carried the
case from the deck to the train; as it neared London the
sun broke out.   At Charing Cross, London's bustle and
noise had not begun; only the officials and a few
passengers were about; when they saw the twenty or
thirty assembled with great wreaths, waiting to do
honour to the dead, those near stood still and the men
bared their heads, as the coffin, now covered with flowers,
surmounted with a large brass crucifix, and accompanied
by the procession of friends, whose whole demeanour
spoke of love and grief, was borne towards the hearse.

Three mourning coaches followed, and as the funeral
began to move slowly up Roehampton lane, the convent
bell was heard tolling, for an hour ago a telephone from
Charing Cross had warned the expectant community.
The Superiors of the house were at the door; on either
side of the cloister were standing the nuns and novices,
holding lighted candles, further down were the children,
dressed in white, with mourning bands upon one arm.

"The morning was radiant; the air was still; we could hear the
tramp of horses far away, and I thought of the many times we had
stood here in the old days with joyful hearts to welcome her. . . .
But now, all that I could pray for was that her spirit might come
and dwell amongst us, and that we might always be a joy and
comfort to her."

A sunbeam fell upon the brass crucifix and made
a dazzling light as the coffin was carried in.   It was laid
upon trestles in the chapel of the Sacred Heart, and
covered with a pall.   Father William Kerr,—how old a
friend! began Mass at once in front of the catafalque; his
voice was low and broken, for he was full of sorrow.

It was now half past eight, Ascension Day, and the

anniversary of Mother Barat's own death, May 25th, 1865, which day had, in that year also, coincided with the feast of the Ascension. The side-chapel of the Sacred Heart, separated from the main chapel by a large open screen of gilt ironwork, had quite recently been painted throughout in a rich harmonious scheme of colour. Many had expressed their wish that Mother Digby could come to Roehampton and see this decoration for herself. And now she was resting in the midst.

The festal carpets were down in both chapels, the main alter was aglow with pink flowers, and with lights when the Mass of the Ascension began at nine o'clock. The triumphant chants sounded, and the "Alleluias," and then the Blessed Sacrament was exposed, close to the open screen and the catafalque. The sun streamed into the chapel, making the lights in the great candelabra look dim ; superb flowers completely covered the pall, wreaths and crosses, and great sprays of beautiful blossoms. The children flocked in when they could, full of awe and sympathy, praying devoutly ; the eyes of the little ones were deep with wonder. Already startling news had come of a grace obtained at Mother Digby's intercession, and her promise to help her children from heaven seemed to have begun its fulfilment.

Late in the afternoon vespers for the dead was chanted in the main chapel. It was like the feast of All Souls succeeding All Saints. The chancel arch, windows, and tribune, were draped with black, looped up with golden ropes. On one side of the sanctuary were arranged the Bishop's throne and canopy in purple and gold ; the catafalque, with tall tapers on either side, was carried into the church, and solemn watch was kept all night.

After the Requiem next morning, sung before the Bishop of Southwark, six hundred people followed the funeral procession. There were monks and nuns of various Orders, besides a hundred and seventy of the *Sacred Heart*, and friends from all parts of England. Who of those present can say what they felt, whilst Mother Digby was being carried past her own window,

2 B

as the students sang out slowly: *In Paradisum deducant te angeli.*[1] Light clouds screened the procession from the sun; the may and cherry trees were in bloom, and a gentle breeze carpetted the path with petals. Outside the cemetery gate were kneeling the infants of the elementary school, from three years old; their heads bowed low, their hands grasping flowers, and crossed upon their breasts.

Facing the great crucifix, and in the centre of the cemetery, was the open grave, fringed with upright lilies, and lined with cypress branches. At the head of the grave was the cross-bearer, and two acolytes; at the foot stood an impressive group: the Bishop in cope and mitre, with his canons in purple, many priests in white cottas, and some black-robed Jesuits. At angles of the cemetery were massed the children, and the students from St Charles' College; the nuns and novices, carrying lighted candles, faced the entrance.

Cum sanctis tuis in aeternum[2]; how the words rang out! At the *Benedictus*, all at once the sunbeams appeared; the blackbirds and a thrush accompanied the chant, whilst a white butterfly fluttered over the grave. The canticle ended, by a happy mistake of the singers, with a *Gloria Patri!*

But, when the coffin was lowered into the earth, tears fell, and some sobs could no longer be repressed. Each religious in turn sprinkled it with holy water. Then the little ones of the elementary school—it was their own idea—came up, kissed the flowers they held, flung them on the coffin, and so completely covered it.

By three o'clock that afternoon a cross had been set up over the grave; a palmtree overshadowed it, and a pall of flowers veiled the new-turned sods.

But it was not here, after all, that Mabel Digby was to sleep her last sleep. Those who loved her had a better thought. Application was made to the necessary authorities, civil and ecclesiastical, and permission came that she should be buried within the precincts of the sanctuary itself.

[1] May the angels conduct thee to paradise.   [2] With Thy saints for ever.

So her remains were transported once more, back to the chapel of the Sacred Heart that had, unknowingly, been so well prepared to form a great sarcophagus. She lies between the altar of that chapel and the main altar close by. Several bodies of the saints from the catacombs, and other great relics, are on her right hand and on her left; she rests where in life she loved best to be —close to the Most Holy.

CHAPTER XXVII

EPITAPHS

"Of time no more to fear the storms and showers,
Of one supernal joy to feel no dearth."
—KENELM DIGBY, *Temple of Memory* (Longmans, 1875), Canto xii.

PRESENTLY came from every house more lengthy tributes of her children to their Mother.

Belgian letters say :

"All her great family are near her now—She seemed to me always living high above all that passes, and to me her teachings are still strength and law." From Australia came: "It is a serene sorrow, that brings us nigh to heaven;" from Japan: "The cable arrived after the hour of the great evening silence; we passed it from hand to hand, and each of us offered to our Lord alone the first effusion of our sorrow." From Vienna, and the daughter of Montalembert: "Heaven had given us a Mother equal to all that she must bear in order to safeguard the Society in face of circumstances so formidable. What a grief for those whom she has left!" from Havana, "Lost is not the word, Oh no! I can see her still, praying before the tabernacle;" from America: "She was faithful and strong, and God was with her!" from Montreal, "She sees all still from above!"

Nor were other countries silent, but more here would be tedious.

The condolences from outsiders, and from all points of the compass, added nothing to what her daughters knew of her already. But most touching and intimate are the remembrances from other religious orders of women: from the Superiors General of the Sisters of Charity, of the Sisters of the Assumption, of the Sisters of St Joseph of Cluny, of the Religious of the Sacred Hearts of Jesus and Mary at Beirut, of the Institut

388

St Julienne; from the Mother Abbess of the Trappist nuns at Ubexy, Vosges, from the Mother Prior of the Carmelites in Paris, and from many Superiors and others.

The regrets of France are numerous and forcible, and the most eloquent those oı Mgr. Baunard, who, when he delivered her funeral allocution on June 2nd, had just celebrated the diamond jubilee of his priesthood, and completed his book: *Le Vieillard.* He recalled, as did all Frenchmen who spoke of her, the ambulance at Marmoutier, in the "Terrible Year"; and adds:

"Sur les hauteurs de cette âme extraordinaire se dessinent trois grands pics: 1ᵉ Sa conversion et sa vocation. 2ᵉ Sa mission de supérieure Générale. 3ᵉ La béatification de cette Constitution du *Sacré Coeur* dans l'exil, ce qui lui a valu le nom de *seconde Fondatrice.*" [1]

In a long article by M. de Grandmaison in the *Univers* is found:

"She gave all who knew her the impression of such intellectual vitality, that her sudden departure appears to be no more than a temporary absence. . . . She combined tenacity to duty with the calm of the English temperament, and her exquisite tenderness of soul was not obscured by a sensibility that would have dimmed her clear vision, and made her firm hand tremble. . . . The vigour of her thought was tempered by the gentleness of her deep-blue eyes, and her holiness inspired all who knew her with confidence. . . ."

"How strikingly," says *La Croix* of June 23; "do the mind and character of the late Superior General of the *Sacred Heart* contradict the loud-voiced assertion of 1904, as to the diminution, suppression, annihilation, of all individuality as the resultant of the religious vows!" [2]

From every part of France came the letters of Bishops, Provincials, heads of Orders, chaplains, cúrés. Other independent testimony strikes always the same notes: "her great heart—her lucid mind—her practical sense—

[1] Upon the heights of this extraordinary soul three lofty peaks predominate: Her conversion and vocation—her mission as Superior General—and the Beatification, so to say, of the Society of the Sacred Heart through its exile, which has obtained for her the name of *Second Foundress.*

[2] *See* p. 292.

her intrepid courage—the unalterable serenity with which she faced the storm."

The merit of her circular letters is touched on :

"In a style simple and concise, she expressed thoughts that were deep and clear, lofty and strong as her own soul."

Of her spiritual life, others added :

"But she was, despite all our human illusions, as well suited to heaven as to earth.   When I think of her, the image of the strong woman rises at once before me ; but her characteristic, nevertheless, was not strength, but love.   I shall never forget the impression made on me by this soul, so humble, so great, so strong, so gentle, so united to God.   She had throughout but a single end in view : the glory of the Sacred Heart."

And they say further :

"She was the safe and valiant pilot—the admiral on his own quarter-deck.—Rare are the generals who can transform all their defeats into as many striking victories ! She fell at her post.— *Vie de soldat ! 'mort de capitaine !*—Thus died this eminent soul, powerful in virtue and in deeds.—Your Society will not only preserve her memory, it will feel for long the effects of her action."

Lastly comes the cry :

"France is her great ruined house—Your place is empty in France ! France has need of you, and calls you back ! "

There are, too, grateful letters from those of the same nationality sustained by Mother Digby in every sort of need, from the young priest, the expense of whose studies she defrayed, to the aged widow whose trembling hand traces the account of almost lifelong friendship :

"She was an incomparable mother ! I hear still the charm of her voice softening for me the griefs of life ! "

An Italian, whose story has been told already,[1] came to pour out her grief to the nuns in a voice broken by sobs :   "Ah, how well she spoke to me of God ! "

[1] *See* p. 246.

"I enjoyed an unbroken friendship of many years with Mother Digby [writes an Irish lady.] How saintly she was, and yet how simple! How she enjoyed any amusing incident! What an interest she took in all my affairs! The blank can never be filled up."

A few from the American tributes follow :

"She was a great woman, [writes the Rector of the Jesitus College at Cincinnati,] a master mind, and a heroic soul. To an outsider, your Society seems to have sustained an irreparable loss—" "It is glorious [says the late Father Pardow] to know that our Lord has had such followers!"

At St Joseph's, Missouri, where she had given the parochial school to the diocese, solemn High Mass was offered for her in the Cathedral and the Rt. Revd. Bishop Burke said of her :

"*Tanto nomine nullum par eloquium.* Her unwritten epitaph will be found in every Catholic heart in St Joseph's . . . she has left in our midst a perpetual monument of her world-wide zeal, every stone of which is a living immortal soul."

Mother Digby had survived her oldest and most eminent friends in Italy; amongst the Cardinals, the names of Mazella, Ferrata, Monaco La Valletta, and Angelo di Pietro stand out. Cardinal Vannutelli, and Cardinal Merry del Val, spoke their sympathy and recognition of her life devoted to God's service.

In England, too, few old friends were now left. Mrs John Hungerford Pollen wrote :

"We do indeed feel a loss, but the gain, the deserved crown, is to her. Her life was a precious gift of God to all of you ; He will make even her death a benefit; it could not be otherwise to her much-loved Order, for she will serve it still. . . . Her last words will be your watchwords."

And General Lord Ralph Kerr : . . .

"May I offer to you and yours my sympathy in your great loss. Mother Digby has been a watchword for so very many years. It seems like the extinction of a star in heaven!"

The Revd. Edward Murnane, of Bermondsey, says:

"The news of dear Mother General's death, sad for her friends, but glorious for her, reached me before your letter, and I at once began a triduum of Masses for I am trying to repay a debt of gratitude. She is helping me now, as she ever helped me on earth, when I needed counsel. She was to me the faithful friend to whom I could ever turn, and I feel she is still the same in heaven, and have been praying to, as well as for her! She is constantly in my thoughts; and if, as I think, in every religious soul the life of our Lord is traced in part, then to her was given the period of the Passion."

But the English tribute most valued in English eyes will be that of the Cardinal of Westminster. From his address to the students of St Charles, June 20th, 1911, are taken these grave and measured words:

. . . . "We meet to-day under the shadow of a great sorrow, which has befallen the Society of the Sacred Heart—a sorrow of a kind that must come to us over and over again as life goes on; an inevitable sorrow, but none the less keenly felt. . . . When the first feeling of loss for a great and valued friend is over there comes another that can hardly be realised in the first moment, and that is one of consolation and of strength. We know that the life we loved was lived and accomplished as God would have it. Every life on earth is uncertain until its whole course is run; even the holiest and the best *may* deflect, in some measure, from its high calling and its generous response; only when it is finished have we the complete sense of security; and then we know and rest happily in the thought that the life has obtained the reward God intended for it." . . .

Very few lives have so many lessons in them as that of the late Mother General of the Society of the Sacred Heart. But there is one thought from it that I would put before you most especially. She was raised up by God to govern that Society at a moment of enormous difficulty —seldom have so many and so great had to be faced by the head of a religious Order. They were sufficient, and more than sufficient, to crush the energy and the initiative of many a brave heart, of many near and dear to God. Holy people have often before now resigned themselves to accept what appeared to be inevitable, saying that it must be God's will, that there is nothing to do but to suffer, under the adverse circumstances. We may find ourselves doing that in the lesser occasions that present themselves to us, justifying ourselves in accepting the overthrow of our aspirations, and doing nothing when the difficulties are great. Such was not the life of Reverend Mother Digby. She did not let a single obstacle—and she met apparently insuperable ones—lessen her energy, or weaken her quiet but firm determination ; and so, under God, she carried out her great work. Not only did she not allow a single house of the Society of the Sacred Heart—the work of one hundred years—to be lost, for she replaced every one that was closed, but she has left a larger number now at her death than she found when she took office as Mother General. She has left a magnificent example to her own children, and to all those who come under their influence.

"The 'giving up' policy is pure cowardice ; displeasing to our Lord, and fatal to our power of doing good. It is quite true that God may intend some of our dearest projects never to be realised ; their conception and the strong desire to carry them out may have been all He wanted us to get from them. But know, that He does not mean us to be idle. . . . He expects us to pray, and, by prayer and consideration to find help against the difficulties He allows during our time of probation.

"As the years go on, you will find plenty of opportunities of carrying out in a small way this lesson, that we learn from Reverend Mother Digby's life : learn the lesson — learn the courage that comes from hope and trust in God."

Upon the marble slab that covers Mabel Digby's tomb is inscribed:

MARIA · JOSEPHA · MABEL · DIGBY

DOMO · WESTMONASTERIENSI · IN · ANGLIA

E · SOCIETATE · SORORVM · A · SACRO · CORDE · IESV

OMNI · VIRTVTVM · GENERE · IVGITER · PRAESTANS

TVM · MAXIME · SEXDECIM · POSTREMIS · VITAE · ANNIS

MATRIS · MAXIMAE · MAGISTERIO · FUNGENS

SPIRITV · CONSILII · AC · FORTITVDINIS

PRAESTANTISSIMA · INCLARVIT

QVVM · EX · TVRBVLENTISSIMA

PER · GALLIAS · TEMPESTATE

VNO · FERE · IMPETV · QUINQUE

ET · QVADRAGINTA · DOMICILIA

ABREPTA · SOCIETATE · ATQVE · EX · SVIS · SEDIBVS

EXTVRBATAE · AD · DVO · MILIA · SACRARVM · VIRGINVM

AT · PRAESENTI · TANTAE · MATRIS · OPE · AC · DILIGENTIA

DOMVI · PARISIACAE · PRINCIPI

ALTERA · IN · BELGIO · SUFFECTA

PARATAQVE · IBI · ALIBIQVE

SORORIBVS · APTA · CONFVGIA

QVIN · ET · IN · LONGISSIMIS · REGIONIBVS

PLVRIMAS · INTER · DIFFICVLTATES

NOVA · COLLEGIA · AC · MONASTERIA · ERECTA

NEC · INTERMISSA · VOTA · AC · STVDIA

VT · VENERANDAE · AVCTORI · TOTIVS · SODALITII

MAGDALENAE · SOPHIAE · BARAT

CAELESTIVM · BEATORVM · HONORES · DECERNERENTVR

QUIEVIT · IN · SACRO · CORDE · IESV

DIE · XII · KAL · IVN · AN · M C M X I

VIXIT · ANNOS · LXXVI · DIES · XLIV [1]

[1] Mary Josephine Mabel Digby, born at Westminster in England, Religious of the Society of the Sacred Heart of Jesus. Ever eminent in the practice of all virtue, she especially excelled whilst, for the last sixteen years of her life, endued with the spirit of counsel and of fortitude, she filled the office of Mother General. For, when a devastating storm beating over France swept away, as it were in one fell rush, five and forty convents of her Society and drove forth homeless two thousand consecrated virgins, the skill and diligence of this great mother not only set up in Belgium a Mother House replacing that of Paris, but there and elsewhere, even in the uttermost ends of the earth, despite very many difficulties, built up new colleges and convents, ensuring fitting shelter to all. Nor did she cease from prayers and toil, until the Venerable Foundress of the Society, Magdalen Sophie Barat, had come to be numbered among those honoured as Blessed in Heaven. She fell asleep in the Sacred Heart of Jesus on the twenty-first day of May in the year of our Lord one thousand nine hundred and eleven, having lived seventy-six years forty-four days.

CHAPTER XXVIII

SOME FAMILIAR SAYINGS OF MOTHER DIGBY

" Truly when I hear Laelia, (for women more easily preserve uncorrupt antiquity, because, being unacquainted with the conversation of many, they always hold the things which they have first learned,) I listened to her as if I were hearing Plautus or Naevius; the sound of her voice is so just and simple, not being infected with the least ostentation, or desire of imitation, that I feel convinced it was thus her father used to speak—thus her ancestors." — KENELM DIGBY, *Godefridus* (Lumley, 1841), p. 39.

1. THE eye of God is like a searchlight; but, unlike the searchlight, it loves also, and purifies.

2. O! love the truth! Let us profit by warnings, by reproaches, above all, whilst we are young!

3. We must open not only the doors, but the windows of our souls to the truth.

4. Keep at a certain distance from yourself; it gives perspective.

5. We must, in going to the infirmary, beware of *Brother Ass;* not be led by him, but lead him.

6. Do not trouble yourself about your health. As soon as you do that, you lose it!

7. A sure way to shorten life, is to surround oneself with little precautions.

8. We are in this world with a body full of pain; we must carry it cheerfully.

9. To complain is to accentuate suffering. You thus give it a sort of bodily shape.

10. People can bear more than they think; above all if they accept suffering simply, without struggling to get rid of it.

11. Trouble and sorrow generally bring us nearer to God, but sometimes it is wounded self-love that makes us long for death. There is an old proverb: "Beware of sighing for Heaven from beneath the clouds."

12. Don't put up an umbrella between you and **God** in bad weather!

13. You must *give* your hearts to God, and not *let them for the season.*

14. Do you always wish Him to pay you in ready money?

15. Give and work because "the Lord hath need of it"; don't look only at "the good day's wages for a good day's work."

16. We must be pilgrims upon earth, not tourists.

17. How small and impotent we get when we look at things from a human side!

18. Live always in an express train which passes by the small stations.

19. We want an armed peace!

20. There are three degrees of willing : I should like— I wish—*I will.* The last is the one we want!

21. Give me the weakest will—give me a reed, but fill it with perfect trust in God, and it will succeed.

22. There are possible things: do them; impossible things: ask for them in prayer.

23. We must make a throne for God in our hearts, and go there often to adore.

24. We must purify the affections of the soul, not kill them. God does not wish to be served by corpses!

25. The mind may be filled with useless furniture, with scruples that deform, dreams that distract and enervate. But the visit of God drives out all this lumber, and renders the imagination fit to reflect the calm and serene images of eternity.

26. By silence, our difficulties, our trials, our sorrows, are set apart, consecrated, given to God. *Tibi silentia laus!*[1]

27. Let us remember that the prophet of old walked not in the sweetness but in the strength of the heavenly food.

28. *You must be joyful.* "What do you call joy?" The harmony of all our faculties in the will of God."

29. You are God's thing, and He takes care of His own belongings.

[1] Silence is Thy praise!

INDEX

ABBADIE, Family of d', 34-5, 99.
Adelaide, Bp. of, 171.
Allies, Mr T.W., 136-7, 148, 149-51.
Amette, see Paris.
Amigo, see Southwark.
Amycla, Mgr. Weathers, Bp. of, 182.
Anderdon, Father, 147.
André, M., 320-1.
Annonay, Mgr. Bonnet, Bp. of, 287.
Ars, Curé d', 19.
Aspinall, Mr, 116.
Assumption, Little Sisters of the, 280.
——, Nuns of the, 224.
Autun, Mgr. Perraud, Bp. of, 222, and see Legraive.
Avellaneda, M. Marco, 342.
Averandi, Mgr., 258.
Avignon, Bp. of, 267.

BALBO, Contessa, 283.
Barat, Mother, character and career, 50—work of her Institute, 208, 269-70 — admits Mother Digby, 44 — recognizes her worth, 49, 70—knew the secret of her conversion, 24—intercourse with M. D. as a novice, 50, 53-5—as a young religious, 60, 69, 70—acquires Marmoutier, 28, 91 —and the Hotel Biron, 210—visits England; sympathy with the English, 122—Beatification of, 319-20, 332-3, 336 — her body found intact, 183, 333-4—removed by M. D. to Belgium, 299—tomb, 337-8—portrait, 335-6 —biographies, 128, 337.
Barelle, Père, 29, 40.
Baunard, Mgr., 389
Beauregard, M. de, 295.
Beauvais, Mgr. Fuzet, Bp. of, 222.
Belfour, Père, 40, 41.
Bentley, John, 178.
Beverley, Mgr. Cornthwaite Bp. of, 162.
Birmingham, Mgr. Ullathorne, Bp. of, 136.
Blois, M. de, 275.
Bombay, Mgr. Porter, Abp. of, 174.
Bonaparte, Card., 50.

Bonaparte, Mme. Constance, 49-50.
Bonnet, see Annonay.
Bordier, M., 36.
Bosredont, Mother de, 44, 46, 48-9, 55, 58-9, 91.
Bouillet, Dr, 44.
Boulangé, Père, 307.
Bourgeois, M., 225, 235.
Bourke, Captain, 196.
Bourne, Card., 392.
Boutard, M., 295.
Boyer de Bouillane, M., 276, 320-1.
Bretonneau, Dr, 27, 40.
Briançon, Comtesse de, 225.
Browne, see Cloyne.
Brzozowska, Mother, 239-40.
Buccleuch, Duchess of, 118, 126.
Buisson, M. Ferdinand, 287, 291-4, 296, 331.
Burke, F. Thomas, 160, 186.
——, see Missouri.
Butt, see Southwark.

CALLEGARI, Card., 313.
Cambrai, Abp. of, 222.
Canrobert, Gen., 245.
Carmelites, 37, 40, 271, 276, 280, 380, 389.
Carnot, M., 213.
Carr, see Melbourne.
Casimir-Périer, M., 213.
Castelbajac, Marquis de, 13.
——, Mlle. de, 13-14, 19, 25, 26
Chadwick, see Hexham.
Châlons, Mgr., Latty, Bp. of, 227-8.
Charity, Srs. of, 40, 271, 343, 388.
Charles X., 3.
Chevreuse, Duchesse de, 219.
Clark, Sir A., 167.
Clémenceau, M., 321.
Clémentine, Princesse, 316.
Clifford, Lord, 147.
Cloyne, Mgr. Browne, Bp. of, 283.
Cochin, M. Denis, 326.
Coffin, see Southwark.
Combes, M., enters the political scene, 225, 275—expels unauthorized Congregations, 280, 285-6, 319—refuses

Combes—*continued*
  authorization, 286—declares his anti-
  clericalism, 286—declares war upon
  all the Congregations, 292, 310, 319;
  331 footnote—praises Mother Barat,
  310—M. D.'s attitude towards him,
  311.
Coppens, Mother, 49.
Cornthwaite, *see* Beverley.
Courtois, Mother, 67.
Craven, Mrs, 126-7.
Crémieux, M., 106.
Cullen, Mgr., 152.
Currie, Mrs, 127, 252, 284.
Curzon, Mlle. de, 220.
Cuverville, Adm., 275.

DAGNEIROLLES, *see* Rolland.
Danell, *see* Southwark.
Darras, Abbé, 65.
Delahaye, M., 288.
Denbigh, Lady, 127.
Desmarquest, Mother, 49.
Desoudin, Mother, 212-2, 216, 231,
  233-5.
Diaz, President, 258-9.
Digby Family, Ch. I., II., 27.
——, Simon, Ch. I., II., 45—his death,
  58—M. D.'s mysterious assurance,
  58, 69, 251.
——, Mrs, Ch. I.-IV., 57—intercourse
  with M. D. at the convent, 49, 53,
  57, 73, 175—intercourse with Eva
  D., 16, 98-100—character and death,
  175.
——, Kenelm Roy, 2, 13, 27—death,
  58.
——, Essex, 2, 7, 13, 27—conversion,
  101, death, 373.
——, Eva, as a child, 2, 13, 16, 27-8,
  48—conversion, 17—death, 98-101.
——, Geraldine, Ch. I., II., 2, 6, 8—
  conversion, 15-6 — influence on
  M. D., 18-24—home life, 33ff—
  character and death, 321.
——, Kenelm (1800-1880), character
  and career, 3—influence upon the
  Digby family, 9, 10—his daughter's
  vocation, 52.
——, Marcella, 52.
——, Jane, 120.
DIGBY, MABEL, birth 1835, 1—
  strong individuality, 5ff—influence
  of Kenelm Digby, 9—life in France,
  12—friendship with the Empress
  Eugénie, 13—mysterious conversion
  1853, 20—change of conduct, 25—
  religious vocation, 29—opposition,
  29ff—friendship with M. d'Abbadie,
  34—M. Dupont, 35—Père Félix,

41—Cardinal Langénieux, 45—and
Fr. Gordon of the Oratory, 45
—enters the Society of the Sacred
Heart 1857, 45—early promise, 47
—first acquaintance with Mother
Barat, 50 — Mistress General at
Marmoutier, 57 — influence, 61—
talent for nursing, 66 — admitted
to final vows, 1859, 70—superior
of Marmoutier, 1865, 72—character
of her rule, 74—antiquarian dis-
coveries, 92—builds a new convent,
94—relations with Card. Guibert,
96—calumnies, 97—Marmoutier,
an ambulance in 1870, 102—superior
at Roehampton, 1872, 116—changes
effected, 120—the school, with
Mother Kerr, 123—relations with
the Children of Mary, 126—friendship with Lady G. Fullerton, 127—
with Lady Lothian, 132—fruitless
negotiations with Card. Manning,
133—undertakes training College,
1874, carries it through against formidable obstacles, 138 — ultimate
success, 151—the Irish convents,
152—demands for an Irish vicariate,
157 — her view prevails, 161—
foundation at Brighton, 162—critical
state of health, 166—accident, 167—
cure, 1879, 168—seven foundations in
Oceania, 172—illness, 176—acquires
the Hammersmith Seminary, 1892,
178—goes to Rome, and commences
her friendly relations with Leo XIII.,
180—Review of her work, 185—of
her training of young religious, 188
—M. D. with the lay Sisters, 190—
with children, 191—characteristics
of her letters, 193, 194, 345—conversation, 196—charity and liberality, 197—relations with the world,
198—her limitations, 202—appointed
Assistant General in France, 1894,
205—critical position of the Congregation, 206—her relations with
the authorities, 211 — Election as
Superior General, 1895, 215—relations with the French Children of
Mary, 218—financial perils, 221—
visits Italy, 225—relations with the
General of the Jesuits, 226—with
Leo XIII., 227—first acquaintance
with Card. Sarto, 229—foundation
at Venice, 231—journeys throughout
Europe, 231—her physical sufferings,
232—at the point of death, 239—
visits America, 1898, 251, 262—
American appreciation of her, 263—
returns to France, 265—meets the

DIGBY, MABEL—*continued*
attacks upon Congregational teaching by holding a council of studies, 268 —letter from Leo XIII. to M. Digby, 268—Centenary of the Society S. H., 1900, 270—The law of Waldeck-Rousseau in 1901, 272—dangers that threaten, 276—refuses to secularize the French religious, 277—M. Combes suppresses the unauthorized convents, 280—M. D. establishes new convents in Spain, and Naples, 282 — last interview with Leo XIII., 289—Buisson law against the Congregations, 1904, 291—efforts of M. Gailhard Bancel and others to save them, 294—M. D. prepares for exile, 297—removes the body of the Foundress, 299—holds a fifteenth General Congregation, 300 — the liquidator, 303—self-sacrifice of her lawyers, 305—life of privation, 306 — expulsions throughout France despite public protests, 306ff—the guardians refuse to leave, 308—45 new foundations in every part of the world, 311—Pius X. carries on the kindness of Leo XIII.—last visit to Rome 1905, 323—physical catastrophes affecting her houses, 325—the Cardinal of Paris, expelled from his palace, greets the nuns, 326—M. D. is driven from the Motherhouse 1906, protest, 328—Conflans, 329—forwards the Beatification of Mother Barat, a cause greatly forwarded by herself, 1908, 332—the body of the Beata exhumed in her presence and found still incorrupt, 333—M. D. again at the point of death, 336—foundations in the New World, 338 — in Japan, 339 — discerns new dangers, 341 — testimonies to her influence, 342-3—leaves France for ever, 1908, 343—Characteristics of her rule, 346ff—devotion to the Society S. H., 346—her training of her daughters, 348—firmness, 349—letters, 349—generosity, 351—intellectual power and education, 354 — salient virtues, humility, love of suffering, serenity, 363 — limitations, 368 — spirit of prayer, 369—last months, 372—last illness, 379—death, 383—body conveyed to England, 383—interment, 387.

Di Pietro, Card., 235, 391.
Dreyfus Case, 244-5, 297.
Drummond, Mr W., 3.

Du Camp, M., 218.
Du Chélas, Mother, 371.
Duchesne, Mother, 251, 254-5, 261, 373.
Dufour, d'Astafort, Mother, 63, 335.
Dumazeaud, Mother, 58.
Dupanloup, *see* Orleans.
Dupont, M., 35-7, 85, 92-3.
Duret, Dr, 307.
Du Rousier, Mother, 82.
Duruy, M., 208.

ERRINGTON, Mother, 174, 186, 262, 284.
Estoile, de l', *see* Malmusse.
Eugénie, Empress, 13-4, 18, 103, 170.

FAURE, M., 214.
Feilding, Lady C., 127.
Félix, Père, 41-4, 49, 55.
Ferrand, Dr, 232, 271.
Ferrata, Card., 216, 391.
Fesch, Card., 50.
Filling, Mother, 105, 107-8.
Fitzgerald family, 172-3.
Fitzsimon, Julia, 143.
Fourniers, Père, 217.
Franciscaines, Dames, 280.
Frederick Charles, Prince, 104, 110.
Froude, *see* Hügel.
Fullerton, Lady G., career, reminiscences, 127—connection with Society S. H. and with M. D., 128-9, 131, 133, 173—interment at Roehampton, 174.
Fuzet, *see* Beauvais.

GAGLIARDI, M., 336.
Gailhard-Bancel, M., 288, 294-5, 331.
Gallwey, Father, 128, 131, 166, 177, 180.
Gamard, Père, 54.
Garcia, Mrs, 127.
Gazelli, Mother, 60, 66, 69, 72-4, 216.
Genty, Abbé, 38, 39.
Geslin de Bourgogne, Gen., 294.
Glasgow, Bp. of, 162.
Goblet, M., 222, 286.
Goetz, Mother, character, 51—second Superior General, 72—training of M. D., 24, 50, 51, 54, 70—appoints M. D. Superior, 72—visits Marmoutier, 72—visits England, 129—sends M. D. to England, 129.
Good Samaritan, Sisters of the, 171.
Goold family, 116-7, 124.
Gordon, Father, 45.
Gouvion St Cyr, Marquise, 219.
Grandmaison, M. de, 337, 389.
Grant, *see* Southwark.
Guadalajara, Bp. of, 340-1.

Guibert, Card., 93-8.
Guyot-Sionnest, M., 303-5, 313.

HALLAM, Henry, 4.
Hanotaux, M., 228.
Harper, Dr, 164-7, 172.
Haversham, Baron, 1.
Hebron, Mgr. Mermillod, Bp. of, 86-7.
Hermann, Père, 17.
Hexham and Newcastle, Mgr. Chadwick, Bp. of, 162.
Hilson, Dr, 375-6
Holguin, Gen. jorge, 339.
Hoskier, Mme., 220.
Howard of Glossop, Lord, 147.
Hügel, Baroness Anatole von, 201-2.
Huyebrechts, Dr, 378.

IMPERIAL, Prince, 170.

JEANNEROT, Gen., 294.
Jenner, Sir W., 167.
Joseph of Cluny, Srs. of St, 388.
Juet, Abbé, 97-8.
Julienne, Nuns of the Institut Ste., 389.

KENNEY, Mother, 81, 86.
Kerr, Mme. C., 58-9, 68, 80.
——, Mother H., character, 123, 173, 199 — Mistress General, 123-5 — friendship with M. D., 123, 134, 137, 168, 188, 198, 202 — death, 173 — biography, 173-4.
——, General Lord Ralph, 391.
——, Father, W., 177, 384.
Kieffer, Soeur, 343.
Kieran, Mother, 117-8, 172.
Kirwan, Lady V., 127.

LABOURÉ, Card., 367.
Lacey, see Middlesborough.
Lajuinais, Comte de, 295.
Lamarzelle, M. de, 275.
Langénieux, Card., 45, 222, 277.
Laprimaudaye, Mother L., 172.
Lasies, M., 295.
Latty, see Châlons.
La Valetta, Card. Monaco, 235, 391.
Lebel, M., 291.
Lefèvre, Abbé, 215.
Legraive, see Malines.
Lehon, Mother, third Superior General, in 1874, character and appearance, 204, 213, 298 — intercourse with M. D., 80, 169 — visits Marmoutier, 82 — appreciation of M. D., 209 — instals M. D. at Roehampton, 116, 119, 171 — visits and decision as to the Irish Vicariate, 161 — during the siege of Paris, 104, 112 — holds

M. Barat's hand in hers, 184 — death, 204.
Lemaître, M., 280.
Leo XIII., reminiscences concerning, 180, 227, 243, 315, 342 — intercourse with M. D., 180, 229, 237, 247 — appreciation of her, 228, 229 — supports her action, 229, 278 — letter to her, 268-270 — last audience with him, 289-90 — intercourse with, or benefits to, the Society of the S. H., 171, 204, 215, 236-8, 271, 282-3 — attitude towards the French Congregations, 223, 228, 245, 266-7, 275.
Leopold, King, 316
Lerolle, M., 301.
Le Roy-Ladurie, Commandant, 281.
Leslie, Mother, 32-3, 38, 59, 68, 137-8, 143.
Logue, Card., 283.
London, Bp. of, 147.
Londonderry, Lady, 126, 174.
Lopez, Col., 259.
Lothian, Lady, character, 68, 118, 202 — reminiscences of, 126, 135 — intercourse with M. D., 64, 68, 80, 132, 139, 162-3 — death, 163.
Loubet, M., 280, 295, 301.
Louchet, M, 222.
Lualdi, see Palermo.
Luppé, Countess L. de, 218, 220.

M'CABE, Card., 160.
Macchi, Mother, 367.
M'Gettigan, Primate of All Ireland, Dr., 155.
Macmullen, Canon, 147.
Malines, Card. Mercier, Abp. of, 334.
——, Mgr. Legraive, Bp. Auxiliary of, 375.
Mallac family, 52-3, 61.
Malmusse, Me de, 48-9
Manning, Card., 122, 131, 149, 177-8.
Marcère, M. de, 275.
Maria Christina, Queen, 249, 325.
Marie du Divin Coeur, Soeur, 268.
—— Sacré Coeur, Soeur, 266-7.
Martin, V. R. Father, 226-7, 325.
Maurice, Baron de Sainte, 25.
Maximilian, Emperor, 259.
Mazella, Card., 238, 391.
Meignan, see Tours.
Melbourne, Mgr. Carr, Bp. of, 172.
Méline, M., 235.
Mercier, see Malines.
Mercy, Sisters of, 131.
Mermillod, see Hebron.
Merry del Val, Card., 391.
Mexico, Abp. of, 258.

Middlesborough, Mgr. Lacey, Bp. of, 162.

Missouri, Mgr. Burke, Bp. of, 263, 391.

Monod, M. 286.

Montalembert, Comte de [1810-1870], 52, 271.

——, Comte de, 307-8.

——, Mother de, 52, 115, 271, 388.

Montblanc, see Tours.

Montmartre, Pères de, 271.

Montmorency, Mathieu de, 43.

Montpellier, Mgr. Thibaut, Bp. of, 17, 20, 23-5, 55.

Moran, Card., 171.

Mori, Contessa, 230.

Morlot, Card. Abp. of Paris, 49—friendship for the Digbys, 27, 59—defends M. D.'s vocation, 44-5, 48—gifts to Marmoutier, 91.

Morris, Father, 171, 174, 177, 181-3.

Morse family, Ch. I.

——, Bd. Henry, 183.

Mourier, Père, 215.

Mun, Comte de, 274.

Murnane, Father, 392.

NAPOLEON, Louis, 13, 50, 102-3.

Neill, Mr, 148.

Newburgh, Lady, 126, 174.

Nolan, Mother, 38-9.

Norfolk, Duke of, 147.

Notre Dame, Sisters of, 136, 139, 150-1

OLIVAINT, Père, 101, 113, 218.

Orleans, Mgr. Dupanloup, Bp. of, 85, 209.

Outremont, Mgr. d', 45, 83.

PALERMO, Mgr. Lualdi, Bp. of, 340.

Palmer, Mr W., 37.

Paris, Mgr. Amette, Abp. of, 336.

Pascot, Mlle. Berthe, 49.

Pecci, see Leo.

Pereira, Hon. Mrs, 127.

Perosi, Signor, 230.

Perpignan, Bp. of, 322

Perraud, see Autun.

Petre, Lord, 147, 149.

Pie, Card., 243, 341-2.

Pierre, Soeur St, 37.

Pietro, Cardinal di, 235, 247, 252.

Pius X., relations with M. D. and her Society, as Patriarch of Venice, 229-31—as Pope, 290, 318-20, 323-4, 332-3—appreciation of M. D., 336.

Pollen, John H., 68, 148, 182, 201, 216-7, 284.

——, Mrs John H., 391.

Pomereu, Comte de, 295.

Porter, see Bombay.

Prévost, Mother, 42-3, 49, 50.

Prisco, Card., 282.

Puebla, Abp. of, 258.

Pusey, Dr, 179.

RAM, Mrs Abel, 203.

Ramière, Père, 23.

Rampolla, Card., 224.

Ratisbonne, Père, 19, 24.

Ravignan, Père de, 54, 218.

Reille, Baron, 295.

Reinach, M., 222.

Reyes, President, 339.

Rheims, see Langénieux.

Ribot, M., 221-2, 286.

Richard, Card., Character and career, 214—at the Motherhouse, 213-4, 270, 300-1—presides over M. D.'s election as Sup. Gen., 215-6—defends the Congregations, 222—urges secularization upon M. D., 277—persecuted by Government, 326-7—visit of condolence to M. D., 329—death, 329.

Richards, Canon, 147.

Ripon, Lord, 128, 147, 149, 151.

Robertson, Mr, 118-9.

Rochefoucauld d'Estissac, Duchesse de la, 219.

Rochequairie, Mother de, 73, 75, 77, 84, 94.

Rolland de Blomac, Baronne de, 18-20, 25.

SACRED HEARTS of J. and M., Religious of the, 388.

Saint-Rémy, Lieut.-Col. de, 281.

Salvo, Marquise de, 127.

Sancha, Card., 282.

Sarto, see Pius X.

Sartorius, Mother von, 4th Superior General, 204—character and career, 211-13—novice with M. D., 52—death, 215.

Schüller, Mathieu, 216, 284.

Schurmanns, Père, 379.

Sciout, Mother, 79-80.

Séez, Mgr. Tregaro, Bp. of, 223.

Séguin, M., 288.

Selosse, M., 307.

Simon, M. Jules, 235

Smith, Mrs V., 127.

Somerville, Revd. W. J., 139.

Southwark, Mgr. Butt, Bp. of, 177, 199.

——, Mgr. Amigo, Bp. of, 385.

——, Mgr. Coffin, Bp. of, 172, 177.

——, Mgr. Danell, Bp. of, 131, 138, 143, 172.

Southwark, Mgr. Grant, Bp. of, 131.
Spencer, Fr. Ignatius, 122.
Spuller, M., 213, 235.
Surat, Mgr., 113.
Sydney, Mgr. Vaughan, Abp. of, 171.

TAMISIER, Mlle., 219.
Tarnow, Bp. of, 283.
Taylor, Mr, 4.
Thibaut, *see* Montpellier.
Thiene, Comte de, 27.
Thomas, Abbé, 215.
——, M., 303.
Tinling, Canon, 146, 150.
Tollu, M., 303, 305.
Tours, Mgr. de Montblanc, Abp. of, 38.
——, Mgr. Meignan Abp. of, 224.
Trappist nuns, 389.
Tregaro, *see* Séez.
Trochu, Gen., 245.
T'serclaes, Mother de, 242-3.

ULLATHORNE, *see* Birmingham.

VALETTA, Card. La, 235.
Vallée Poussin, Mme. de la, 280.
Vandeuvre, Mother de, 312.
Vannutelli, Card., 391

Varin, Père, 218.
Vaughan, Card., 177-179.
——, *see* Sydney.
Vendôme, Duchesse de, 336, 338.
Vercruysse, Mother, 94, 109, 169.
Victoria, Queen, 3.
Vilain XIIII., Comte, 315.
Vinall, Mother, 179-80.
Visitation, nuns of the, 271.
Viviani, M., 274.

WALDECK - ROUSSEAU, war on the Congregations, 265—Bill of 1901, 272-5—resignation,279—tries to save the Congregations, 286—death, 305
Wallon, M., 301
Ward, Mother M., 174-5, 202.
Weathers, *see* Amycla.
Weld, Mgr., 178.
Wenham, Canon, 142, 146-7, 151.
Wilberforce, Bp., 179
Windsor, Dean of, 147
Wiseman, Card., 122, 130-1
Wynn, Father, 366
Wynne, Father, 122

ZAEPFFEL, Mother, 61, 72-4, 84
Zurlinden, Gen., 244.

PRINTED AT THE EDINBURGH PRESS, 9 AND 11 YOUNG STREET.